ARTICULATIONS:
A UNLV Rhetoric and Reader

UNIVERSITY OF NEVADA, LAS VEGAS

This volume has been customized by the school for which it was published, to give you the best educational value. Chapters and pages may have been altered, added, deleted, or rearranged. Pagination and chapter numbers may be non-sequential. This volume is meant solely for use at this school.

NORTON
CUSTOM

First Edition
Editor: Marilyn Moller
Custom editor: Katie Hannah
Custom editorial assistant: Laura Dragonette
Editorial assistants: Erica Wnek, Tenyia Lee
Managing editor: Marian Johnson
Developmental editor: John Elliott
Project editor: Rebecca Homiski
Custom project editor: Hannah Bachman
Marketing manager: Lib Triplett
Emedia editor: Cliff Landesman
Photo editor: Trish Marx
Production manager: Jane Searle
Custom production manager: Diana Spiegle
Design director: Rubina Yeh
Designer: Jo Anne Metsch
Composition and layout: Carole Desnoes
Manufacturing: RR Donnelley Crawfordsville

ISBN 978-0-393-27743-2

W. W. Norton & Company, Inc., 500 Fifth Avenue, New York, NY 10110
www.wwnorton.com

W. W. Norton & Company, Ltd., Castle House, 75/76 Wells Street, London WIT 3QT
1 2 3 4 5 6 7 8 9 0

CONTENTS

Readings 327

Dear students,

Welcome to UNLV and to your first required composition class. You are probably both excited and a little nervous about coming to college, wondering what you will learn, who you will meet, and whether or not you are prepared for the work that will be required. Be assured that we are here to help you.

This course is designed to help you develop the critical reading and writing skills that you will need in a variety of contexts, not just in your college classes, but also in your career and personal life. We cannot anticipate every writing situation you will encounter, and we cannot give you a simple formula or list of rules to follow in order to create effective documents. Instead, we will help you consider the choices that influence meaning, both when creating and interpreting a text.

As part of that goal, we have compiled this textbook from multiple sources. Not only the selected readings, but also the chapters that explain reading, thinking, and writing strategies were written by diverse authors and were originally published in different books.

Sometimes, that may seem a little confusing, especially if an author refers to other passages they have written that are not in our book, or if two authors use slightly different vocabulary to talk about the same concepts. A little confusion, however, isn't bad if it causes us to think a little more. The harder we work to learn a concept or skill or idea, the more likely we are to retain it and use it in different contexts.

This ability to take a skill from one context, in this case from your English class, and use it someplace else is called *transfer*, and it is a critical ingredient in your development as a life-long learner. One of the most important skills needed to accomplish this goal is reflected in the title of this book: *Articulations*. Articulations are points of connection, places where two different bones or architectural structures or ideas come together to create something new and useful and sometimes beautiful. The goal of this book and this class is to help you find the articulations, the connections between what you know and what you don't know, the connections between rhetoric and your own discipline, and the connections between academic literacy and literacy in professional, personal, and civic settings.

This may be a new kind of thinking for you, and sometimes you may struggle. Don't get discouraged; struggle is a normal part of the learning process. Also keep in mind that we have many resources on campus to help you. Your instructor is available, not only during class time, but during office hours. The Writing Center provides trained consultants who can help you see your writing through new eyes and work through the writing process. The OIT Help Desk can provide technical support if you need help with Word or WebCampus or your ACE or Rebelmail accounts.

If you have questions or concerns that these resources can't answer, come see us in the English Composition Office. We are located on the second floor of the RLL, the building on the cover of this textbook, just as you come up the stairs or get off the elevator. We are here to help you have a great experience in ENG 101 or ENG 101E/F.

Sincerely,

Elaine Bunker, *Assistant Director of English Composition*
and lead instructor for ENG 101E/F

Karen Roop, *Assistant Director of English Composition*
and lead instructor for ENG 101

ONE

Thinking Rhetorically

The only real alternative to war is rhetoric.

—WAYNE BOOTH

PROFESSOR WAYNE BOOTH made this statement at a national conference of scholars and teachers of writing held only months after 9/11, and it quickly drew a range of responses: Just what did Booth mean by this stark statement? How could rhetoric—the art and practice of persuasion—act as a counter to war?

Throughout his long career, Booth explored these questions, identifying rhetoric as an ethical art that begins with deep and intense listening and that searches for mutual understanding and common ground as an alternative to violence and war. Put another way, two of the most potent tools we have for persuasion are language and violence: When words fail us, violence often wins the day. Booth, a noted critic and scholar, sees the careful, ethical use of language as our best approach to keeping violence and war at bay. Years later, Booth's words echoed again, during the start of the Arab Spring of 2011 as a vast gathering of Egyptian citizens protested in Cairo's Tahrir Square, using rhetorical means of persuasion—including posters, tweets, *Facebook* status updates, songs, and more—to eventually persuade President Hosni Mubarak to step down.

So how can you go about developing your own careful, ethical use of language? Our short answer: by learning to think and act rhetorically, that is, by developing habits of mind that begin with listening and searching for

Protestors in Cairo's Tahrir Square use banners, flags, raised fists, and their own voices to communicate their positions.

understanding before you decide what you yourself think and try to persuade others to listen to and act on what you say.

Learning to think rhetorically will serve you well as you negotiate your way through the complexities of life in today's world. In many situations in your everyday life, you'll need to communicate successfully with others in order to get things done, and done in a responsible and ethical way. On the job, for example, you may need to bring coworkers to consensus on how best to raise productivity when there is little, if any, money for raises. Or in your college community, you may find yourself negotiating difficult waters. When a group of students became aware of how little the temporary workers on their campus were paid, for example, they met with the workers, listening hard and gathering information. They then mounted a campaign using flyers, newsletters, photographs, speeches, and sit-ins—in other words, using the available means of persuasion—to win attention and convince the administration to raise the workers' pay. These students were thinking and acting rhetorically, and doing so responsibly and ethically.

Note that these students, like the protesters in Tahrir Square, worked closely together, both with the workers and with each other. In other words, none of us can manage such actions all by ourselves; we need to engage in

Students use posters and face-to-face conversation to protest the low wages paid to campus workers at Harvard.

conversation with others. Perhaps that's what philosopher Kenneth Burke had in mind when he created his famous "parlor" metaphor for life:

> Imagine that you enter a parlor. You come late. When you arrive, others have long preceded you, and they are engaged in a heated discussion, a discussion too heated for them to pause and tell you exactly what it is about. . . . You listen for a while, until you decide that you have caught the tenor of the argument; then you put in your oar.
>
> —KENNETH BURKE, *The Philosophy of Literary Form*

In this parable, each of us is much like the person arriving late to a room full of animated conversation; we don't understand what is going on. Yet instead of butting in or trying to take over, we listen closely until we catch on to what people are saying. Then we join in, using language and rhetorical strategies to engage with others as we add our own voices to the conversation.

This book aims to teach you to *think and act rhetorically*—to listen carefully and then to "put in your oar," join conversations about important issues, and develop strong critical and ethical habits of mind that will help you engage with others in responsible ways. In this chapter, you'll learn more about several specific practices that will help you develop the habit of thinking rhetorically.

First, Listen

*We have two ears
and one mouth
so we may listen
more and talk less.*
—EPICTETUS

Thinking rhetorically begins with listening, with being willing to hear the words of others in an open and understanding way. It means paying attention to what others say *as a way* of getting started on your own contributions to the conversation. Think of the times you are grateful to others for listening closely to you: when you are talking through a conflict with a family member or even when you are trying to explain to a salesperson just what it is you are looking for. On those occasions, you want the person you are addressing to really listen.

Hear What Others Are Saying—and Think about Why

When you enter any conversation, whether academic, professional, or personal, take the time needed to understand what is being said rather than rushing to a conclusion or a judgment. Listen carefully to what others are saying and consider what motivates them to do so: Where are they coming from?

Developing such habits of mind will be useful to you almost every day, whether you are participating in a class discussion, negotiating with friends over what film is most worth seeing, or studying a local ballot issue to decide how you'll vote. In each case, thinking rhetorically means being flexible and fair, able to hear and consider varying—and sometimes conflicting—points of view.

In ancient Rome, Cicero argued that considering alternative points of view and counterarguments was key to making a successful argument, and it is just as important today. Even when you disagree with a point of view—perhaps especially when you disagree with it—allow yourself to see the issue from the viewpoint of its advocates before you reject their positions. You may be convinced that hydrogen fuel will be the solution to global warming—but check your enthusiasm for it until you have thought hard about others' perspectives and carefully considered alternative solutions.

Thinking hard about others' views also includes considering the larger context and how it shapes what they are saying. This aspect of rhetorical thinking goes beyond the kind of close reading you probably learned to do in high school literature classes, where you looked very closely at a particular text and interpreted it on its own terms, without looking at secondary sources or outside influences. When you think rhetorically, you take a step further and put that close analysis into a larger context—historical, political, or cultural, for example.

In analyzing the issue of gay marriage, for instance, you would not merely consider your own thinking or do a close reading of texts that address the issue. In addition, you would look at the whole debate in context by considering its historical development over time, thinking about the broader political agendas of both those who advocate for and oppose gay marriage, asking what economic ramifications adopting—or rejecting—gay marriage might have, examining the role of religion in the debate, and so on. In short, you would try to see the issue from as many different perspectives and in as broad a context as possible before you formulate your own stance. When you write, you draw on these sources—what others have said about the issue—to support your own position and consider counterarguments to it.

What Do You Think—and Why?

Examining all points of view, all angles, on any issue will engage you in some tough thinking about your own stance—literally, where you are coming from on an issue—and why you think as you do. Such self-scrutiny can eventually clarify your stance or perhaps even change your mind; in either case, you stand to gain. Just as you need to think hard about the motivations of others, it's important to examine your own motivations in detail, asking yourself what influences in your life lead you to think as you do or to take certain positions. Then you can reconsider your motivations and reflect on their relationship to those of others, including your audience—those you wish to engage in conversation or debate.

In your college assignments, you probably have multiple motivations and purposes, one of which is to convince your instructor that you are a serious and hardworking student. But think about additional purposes as well: What could you learn from doing the assignment? How can doing it help you attain goals you have?

Beyond the classroom, examining your own stance and motivation is equally important. Suppose you are urging fellow members of a campus group to raise money for AIDS research. On one level, you are dedicated to helping science find a means of eradicating this disease. But when you think a bit harder, you might find that you have additional motivations: to oppose those who would rather raise money for a social event, to be able to list this fund-raising for science on your résumé, perhaps to change the organization's direction. As this example shows, examining what you think and why helps you to challenge your own position—and to make sure that your approach to the topic is appropriate and effective.

Do Your Homework

Rhetorical thinking calls on you to do some homework, to find out everything you can about what's been said about your topic, to analyze what you find—and then to synthesize that information to inform your own ideas. To put it another way, you want your own thinking to be deeply informed, to reflect more than just your own opinion.

To take an everyday example, you should do some pretty serious thinking when deciding on a major purchase, such as a new car. You'll want to begin by considering the purchase in the larger context of your life. What motivates you to buy a car? Do you need one for work? Do you want it in part as a status symbol? Are you concerned about the environment and want to switch to an electric vehicle? Who besides you might be affected by this decision? A thoughtful analysis of the context and your specific motivations and purposes can guide you in drawing up a preliminary list of cars to consider.

Then you'll need to do some research, checking out reports on safety records, efficiency, cost, and so on. Sometimes it can be hard to evaluate such sources: How much should you trust the mileage statistics provided by the carmaker, for example? For this reason you should consult multiple sources and check them against one another.

You will also want to consider your findings in light of your priorities. Cost, for instance, may not be as high on your priority list as energy efficiency. Such careful thinking will help you come to a sound decision, and then to explain it to others. If your parents, for instance, are helping you buy the car, you'll want to consider what their responses to your decision will be, anticipating questions they may ask and how to respond.

TAKE A LOOK at the 2011 Super Bowl Chrysler ad at wwnorton.com/write/everyone links. You'll see many scenes from Detroit, and here are some of the words in the ad: "What does this city know about luxury? What does a town that's been to hell and back know about the finer things in life? I'll tell you, more than most!" What kind of rhetorical thinking did the ad writers do? Who was their target audience, and how did they go about appealing to them? This was an award-winning ad—but how successful do you think it was as an ad? In other words, did it sell a lot of cars? If you were going to write an ad for a car you like, what words would you use, and why?

Doing your homework also means taking an analytic approach, focusing on *how* various rhetorical strategies and appeals work to persuade you. You may have been bowled over by a powerful advertisement for a new car—one you saw on Super Bowl Sunday that has been in your mind ever since. So what made that advertisement so memorable? To answer that question, you'll need to study the ad closely, determining just what qualities—a clever script? memorable music? celebrity actors? a provocative message?—worked to create the effect the ad had on you. This is the kind of analysis and research you will do when you engage in rhetorical thinking.

Give Credit

As part of engaging with what others have thought and said, you'll want to give credit where credit is due. Acknowledging the work of others will help build your own ethos, or character, showing that you have not only done your homework but that you want to credit those who have influenced you. The great physicist and astronomer Isaac Newton demonstrated the art of giving credit when he wrote to his rival Robert Hooke in 1676, saying:

> What Descartes did was a good step. You have added much in several ways, and especially in taking the colours of thin plates into philosophical consideration. If I have seen a little further it is by standing on the shoulders of giants.   —ISAAC NEWTON, letter to Robert Hooke

In this letter, Newton acknowledges the work of Descartes as well as of Hooke before saying, with a fair amount of modesty, that his own advancements were made possible by their work. In doing so, he is thinking—and acting—rhetorically.

You can give credit informally, as Newton did in this letter, or you can do so formally with a full citation. Which method you choose will depend on your purpose and context. Academic writing, for instance, usually calls for formal citations, but if you are writing for a personal blog, you might embed a link that connects to another's work—or just give an informal shout-out to a friend who contributed to your thinking. In each case, you'll want to be specific about what ideas or words you've drawn from others, as Newton does in referring to Hooke's consideration of the colors of thin plates. Such care in crediting your sources contributes to your credibility—and is an important part of ethical, careful rhetorical thinking.

Be Imaginative

Remember that intuition and imagination can often lead to great insights. While you want to think analytically and carefully, don't be afraid to take chances. A little imagination can lead you to new ideas—about a topic you're studying and about how to approach the topic in a way that will interest others. Such insights and intuitions can often pay off big-time. One student athlete we know was interested in how the mass media covered the Olympics, and he began doing research on the coverage in *Sports Illustrated* from different periods. So far, so good: He was gathering information and would be able to write an essay showing that the magazine had been a major promoter of the Olympics.

While looking through old issues of *Sports Illustrated*, however, he kept feeling that something he was seeing in the early issues was different from current issues of the magazine . . . something that felt important to him

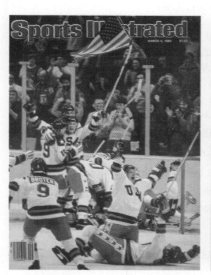 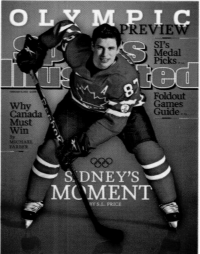

Two *Sports Illustrated* covers depicting hockey players in the Winter Olympics. The cover on the left, from 1980, showcases the U.S. team's "miracle on ice" victory win over the heavily favored USSR team. The one on the right, from 2010, pictures Canada's superstar Sidney "Sid the Kid" Crosby, who scored the game-winning shot in the gold medal game against the United States.

though he couldn't quite articulate it. This hunch led him to make an imaginative leap, to articulate for himself what that difference was. Excited that he was on to something, he returned to his chronological examination of the magazine. On closer inspection, he found that over the decades of its Olympics coverage, that magazine had slowly but surely moved from focusing on teams to depicting *only* individual stars. This discovery led him to make an argument he would never have made had he not paid attention to his imagination, to his creative hunch—that the evolution of sports from a focus on the team to a focus on individual stars is perfectly captured in the pages of *Sports Illustrated*. It also helped him write a much more interesting—and more persuasive—essay, one that captured the attention not only of his instructor and classmates but of a local sports newsmagazine, which reprinted his essay along with a picture of its author. Like this student, you can benefit by using your imagination and listening to your inner hunches. They can pay off for you as they did for him.

Put in Your Oar

So rhetorical thinking offers a way of coming to any situation with a tool kit of strategies that will help you understand that situation and "put in your oar" to act effectively within it. When you think rhetorically, you ask yourself certain questions:

- How do you want to come across to your audience?
- How can you appear knowledgeable, fair, and well informed?
- What can you do to represent yourself in a positive way?
- What can you do to show respect both for your audience and for those whose work and thinking you engage with?
- How can you demonstrate that you have your audience's best interests at heart?

This kind of rhetorical thinking will help ensure that your words will be listened to and taken seriously.

We can find examples of such a rhetorical approach in all fields of study and in all walks of life. Take, for instance, the landmark essay by James Watson and Francis Crick on the discovery of DNA, published in *Na-*

ture in 1953. This essay shows Watson and Crick to be thinking rhetorically throughout, acutely aware of their audience (major scientists throughout the world) as well as of competitors who were simultaneously working on the same issue.

Here is Wayne Booth's analysis of Watson and Crick's use of rhetoric:

> In [Watson and Crick's] report, what do we find? Actually scores of *rhetorical* choices that they made to strengthen the appeal of their scientific claim. (Biographies and autobiographies have by now revealed that they did a lot of conscientious revising, not of the data but of the mode of presentation; and their lives were filled, before and after the triumph, with a great deal of rhetoric-charged conflict.) We could easily compose a dozen different versions of their report, all proclaiming the same scientific results. But most alternatives would prove less engaging to the intended audience. They open, for example, with

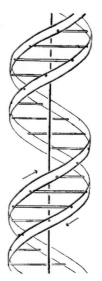

>> "*We wish to suggest* a structure" that has "*novel* features which are of *considerable* biological *interest.*" *(My italics, of course)*

> Why didn't they say, instead: "We shall here demonstrate a *startling, totally new structure* that will *shatter* everyone's conception of the biological world"? Well, obviously their rhetorical choice presents an ethos much more attractive to most cautious readers than does my exaggerated alternative. A bit later they say

>> "We have made the *usual chemical assumptions,* namely . . ."

> Why didn't they say, "*As we all know*"? Both expressions acknowledge reliance on warrants, commonplaces within a given rhetorical domain. But their version sounds more thoughtful and authoritative, especially with the word "chemical." Referring to Pauling and Corey, they say

>> "They *kindly* have made their manuscript available."

> Okay, guys, drop the rhetoric and just cut that word "kindly." What has that got to do with your scientific case? Well, it obviously strengthens the authors' ethos: we are nice guys dealing trustfully with other nice guys, in a rhetorical community.

> And on they go, with "*In our opinion*" (rather than "We proclaim" or "We insist" or "We have miraculously discovered"): again ethos—we're

The original sketch showing the structure of DNA that appeared in Watson and Crick's article.

not dogmatic); and Fraser's "*suggested*" structure is "*rather ill-defined*" (rather than "his structure is stupid" or "obviously faulty"—we *are* nice guys, right?)

And on to scores of other such choices.

—WAYNE BOOTH, *The Rhetoric of Rhetoric*

Booth shows in each instance how Watson and Crick's exquisite understanding of their rhetorical situation—especially of their audience and of the stakes involved in making their claim—had a great deal to do with how that claim was received. (They won the Nobel Prize!)

As the example of Watson and Crick illustrates, rhetorical thinking involves certain habits of mind that can and should lead to something—often to an action, to making something happen. And when it comes to taking action, those who think rhetorically are in a very strong position. They have listened attentively and thought carefully and methodically; viewed their topic from many alternate perspectives; done their homework; and engaged with the words and thoughts of others. This kind of rhetorical thinking will help you to get in on conversations—and will increase the likelihood that your ideas will be heard and will inspire actions that take root and prosper.

Indeed, the ability to think rhetorically is of great importance in today's global world, as Professors Gerald Graff and Cathy Birkenstein explain:

The ability to enter complex, many-sided conversations has taken on a special urgency in today's diverse, post-9/11 world, where the future for all of us may depend on our ability to put ourselves in the shoes of those who think very differently from us. Listening carefully to others, including those who disagree with us, and then engaging with them thoughtfully and respectfully . . . can help us see beyond our own pet beliefs, which may not be shared by everyone. The mere act of acknowledging that someone might disagree with us may not seem like a way to change the world; but it does have the potential to jog us out of our comfort zones, to get us thinking critically about our own beliefs, and perhaps even to change our minds.

—GERALD GRAFF AND CATHY BIRKENSTEIN, *"They Say / I Say"*

In the long run, if enough of us learn to think rhetorically, we just might achieve Booth's goal—to use words (and images) in thoughtful and constructive ways as an alternative to violence and war.

TWO

Rhetorical Situations

AS PART OF A COLLEGE APPLICATION, a high school student writes a personal statement about what she plans to study, and why. A baseball fan posts a piece on a New York Yankees blog analyzing data to show why a beloved pitcher probably won't be elected to the Hall of Fame. Eighty-seven readers respond, some praising his analysis, others questioning his conclusions and offering their own analyses. The officers of a small company address the annual shareholders' meeting to report on how the firm is doing, using *PowerPoint* slides to call attention to their most important points. They take questions afterward, and two people raise their hands. Our baseball fan sees on *Twitter* that the Yankees have signed a star pitcher he thinks they don't really need—and fires off a tweet saying so. The student in our first example takes a deep breath and logs on to the website of the college she wants to attend to see if she's been accepted. Good news: She's in. Come September she's at the library, working on an essay for her first-year composition course—and texting her friends as she works.

In each of these scenarios, an author is writing (or speaking from written notes) in a different set of specific circumstances—addressing certain audiences for a particular purpose, using certain technologies, and so on. So it is whenever we write. Whether we're texting a friend, outlining an oral presentation, or writing an essay, we do so within a specific rhetorical situation. We have a purpose, an audience, a stance, a genre, a medium, a design—all of which exist in some larger context. This chapter covers each of these ele-

Three different rhetorical situations: a lone writer texting (*top left*); a student giving an oral presentation in class (*top right*); and members of a community group collaborating on a group project (*bottom left*).

ments and provides prompts to help you think about some of the choices you have as you negotiate your own rhetorical situations.

Every rhetorical situation presents its own unique constraints and opportunities, and as authors, we need to think strategically about our own situation. Adding to a class wiki presents a different challenge from writing an in-class essay exam, putting together a résumé and cover letter for a job, or working with fellow members of a campus choir to draft a grant proposal to the student government requesting funding so the choir can go on tour the following year. A group of neighbors developing a proposal to present at a community meeting will need to attend to both the written text they will submit and the oral arguments they will make. They may also need to create slides or other visuals to support their proposal.

The workplace creates still other kinds of rhetorical situations with their own distinctive features. Reporters, for instance, must always consider their deadlines as well as their ethical obligations—to the public, to the persons or institutions they write about, and to the story they are reporting. A reporter working for six months to investigate corporate wrongdoing faces different challenges from one who covers local sports day to day. The medium—print, video, radio, podcast, blog, or some combination of these or other media—also influences how reporters write their stories.

Think about Your Own Rhetorical Situation

It is important to start thinking about your rhetorical situation early in your writing process. As a student, you'll often be given assignments with very specific guidelines—to follow the conventions of a particular genre, in a certain medium, by a specific date. Nevertheless, even the most fully developed assignment cannot address every aspect of any particular rhetorical situation.

Effective writers—whether students, journalists, teachers, or your mom—know how to analyze their rhetorical situation. They may conduct this analysis unconsciously and instinctively, drawing upon the rhetorical common sense they have developed as writers, readers, speakers, and listeners. Particularly when you are writing in a new genre or discipline, though—a situation that you'll surely face as a college student—it can be helpful to analyze your rhetorical situation more systematically.

THINK ABOUT YOUR GENRE

- *Have you been assigned a specific genre?* If not, do any words in the assignment imply a certain genre? *Evaluate* may signal a review, for example, and *explain why* could indicate a causal analysis.

- *If you get to choose your genre,* consider your purpose. If you want to convince readers to recycle their trash, you would likely write an argument. If, however, you want to explain how to go about recycling, your purpose would call for a process analysis.

- *Does your genre require a certain organization?* A process analysis, for instance, is often organized chronologically, whereas an annotated bibliography is almost always organized alphabetically.

- *How does your genre affect your tone?* A lab report, for example, generally calls for a different tone than a film review.

- *Are certain design features expected in your genre?* You would likely need to include images in a review of an art show, for instance, or be required to use a certain font size for a research paper.

THINK ABOUT YOUR AUDIENCE

- *Who is your intended audience?* An instructor? A supervisor? Classmates? Members of a particular organization? Visitors to a website? Who else might see or hear what you say?

- *How are members of your audience like and unlike you?* Consider demographics such as age, gender, religion, income, education, occupation, or political attitudes.

- *What's your relationship with your audience?* An instructor or supervisor, for example, holds considerable authority over you. Other audiences may be friends, coworkers, or (especially online) complete strangers. What expectations about the text might they have because of your relationship? You'd need to be careful not to sound too informal to a committee considering you for a scholarship, or too bossy to a group of friends.

- *If you have a choice of medium,* which one(s) would best reach your intended audience?

- *What do you want your audience to think or do* as a result of what you say? Take your ideas seriously? Respond to you? Take some kind of action? How will you signal to them what you want?

- *Can you assume your audience will be interested* in what you say, or will you need to get them interested? Are they likely to resist any of your ideas?

- *How much does your audience know about your topic?* How much background information do they need? Will they expect—or be put off by— the use of technical jargon? Will you need to define any terms?

- *Will your audience expect a particular genre?* If you're writing about Mozart for a music class, you might analyze something he wrote; if, however, you're posting comments on *Amazon* about a new CD, you'd be more likely to write some kind of review.

THINK ABOUT YOUR PURPOSE

- *How would you describe your own motivation for writing?* To fulfill a course assignment? To meet a personal or professional commitment? To express your ideas to someone? For fun?

- *What is your primary goal?* To inform your audience about something? To persuade them to think a certain way? To call them to action? To entertain them? Something else? Do you have other goals as well?

- *How do your goals influence your choice of genre, medium, and design?* For example, if you want to persuade neighbors to recycle, you may choose to make colorful posters for display in public places. If you want to inform a corporation about what recycling programs accomplish, you may want to write a report using charts and examples.

THINK ABOUT YOUR STANCE

- *What's your attitude toward your topic?* Objective? Strongly supportive? Mildly skeptical? Amused? Angry?

- *What's your relationship with your audience?* Do you know them? Are they teachers? friends? strangers? How do you want to be seen by them—as a serious student? an effective leader? an informed citizen?

- *How can you best convey your stance in your writing?* What tone do you want it to have?

- *How will your stance and tone be received by your audience?* Will they be surprised by it?

THINK ABOUT THE LARGER CONTEXT

- *What else has been said about your topic,* and how does that affect what you will say? What would be the most effective way for you to add your voice to the conversation?

- *Do you have any constraints?* When is this writing due? Given your current to-do list and the nature and significance of this project, how much time and energy can you put into it?

- *How much independence do you have as a writer* in this situation? To what extent do you need to meet the expectations of others, such as an instructor or supervisor? If this writing is an assignment, how can you approach it in a way that makes it matter to you?

THINK ABOUT YOUR MEDIUM AND DESIGN

- *If you get to choose your medium,* which one will work best for your audience and purpose? Print? Spoken? Digital? Some combination?

- *How will the medium determine what you can and cannot do?* For example, if you're writing on *Facebook,* how might the medium influence your tone? If you're submitting an essay online, you could include video, but if you were writing the same essay in print, you'd only be able to include a still shot from the video.

- *Does your medium favor certain conventions?* Paragraphs work well in print, but *PowerPoint* presentations usually rely on bulleted phrases instead. If you are writing online, you can include links to sources and background information.

- *What's the look most appropriate to your rhetorical situation?* Serious? Warm and inviting? Whimsical? What design elements will help you project that look?

- *Should you include visuals?* Is there anything in your text that would benefit from them? Will your audience expect them? What kind would be appropriate—photographs? video? maps? Is there any statistical material that would be easier to understand as a table, chart, or graph?

- *If you're writing a spoken or digital text,* should you include audio or video?

MAKE A LIST of all the writing that you remember doing in the last week. Be sure to include everything from texting and tweeting to more formal academic or work-related writing. Choose three examples that strike you as quite different from one another and write an analysis of the rhetorical situation you faced for each one, drawing upon the guidelines in this chapter.

THREE

Meeting the Demands of Academic Writing

"It's Like Learning a New Language"

ELLEN MACNAMARA ARRIVED AT COLLEGE excited but also anxious. She had grown up in a small town far from the college, had not taken calculus, and had never written more than a five-paragraph essay. So when she got her first college writing assignment—in a political science class, to write a ten-page essay on how the relationship among the three branches of the U.S. government has evolved—she felt a little panic. She had read all her assignments and done some research, and she had even met with her instructor during office hours. She had quite a bit of material. But when she started to write, it just didn't sound right. She wasn't sure what college writing sounded like, but this wasn't it. Following her instructor's advice, Mac-Namara studied several of the political science articles that were on her course reading list. Compared to her usual writing, they were much more formal, full of long words and complicated sentences. What she eventually came up with wasn't a particularly good paper (and she knew it), but it served its purpose: It had gotten her thinking about college-level writing. Looking back at the work she had done to get this far, she thought, "Wow, this is almost like learning a new language."

MacNamara had a point. Many students have experiences similar to hers, especially multilingual students who've grown up in other cultures. One Romanian student we know puts it this way:

> In my country we care very much about the beauty of what we write. Even with academic and business writing, we try to make our texts poetic in some way. When I got to the U.S.A., I discovered that writing that I thought was beautiful struck my teachers as wordy and off task. I was surprised about this.

This student, like Ellen MacNamara, needed to set about learning a new language—in this case, the language of U.S. academic writing.

So Just What Is Academic Writing?

Academic writing is the writing you do for school. It follows a fairly strict set of conventions, such as using standard edited English, following logical patterns of organization, and providing support for the points you make. But academic writing reaches beyond the classroom: It's used in many journals, newspapers, and books as well as on the web, especially in many blogs. So "academic writing" is a broad category, one flexible enough to accommodate differences across disciplines, for example, while still remaining recognizably "academic." This chapter considers some of the assumptions that lie behind academic writing in the United States and describes some of the most common characteristics of that writing.

We're giving so much attention to academic writing for a couple of important reasons: First, becoming fluent in it will be of great help to you both in college and well beyond; and second, it poses challenges to both native and nonnative speakers of English. We want to acknowledge these challenges without making them sound like it takes a rocket scientist to meet them. Instead, we want to try to demystify some of the assumptions and conventions of academic writing and get you started thinking about how to use them to your advantage.

Joining U.S. Academic Conversations

If you are new to college, you need to learn to "talk the talk" of academic writing as soon as possible, so that you can join the conversations in progress all around you. Doing so calls for understanding some common expectations that most if not all of your instructors hold.

You're expected to respond. One important assumption underlying the kind of writing expected in American colleges is that reading and writing are active processes in which students not only absorb information but also respond to and even question it. Not all educational systems view reading and writing in this way. In some cultures, students are penalized if they attempt to read established texts critically or to disagree with authorities or insert their own views. If you are from such a background, you may find it difficult to engage in this kind of active reading and writing. It may feel rude, disrespectful, or risky, particularly if such engagement would result in a reprimand in your home culture.

Remember, however, that the kind of engagement your instructors want is not hostile or combative, not about showing off by beating down the ideas of others. Rather, they expect you to demonstrate your active engagement with the texts you read—and an awareness that in doing so you are joining an academic conversation, one that has been going on for a long time and that will continue. It's fine to express strong opinions, but it's also important to remember—and acknowledge—that there is almost surely some value in perspectives other than your own.

You're expected to ask questions. Because U.S. culture emphasizes individual achievement so much, students are expected to develop authority and independence, often by asking questions. In contrast to cultures where the best students never ask questions because they have already studied the material and worked hard to learn it, in American academic contexts, students are expected to ask questions. In other words, don't assume you have to figure everything out by yourself. Do take responsibility for your own learning whenever possible, but it's fine to ask questions, especially specific questions about assignments.

You're expected to say what *you* think. American instructors expect that students will progress from relying on the thoughts of others to formulating ideas and arguments of their own. One important way to make that move is to engage in dialogue with other students and teachers. In these dialogues, teachers are not looking for you to express the "right" position; instead, they're looking for you to say what *you* think and provide adequate and appropriate support for what you say.

You're expected to focus from the start. In contrast to many cultures, where writers start with fairly general background information for readers, American academic writing focuses in on the topic at hand from the start. Thus, even in the introduction of an essay, you begin at a relatively focused level, providing even greater detail in the paragraphs that follow. The point is not to provide evidence of how much you know but instead to provide as much specific information as is required for the audience to understand the point without having to work very hard.

Because American academic writers generally open their discussions at a fairly specific level, you wouldn't want to begin with a sentence like "All over the world and in many places, there are families," a thesis statement in an essay one of us once received from a native speaker of Arabic. (Translated into Arabic, this would make a beautiful sentence and an appropriate opening statement for a student essay.) Students educated in Spanish or Portuguese and, to an even greater extent, those educated in Arabic are accustomed to providing a great deal more background information than those educated in English do. If you are from one of these cultural backgrounds, do not be surprised if your instructor encourages you to delete most of the first few pages of a draft, for example, and to begin instead by addressing your topic more directly and specifically.

You're expected to state your point explicitly. In U.S. academic English, writers are expected to provide direct and explicit statements that lead readers, step by step, through the text—in contrast to cultures that value indirectness, circling around the topic rather than addressing it head-on. A Brazilian student we knew found it especially hard to state the major point of an essay up front and explicitly. From his cultural perspective, it made far more sense to develop an argument by building a sense of suspense and stating his position only at the end of the essay. As he said, "It took a lot of practice for me to learn how to write the very direct way that professors in the U.S.A. want."

All these expectations suggest that American academic discourse puts much of the burden for successful communication on the author rather than on members of the audience. So with these expectations in mind, let's take a close look at seven common characteristics of U.S. academic writing.

Academic writers at work in India, Chile, Italy, Burkina Faso, Thailand, and the United States.

CHARACTERISTIC FEATURES

Although no list of characteristics can describe all the kinds of texts you'll read or write in college, particularly given differences among disciplines, we can offer a list of conventional features that captures most, if not all, of what your professors will expect in the writing you do in their classes.

- Use standard edited English.
- Use clear and recognizable patterns of organization.
- Mark logical relationships between ideas.
- State claims explicitly and provide appropriate support.
- Present your ideas as a response to others.
- Express ideas clearly and directly.
- Be aware of how genres and conventions vary across disciplines.
- Document sources using the appropriate citation style.

Use Standard Edited English

Academic writing almost always follows the conventions of standard edited English in terms of spelling, grammar, and punctuation. In addition, it is more rather than less formal. Thus, the kind of abbreviations and other shortcuts you use all the time in text messaging or posting to social media sites usually aren't appropriate in academic writing: You'll have to write out "with respect to" rather than "wrt," and you'll also want to avoid ☺ and other emoticons. Likewise, slang isn't usually appropriate. In some contexts, you'll discover that even contractions aren't appropriate—although we use them in this book because we're aiming for a conversational tone, one that is formal to some degree but not stuffy. As you can probably tell, defining standard edited English is in many ways a matter of cataloging things you *shouldn't* do.

Additionally, however, thinking about the label itself—standard edited English—will give you some insights into the goal you are trying to accomplish. In general, the "standard" variety of any language is the one used in formal contexts, including academic ones, by people who are well educated; thus, the ability to use the standard variety of a language marks its user as educated.

The logic behind a standard language is simple and useful: If everyone can agree on and follow the same basic conventions, whether for spelling or subject-verb agreement, we'll be able to communicate successfully with a much broader range of people. It's a good principle in theory, but as you know if you have been to Canada or the United Kingdom, "standard" English varies from country to country. Moreover, standards change over time. So while having a "standard" set of conventions is valuable in many ways, it can't guarantee perfect communication.

"Edited," the second term of the label "standard edited English," reminds you that this variety of English is one that has been looked at very carefully. Many writers, especially those who grew up speaking a variety of English other than the standard and those whose first language is not English, reread their writing several times with great care before submitting it to ensure, for example, that every verb agrees with its subject. This is, of course, the role that good editors play: They read someone else's work and make suggestions about how to improve the quality, whether at the level of the sentence, the paragraph, or the text as a whole. Few of us pay such careful attention to our writing when we tweet, text, or email—but we *all* need to do so with our academic writing.

Use Clear and Recognizable Patterns of Organization

Academic writing is organized in a way that's clear and easy for readers to recognize. In fact, writers generally describe the pattern explicitly early in a text by including a thesis sentence that states the main point and says how the text is structured.

At the level of the paragraph, the opening sentence generally serves as a topic sentence, which announces what the paragraph is about. Readers of academic writing expect such signals for the text as a whole and for each paragraph, even within shorter texts like essay exams. Sometimes you'll want to include headings to make it easy for readers to locate sections of text.

Readers of academic writing expect the organization of the text not only to be clear but also to follow some kind of logical progression. For example:

- Beginning with the simplest ideas and then moving step by step to the most complex ideas
- Starting with the weakest claims or evidence and progressing to the strongest ones

- Treating some topics early in the text because readers must have them as background to understand ideas introduced later
- Arranging the text chronologically, starting with the earliest events and ending with the latest ones

Some academic documents, including most journals in the sciences and social sciences, require a specific organization known as IMRAD for its specific headings: introduction, methods, results, and discussion. Although there are many possible logical patterns to use, readers will expect to be able to see that pattern with little or no difficulty. Likewise, they generally expect the transitions between sections and ideas to be indicated in some way, whether with words like *first, next,* or *finally,* or even with full sentences like "Having considered three reasons to support this position, here are some alternative positions."

Finally, remember that you need to conclude your text by somehow reminding your readers of the main point(s) you want them to take away. Often, these reminders explicitly link the conclusion back to a thesis statement or introduction.

Mark Logical Relationships between Ideas

One more thing expected of academic writers is to make clear how your ideas relate to one another. Thus, in addition to marking the structure of the text, you need to mark the links between ideas and to do so explicitly. If you say in casual conversation, "It was raining, and we didn't go on the picnic," listeners will interpret *and* to mean *so* or *therefore.* In academic writing, however, you have to help readers understand how your ideas are related to one another. For this reason, you'll want to use transitions like *therefore, however,* or *in addition.* Marking the relationships among your ideas clearly and explicitly helps readers recognize and appreciate the logic of your arguments.

State Claims Explicitly and Provide Appropriate Support

One of the most important conventions of academic writing is to present claims explicitly and support them with evidence, such as examples or statistics, or by citing authorities of various kinds. Notice the two distinct parts: presenting claims clearly and supporting them appropriately. In academic writing, authors don't generally give hints; instead, they state what is on their minds, often in a thesis statement. If you are from a culture that values indirection and communicates by hinting or by repeating proverbs or telling stories to make a point, you'll need to work to be sure that you have stated your claims explicitly. Don't assume that readers will be able to understand what you're saying, especially if they do not have the same cultural background knowledge that you do.

Qualify your statements. It's important to note that being clear and explicit doesn't mean being dogmatic or stubborn. You'll generally want to qualify your claims by using qualifying words like *frequently, often, generally, sometimes,* or *rarely* to indicate how strong a claim you are making. Note as well that it is much easier to provide adequate support for a qualified claim than it is to provide support for an unqualified claim.

Choose evidence your audience will trust. Whatever your claim, you'll need to look for evidence that will be considered trustworthy and persuasive by your audience. And keep in mind that what counts as acceptable and appropriate evidence in academic writing often differs from what works in other contexts. Generally, for example, you wouldn't cite sacred religious texts as a primary source for academic arguments.

Consider multiple perspectives. Similarly, you should be aware that your readers may have range of opinions on any topic, and you should write accordingly. Thus, citing only sources that reflect one perspective won't be sufficient in most academic contexts. Be sure to consider and acknowledge counterarguments and viewpoints other than your own.

Organize information strategically. One common way of supporting a claim is by moving from a general statement to more specific information. When you see words like *for example* or *for instance,* the author is moving from a more general statement to a more specific example.

In considering what kind of evidence to use in supporting your claims, remember that the goal is not to amass and present large quantities of evidence but instead to sift through all the available evidence, choose the evidence that will be most persuasive to your audience, and arrange and present it all strategically. Resist the temptation to include information or anecdotes that are not directly relevant to your topic or contribute to your argument. Your instructor will likely refer to these as digressions or as "getting off topic" and encourage you to delete them.

Present Your Ideas as a Response to Others

The best academic writers do more than just make well-supported claims. They present their ideas as a response to what else has been said (or might be said) about their topic. One common pattern, introduced by Professors Gerald Graff and Cathy Birkenstein, is to start with what others are saying and then to present your ideas as a response. If, as noted earlier in this chapter, academic writing is a way of entering a conversation—of engaging with the ideas of others—you need to include their ideas in with your own.

In fact, providing support for your claims will often involve synthesis: weaving the ideas and even the words of others into the argument you are making. And since academic arguments are part of a larger conversation, all of us in some important ways are always responding to and borrowing from others, even as we develop our own ideas and present them to others.

Express Your Ideas Clearly and Directly

Another characteristic of academic writing is clarity. You want to be sure that readers can understand exactly what you are writing about. Have you ever begun a sentence by writing "This shows . . ." only to have your teacher ask, "What does *this* refer to?" Such a comment would be evidence that the teacher, as reader, wasn't sure what the author—you—was referring to: this argument? this evidence? this analysis? this figure? this claim? You'll also want to define terms you use, both to be sure readers will not be confused and to clarify your own positions—much as we defined "standard edited English" earlier in this chapter.

Clarity of expression in academic writing also means being direct and concise. Academic writers in the United States, for example, avoid highly elaborate sentence structures or flowery language, and they don't let the metaphors and similes they use get the best of them either, as this author did:

> Cheryl's mind turned like the vanes of a wind-powered turbine, chopping her sparrow-like thoughts into bloody pieces that fell onto a growing pile of forgotten memories.

In fact, this sentence was the winner of an annual "bad writing" contest in which writers try to write the worst sentence they possibly can. It's easy to see why this one was a winner: It has way too much figurative language—

wind-powered turbines that chop, sparrows that bleed, thoughts in a pile, memories that are forgotten—and the metaphors get in the way of one another. Use metaphors sparingly in academic writing, and be very careful that they don't distract from what you're trying to say. Here's one way the prize-winning sentence might be revised to be clearer and more direct: "Cheryl's mind worked incessantly, thought after thought piling up until she couldn't keep track of them all."

Be Aware of How Genres and Conventions Vary across Disciplines

While we can identify common characteristics of all academic writing, it is important to note that some genres and conventions vary across disciplines. Thus, an analytic essay in psychology is similar to one in a literature class, but it is also different in crucial ways. The same will be true for lab reports or position papers in various fields. In this regard, different disciplines are like different cultures, sharing many things but unique in specific ways. Therefore, part of becoming a biologist or an engineer—or even an electrical engineer instead of a civil engineer—will require learning its particular rules and rituals as well as its preferred ways of presenting, organizing, and documenting information.

You'll also find that some rhetorical moves vary across genres. In the humanities, for example, writers often use a quotation to open an essay, as a way of launching an argument—or to close one, as a way of inspiring the audience. Such a move occurs far less often, if at all, in the sciences or social sciences.

Despite these differences in genres across academic disciplines, you'll also find there are some common rhetorical moves you'll make in much of the academic writing you do. Thus, you'll find that short essays and research articles generally open with three such moves:

- First, you give the context or general topic of whatever you are writing; frequently, you will do this by discussing the existing research or commentary on the topic you are writing about.
- Second, you point out some aspect of this topic that merits additional attention, often because it is poorly understood or because there is a problem that needs to be solved—that is, you'll show there is a problem or gap of some kind in our understanding.

- Finally, you'll explain how your text addresses that problem or fills that gap. Notice that this often happens within the first paragraph or two of the text.

By contrast, in writing a response to a question on a timed exam, you might restate the question in some way, using it as the opening line of your response and a thesis statement or topic sentence. For example, if you get an essay exam question asking "How are West African influences evident in coastal southeastern areas of the United States today?" you might begin your response by turning the question into a statement like this: "West African influences to language, music, and food are still very visible in coastal areas of the southeastern United States." You should not spend several sentences introducing your topic while the clock ticks; to do so would be to waste valuable time.

With experience, you will learn the genres and conventions you need to know, especially within your major.

Document Sources Using the Appropriate Citation Style

Finally, academic writers credit and document all sources carefully. If becoming fluent in academic discourse is a challenge for all of us, understanding how Western academic culture defines intellectual property and plagiarism is even more complicated. Although you will never need to provide a source for historical events that no one disputes (for example, that the U.S. Declaration of Independence was signed on July 4, 1776, in Philadelphia), you will need to provide documentation for words, ideas, or organizational patterns that you get from others, including any information (words or images) you find on the internet.

What Else Do You Need to Learn about Academic Writing?

While we hope this brief list gives you a good idea of the major features of academic writing in the United States, you'll likely still find yourself asking questions. Just what does a direct and concise style look like? How much and what kinds of evidence are necessary to support a claim sufficiently? How much documentation is sufficient? Should a review of literature primarily describe and summarize existing research, or should it go one step further and critique this research? You will begin to learn the answers to these questions in time, as you advance through college, and especially when you choose your major. But don't be surprised that the immediate answer to all these questions will very often be, "It depends." And "it" will always depend on what your purpose is in writing and on the audience you wish to reach.

In the meantime, even as you work to become fluent in U.S. academic writing, it's worth returning to a note we have sounded frequently in this chapter: The U.S. way of writing academically is not the *only* way. Nor is it a *better* way. Rather, it is a *different* way. As you learn about and experience other cultures and languages, you may have an opportunity to learn and practice the conventions those cultures use to guide their own forms of academic writing. When you do so, you'll be learning yet another "new" language, just as you have learned the "academic writing" language of the United States.

FOUR

Reading with a Critical Eye

READING STRATEGIES

We read newspapers and websites to learn about the events of the day. We read cookbooks to find out how to make brownies and textbooks to learn about history, chemistry, and other academic topics. We read short stories for pleasure—and, in literature classes, to analyze plot, setting, character, and theme. And as writers, we read our own drafts to make sure they say what we mean and to make sure they're correct. In other words, we read in various ways for many different purposes. But almost all of us could benefit from learning to read more effectively.

Taking Stock of Your Reading

One way to become a better reader is to understand your reading process; if you know what you do when you read, you're in a better position to decide what you need to change or improve. Consider the answers to the following questions:

- What do you read—for pleasure? for work? for school? for something else? Consider all the sorts of reading you do: books, magazines, newspapers, websites, Facebook, texting, blogs, instructions.

- When you're facing a reading assignment, what do you do? Do you do certain things to get comfortable? Do you play music or seek quiet? Do you plan your reading time or set reading goals for yourself? Do you flip through or skim the text before settling down to read it or just start at the beginning and work through it?

- When you begin to read something for an assignment, do you make sure you understand the purpose of the assignment—why you must read this text? Do you ever ask your instructor (or whoever else assigned the reading) what its purpose is?

- How do you motivate yourself to read material you don't have any interest in? How do you deal with boredom while reading?

- Does your mind wander? If you realize that you haven't been paying attention and don't know what you just read, what do you do?

- Do you ever highlight, underline, or annotate text as you read? Do you take notes? If so, what do you mark or write down? Why?

- When you read text you don't understand, what do you do?

- As you anticipate and read an assigned text, what attitudes or feelings do you typically have? If they differ from reading to reading, why do they?

- What do you do when you've finished reading an assigned text? Write out notes? Think about what you've just read? Move on to the next task? Something else?

- How well do your reading processes work for you, both in school and otherwise? What would you like to change?

The rest of this chapter offers advice and strategies that you may find helpful as you work to improve your reading skills.

Reading Strategically

Academic reading is challenging because it makes several demands on you at once. Textbooks present new vocabulary and concepts, and picking out the main ideas can be difficult. Scholarly articles present content and arguments you need to understand, but they often assume readers already know key concepts and vocabulary and so don't generally provide background information. As you read more texts in an academic field and participate in its conversations, the reading will become easier, but in the meantime you can develop strategies that will help you to read carefully and critically.

Different texts require different kinds of effort. Some texts can be read fairly quickly, if you're reading to get a general overview. Most of the time, though, you need to read carefully, matching the pace of your reading to the difficulty of the text. To read with a critical eye, you can't be in too much of a hurry. You'll likely need to skim the text for an overview of the basic ideas and then go back to read carefully. And then you may read the text again. That is true for visual as well as verbal texts—you'll often need to get an overview of a text and then reread to pay close attention to its details.

Preparing to Read

To learn, we need to place new information into a context of what we already know. For example, to understand photosynthesis, we need to already know something about plants, energy, and air, among other things. To learn a new language, we draw on similarities and differences between it and any other languages we know. A method of bringing to conscious attention our current knowledge on a topic and of helping us articulate our purposes for reading is a list-making process called KWL+. To use it, create a table with three columns:

K: What I Know	W: What I Want to Know	L: What I Learned

Before you begin reading a text, list in the "K" column what you already know about the topic. Brainstorm ideas, and list terms or phrases that come to mind. Then group them into categories. Also before reading, or after reading the first few paragraphs, list in the "W" column questions you have that you expect, want, or hope to be answered as you read. Number or reorder the questions by their importance to you.

Then read the text. As you read or afterward, list in the "L" column what you learned from the text. Compare your "L" list with your "W" list to see what you still want or need to know (the "+")—and what you learned that you didn't expect.

Previewing a Text

It's usually a good idea to start by skimming a text: read the title and sub-title, any headings, the first and last paragraphs, the first sentences of all the other paragraphs. Study any illustrations and other visuals. Your goal is to get a sense of where the text is heading. At this point, don't stop to look up unfamiliar words; just mark them somehow (such as with underlining, highlighting, or electronic annotations), and look them up later.

Considering the Rhetorical Situation

As a reader, you need to think about the message that the writer wants to articulate, the intended audience, and the larger context in which the text was created.

Purpose   What is the writer's purpose? To entertain? inform? persuade read-ers to think something or take some action? What is *your* purpose for reading this text?

Audience   Who is the intended audience? Are you a member of that group? If not, should you expect that you'll need to look up unfamiliar terms or concepts or that you'll run into assumptions you don't necessar-ily share?

Genre   What is the genre? Is it a report? an argument? an analysis? some-thing else? Knowing the genre can help you anticipate certain key features.

Stance   Who is the writer, and what is his or her stance? Critical? Curious? Opinionated? Objective? Passionate? Indifferent? Something else? Knowing the stance affects the way you understand a text, wheth-er you're inclined to agree or disagree, to take it seriously, and so on.

Media /   What is the medium, and how does it affect the way you read? If
Design   it's a print text, what do you know about the publisher? If it's on the web, who sponsors the site, and when was it last updated? Are there any headings, summaries, color, or boxes that highlight key parts of the text?

Thinking about Your Initial Response

It's usually good to read a text first just to get a sense of it. Some readers find it helps to make brief notes about their first response to a text, noting their reaction and thinking a little about why they reacted as they did:

- *What are your initial reactions?* Describe both your intellectual reaction and any emotional reaction. Identify places in the text that caused you to react as you did. If you had no particular reaction, note that.

- *What accounts for your reaction?* Do you agree or disagree with the writer or have a different perspective? Why? Are your reactions rooted in personal experiences? positions you hold? As much as possible, you want to keep your opinions from coloring your analysis, so it's important to try to identify those opinions up front.

Annotating

Many readers find it helps to annotate as they read: highlighting key words, phrases, sentences; connecting ideas with lines or symbols; writing comments or questions in the margin or on sticky notes; circling new words so you can look up the definitions later; noting anything that seems noteworthy or questionable. Annotating forces you to read for more than just the surface meaning. Especially when you are going to be writing about or responding to a text, annotating creates a record of things you may want to refer to.

Annotate as if you're having a conversation with the author, someone you take seriously but whose words you do not accept without question. Put your part of the conversation in the margin, asking questions, talking back: "What's this mean?" "So what?" "Says who?" "Where's evidence?" "Yes!" "Whoa!" or even ☺ or ☹ or texting shorthand like LOL or INTRSTN. If you're using online sources, you may be able to copy them and annotate them electronically. If so, make your annotations a different color from the text itself.

What you annotate depends on your purpose or what you're most interested in. If you're analyzing an argument, you would probably underline any thesis statement and then the reasons and evidence that support the statement. It might help to restate those ideas in your own words, in the margins—in order to put them in your own words, you need to understand them! If you are trying to identify patterns, you might highlight each pattern in a different color or mark it with a sticky note and write any questions or notes about it in that color.

There are some texts that you cannot annotate, of course: library books, some materials you read on the web, and so on. Then you will need to use sticky notes or make notes elsewhere, and you might find it useful to keep a reading log for that purpose.

Coding

You may also find it useful to record your responses to your reading as you go through a text by using a coding system—for example, using "X" or "?" to indicate passages that contradict your assumptions or puzzle you. You can make up your own coding system, of course, but you could start with this one*:

- ✔ Confirms what you thought
- X Contradicts what you thought
- ? Puzzles you
- ?? Confuses you
- ☆ Strikes you as important
- → Is new or interesting to you

You might also circle new words that you'll want to look up later and highlight or underline key phrases.

A Sample Annotated Text

HERE IS an annotated passage from Lawrence Lessig's essay "Some Like It Hot." These annotations rephrase key definitions, identify the essay's thesis and main ideas, ask questions, and comment on issues raised in the essay. Annotating the entire essay would provide a look at Lessig's ideas and a record of the experience of reading the essay—useful for both understanding it and analyzing it.

*Adapted from *Subjects Matter: Every Teacher's Guide to Content-Area Reading* by Harvey Daniels and Steven Zemelman.

If piracy means using the creative property of others without their permission, then the history of the content industry is a history of piracy. Every important sector of big media today — film, music, radio, and cable TV — was born of a kind of piracy. The consistent story is how each generation welcomes the pirates from the last. Each generation — until now.

The Hollywood film industry was built by fleeing pirates. Creators and directors migrated from the East Coast to California in the early twentieth century in part to escape controls that film patents granted the inventor Thomas Edison. These controls were exercised through the Motion Pictures Patents Company, a monopoly "trust" based on Edison's creative property and formed to vigorously protect his patent rights.

California was remote enough from Edison's reach that filmmakers like Fox and Paramount could move there and, without fear of the law, pirate his inventions. Hollywood grew quickly, and enforcement of federal law eventually spread west. But because patents granted their holders a truly "limited" monopoly of just seventeen years (at that time), the patents had expired by the time enough federal marshals appeared. A new industry had been founded, in part from the piracy of Edison's creative property.

Meanwhile, the record industry grew out of another kind of piracy. At the time that Edison and Henri Fourneaux invented machines for reproducing music (Edison the phonograph; Fourneaux the player piano), the law gave composers the exclusive right to control copies and public performances of their music. Thus, in 1900, if I wanted a copy of Phil Russel's 1899 hit, "Happy Mose," the law said I would have to pay for the right to get a copy of the score, and I would also have to pay for the right to perform it publicly.

But what if I wanted to record "Happy Mose" using Edison's phonograph or Fourneaux's player piano? Here the law stumbled. If I simply sang the piece into a recording device in my home, it wasn't clear that I owed the composer anything. And more important, it wasn't clear whether I owed the composer anything if I then made copies of those recordings. Because of this gap in the law, I could effectively use someone else's song without paying the composer anything. The composers (and publishers) were none too happy about this capacity to pirate.

Piracy—unauthorized use of the artistic work of others.

"Content industry"—new term. Film, music, and so on? Doesn't include books and magazines?

Thesis: "Big media" are all based on piracy.

Hollywood film industry started in order to avoid Edison's patents. What were they for? Cameras and projectors? Is this true?

Record-industry piracy.

Player pianos?

Is copyright law different for books and other printed matter?

In 1909, Congress closed the gap in favor of the composer and the recording artist, amending copyright law to make sure that composers would be paid for "mechanical reproductions" of their music. But rather than simply granting the composer complete control over the right to make such reproductions, Congress gave recording artists a right to record the music, at a price set by Congress, after the composer allowed it to be recorded once. This is the part of copyright law that makes cover songs possible. Once a composer authorizes a recording of his song, others are free to record the same song, so long as they pay the original composer a fee set by the law. So, by limiting musicians' rights — by partially pirating their creative work — record producers and the public benefit.   — LAWRENCE LESSIG, "Some Like It Hot"

Partial piracy? Not sure about this—when artists use a song, they pay a fee but don't need permission. The composer doesn't have complete control. So it's piracy, but not completely

Playing the Believing and Doubting Game

One way to think about your response to a text is to list or freewrite as many reasons as you can think of for believing what the writer says and then as many as you can for doubting it. First, write as if you agree with everything in the writer's argument; look at the world from his or her perspective, trying to understand the writer's premises and reasons for arguing as he or she does even if you strongly disagree. Then, write as if you doubt everything in the text: try to find every flaw in the argument, every possible way it can be refuted—even if you totally agree with it. Developed by writing theorist Peter Elbow, the believing and doubting game helps you consider new ideas and question ideas you already have—and at the same time see where you stand in relation to the ideas in the text you're reading.

Reflecting, Rereading, Persisting

Let's face it: Some texts are difficult. You may have no interest in the subject matter, or understanding the text requires knowledge you don't have, or you don't have a clear sense of why you have to read the text at all. Whatever the reason, reading such texts can be a challenge. Here are some tips for dealing with them:

Look for something familiar. Difficult texts are often difficult and seem boring because we don't know what we need to know in order to read them effectively. By skimming the headings, the abstract or introduction, and the conclusion, you may find something that relates to knowledge you already have—and being aware of that prior knowledge can help you see how this new material relates to it.

Reread. Reading a text the first time through is like driving to an unfamiliar destination on roads you've never traveled: you don't know where you're headed, you don't recognize anything along the way, and you're not sure how long getting there will take. As you drive the route again, though, you see landmarks along the way; you know where you're going. When you must read a difficult text, sometimes you need to get through it once just to understand what it is saying. On the second reading, look for parts of the text that relate to other parts, to other texts or course information, or to other knowledge you have.

Be persistent. Studies reveal that students who do not do well in school attempt to read a difficult text and respond, "I don't understand this text. I'm too dumb to get it." And they quit reading. Successful students, on the other hand, see difficult texts as challenges: "I'm going to keep working on this text until I make sense of it." Remember that reading is an active process, and the more you work to control your reading processes, the more successful you will be.

Thinking about How the Text Works: What It Says, What It Does

Sometimes you'll need to think about how a text works, how its parts fit together. You may be assigned to analyze a text, or you may just need to make sense of a difficult text, to think about how the ideas all relate to one another. Whatever your purpose, a good way to think about a text's structure is by outlining it, paragraph by paragraph. If you're interested in analyzing its ideas, look at what each paragraph says; if, on the other hand, you're concerned with how the ideas are presented, pay attention to what each paragraph does.

What it says. Write a sentence that identifies what each paragraph says. Once you've done that for the whole text, look for patterns in the topics the writer addresses. Pay attention to the order in which the topics are presented. Also look for gaps, ideas the writer has left unsaid. Such paragraph-by-paragraph outlining of the content can help you see how the writer has arranged ideas and how that arrangement builds an argument or develops a topic. Here, for example, is such an outline of this excerpt from Lawrence Lessig's essay (the left column refers to paragraph order in the excerpt on pp. 39–40):

1   Every major type of media bases its development on piracy, the unauthorized use of artists' work.

2–3   To escape patents that restricted the copying of innovations in filmmaking, the movie industry moved from the East Coast to California.

4–5   Copyright law gave composers control over the performance of their music—but because it didn't cover the recording of music and the sale of copies of the recordings, it allowed piracy in the record industry.

6   Congress eventually changed the law, allowing musicians to record a song without the composer's permission if they paid the composer a fee.

What it does. Identify the function of each paragraph. Starting with the first paragraph, ask, What does this paragraph do? Does it introduce a topic? provide background for a topic to come? describe something? define something? entice me to read further? something else? What does the second paragraph do? the third? As you go through the text, you may identify groups of paragraphs that have a single purpose. For an example, look at this functional outline of Lessig's essay (again, the numbers on the left refer to the paragraphs):

1   Defines the key term, *piracy*, and illustrates the thesis using the history of four media industries in the United States.

2–3   Tells the history of the first medium, film, by focusing on piracy as a major factor in its development.

4–6   Tells the history of the second medium, the recording industry, again by focusing on the role of piracy in its development.

Summarizing

Summarizing a text can help you both to see the relationships among its ideas and to understand what it's saying. When you summarize, you restate a text's main ideas in your own words, leaving out most examples and other details. Here's a summary of the full version of Lawrence Lessig's essay:

> In his essay "Some Like It Hot," Lawrence Lessig argues that the development of every major media industry is based on piracy, the unauthorized use of artists' or inventors' work. First, the film industry flourished by evading restrictions on the copying of innovations in filmmaking. Then, the recording industry benefited from copyright laws that gave composers control over the performance of their music but not over the recording of it or the sale of the recordings. A law passed in 1909 in effect allows musicians to record a song without the composer's permission if they pay the composer a fee. According to Lessig, radio broadcasters benefit from piracy, too, every time they play a song recorded by someone other than the composer: they pay the composer a fee but not the recording artist. Finally, when it first started operating, cable TV benefited from piracy — by paying the networks nothing for their broadcasts. Congress eventually extended the copyright law, forcing cable companies to pay for the content they broadcast — but at a price controlled by Congress so that the networks wouldn't be able to drive the cable companies out of business. Peer-to-peer file sharing, like the early media industries, is being used to share artistic content and avoid industry controls on that sharing. It benefits the public by allowing access to music that is out of print, that copyright holders want to share, and that is no longer copyrighted. Therefore, Lessig argues, the public needs to figure out how to make file-sharing work without penalizing musicians by pirating their songs. Copyright law must balance the protection of artists' work with the encouragement of technological innovation.

Identifying Patterns

Look for notable patterns in the text: recurring words and their synonyms, as well as repeated phrases, metaphors and other images, and types of sentences. Some readers find it helps to highlight patterns in various colors. Does the author repeatedly rely on any particular writing strategies: narration? comparison? Something else?

It might be important to consider the kind of evidence offered: Is it more opinion than fact? Nothing but statistics? If many sources are cited, is the information presented in any predominant patterns: as quotations? paraphrases? summaries? Are there repeated references to certain experts or sources?

In visual texts, look for patterns of color, shape, and line. What's in the foreground, and what's in the background? What's completely visible, partly visible, or invisible? In both verbal and visual texts, look for omissions and anomalies. What isn't there that you would expect to find? Is there anything that doesn't really fit in?

If you discover patterns, then you need to consider what, if anything, they mean in terms of what the writer is saying. What do they reveal about the writer's underlying premises and beliefs? What do they tell you about the writer's strategies for persuading readers to accept the truth of what he or she is saying?

See how color coding William Safire's essay on the Gettysburg Address reveals several patterns in the language Safire uses. In this excerpt from the essay, which appears in full in the Readings, religious references are colored yellow; references to a "national spirit," green; references to life, death, and rebirth, blue; and places where he directly addresses the reader, gray.

> But the selection of this poetic political sermon as the oratorical center-piece of our observance need not be only an exercise. . . . now, as then, a national spirit rose from the ashes of destruction.
>
> Here is how to listen to Lincoln's all-too-familiar speech with new ears.
>
> In those 266 words, you will hear the word *dedicate* five times. . . .
>
> Those five pillars of dedication rested on a fundament of religious metaphor. From a president not known for his piety—indeed, often criticized for his supposed lack of faith—came a speech rooted in the theme of national resurrection. The speech is grounded in conception, birth, death, and rebirth.
>
> Consider the barrage of images of birth in the opening sentence. . . .
>
> Finally, the nation's spirit rises from this scene of death: "that this nation, under God, shall have a new birth of freedom." Conception, birth, death, rebirth. The nation, purified in this fiery trial of war, is res-urrected. Through the sacrifice of its sons, the sundered nation would be reborn as one. . . .
>
> Do not listen on Sept. 11 only to Lincoln's famous words and com-

forting cadences. Think about how Lincoln's message encompasses but goes beyond paying "fitting and proper" respect to the dead and the bereaved. His sermon at Gettysburg reminds "us the living" of our "unfinished work" and "the great task remaining before us"—to resolve that this generation's response to the deaths of thousands of our people leads to "a new birth of freedom."

The color coding helps us to see patterns in Safire's language, just as Safire reveals patterns in Lincoln's words. He offers an interpretation of Lincoln's address as a "poetic political sermon," and the words he uses throughout support that interpretation. At the end, he repeats the assertion that Lincoln's address is a sermon, inviting us to consider it differently. Safire's repeated commands ("Consider," "Do not listen," "Think about") offer additional insight into how he wishes to position himself in relation to his readers.

Count up the parts. This is a two-step process. First, you count things: how many of this, how many of that. After you count, see what you can conclude about the writing. You may want to work with others, dividing up the counting.

- *Count words.* Count one-, two-, three-syllable words, repeated words, active and passive verbs, prepositions, jargon or specialized terms.

- *Count sentences.* Count the number of words in each sentence and the average number of words per sentence. Count the number of sentences in each paragraph. Count the number of simple sentences, compound sentences, complex sentences, and fragments. Count repeated phrases.

- *Count paragraphs.* Count the number of paragraphs, the average number of words and sentences per paragraph, the shortest and longest paragraphs. Consider the position of the longest and shortest paragraphs. Find parallel paragraph structures.

- *Count images.* List or mark images, similes, metaphors, and other figures of speech. Categorize them by meaning as well as type.

What do your findings tell you about the text? What generalizations can you make about it? Why did the author choose the words or images he or she used and in those combinations? What do those words tell you about the writer—or about his or her stance? Do your findings suggest a strategy, a plan for your analysis? For instance, Safire counts the number of times Lincoln uses *dedicate* and images of birth, death, and rebirth to argue something about Lincoln's speech and what it should mean to Safire's audience on the anniversary of 9/11.

Analyzing the Argument

All texts make some kind of argument, claiming something and then offering reasons and evidence as support for the claim. As a critical reader, you need to look closely at the argument a text makes—to recognize all the claims it makes, consider the support it offers for those claims, and decide how you want to respond. What do you think, and why? Here are some questions to consider when analyzing the argument:

- *What claim is the text making?* What is the writer's main point? Is it stated as a thesis or only implied? Is it qualified somehow? If not, should it have been?

- *How is the claim supported?* What reasons does the writer provide for the claim, and what evidence is given for the reasons? What kind of evidence is it: facts? statistics? examples? expert opinion? images? How convincing do you find the reasons and evidence? Is there enough evidence?

- *What appeals besides logical ones are used?* Does the writer appeal to readers' emotions? Try to establish common ground? Demonstrate his or her credibility as trustworthy and knowledgeable? How successful are these appeals?

- *Are any counterarguments acknowledged?* If so, are they presented accurately and respectfully? Does the writer accommodate them or try to refute them? How successfully does he or she deal with them?

- *What outside sources of information does the writer cite?* What kinds of sources are they, and how credible do they seem? Are they current and authoritative? How well do they support the argument?

- *What stance does the writer take toward readers?* What attitudes does it assume they hold? Do you feel that you are part of the intended audience? How can you tell?

Check for fallacies. Fallacies are arguments that involve faulty reasoning. Because they often seem plausible, they can be persuasive. It is important, therefore, that you question the legitimacy of such reasoning when you run across it.

Considering the Larger Context

All texts are part of ongoing conversations with other texts that have dealt with the same topic. An essay arguing for handgun trigger locks is part of an ongoing conversation about gun control, which is itself part of a conversation on individual rights and responsibilities. Academic texts document their sources in part to show their relationship to the ongoing scholarly conversations on a particular topic. Academic reading usually challenges you to become aware of those conversations. And, in fact, any time you're reading to learn, you're probably reading for some larger context. Whatever your reading goals, being aware of that larger context can help you better understand what you're reading. Here are some specific aspects of the text to pay attention to:

- *Who else cares about this topic?* Especially when you're reading in order to learn about a topic, the texts you read will often reveal which people or groups are part of the conversation—and might be sources of further reading. For example, an essay describing the formation of Mammoth Cave could be of interest to geologists, spelunkers, travel writers, or tourists. If you're reading such an essay while doing research on the cave, you should consider how the audience addressed determines the nature of the information provided—and its suitability as a source for your research.

- *Ideas.* Does the text refer to any concepts or ideas that give you some sense that it's part of a larger conversation? An argument on airport security measures, for example, is part of larger conversations about government response to terrorism, the limits of freedom in a democracy, and the possibilities of using technology to detect weapons and explosives, among others.

- *Terms.* Is there any terminology or specialized language that reflects the writer's allegiance to a particular group or academic discipline? If you run across words like *false consciousness, ideology,* and *hegemony,* for example, you might guess the text was written by a Marxist scholar.

- *Citations.* Whom does the writer cite? Do the other writers have a particular academic specialty, belong to an identifiable intellectual school, share similar political leanings? If an article on politics cites Paul Krugman and Barbara Ehrenreich in support of its argument, you might assume the writer holds liberal opinions; if it cites Michelle Malkin and Sean Hannity, the writer is likely a conservative.

ENGAGING CRITICALLY WITH TEXTS

	As a Reader	As a Writer/Designer
Writer/ Designer	• Who composed this text? • What else has this person composed? • What social, historical, cultural, or economic influences can you identify? • What point of view does he or she adopt?	• How do you wish to represent yourself in your text? • How can you convince your audience that you are worth taking seriously? • What's your point of view?
Purpose	• What does the author/designer hope to accomplish? • What social, political, or economic influences can you identify?	• What do you want to communicate? • What is your most important goal?
Medium/ Genre	• What media are used—print? electronic? handwriting? type? paint? film? • What is the genre—essay? journal? letter? story? poem? ad? painting? photograph? collage? something else?	• What media will you use— print? electronic? handwriting? film? paint? type? • What is the genre—essay? journal? ad? letter? painting? photograph? collage? story? something else?

	As a Reader	As a Writer/Designer
Subject	• What is the text about? • What statement does the text make, and how is that message supported? • What other texts exist on this topic and what other texts are referred to?	• What is your text about? • What other texts should you refer to? • Where will you find facts, examples, images, and other material?
Audience	• What is your initial reaction? • What is the audience assumed to know or believe? • Who is the intended audience? Are you a member of this group?	• Who is your intended audience? • What are they likely to know and believe about your subject? • How can you interest them in your subject?
Organization	• How is the text organized? • Is the arrangement what you would expect or is it a surprise? • What is included? excluded? emphasized? not emphasized?	• How will you organize your text? • Is a particular organization required, or do you have some choice? • What will you emphasize? What then might you pay less attention to?
Style/Tone	• How would you character-ize the style—academic? hip? formal? informal? • How would you characterize the tone—serious? humorous? satiric? something else?	• What style are you aiming for—formal? informal? academic? fanciful? • What tone should you adopt—serious? witty? light-hearted? something else?

FIVE

Looking Closely
at Visual Texts

OF THE MANY PRESS IMAGES following the September 11, 2001, attack on New York City's World Trade Center, Thomas Franklin's photo of three firefighters raising the American flag against a backdrop of gray dust and twisted steel may be the best known. Many compared it to Joseph Rosenthal's 1945 Pulitzer-Prize–winning picture of American marines raising the U.S. flag on Mount Suribachi, Iwo Jima. In the days and weeks following the Trade Center attack, those two photos appeared side by side in newspapers and magazines, on posters, Web sites, and office walls. To some, the photos together represented hope in the face of disaster. For others, the two images identified that moment in 2001 as a declaration of war and New York City firefighters as new soldiers in that war. Still others saw the comparison as a distortion of the events of September 11.

Even if it had not been placed next to Rosenthal's photo, the image of the firefighters very likely would have become central to what the U.S. press called the "nation's mood" following September 11. Franklin has said that he knew he had an important shot even as he was taking it. How one picture can make such an impact—how an image carries and conveys meaning—is the subject of this chapter

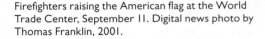

U.S. Marines raising the flag on Mount Surabachi, Iwo Jima. News photo by Joseph Rosenthal, 1945.

Firefighters raising the American flag at the World Trade Center, September 11. Digital news photo by Thomas Franklin, 2001.

READING TEXT

As we read a message, most of us don't think much about how it was put together. This is especially true of visual messages. They seem to communicate naturally, even simply. Yet, as we have seen, visual messages have much in common with verbal ones. They consist of a complex of elements, including how and why the image was made, who made it, how an audience reads it, and where it appears. We call these elements the immediate and the broader contexts; they influence the creation of a message and how audiences receive it.

Immediate Context

The immediate context is anyone or anything that has an immediate role in forming the message. As with verbal texts, visual texts have an author (or authors), an audience, a subject, and a purpose. Whoever made the image had to decide what technology to use (medium) and what kind of image it would be (genre). Visual messages, also like verbal ones, present a point of view and involve a conscious selection of materials, as well as decisions about what to emphasize or focus on and how to arrange or organize the information.

Broader Context

The broader context includes larger questions about the cultural, economic, social, and historic circumstances in which the image was produced and, later, read.

Most of us don't separate the immediate from the broader context when we read. If you are to understand how images communicate meaning, however, you will want to look closer—think about both. Notice how such an analysis might work with the two photos that open this chapter.

Who is the author? For some images, this question is a simple one. For example, Thomas Franklin took the photo of firefighters raising the flag at the World Trade Center site. At the time, Franklin was a photographer for New Jersey's *Bergen County Record*. Joseph Rosenthal, who took the photo at Iwo Jima, was a World War II war correspondent. As photojournalists, each was looking for newsworthy images. For both Franklin and Rosenthal, then, the photos began as events related to their work.

Other images are not as easily identified with an individual author or a particular event. Billboards, postcards, stamps, logos, book covers, and product labels are images we see and read every day. We rarely know who created them, but even when we cannot name the individual responsible for a text, we can identify something about that author. We can guess, for example, that a CD cover was probably created by a graphic designer, a digital artist, or a team of designers hired by the recording company to make a message that will attract attention and suggest the type of music on the CD.

In many cases, it matters less whether or not we can actually name an individual author than whether we can identify purpose and point of view. For example, most readers don't think much about an individual author when they look at a commercial for ESPN, but everyone knows that it is an advertisement for a sports network told from the point of view of that network. A commercial for PBS is likely to have a very different look because it has a different point of view and targets a different audience.

Two U.S. commemorative stamps, based on the Iwo Jima photo. The vertical stamp was issued in 1945; the horizontal stamp, in 1995. Notice how the shape of the stamp affects the arrangement, and the emphasis: the vertical stamp emphasizes the flag, whereas the horizontal one emphasizes the soldiers struggling to raise the flag. See also how the horizontal cropping did not accommodate the original flag, and a new larger flag was inserted.

Marines raise flag on Iwo Jima, Feb. 23, 1945

What is the purpose? Asking about purpose might also seem like a straightforward question, but you will quickly discover that most communication has more than one purpose and that the purpose shifts as a text is placed in different contexts. It is obvious, for example, that the Franklin and Rosenthal photos were initially taken as visual representations of news events. It is the job of photojournalists to report the news through pictures.

However, once the firefighters photo is reproduced on a T-shirt by a designer, for example, the purpose shifts. It becomes a kind of memorial, a way of identifying loyalties, and even a fashion statement. That same photo is presented in this textbook as an example of a familiar and complex piece of visual communication. It is the same image, but it takes on additional meaning as its purpose changes with use and reuse.

The same can be said of the Iwo Jima photo. Almost immediately after it was first published, it was being used for a number of different purposes. Only five months after the picture first appeared in newspapers, the U.S. Post Office issued a stamp featuring it. By 1995, when a second version of the stamp appeared, even those Americans who knew nothing about the image had probably seen it in countless versions, including the memorial statue that now stands in Washington, D.C.

In 1945, the stamp was produced as a memorial representing courage under fire. In 1995, it was a piece of history. For stamp collectors, the image is an artifact. A postage stamp itself is simply a proof of purchase, but an individual stamp design either survives—becomes popular—or not, depending on how many people decide to buy it.

The Iwo Jima photo remained a familiar image throughout the twentieth century, even showing up in folk art, such as a cigarette machine triptych purchased in South Carolina in 2000.

Image Conscious

Look around and note down all the images that surround you—calendars, photographs, posters, screen savers. To what extent can you identify an author for these texts? Even if you cannot name a person or design team, what could you say about the author's point of view and purpose?

Folk art triptych juxtaposing the Iwo Jima photo with various other iconic images—
Dana Carvey as Garth in *Wayne's World*, The Rock, among others, 2000.

Whatever else the artist had in mind in placing Rosenthal's photo in this particular triptych, it is certain that reporting the news is no longer the purpose the photo serves in this context.

What are the medium and genre? The way a message is created as well as what kind of message it is affects the way we read. For example, a letter seems different depending on whether it is received as an email message or a note in a greeting card, whether it is handwritten on delicate stationary or typed as a formal memo with a company logo printed at the top. Each of these involves a different medium, set in a different genre.

When we use the term medium, we are talking about the technology used to create and communicate a text. Movies, television, film photography, digital photography, watercolor painting, and charcoal drawing are all examples of different visual media. They all use different technologies. The Franklin and Rosenthal images, though both photographs, were produced using different media. Franklin's photo is digital; Rosenthal's is film. Both, however, are the same genre (or type) of photo: news photos.

The meaning we take from an image has as much to do with its genre— what kind of an image it is—as with the technology used to make it. News photos, for example, are typically read as objective records (whether they are or not), whereas paintings are considered interpretations. A film or television drama is a fiction, an interpretation of reality—though it might look very realistic. An advertisement is selling you something. Knowing the genre helps readers identify what the message is supposed to be. For example, not many readers would look at an ad for toothpaste and mistake it for a scientific report, but the advertiser tries to give it as much truth value as

Image Conscious
Cover the flag in the Rosenthal and the Franklin photos so that you can see only the men. Once you eliminate the flag, how does each photo change? Without the flag, what is the subject? What is each photo's new symbolic significance?

possible, perhaps using some of the conventions of the genre of scientific reports (charts and graphs, for example), so that readers think about the science in the ad more than its commercial purpose.

What is the subject? Look again at the Iwo Jima photo. Two days after its publication, Congress already was talking about it as a model for a memorial statue. Somehow, in addition to recording a single moment in time, the photo also carries a symbolic and emotional message. The same is true of Franklin's firefighter photo. Within months after it had appeared, the photo was being talked of as a model for a future memorial. Its symbolic significance was obvious to everyone who saw it.

How is that possible? To begin with, the subject of both photos was newsworthy. The public wanted to see the real people, places, and events depicted. Many news photos are significant solely on the basis of what they depict and the context in which they depict it. As press photos, then, both simply showed people at the actual scenes of events of international significance.

In addition, the subjects of these photos carried a powerful emotional impact. Both depicted a moment of triumph after devastating defeat. The 1945 battle that ended with a marine victory on Mount Suribachi had gone on for four days in some of the fiercest fighting of World War II. By the time Rosenthal took his picture, 40 percent of the company engaged in this battle had been killed. Similarly, the firefighter photo was taken on the evening of September 11, 2001, at the end of a day of national tragedy. In Franklin's words, the photo "had drama, spirit, and courage in the face of disaster."

So, the subject depicted by each photo and the significance of that subject are key elements we need to consider as we read these images.

Both photos carry strong symbolic meaning. The U.S. flag, an easily recognized symbol of U.S. patriotism and nationhood, is at the top and is the focus of both images. The individuals in each photo also carry symbolic significance: marines and firefighters are historically associated with courage and self-sacrifice.

Not everyone who sees these images will have positive associations with patriotism, the flag, or marines and firefighters, however. That is why it is very important to consider the audience when you think about how an image communicates meaning.

Who is the audience? You can sometimes identify the intended audience for an image very precisely, but that is not always the case, and it might not be necessary. It is necessary, however, to think about how an author might expect an audience to receive the work. A photojournalist expects the audience to be readers of the news publication in which the photo appears. Ideally, that audience will accept the photo as a piece of news—a faithful reproduction of something that actually happened. The news photo allows readers to witness an event they would not be able to see for themselves.

Of course, no designer or author can control audience response. The best you can do is know something about the audience you are aiming for and make choices based on what you know. That is what happened when the Franklin and Rosenthal pictures were placed side by side on posters after the World Trade Center attack. These posters were designed for an audience that would see the two moments (1945 and 2001) as corresponding—not just in the way the photos looked but in their reference to war and tragedy and triumph. Those who did not see the correspondence or who did not agree that the September 11 attack was analogous to World War II very likely dismissed the message of the poster as overly simple—even manipulative.

How is it arranged? When we talk about arrangement, or composition, we mean the way an image is organized within its frame or visual space. In the case of these two photos, the arrangement is a classic and stable triangle, with the flag forming the apex and the figures below forming the base. Like verbal composition, visual composition is a process of selection and emphasis—what is included in the space and what is left out, what is placed in the foreground (at the front of the picture) and what is relegated to the background. In other words, the way a text is arranged or organized suggests what the author believes is important about the subject and influences the way the audience reads the text.

Designers and visual artists must choose between a closed or open form when they compose an image. With a closed form the entire image is inside the visual frame and the viewer's attention is focused within the picture. The Rosenthal and Franklin photos are arranged in very similar ways and both are closed forms. As you can see in this diagram of the Rosenthal photo, the men at the base seem to be moving in a mass toward the flag, which then forms the top of the closed triangular form. A similar form is made in the composition of the Franklin photo on page 52. An open form is one that suggests that there's something more outside the visual frame. The im-

Diagram of closed form in the Rosenthal photograph.

Billboard, New York City, 2002. The runner's arm extending off the frame, along with the half-missing *swoosh*, creates a sense of movement.

age might be cut off at the edges, or a person in the image might be looking at something outside the image—even at the camera, making it seem as though the viewer is a part of the world of the image. We see this kind of composition quite often in contemporary advertising such as the Nike ad, in which the model is literally stretching out of the frame. We know he is moving. He isn't looking at the camera but concentrating on what's ahead—and outside—of the frame.

The Sherman Monument, by Augustus Saint-Gaudens. New York City.

An open form suggests that the image is not completely self-contained, that there is something more beyond the visual space that viewers should be thinking about. Even a memorial statue, like this one, can be arranged in an open form, when it directs our attention forward, beyond the artwork itself.

Advertisers are very careful about how they compose their visual texts because they need to make sure their message comes across. In the Nike ad, for example, the most

On the left, the original Iwo Jima photo, by Joseph Rosenthal, 1945. On the right, the final cropping of the photo, by Rosenthal. Notice that the soldiers are now centered in the image, giving them greater emphasis.

important part of the message is the suggestion that wearing Nike products gives us energy, speed, and a great body. Readers of ads generally know that they are dealing with a message that is carefully constructed in order to put the product in the best light.

Most readers don't think of news photographs as carefully arranged. News photos are assumed to be moments in time captured just as events happened, with little thought about composition beyond the quick decisions a skilled photographer might make while looking through the viewfinder. And yet even here composition is rarely a matter of chance. The Iwo Jima photo, for example, was cropped from its original longer shot, which had much more sky and landscape, making a tighter, more closed composition—and a greater visual impact.

What is the historical context? All texts are created at a time, in a place, and sometimes in response to specific events or feelings. Visual texts, like all others, derive their meaning partially from their historic context. We have already seen some of that in our discussion of two photographs. To read either the Franklin or Rosenthal photograph, it helps to understand events in history, but, again, the historic context will not guarantee a single reading of these photos.

On the one hand, many Americans know that the Iwo Jima photo was taken during World War II. However, because most of us do not know the details of the event depicted, the image has come to be understood as a generalized reference to Americans at war, perhaps to heroism or to the horrors of war. The firefighter photo, on the other hand, is still current. Most of us know some details of the events of that day, and that knowledge affects the way we read the image.

Not all images have such an easily defined historic context, but all are created at a particular historical moment and all are read at particular moments in time. The way readers understand an image will depend on when they read it, when it was made, and what was happening in the world at the time.

What are the cultural and social contexts? In addition to having historical contexts, images take on meaning within certain cultural and social contexts. Our two photos are good examples. Firefighters have traditionally been considered heroes in U.S. culture, which is why television producers and filmmakers often position them at the center of the action willing to sacrifice themselves to save others. In that way they are like soldiers—or, at least, like the idealized soldiers of movies and novels.

Moreover, the firefighter photo takes on much of its meaning because it reminds viewers—especially once it is compared to the Iwo Jima photo—of World War II and other battles that Americans have fought. Once the reference to World War II—a war some have called America's last "good war"—is made, the image evokes some of the pride that Americans felt at winning the war with Hitler. The meaning of the photo, then, begins to shift from an inspiring moment at the end of a long day of catastrophe to what the press quickly began to call "America's New War." All of the films and photos and novels that we have seen and read about World War II and especially about Iwo Jima influence how we understand this new image. It might even bring to mind John Wayne in the 1950s film *The Sands of Iwo Jima*. Of course, if you are not familiar with the Rosenthal photo or have never thought of World War II or of any war as a "good" war, or if you are from a different culture entirely, the meaning you take from the firefighter image will differ. You will still very likely see it as a patriotic image, but patriotism in this form might not appeal to you.

Considering cultural and social contexts is especially important in analyzing advertisements. Beauty products, for example, often focus on ideal male and female forms. One way to read the image shown here would be to consider how ads often distort female beauty or promise the impossible,

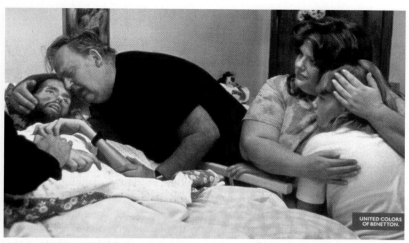

United Colors of Benetton's "Faces of AIDS" campaign, 1992.

featuring close-ups of models airbrushed to conform to cultural ideals of perfection.

What is the economic context? Thinking about the economic context can help you more fully read a text. Consider, for example, how powerful news photos help to sell newspapers. That is one reason the two photos we have focused on here have been reprinted so often. A photo with wide distribution can affect the way that the public sees or understands an event—something we need to keep in mind when thinking about what such an image means.

The economics of advertising seems obvious: advertisers spend money to influence our purchases. But what if an advertiser doesn't seem to be selling us something? What if an advertiser seems to be presenting a message about hunger or human rights or violence in the streets? The United Colors of Benetton has become famous for "message" ads such as the one reprinted above featuring dying AIDS activist David Kirby. This image is shocking; it forces readers to think about what is going on in the picture and perhaps even to become more aware of issues surrounding AIDS. In fact, this particular ad is part of the United Colors of Benetton's institutional campaign, not their product campaign. Yet it is still an ad by a company that sells clothing. If we think of them as a socially responsible company, will we think it socially responsible to buy their clothes?

ANALYZING VISUAL TEXTS

Not all texts are as richly complex as the two we have focused on in this chapter, but they all can be understood in terms of author; purpose; audience; composition; medium; genre; social, cultural, historical, and economic contexts; and so on. When you analyze a visual text, you will likely begin with your personal response and then consider the text's immediate and broader contexts.

What is your personal response? Images often evoke memories or quick reactions. Take a moment to write about your response to Franklin's photo and then compare your response with fellow students. Although there are likely to be many similar responses to a photo such as this one, there will also be responses that differ significantly from yours. The fact that people have different reactions should not be surprising given that the way we read or react to a text depends on what we bring to it. For example, if you live in New York City, if you are a firefighter, or if you lost friends or family in the September 11 attack, your response is likely to be very different from the response of someone who does not have your experience.

Think, as well, of your response to the Iwo Jima photo. Is it the same as your response to the firefighter photo? If you were to ask a World War II veteran for a response to Rosenthal's image—which, of course, you could do—how would his or her reaction differ from yours? Very likely, the veteran would know a lot about the Iwo Jima photo—and would, of course, have different memories and thus a different response to the photo than you do.

Most of us have some response to everything we see—even if that response is indifference. We are not likely to know immediately how an image evokes that response, however. In order to account for how an image conveys a message or evokes a response, you will need to understand how different elements come together as a visual language. Some of those elements are embodied in the image itself, whereas others come from outside the image.

How does the text work? To read any text, a reader pulls meaning from a system of signs: letters, words, sentences, paragraphs, shapes, colors, pictures. In verbal texts, even the typeface and page design contribute to meaning, but here we will focus mostly on visual texts—photographs, postcards, advertisements, and so on. When we examine how a sign carries and conveys meaning, we are engaging in analysis. Visual analysis, like any analysis, begins with a single question: How does it work?

Take, for example, our analysis of the firefighter photo. As we wrote about that image, we noted its subject matter: three firefighters raising the American flag at the wreckage of the World Trade Center on the evening of September 11, 2001. We noticed the composition, how the arrangement of the men and flag contributed to the photo's meaning. We could also consider the medium by which it was produced (digital photography) and the fact that digital imaging can be easily manipulated and so does not carry as much truth value as film photography traditionally has.

We made a point to identify the genre as a news photo. Genre is important in this case because a news photo carries more authority than an art photo or a studio portrait. Think, for example, about your high school yearbook photo. If you had your senior picture taken at a studio, you were posed in clothes you chose for the occasion. You were prepared to be photographed so that your parents could send the picture to friends and put it up on the wall. The photo might have been airbrushed to remove any blemishes. That is a very different kind of photo from one that a friend might have taken of you at a party later that same day. You are the same person in both photos, but the two are read differently—the first as an ideal portrait of you, the second as a candid snapshot.

As a news photo, the Franklin image promises to show us the truth about an event. We don't expect it to be posed or retouched. We count on photojournalists to show us "the real story." But, put the photo on a T-shirt or in a textbook, and it takes on additional cultural meaning as a national icon, a piece of history, and a photo significant enough to reprint in a school book. Each time the photo shifts from one medium and genre to another—and especially when it is reproduced thousands of times—it takes on additional meaning.

The same high school student shown in a candid photograph and a formal studio photograph.

WRITING UP AN ANALYSIS

The list of questions on the following pages provides a good start for a written analysis. You may wish to make notes in response to them. But remember that notes are just the beginning of your work. To complete your analysis, you will have to go back through your notes, decide what to focus on for your analysis, and choose the information and ideas that will support your conclusions.

SNAPSHOT

Social, cultural, historical, and economic context help shape the way we read all visual texts, even the most casual family snapshots. Locate old photos of family or friends or just ones that you can find in magazines like Look or the Saturday Evening Post in your local library. Notice how details in the photos "date" them or suggest a certain level of income or a particular event (like graduation or prom or a family picnic). Then, take your own snapshot of family members or friends. In a one-page discussion of the photo, point out what details in your snapshot will, eventually, "date" it.

When you write up an analysis, you won't be able to pay attention to all of these elements for every image, but you can focus on several of them to explain how an image works—how it conveys meaning, or how it is possible for you and your friends to have different responses to the same image, or why some images are easy to read while others take more time and seem difficult to understand.

Some Questions for Analyzing Images

- What is your first response?
- What is the subject or content?
- What is the primary purpose? Are there additional purposes you need to consider?
- How is the image arranged in the visual space? Can you diagram its

overall composition? What effect does this arrangement have on the way you read this image?

- What strikes you as important, interesting, or emotionally moving in the image? Can you identify elements of the image that could be seen as symbolic?

- What is the medium and what do you normally expect from images in this medium?

- What is the genre? Does the image conform to the conventions of that genre or does it break from the expectations? (We expect something different from a museum painting for example, than from a cartoon. And we expect cartoons on the comics page to be different from those on the editorial page.)

- Can you identify the author? If so, what else has he or she done? Is this image like the author's other work or is it different? What accounts for the difference?

- How do you think others read this image? (Ask students, friends, relatives, or coworkers for their responses to the image.)

- What are the larger historical, political, social, cultural, and economic contexts of the image?

- Where does the image come from? (For example, is it from a magazine? What magazine? What do you know about the audience for that magazine?)

- Is this a serious or comic image? How do you know?

- What does the image remind you of? Have you seen anything like it somewhere else? Where? How is this image similar to those others? How does it differ?

- Does the image include words or a caption? How are those words used? Do they simply identify the image? Are they part of the image? What do they contribute to the overall message?

SIX

Writing Analytically

ANALYZE THIS. ANALYZE THAT. These are more than the titles of two movies starring Robert DeNiro and Billy Crystal. Analysis is a necessary step in much of the thinking that we do, and that we do every day. What should you wear today? T-shirt and hoodie? Sweatshirt? Your new red sweater? You look closely at the weather, what you will be doing, the people you will be with (and might want to impress, or not), and then decide based on those factors. You may not consciously think of it as analysis, but that's what you've done.

When you analyze something, you break it down into its component parts and think about those parts methodically in order to understand it in some way. Case in point: You want a new gaming system, but should you get a PlayStation 3? Nintendo Wii? Xbox 360? Or maybe something more portable, a Sony PSP-3000 or a Nintendo DSi? You might check websites like *TestFreaks*, which provide information based on expert analyses of each system, or you might conduct your own analysis. What kinds of games do you play? Party games? Arcade games? Online games? Which is more important to you: an easy-to-use interface or high-end HD graphics? big-name titles or an all-purpose entertainment center? These are some of the ways you might analyze the various systems, first to understand what they offer and then to decide which one you want to buy.

Since our world is awash in information, the ability to read it closely, examine it critically, and decide how—or whether—to accept or act on it becomes a survival skill. To navigate this sea of information, we rely on our ability to analyze.

You have probably analyzed literary texts in English classes; perhaps you've analyzed films or song lyrics. In many college classes, you'll be expected to conduct different sorts of analyses—rhetorical, causal, process, data, and more. Analysis is critical to every academic discipline, useful in every professional field, and employed by each of us in our everyday lives. It's essential to understanding and to decision making. This chapter provides guidelines for conducting an analysis and writing analytically.

⟋⟍ *THINK ABOUT your own use of analysis. How many decisions—large and small—have you made in the last week? in the last month? in the last year? From small (what to have for breakfast) to major (which college to attend), make a chart listing a representative sample of these decisions and what areas of your life they affected; then note the information you gathered in each case before you decided. What does this chart tell you about your interests, activities, and priorities? You've just completed an analysis.*

Across Academic Fields

Some form of analysis can be found in every academic discipline. In a *history* class, you may be asked to analyze how Russia defeated Napoleon's army in 1812. In *biology*, you might analyze how the body responds to exercise. In *economics*, you might analyze the trade-off between unemployment and inflation rates. In a *technical communication* course, you might analyze a corporate website to understand how it appeals to various audiences. In your *composition* course, you'll analyze your own writing for many purposes, from thinking about how you've appealed to your audience to how you need to revise a draft. So many courses require analysis because looking closely and methodically at something—a text, a process, a philosophy—helps you discover connections between ideas and think about how things work, what they mean, and why.

Across Media

Your medium affects the way you present your analysis. In *print,* much of your analysis may be in paragraphs, but you might include photographs, tables, or graphs such as a flowchart to analyze a process. If you're analyzing something in an *oral presentation* you might show data in a handout or on presentation slides—and you would need to add some signpost language to

THINK BEYOND WORDS

WATCH THE VIDEO of a TED talk by statistician Nate Silver on whether race affects voting. He includes slides with lists, bar graphs, photos, and maps—and a space below the video invites readers to comment. How much do the visuals contribute to his analysis? TED talks are intended to focus on "ideas worth spreading." Write a tweet about something Silver said in his talk that you find thought-provoking: your challenge will be to make it clear and interesting in 140 characters. Go to wwnorton. com/write/everyonelinks to view the video.

help your audience follow your analysis. A *digital text* allows you to blend paragraphs, charts, images, audio, and video—and does so in a way that lets readers click on various parts as they wish. And some digital texts—blogs, listservs, tweets—allow readers to comment; in effect, to become authors themselves. You won't always be able to choose, but when you do, you'll want to choose the medium that enables you to most effectively make your point for the specific audience you are trying to reach.

Across Cultures and Communities

Human nature being what it is, communicating with people from other communities or cultures challenges us to examine our assumptions and think about our usual ways of operating. Analyzing something from (or for) another culture or community may require extra effort at understanding beliefs, assumptions, and practices that we are not familiar with. We need to be careful not to look at things only through our own frames of reference.

Sheikh Jamal Rahman, Pastor Don Mackenzie, and Rabbi Ted Falcon embody this extra effort. In their book, *Getting to the Heart of Interfaith: The Eye-Opening, Hope-Filled Friendship of a Pastor, a Rabbi and a Sheikh*, they have taken on the challenge of working toward interfaith understanding, saying that religion today "seems to be fuelling hatred rather than expanding love" and that in order to heal the divisions between us, we must "find ways of entering into conversation with those different from us." And they say that analysis—what they call "inquiring more deeply"—is essential to their ongoing journey toward understanding issues central to each faith.

All three agree it's critical to discuss the difficult and contentious ideas in faith. For the minister, one "untruth" is that "Christianity is the only way to God." For the rabbi, it is the notion of Jews as "the chosen people." And for the sheikh, it is the "sword verses" in the Koran, like "kill the unbeliever," which when taken out of context cause misunderstanding.

Their book embodies cultural sensitivity and describes the process of creating a text that's respectful of their different faiths. Reading a sentence that the sheikh had written about the security wall in Israel, the rabbi announced, "If that line is in the book, I'm not in the book." Then they analyzed the sentence, discussing it vigorously, and Sheikh Rahman revised the wording to be "respectful of [both] their principles."

Having respect for the principles, values, and beliefs of others means recognizing and respecting differences among cultures. The best way to demonstrate cultural sensitivity is to use precise language that avoids negative descriptions or stereotypes about age, class, gender, religion, race, ethnicity, and such—in short, by carefully selecting the words you use.

Across Genres

Seldom does any piece of writing consist solely of one genre; in many cases, it will contain multiple genres. You might use a short narrative as an introductory element in a process analysis. To argue a position on an issue, you'll need to analyze that issue before you can take a stand on it. You sometimes can't compose a report until you have analyzed the data or the information that the report is to be based on. And a review—whether it's of a film, a website, a book, or something else—depends on your analysis of the material before you evaluate it.

LOOK FOR analysis in everyday use. Find two consumer-oriented websites that analyze something you're interested in—laptop computers, cell phones, cars, places you might like to go, things you might like to do. Study the analyses and decide which one is more useful, and then try to figure out what makes it better. Is it the language? the images? the amount of detail? the format? How might you change the other one to make it more effective?

CHARACTERISTIC FEATURES

While there are nearly as many different kinds of analysis as there are things to be analyzed, we can identify five common elements that analyses share across disciplines, media, cultures, and communities:

- A question that prompts you to take a closer look
- Some description of the subject you are analyzing
- Evidence drawn from close examination of the subject
- Insight gained from your analysis
- Clear, precise language

A Question That Prompts You to Take a Closer Look

If you look at the examples cited earlier in this chapter, you'll note that each is driven by a question that doesn't have a single "right" answer. Which gaming system best meets your needs? What should you wear? Which college offers the best education for the future you desire? How can we begin to achieve interfaith understanding? Each question requires some kind of analysis. While an author may not explicitly articulate such a question, it will drive the analysis—and the writing based on the analysis. In an essay about how partisan politics are driving opinions of President Obama, see how nationally syndicated columnist David Brooks starts by asking a question:

> Who is Barack Obama?
>
> If you ask a conservative Republican, you are likely to hear that Obama is a skilled politician who campaigned as a centrist but is governing as a big-government liberal. He plays by ruthless, Chicago politics rules. He is arrogant toward foes, condescending toward allies and runs a partisan political machine.
>
> If you ask a liberal Democrat, you are likely to hear that Obama is an inspiring but overly intellectual leader who has trouble making up his mind and fighting for his positions. He has not defined a clear mission. He has allowed the Republicans to dominate debate. He is too quick to compromise and too cerebral to push things through.
>
> You'll notice first that these two viewpoints are diametrically opposed. You'll observe, second, that they are entirely predictable. Political partisans always imagine the other side is ruthlessly effective and that the public would be with them if only their side had better messaging. And finally, you'll notice that both views distort reality. They tell you more about the information cocoons that partisans live in these days than about Obama himself.   —DAVID BROOKS, "Getting Obama Right"

To begin answering his opening question, Brooks offers brief summaries of both partisan opinions on Obama's leadership; then he takes a closer look, giving us a brief analysis of those opinions. You might not always start an analytical essay as Brooks does, by asking an explicit question, but your analysis will always be prompted by a question of some kind.

Some Description of the Subject You Are Analyzing

You need to describe what you are analyzing. How much description you need depends on your subject, your audience, and the medium you've chosen to compose in. For example, if you are analyzing the *Twilight* novels and movies for a class on vampires in film and literature, you can assume that most of your readers will be familiar with them, but you'll need to add extra details for readers who may not have seen or read the specific texts you refer to. If you are writing a paper for a psychology class on the impact of the film on those who are "*Twilight* addicted," however, you will have to describe that impact, as Christine Spines does in a piece written for the *Los Angeles Times* in 2010:

> Chrystal Johnson didn't think there was anything unhealthy about her all-consuming fixation with *The Twilight Saga*—until she discovered it was sucking the life out of her marriage.
>
> "I found poems my husband had written in his journal about how I had fallen for a 'golden-eyed vampire,'" says Johnson, a 31-year-old accountant from Mesa, Arizona, who became so enthralled by the blockbuster series of young adult novels and movies that she found herself staying up all night, re-reading juicy chapters and chatting about casting news and the are-they-or-aren't-they romance between the stars of the films, Kristen Stewart and Robert Pattinson.
>
> "*Twilight* was always on my mind, to the point where I couldn't function," Johnson says.
>
> —CHRISTINE SPINES, "When *Twilight* Fandom Becomes Addiction"

Robert Pattinson as the "golden-eyed vampire."

After this introduction, Spines adds more descriptive detail about the addictive behavior. She cites a professor of communication studies who says that "getting up at 4 a.m." to read or watch movies is "sacrificing marriage ... [and] sounds like addictive behavior." She also quotes one of the fans who slept for days outside the Nokia Theatre in Los Angeles, just hoping to see the stars at the premiere of *Twilight*: "This is the first time I've been this passionate about anything. . . . I've read each of the books at least eight or nine times and I've watched each of the movies over 300 times."

Spines provides this detail because she is writing for a newspaper whose readers may know little or nothing about her subject and need it described in some detail in order to understand her analysis. Citing an academic expert and someone who has firsthand experience with the be-havior gives her credibility. In a similar situation, when you're composing a text that will be read by an audience that you don't know well, you'll also need to provide necessary description and details. If your analysis is going to appear on the internet, you might provide an image or graph-ic, embed a video, or include a link to a site offering more information on your subject.

Evidence Drawn from Close Examination of the Subject

Examining the subject of your analysis carefully and in detail and then thinking critically about what you find will help you discover key elements, patterns, and relationships in your subject—all of which provide you with the evidence on which to build your analysis. For example, if you are ana-lyzing a poem, you might examine word choice, rhyme scheme, figurative language, repetition, and imagery. If you are analyzing an ad in a magazine, you might look at the placement of figures or objects, the use of color, and the choice of fonts. Each element contributes something significant to the whole; each carries some part of the message being conveyed. Following are discussions and examples of four common kinds of analysis: rhetorical analysis, process analysis, causal analysis, and data analysis.

Rhetorical analysis. This kind of analysis can focus on a written text, a visual text, an audio text, or one that combines words, images, and sound. All of these are rhetorical analyses; that is, they all take a close look at how an author, designer, or artist communicates a message to an audience. Whether they are using words or images, adjusting font sizes or colors, they all are trying to persuade a particular audience to have a particular reaction to a particular message—theirs.

See how the following example from an article in the online magazine *Macworld* analyzes the core of Apple's "exceptional advertising . . . that in-definable element of cool," something that "Dell, Microsoft, and Hewlett-Packard lack":

> Despite their differences, Apple ads have in common at least one major advantage over many competitors' commercials: regardless of whether you love or hate the spots, you'll likely *remember* them, and that's the first step to building a successful image. . . .

Apple's current campaign for the Mac, "Get a Mac," conveys just as simple and straightforward a message as the name would suggest. It's a deliberate attempt to appeal to the vast majority of computer users who, as Apple sees it, are using a Windows machine either because they aren't aware they have an alternative or because they're nursing some erroneous preconceptions about Macs.

The ads, which first began airing in May 2006, feature actors Justin Long and John Hodgman as the Mac and PC, respectively—anthropo-morphized versions of the long-warring computer platforms.

Aside from a brief shot at the end of the spots, you won't see any actual computers in the "Get a Mac" ads. And there's a good reason for that—computer features are hard to show off in a small space in 30-second segments. Instead, Apple illustrates features by putting the characters into humorous situations. For example, when the PC sports a leg cast due to someone tripping over his power cord, it gives the Mac a chance to bring up the detachable MagSafe adapter.

The result: The ad spells out the Mac's advantages in a way that's both accessible and memorable for the average user. . . .

Because of the "Get a Mac" campaign's reliance on dialogue, Apple has also localized them for other markets. Both the U.K. and Japan now have their own version of the "Get a Mac" ads, with native actors and situations tuned to the nuances of those cultures. It's all part of the at-tention to detail that Apple knows it needs in order to compete globally.

—DAN MOREN, "Analysis: The Many Faces of Apple Advertising"

In the rest of his article, Moren takes us methodically through the ad cam-paigns for other Apple products to provide more evidence for his opening claim that Apple's ads are inherently memorable. And because this article was written for an online publication, he can use multiple media to demon-strate his points. He includes hyperlinks to the online ads, so we can actu-ally listen to the dialogue and see for ourselves that round-faced, balding, pudgy PC is a bit stodgy, dressed in a brown blazer and slacks with white shirt and tie, while lean, shaggy-haired Mac is quintessentially cool, in jeans and a casual shirt, hands tucked into his pockets. Moren also points out an example of how using actors allows for a humorous demonstration of an appealing gadget that's available with a Mac: "When the PC sports a leg cast due to someone tripping over his power cord, it gives the Mac a chance to bring up the detachable MagSafe adapter."

Note how the author moves from a broad statement—"Apple ads have

John Hodgman and Justin Long as PC and Mac in Apple's "Get a Mac" campaign.

in common at least one major advantage over many competitors' commercials: regardless of whether you love or hate the spots, you'll likely *remember* them, and that's the first step to building a successful image"—to the supporting evidence, discovered by looking closely at the ads and identifying their essential components and the way each one contributes to make the ads "one of the best campaigns of all time."

To see the ads, go to wwnorton.com/ write/everyonelinks and check out the "'Get a Mac' Collection" link.

Process analysis. The following example analyzes a process—how skaters make high-speed turns. This is the most critical element in speed skating, for being able to consistently make fast turns without slipping and losing ground can be the difference between winning and losing. This analysis from *Science Buddies,* a website for students and parents, closely examines the key steps of the process. Note how the author provides some information about the basic physics of speed and turns and then systematically explains how each element of the action—speed, angle, push back force from the surface—contributes to the total turn.

Check out the link to the entire piece at wwnorton.com/ write/everyonelinks.

> Whether it's ice, wood, or a paved surface, the science that governs a skater's ability to turn is essentially the same. It's based on a couple of basic laws of physics that describe speed and the circular motion of turns. The first is Newton's *law of inertia* that says a body in motion will stay in motion unless there is some outside force that changes it. To skaters hoping to make a turn after they speed down the straightaway, that means the force of inertia would tend to keep them going straight ahead if there wasn't a greater force to make them change direction and begin turning.
>
> The force that causes the change in direction comes from the skater's blades or wheels as they cross over at an angle in front of the skater leaning to make a turn. Newton's *law of reaction* explains that the push from the skater's skates generates an equal but opposite push back from the ice or floor. This push back force draws the skater in towards the track and is described as a "center seeking" or *centripetal* type of force. It's the reason why turns are possible in any sport. The wheels of a bicycle, for example, also angle into the road surface when the cyclist leans to begin a turn. As the road pushes back on both bike and rider, it supplies the inward centripetal force to generate the turning motion.
>
> The more a skater leans into a turn, the more powerful the push from the skate, and the greater centripetal force produced to carry the skater through the turn. Leaning in also creates a smaller arc, or tighter turn,

Lee Jung-su, Lee Ho-suk, and Apolo Anton Ohno skate for the finish line during the last turn of the men's 1,000-meter short track speed skating finals at the Vancouver 2010 Winter Olympics.

making for a shorter distance and a faster path around the turn. However, there's a catch. As the skater leans more and more into the track, the balancing point of the body, or the skater's *center of gravity*, also shifts more and more to the side. If it shifts too far, the skater no longer can maintain balance and ends up splayed out onto the rink rather than happily heading round the turn to the finishing line.

So success in turns, especially fast ones, means skaters must constantly find their center of gravity while teetering on the edge of their skates. To make the turn at all requires that the skater push the skates against the ice with sufficient power to generate enough inward centripetal force to counter the inertia of skating straight ahead. And to keep up speed in a race, a skater must calculate and execute the shortest, or tightest, turns possible around the track.

—DARLENE JENKINS, "Tightening the Turns in Speed Skating:
Lessons in Centripetal Force and Balance"

This kind of close examination of the subject is the heart of analysis. Darlene Jenkins explains the key elements in the process of making a high-speed turn—speed, angle, push back force—and also examines the relationships among these elements as she describes what happens in minute detail, revealing how they all combine to create the pattern of movement that leads to a successful high-speed turn. By including a photograph that shows skaters leaning into a turn, blades and bodies angled precariously, Jenkins emphasizes visually what her words convey, and readers actually see what she's describing.

Causal analysis. You'll often have occasion to analyze causes, to figure out why something occurs or once occurred. Why did the U.S. financial system almost collapse in 2008? What caused the 2011 NBA lockout?

Behavioral ecologist Karen McComb, who studies communication between animals and humans, wanted to understand why cat owners so often respond to purring cats by feeding them. To answer the question of what the cats do to solicit food this way, McComb and a team recorded a number of domestic cats in their homes and discovered what the team termed "solicitation purring"—an urgent high-frequency sound, similar to an infant's cry, that is embedded within the cats' more pleasing and low-pitched purring and that apparently triggered an innate nurturing response in their owners. In an article presenting their findings, the team provided numerical data about the pitch and frequency of different kinds of purring, along with their conclusion about what the data showed: that the similarities in pitch and frequency to the cries of human infants "make them very difficult to ignore."

Using data like these to support an analysis would be common in science classes, while in the humanities and social sciences, you're more likely to write about causes that are plausible or probable than ones that can be measured. In a literature class, for example, you might be asked to analyze the influences that shaped F. Scott Fitzgerald's creation of Jay Gatsby in *The Great Gatsby*—that is, to try to explain what caused Fitzgerald to develop Gatsby the way he did. In a sociology class, you might be asked to analyze what factors contributed to a population decline in a certain neighborhood. In both cases, these causes are probabilities—plausible but not provable.

Go to wwnorton. com/write/ everyonelinks to link to the full article, "The Cry Embedded within the Purr."

Data analysis. Some subjects will require you to analyze data, as in the example below, in which blogger Will Moller analyzes the performances of ten major league baseball pitchers to answer the question of whether New York Yankees pitcher Andy Pettitte is likely to get into baseball's Hall of Fame.

> I prefer to look at Andy versus his peers, because simply put, it would be very odd for 10 pitchers from the same decade to get in (though this number is rather arbitrary). Along that line, who are the best pitchers of Andy's generation, so we can compare them? . . .

	Wins	Win%	WAR	ERA+	IP	K	K/BB	WAR/9IP
Martinez	219	68.7%	89.4	154	2827	3154	4.15	0.28
Clemens	354	65.8%	145.5	143	4917	4672	2.96	0.27
Johnson	303	64.6%	114.8	136	4135	4875	3.26	0.25
Schilling	216	59.7%	86.1	128	3261	3116	4.38	0.24
Maddux	355	61.0%	120.6	132	5008	3371	3.37	0.22
Mussina	270	63.8%	85.6	123	3563	2813	3.58	0.22
Smoltz	213	57.9%	82.5	125	3473	3084	3.05	0.21
Brown	211	59.4%	77.2	127	3256	2397	2.66	0.21
Pettitte	240	63.5%	66.9	117	3055	2251	2.34	0.20
Glavine	305	60.0%	67.1	118	4413	2607	1.74	*0.14*

	Postseason Wins	Postseason Losses	Saves
Martinez	6	4	
Clemens	12	8	
Johnson	7	9	
Schilling	11	2	
Maddux	11	14	
Mussina	7	8	
Smoltz	15	4	158
Brown	5	5	
Pettitte	19	10	
Glavine	14	16	

The above table tells the story pretty well. I've bolded the numbers that are particularly absurd, and italicized one in particular which should act as a veto. Though I imagine most of the readers of this blog know full well what these statistics mean at this point, for those of you who don't, a primer:

WAR stands for Wins Above Replacement, and is a somewhat complicated equation which estimates the true value of a pitcher, taking into account league, ERA, park effects, etc. For instance, a pitcher that wins a game but gives up 15 earned runs has probably lost value in their career WAR, even though they get the shiny addition to their win-loss record. We like WAR around these parts.

ERA+ is a normalized version of ERA centered on 100, basically showing how much better or worse a pitcher was compared to their league average (by ERA). 110, for example, would indicate that the pitch-

Andy Pettitte pitching against the Kansas City Royals in April 2009.

er's ERA was 10% better than average. 95, on the other hand, would be roughly 5% worse than average. This is a good statistic for comparing pitchers between different time periods—a 4.00 ERA in 2000 doesn't mean the same thing as a 4.00 ERA in 1920, for example.

K/BB is how many strikeouts a pitcher had per walk. More is better, less is worse.

As you can see, the above table doesn't do Andy any favors. He's 6th in wins and 5th in winning percentage, but he's 9th in ERA+ and dead last in WAR. His K/BB beats only Tom Glavine, who comes off looking pretty bad on this list. The only thing he has going for him is his playoff record—and frankly, the team he was on won a whole bunch of playoff games while he was on the team, even when he wasn't pitching. Besides, we're pretty much past the point of taking W/L record as a good indication of pitcher skill—why is it that when we slap the word "postseason" onto the statistic, we suddenly devolve 10 years to when such things seemed to matter?   —WILL MOLLER, "A Painful Posting"

Link to Moller's entire piece at wwnorton.com/ write/everyonelinks.

Moller's guiding question, "Should Andy Pettitte be in the Hall of Fame?" is unstated in this excerpt, but it is made clear earlier in the piece. He presents the data in a table for readers to see—and then walks us through his analysis of that data. It's critical when using numerical data like these not only to present the information but also to say what it means. That's a key part of your analysis. Using a table to present data is a good way to include numerical evidence, but be careful that you don't just drop the table in; you need to explain to readers what the data mean, as Moller does. Though he does not state his conclusions explicitly here, his analysis makes clear what he thinks—as does his URL: http://itsaboutthemoney.net/archives/2011/02/04/sorry-andy/. Just as Moller defines abbreviations some readers may not know, you should be careful to explain anything that your audience might not understand.

Insight Gained from Your Analysis

Like all rhetorical acts, analysis has a purpose. One key purpose is to give your audience insight into what you are analyzing. As you examine your subject, you come up with facts, data, and other specific information drawn from the subject—which will lead you to some insight, a deeper understanding of the subject you're analyzing. The insight that you gain will lead you to your thesis. When the "interfaith amigos" mentioned earlier in this chapter analyzed a sentence in their book that offended the rabbi, each gained insight into the others' principles that led to further understanding. In "Getting Obama Right," these concluding lines make clear the insight David Brooks derived from analyzing the perceptions of Obama expressed by both liberal Democrats and conservative Republicans:

> In a sensible country, people would see Obama as a president trying to define a modern brand of moderate progressivism. In a sensible country, Obama would be able to clearly define this project without fear of offending the people he needs to get legislation passed. But we don't live in that country. We live in a country in which many people live in information cocoons in which they only talk to members of their own party and read blogs of their own sect. They come away with perceptions fundamentally at odds with reality, fundamentally misunderstanding the man in the Oval Office.
>
> —DAVID BROOKS, "Getting Obama Right"

From Brooks' insight that both Republicans and Democrats are misreading the facts and presenting a biased view, we get his message: Such misperception is counterproductive to effective government.

Summarizing the study of the way cats manipulate humans noted earlier in this chapter, Karen McComb and her team note parallels between the isolation cry of domestic cats and the distress cry of human infants as a way of understanding why the "cry embedded within the purr" is so successful in motivating owners to feed their cats. They conclude that the cats have learned to communicate their need for attention in ways that are impossible to ignore, ways that prompt caring responses from people. Thus, their work suggests that much can be learned by focusing on animal-human communication from both directions, from animals to humans as well as the reverse.

Remember that any analysis you do needs to have a purpose. In an analysis, your purpose—to discover how cats motivate their owners to provide food on demand, to understand how partisan misperceptions create roadblocks in government, to explain why a favorite baseball player's statistics won't get him into the Hall of Fame—needs to generate a clear point that you make for your audience; in most cases, that point will be the insight you gain from the analysis.

Clear, Precise Language

Since the point of an analysis is to help an audience understand something, you need to pay extra attention to the words you use and the way you explain your findings. You want your audience to follow your analysis easily and not get sidetracked. In presenting your findings, you need to demonstrate that you know what you are talking about. You have studied your subject, looked at it closely, thought about it—*analyzed* it; therefore, you know it well, but most important, you know what you want to say about it and why. Now you have to craft your analysis in such a way that your audience will follow that analysis and understand what it shows.

Analyzing the elements in a text or explaining an intricate process requires you to use precise language that your audience will understand, to describe anything that may be unfamiliar to them, to define terms they may not be familiar with, and to lay out the exact steps in a process.

The analysis of speed skating turns earlier in this chapter was written for an audience of young people and their parents who are interested in science and creating projects for science fairs. The language used to describe the physics that govern the process of turning is appropriate for such an audience—specific and precise but not technical. When the author refers to Newton's law of inertia, she immediately defines *inertia* and then explains what it means for skaters. The important role of centripetal force is explained as "the more a skater leans into turns, the more powerful the push from the skate." Everything is clear because the writer uses simple, everyday words—"tighter turn," "teetering on the edge of their skates"—to convey complex science in a way that is concrete and to the point.

Look also at the analysis of baseball statistics presented earlier in this chapter. Even though it was written for a blog targeting Yankees fans, the author includes a "primer" for those readers who may not understand the kinds of statistics he presents.

You need to consider what your audience knows about your topic and what information you'll need to include to be sure they'll understand what you write. You'll also want to be careful about how you present information. In U.S. academic writing, you are expected to state your conclusions explicitly—in clear, specific language.

WRITING ANALYTICALLY / A Roadmap

Find a topic that matters—to you, and to others

Whether you can choose your topic or have to respond to a specific assignment, make the project interesting—to you and your audience. Find an angle that appeals to your interests, that engages you. No audience will want to hear about something you are not interested in writing.

If you can choose your topic, begin by considering your own interests. What do you like to do? What issues catch your interest? What do you value? If you value courage, you might want to analyze how a particular literary character manifests that trait: Is Harry Potter courageous when he repeatedly confronts Voldemort alone, or is he foolhardy? An interest in sports could lead you to analyze statistical data on a favorite athlete (as Will Moller does) or to analyze the process of doing something in a particular sport (as Darlene Jenkins does). Concern about climate change could lead you to analyze the costs and benefits of alternative energy sources. Whatever your interests, you'll be sure to find some way of conducting rhetorical, process, causal, or data analysis.

If you've been assigned a topic, say to analyze the Gettysburg Address, you might consider the way President Lincoln appealed to his audience. To make the analysis more interesting, you might imagine that Lincoln was giving this speech to an audience of college students today. What advice would you give him about revising in order to reach such an audience? Or perhaps you've been assigned to analyze a physical process—the process of sleeping, for example. You might examine your own sleep habits and see how they compare with the norm for your age group.

Make your topic matter to your audience. Some topics matter to everyone, or nearly everyone; you might be able to identify such topics by checking the media for what's being debated and discussed. But when you're writing about something that may not automatically appeal to a wide audience, it's your responsibility as the writer to make the topic matter to them. Think about Robert Connors' essay on the skunk—not an inherently interesting topic or one that matters widely—but he involves us by showing how he came to care and by analyzing the situation in a way that engages our interest and makes us care, too.

Consider your rhetorical situation

Keep in mind the elements of your particular situation—your audience, your specific purpose, your stance, and so on—and how they will or should influence the choices you make in your writing.

Identify your audience. Who do you want to reach, and how can you shape your analysis so that you get through to them? Karen McComb's analysis of cats purring was for an audience of scientific peers, whereas Robert Connors wrote his piece for *Yankee*, a New England "lifestyle" magazine with articles on travel, home, and food. Very different audiences, very different purposes, very different analyses. In each case, the author could target a specific audience.

However, if you are writing for the web, you will likely reach a broader audience than either of these, and one whose characteristics you can't predict, so you need to keep in mind what additional information you might need to provide—just as Will Moller does in his blog about Andy Pettitte. Even though his primary audience is Yankees fans, he knows that many of them won't know much about statistics, so he provides the definitions they need to understand his analysis. To identify your target audience, you might consider the following questions:

- Who are you trying to reach? And what do you know about them—their age, gender, cultural and linguistic background? Anything else?

- What are they likely to know about your subject, and what background information will you need to provide?

- How will they benefit from the analysis and insight you hope to offer?

- Will your subject matter to them—and if not, how can you make them care about it?

Keeping your likely audience firmly in mind will help you craft an analysis that connects with them.

Articulate your purpose. In all likelihood, you won't be the first or only one to write on your topic, so one broad purpose for writing will be to add your voice to a larger conversation. Following are some questions that can help you narrow your focus and articulate more specific purposes:

- What are you analyzing? A text? A process? Causes? Data?

- What has motivated you to write? Are you responding to some other text or author?

- What do you want to accomplish by analyzing this subject? How can you best achieve your goals?

- What do you want your audience to take away from your analysis?

Think about your stance. What is your attitude toward the subject, and how do you want to come across as an author? Objective? Passionate? Something else? How can your writing reflect that stance? If your subject is surfing and you're writing on a surfers' blog about how to catch a wave, for an audience of beginners, your stance might be that of an experienced surfer, or a former beginner. Your language would probably be informal, with little or no surfing jargon. If, on the other hand, you're writing an article for *Surfing Magazine* analyzing the process Laird Hamilton developed to ride fifty-foot waves, your stance might be that of an objective reporter, and your language would need to be more technical for that well-informed audience. No matter what your stance or target audience, you need to consider what kind of language is appropriate, what terms need to be defined, and how you can establish your authority as an author.

Consider the larger context. If you are analyzing an ad for a composition class, you will want to look at relevant information about the original context. When was the ad created, and who was the target audience? What were the social, economic, and political conditions at the time? All of that is contextual information. If you are preparing a load analysis for an engineering class, you'll need to consider such factors as how, when, and where the structure will be used. Much of the contextual information comes from what others have said about your subject, and your analysis adds to the conversation.

Consider media. Will your analysis be delivered in print? on a website? in an oral presentation? Are you writing for the opinion pages in your campus newspaper? Or are you assigned to give an oral presentation incorporating audio and images? If you get to choose your medium, the choice should depend on how you can best present your subject and achieve your purpose with your intended audience. Whether you have a choice or not, the media you use will affect how you organize and design your analysis.

Consider matters of design. Think about how to best present your information and whether you need to follow any disciplinary conventions. Does your information include data that is easiest to understand in a chart or graph? Would headings help readers follow your analysis? Does your subject require illustrations? What fonts are most appropriate for your subject, your medium, and your audience? Like all of your other writing choices, the design decisions you make can help you achieve your goals.

Analyze your subject

What kind of analysis is needed for your subject and purpose? You may be assigned to conduct a certain kind of analysis, or you may be inspired by a question, as Will Moller was in analyzing data to determine whether Andy Pettitte is likely to be elected to the Hall of Fame. But sometimes you may be asked simply to "analyze x"—an ad, a game, a historical event, several hedge funds—and then you'll need to determine what kind of analysis you'll do. The kind of analysis you need to do—*rhetorical analysis, process analysis, causal analysis, data analysis*—will determine the way you study your subject.

If you're analyzing rhetoric, you need to look at what the text you're examining says and how it supports its claims.

- What question has led you to analyze this text? What specifically are you looking for?

- What claim is the text making—and how does it support that claim?

- If you're analyzing a written text, what reasons and evidence does the author provide for the claim—and do they convince you?

- Does the writer acknowledge or respond to counterarguments or other opinions? If so, are they presented fairly?

- If you're analyzing a visual text, how does it make its point? Where does your eye go first? What's in the foreground, and what's in the background?

- Are there any words that indicate what the author thinks—or wants you to think?

- How does the author establish authority to address the topic?

- Does the text appeal to your emotions? If so, how?

If you're analyzing a process, you'll need to decide whether your analysis will be *informational* or *instructional*. An informational analysis tells how something works; an instructional one tells how to do something. Writing about how solar panels convert sunshine to energy would be informational, whereas writing about how to install solar panels would be instructional— and would need to explicitly identify all materials and conditions needed and then tell readers step-by-step exactly how to carry out the process. Once you've determined what kind of process you're analyzing, you might then consider questions like these:

- What question is prompting your analysis?

- If the process is instructional, what materials are needed?

- What are the steps in the process?

- What order do the steps follow?

Some processes follow a set order (throwing a curve ball, parallel parking a car), whereas others have no fixed order (playing sudoku). Remember that whatever the process, you'll need to present the steps in some kind of order.

If you're analyzing causes, you're looking for answers to why something happened. Why, for instance, did the Penn State University Board of Trustees fire legendary football coach Joe Paterno? Questions about causes can rarely be answered definitively, so if you're writing a causal analysis, you'll usually be arguing that certain causes are the most plausible or the primary ones, and that other possible causes are secondary or less likely. In addition, although an *immediate cause* may be obvious, less obvious *long-term causes* may also have contributed.

In the Paterno case, the Penn State trustees initially said only that they felt it "was necessary to make a change in leadership." At the time, however, some people speculated that Paterno was being blamed for not having done more in light of the sexual assault accusations about a former coach. Others argued that the immediate cause was damage control, that in light of the accusations the trustees felt they needed to "protect the brand" (football brings in $72 million a year to Penn State). Still others pointed out that Penn State had been trying to get Paterno to retire for many years—perhaps a contributing cause. Months later, the trustees named additional reasons, but the initial speculations serve as a good example of the kind of analysis that goes on when people want to know why something happened.

You also need to keep two other considerations in mind when analyzing causes. First, don't confuse coincidence with causation. That two events—such as a new police-patrol policy in a city and a drop in the crime rate—occurred more or less simultaneously, or even that one event preceded the other, does not prove that one *caused* the other. Second, you need to consider all possible causes and provide evidence to support the ones you identify as most plausible. If the city also experienced an economic boom around the same time that the new policy and the drop in crime began, for example, you would need to show (perhaps using evidence from other cities) that good economic conditions do not usually seem to reduce crime rates.

As the preceding example suggests, you'll often need to do some research to be sure you understand all the possible causes and whether they are primary or contributing causes, immediate or long-term causes. Here are some questions that can guide your analysis:

- What question is prompting your analysis?

- List all the causes you can think of. Which ones seem like the primary causes? Which seem to be contributing or secondary causes?

- Is there an immediate cause, something that directly set off whatever happened?

- Think about long-term causes, ones that originated long ago but are ultimately responsible for what happened.

- Might any of the causes on your list be merely coincidences?

- Which are the most plausible causes—and why?

- Do you need to do research to help answer any of these questions?

If you're analyzing data, you're trying to identify patterns in information that you or someone else has gathered. The information collected by the U.S. Census is data. Social scientists might classify that data according to certain criteria, such as numbers of families with children in urban areas, and then analyze those data looking for patterns on which to make claims or predictions about population trends.

In his piece on Andy Pettitte, Will Moller provides readers with numerical data on ten pitchers' performances, data he analyzes to determine whether Pettitte is likely to be nominated to the Hall of Fame. Moller's analysis expressly states his guiding question—"Who are the best pitchers of [Andy Pettitte's] generation, so we can compare them?"—and then answers it by considering each element of the data as it relates to the pitchers' performances.

Although the mathematical nature of some data analysis can often make it more straightforward than other kinds of analysis, identifying statistical patterns and figuring out their significance can be challenging. Here are some questions to consider when analyzing data:

- What question are you trying to answer?

- Are there any existing data that can help you find your answer? If so, will they provide sufficient information, or do you need to find more?

- Is the data up-to-date? trustworthy? Who collected the data, and why?

- Are there other data that tell a different story?

- Do you need to conduct any research of your own to generate the data you need?

- Can you identify patterns in the data? If so, are they patterns you expected, or are any of them surprising?

Determine what your analysis shows

Once you've analyzed your subject, you need to figure out what your analysis shows. What was the question that first prompted your analysis, and how can you now answer that question? What have you discovered about your subject? What have you discovered that interests you—and how can you make it matter to your audience? Write out a tentative thesis, noting what you've analyzed and why, and what conclusions or insights you want to share. Your thesis is your point, the claim you want to make about your subject. Let's say you're writing a rhetorical analysis of the Gettysburg Address. Here's how one author analyzed that speech:

> Following Edward Everett's two-hour oration, President Lincoln spoke eloquently for a mere two minutes, deploying rhetorical devices like repetition, contrast, and rhythm in a way that connected emotionally with his audience.

This sentence tells us that the writer will describe the event, say something about the length of the speech, and explain how specific words and structures resulted in an eloquently simple but profoundly moving speech.

As you formulate your thesis, begin by stating it several different ways and then look for the one that is most interesting to you. Think about your audience and how you can make your analysis most compelling to them. Then list the evidence you found that supports your analysis—examples, quotations, quantitative or qualitative data, and so forth. Which ones will be most persuasive to your audience? Consider other analytical perspectives and how you can account for them. Do you have everything you need, or do you need to do any further research?

Organize and start writing

Once you've carried out your analysis, it's time to start drafting.

Type out your tentative thesis, and keep checking back to be sure that you are supporting it as you draft.

Give evidence that supports your thesis. The kind of evidence will depend on the kind of analysis—examples, statistics, and other data taken from the subject itself as well as from other sources you've consulted.

Cite other sources, but remember that this is *your* analysis. Your audience wants to hear your voice and learn from your insights. At the same time, don't forget to acknowledge other perspectives.

Draft an opening. You might begin by describing *what* you're analyzing and *why*, explaining what question prompted you to take a closer look at your topic. Provide any background information your audience might need. State your thesis: What are you claiming about your subject?

Draft a conclusion. You might end by reiterating what you've learned from your analysis and what you want your audience to understand about your subject. Make sure they know why your analysis matters, both to them and to you.

Look critically at your draft, get response—and revise

Read your draft slowly and carefully to see whether you've made your guiding question clear, described your subject sufficiently, offered enough evidence to support your analysis, and provided your audience with some insight about your subject.

Then ask some others to read and respond to your draft. If your school has a writing center, try to meet with a tutor, taking along any questions you have. Here are some questions that can help you or others read over a draft of analytic writing:

- *Is the guiding question behind your analysis clear?* Is it a question worth considering?

- *How does the opening capture the audience's interest?* Does it indicate why this analysis matters? How else might you begin?

- *Is the subject described in enough detail for your intended audience?* Is there any other information they might need to follow your analysis?

- *What insights have you gained from the analysis?* Have you stated them explicitly? How likely is it that readers will accept your conclusions?

- *Is the point of your analysis clear?* Have you stated the point explicitly in a thesis—and if not, do you need to?

- *What evidence do you provide to support your point?* Is it sufficient?

- *If you've cited any sources, are they credible and convincing?* Have you integrated them smoothly into your text—is it clear what *you* are saying and where (and why) you are citing others? And have you documented any sources you've cited?

- *Have you addressed other perspectives?* Do you need to acknowledge possible counterarguments?

- *How would you describe your tone,* and does it accurately convey your stance? Is it an appropriate tone for your audience and purpose? If not, how could it be improved?

- *How effectively is the analysis designed?* Have you included any images or other visual data—and if so, how do they contribute to the analysis? If not, is there any information that might be easier to understand if presented in a table or chart or accompanied by an image?

- *How is the analysis organized?* Is it easy to follow, with explicit transitions from one point to the next? Are there headings—and if not, would they help? If you're analyzing a process, are the steps in an order that your audience will be able to follow easily?

- *Consider style*—is it appropriate for the audience and purpose? Look at the choice of words and kinds of sentences—are they appropriately formal (or informal)? Could the style be improved in any way?

- *How does the draft conclude?* Is the conclusion forceful and memorable? How else might the analysis conclude?

- *Consider the title.* Does it make clear what the analysis is about, and will it make your intended audience interested in reading on?

Revise your draft in light of your own observations and any feedback you get from others, keeping your audience and purpose firmly in mind. But remember: *You* are the analyst here, so you need to make the decisions.

꩜ *REFLECT ON WHAT YOU'VE LEARNED. Once you've completed your analysis, let it settle for a while and then take time to reflect. How well did you analyze your subject? What insights did your analysis lead to? What additional revisions would you make if you could? Research shows that such reflections help "lock in" what you learn for future use.*

Advertisements R Us

MELISSA RUBIN

ADVERTISEMENTS ARE WRITTEN to persuade us—to make us want to support a certain cause, buy a particular car, drink a specific kind of soda. But *how* do they do it? How do they persuade us? Since the beginning of modern consumer culture, companies have cleverly tailored advertisements to target specific groups. To do so, they include text and images that reflect and appeal to the ideals, values, and stereotypes held by the consumers they wish to attract. As a result, advertisements reveal a lot about society. We can learn a great deal about the prevailing culture by looking closely at the deliberate ways a company crafts an ad to appeal to particular audiences.

This ad from the August 1950 *Coca-Cola Bottler* magazine, a trade magazine for Coca-Cola bottlers (fig. 1), features a larger-than-life red Coca-Cola vending machine with the slogan "Drink Coca-Cola—Work *Refreshed*" (Coca-Cola). Set against a bright blue sky with puffy white clouds, an overlarge open bottle of Coke hovers just to the right and slightly above the vending machine, next to the head of "Sprite Boy," a pixie-ish character and onetime Coke symbol, who sports a bottle cap for a hat. Sprite Boy's left hand gestures past the floating Coke bottle and toward a crowd congregating before the vending machine. The group, overwhelmingly male and apparently all white, includes blue-collar workers in casual clothing, servicemen in uniform, and businessmen in suits in the foreground; the few women displayed are in the background, wearing dresses. The setting is industrialized and urban, as indicated by the factory and smokestacks on the far left side of the scene and by the skyscrapers and apartment building on the right.

Practically since its invention, Coca-Cola has been identified with mainstream America. Born from curiosity and experimentation in an Atlanta pharmacy in 1886, Coke's phenomenal growth paralleled America's in the industrial age. Benefiting from developments in technology and transportation, by 1895 it was "sold and consumed in every state and territory in the United States" (Coca-Cola Company). In 2010, Diet Coke became the second-most-

---

MELISSA RUBIN, an English major at Hofstra University, wrote this analysis using an early draft of this chapter.

Fig. 1. 1950 ad from *Coca-Cola Bottler* magazine (Coca-Cola).

popular carbonated drink in the world . . . behind Coca-Cola (Esterl). In the immediate post-war world, Coke became identified with American optimism and energy, thanks in part to the company's wartime declaration that "every man in uniform gets a bottle of Coca-Cola for 5 cents, wherever he is, and whatever it costs the Company" (Coca-Cola Company). To meet this dictate, bottling plants were built overseas with the result that many people other than Americans first tasted Coke during this war that America won so decisively, and when peace finally came, "the foundations were laid for Coca-Cola to do business overseas" (Coca-Cola Company).

Given the context, just a few years after World War II and at the beginning of the Korean War, the setting clearly reflects the idea that Americans experienced increased industrialization and urbanization as a result of World War II. Factories had sprung up across the country to aid in the war effort, and many rural and small-town Americans had moved to industrial areas and large cities in search of work. In this advertisement, the buildings surround the people, symbolizing a sense of community and the way Americans had come together in a successful effort to win the war.

The ad suggests that Coca-Cola recognized the patriotism inspired by the war and wanted to inspire similar positive feelings about their product. In the center of the ad, the huge red vending machine looks like the biggest skyscraper of all—the dominant feature of the urban industrial landscape. On the upper right, the floating face of Coca-Cola's Sprite Boy towers above the scene. A pale character with wild white hair, hypnotic eyes, and a mysterious smile, Sprite Boy stares straight at readers, his left hand gesturing toward the red machine. Sprite Boy's size and placement in the ad makes him appear godlike, as if he, the embodiment of Coca-Cola, is a powerful force uniting—and refreshing—hardworking Americans. The placement of the vending machine in the center of the ad and the wording on it evoke the idea that drinking Coca-Cola will make a hardworking American feel refreshed while he (and apparently it was rarely she) works and becomes part of a larger community. The text at the bottom of the ad, "A welcome host to workers—*Inviting you to the pause that refreshes with ice-cold Coca-Cola*"—sends the same message to consumers: Coke will refresh and unite working America.

The way that Coca-Cola chooses to place the objects and depict men and women in this ad speaks volumes about American society in the middle of the twentieth century: a white, male-dominated society in which servicemen and veterans were a numerous and prominent presence. The clothing that the men in the foreground wear reflects the assumption that the target demographic for the ad—people who worked in Coca-Cola bottling plants—valued hard workers and servicemen during a time of war. White, uniformed men are placed front and center. One man wears an Army uniform, the one next to him wears a Navy uniform, and the next an Air Force uniform. By placing the servicemen so prominently, Coca-Cola emphasizes their important role in society and underscores the value Americans placed on their veterans at a time when almost all male Americans were subject to the draft and most of them could expect to serve in the military or had already done so. The other men in the foreground—one wearing a blue-collar work uniform and the other formal business attire—are placed on either side of and slightly apart from the soldiers, suggesting that civilian workers played a valuable role in society, but one secondary to that of the military. Placing only a few women dressed in casual day wear in the far background of the image represents the assumption that women played a less important role in society—or at least in the war effort and the workforce, including Coke's.

The conspicuous mixture of stereotypical middle-class and working-class attire is noteworthy because in 1950, the U.S. economy had been marked by years of conflict over labor's unionization efforts and management's opposition to them—often culminating in accommodation between the two sides. The ad seems to suggest that such conflict should be seen as a thing of the past, that men with blue-collar jobs and their bosses are all "workers" whom Coca-Cola, a generous "host," is inviting to share in a break for refreshments. Thus all economic classes, together with a strong military, can unite to build a productive industrial future and a pleasant lifestyle for themselves.

From the perspective of the twenty-first century, this ad is especially interesting because it seems to be looking backward instead of forward in significant ways. By 1950, the highly urban view of American society it presents was starting to be challenged by widespread movement out of central cities to the suburbs, but nothing in the ad hints at this profound change. At the time, offices and factories were still located mostly in urban areas and associated in Americans' minds with cities, and the ad clearly reflects this perspective. In addition, it presents smoke pouring from factory smokestacks in a positive light, with no sign of the environmental damage that such emissions cause, and that would become increasingly clear over the next few decades.

Another important factor to consider: everyone in the ad is white. During the 1950s, there was still a great deal of racial prejudice and segregation in the United States. Coca-Cola was attuned to white society's racial intolerance and chose in this ad to depict what they undoubtedly saw as average Americans,

the primary demographic of the audience for this publication: Coca-Cola employees. While Coke did feature African Americans in some ads during the late
1940s and early 1950s, they were celebrity musicians like Louis Armstrong,
Duke Ellington, Count Basie, or Graham Jackson (the accordion player who
was a huge favorite of Franklin Delano Roosevelt's) or star athletes like Marion
Motley and Bill Willis, the first men to break the color barrier in NFL football
("World of Coca-Cola"). The contrast between these extremes underscores
the prejudice: "ordinary" people are represented by whites, while only exceptional African Americans appear in the company's ads.

In 1950, then, the kind of diversity that Coke wanted to highlight and appeal   10
to was economic (middle-class and working-class) and war-related (civilian
and military). Today, such an ad would probably represent the ethnic diversity
missing from the 1950 version, with smiling young people of diverse skin colors and facial features relaxing with Cokes, probably now in cans rather than
bottles. But the differences in economic, employment, or military status or in
clothing styles that the 1950 ad highlighted would be unlikely to appear, not
because they no longer exist, but because advertisers for products popular
with a broad spectrum of society no longer consider them a useful way to appeal to consumers.

While initially the ads for Coca-Cola reflected the values of the time, their
enormous success eventually meant that Coke ads helped shape the American
identity. In them, Americans always appear smiling, relaxed, carefree, united
in their quest for well-deserved relaxation and refreshment. They drive con-
vertibles, play sports, dance, and obviously enjoy life. The message: theirs is a
life to be envied and emulated, so drink Coca-Cola and live that life yourself.

Works Cited

Coca-Cola. Advertisement. *The Coca-Cola Bottler* 41.6 (1950): n. pag. Web. 5
    May 2011.

Coca-Cola Company. "The Coca-Cola Company Heritage Timeline." *Coca-
    Cola History.* Coca-Cola Company, n.d. Web. 26 June 2011.

Esterl, Mike. "Diet Coke Wins Battle in Cola Wars." *Wall Street Journal.* 17
    Mar. 2011: B1. Print.

"The World of Coca-Cola Self-Guided Tour for Teachers. Highlights: African-
    American History Month." *World of Coca-Cola.* World of Coca-Cola at
    Pemberton Place, n.d. Web. 26 June 2011.

Study Questions

1. What insight does Melissa Rubin offer about the Coca-Cola ad she analyzes, and what evidence does she provide to support her analysis? Has
   she persuaded you to accept her conclusions—and if not, why not?

2. How does she incorporate historical context, and what does that information contribute to her analysis?

3. Rubin's analysis is driven by this question: What can we learn about the
   culture in which a given ad is created by closely examining how that ad
   appeals to particular audiences? What other questions might you try to
   answer by analyzing an ad?

4. This Coca-Cola ad reflects the values of its era. Can you think of a contemporary ad that projects the values of the era we live in? How do the
   two ads compare?

5. Write an analysis of a current ad, looking specifically at how it reflects
   American values in the twenty-first century. Be sure to include the ad
   in your essay.

SEVEN

The Writing Process: An Overview

TO LEARN TO DO ANYTHING WELL, from baking bread to programming a computer, we usually break it down into a series of operations. Writing is no exception. This chapter introduces all the steps of the writing process that will take you from a blank page to a final draft: planning; generating ideas; organizing and drafting; revising your draft as it progresses, both on your own and with the help of others; and editing and proofreading your work into its final form.

Keep in mind, however, that writing is a recursive process—that is, it involves a certain amount of repetition. We plan, we draft, we revise; we plan, we draft, we revise again. Also, we tend to skip around as we write. For example, if we suddenly think of a great new idea, we may go back and redraft what we have already written, perhaps revising it completely. Often, in fact, we engage in the various activities of writing more or less at the same time—and many times we perform these various activities in collaboration with others.

PLANNING

Most of the writing we do—and not just in school—starts with an assignment. An English teacher asks you to analyze a poem by Billy Collins. A college application includes an essay question, asking you to explain why you want to go to that school. A prospective employer wants to know, on a job application form, why he or she should hire you. Before you plunge headlong into any writing assignment, however, you need to think about where you're going. You need to plan.

To plan any piece of writing effectively, think about your purpose in writing, the audience you're writing for, and the nature and scope of your topic. If a topic hasn't already been suggested or assigned to you, of course, you'll have to find one. You'll also need to budget your time.

Managing Your Time

When is the assignment due? As soon as you get a writing assignment, make a note of the deadline. Some teachers deduct points for late papers; some don't accept them at all. Even if your instructor is lenient, learning to meet deadlines is part of surviving in college—and beyond. And remember that it's hard to plan well if you begin an assignment the night before it's due. Especially with research papers and other long-range projects, you should begin early so you have plenty of time to do everything the assignment requires.

What kind of research will you need to do? If you are writing a personal narrative or analyzing a process you know well (such as teaching an Irish setter to catch a Frisbee), you may not need to do much research at all before you begin to write. On the other hand, if you are preparing a full-scale research paper on climate change or the fiction of Henry James, the research may take longer than the actual writing. Most college assignments require at least some research. So as you plan any piece of writing, think about how much and what kind of research you will need to do, and allow plenty of time for that research.

Finding a Topic

Though we often use the words interchangeably, a *subject*, strictly speaking, is a broad field of study or inquiry, whereas a *topic* is a specific area within that field. If you are writing a paper for an ecology class, the subject of your paper is likely to be ecology. However, if your teacher asks what you're planning to write on and you reply simply, "ecology," be prepared for a few more questions.

Even if you said "climate change" or "global warming," your teacher would still want to know just what approach you planned to take. A good topic not only narrows down a general subject to a specific area within that field, it addresses a particular aspect of that more limited area, such as what climate change is or what causes climate change or what effects climate change has on the environment or how to stop climate change.

With many writing assignments, you may be given a specific topic or choice of specific topics. For example, an essay exam in Ecology 101 might ask, "Can climate change be stopped? How? Or why not?" Or it might say, more specifically, "Describe the key principles of the Kyoto Protocol." In a literature course, you might get a topic like this: "The narrator of Henry James's *The Turn of the Screw:* heroine or hysteric?" Or in a political science course, you might be asked to compare Marx's theory of revolution with Lenin's.

When you're given such a specific topic, make sure you read the assignment carefully and know just what you are being asked to do. Pay close attention to how the assignment is worded. Look for key terms like *describe, define, analyze, compare and contrast, evaluate, argue.* Be aware that even short assignments may include more than one of these directives. For example, the same assignment may ask you not only to define climate change but to analyze its causes and effects or to compare and contrast present-day climate conditions with those of an earlier time or to construct an argument about what should be done to stop climate change.

Many teachers provide lists of possible topics. With longer assignments, however, you may have to work out a topic yourself, perhaps after meeting with your teacher. Start the conversation as soon as you get the assignment. Let your instructor know if there are any areas within your field of study you find particularly interesting or would like to learn more about. Ask for guidance and suggestions—and start looking on your own. If your school has a writing center, it might be useful to discuss possible topics with someone there.

THINKING ABOUT PURPOSE AND AUDIENCE

We write for many reasons: to organize and clarify our thoughts, express our feelings, remember people and events, solve problems, persuade others to act or believe as we think they should.

For example, let's look at a passage from a recent government report on climate change:

> Climate change, once considered an issue for a distant future, has moved firmly into the present. Corn producers in Iowa, oyster growers in Washington State, and maple syrup producers in Vermont are all observing climate-related changes that are outside of recent experience. So, too, are coastal planners in Florida, water managers in the arid Southwest, city dwellers from Phoenix to New York, and Native Peoples on tribal lands from Louisiana to Alaska. This National Climate Assessment concludes that the evidence of human-induced climate change continues to strengthen and that impacts are increasing across the country.
>
> —U.S. GLOBAL CHANGE RESEARCH PROGRAM,
> *Climate Change Impacts in the United States: Highlights*

The main purpose of this passage, and the report it introduces, is to persuade the reader that serious climate change, far from an issue to be addressed in the distant future, has already occurred.

As you think about *why* you're writing, however, you also need to consider *who* your readers are. In this report on climate change, for example, the authors speak directly to their intended audience:

> Climate change presents a major challenge for society. This report advances our understanding of that challenge and the need for the American people to prepare for and respond to its far-reaching implications.

The intended audience here is ordinary citizens in communities across the country. Your intended audience can be yourself; someone you know, such as your roommate or your teacher; or someone you can't know immediately and directly, such as "the American people." These different audiences have different needs, which you'll want to take into account as you write. If *you* are the intended audience—as when you write in a diary or journal, or jot down a reminder for yourself—you can be as cryptic as you like:

CC lecture tonight @ 8 in Denney.
Joy @ Blue Dube, get notes, ask her to feed cat.

Once you plan to address someone else in writing, no matter what your purpose, you will need to fill in more blanks for the reader, even if you know that person well and are simply, as in the following example, leaving an informal message:

Joy,

I have to go to a lecture on climate change tonight in Denney. Meet you at the Blue Danube at 6. May I borrow your ecology notes? Please feed Gen. Burnsides for me. Friskies in cabinet above fridge. Half a can. Thanks!

Fred

Obviously, the writer of this message is familiar with his audience. He can assume, for example, that she knows Denney is the name of a building on campus and that General Burnsides is the name of a cat—but even Joy has to be told where the cat food is stashed and how much to serve. When you don't know your audience, or when you can't be sure they know what you're talking about, you need to supply them with even more information.

Questions About Purpose and Audience

What is the occasion for writing? Are you writing a research paper? Applying for a job? Responding to an email? Commenting on a blog? Planning a wedding toast?

What is your purpose? Do you want to tell your readers something they may not know? Entertain them? Convince them to do something? Change their minds?

Who is going to read (or hear) what you write? Your classmates? Your teacher? Readers of a blog? Guests at a wedding?

What do you know about your audience's background? For example, if you are writing an argument on how to stop climate change, you can expect readers who come from coal-mining regions to be more sympathetic if you suggest reducing carbon emissions than if you propose shutting down all coal-burning power plants.

How much does your audience already know about your subject? If you are writing for a general audience, you may need to provide some background information and explain terminology that may be unfamiliar. For example, if you are writing about climate change for a newsmagazine, you might note that sequestration is one way to reduce carbon emissions—and then define *sequestration* for those who don't already know. If you're writing for an audience of environmental scientists, though, you may be able to assume that they are familiar with carbon sequestration and you don't have to define it.

What should you keep in mind about the demographics of your audience? Does the gender of your audience matter? How about their age, level of education, economic status, or religion? Once you have sized up your audience, you're in a better position to generate ideas and evidence that will support what you have to say *and* appeal to that audience.

Who do you want your audience to be? The language you use can let your readers know that you are writing to them—or not. In particular, be careful how you use the personal pronouns *we, us,* and *our.* For instance, if you write, "As Christians, we need to have compassion for others," be sure you want to limit your audience to Christians, for this language excludes anyone who is not.

COLLABORATING WITH OTHERS

From a brief check-in on Facebook or Twitter ("Listening to an *amaazzing* tune by Geeshie Wiley. Who was she?") to a full-scale research project on, for example, early black female blues singers—most of the writing you do in the digital age invites collaboration with others. Whether you're working online or face to face, follow these general guidelines:

Set clear goals and deadlines. One way to do this is to draw up a "contract" that spells out the purpose, scope, and schedule of the project—and have everyone sign it. Update this document periodically.

Be flexible and open minded. The whole point of collaboration is to encourage everyone to contribute. Listen carefully and be respectful of other people's ideas. You're working for consensus, not total agreement.

Appoint a group manager. Although everyone needs to take responsibility for the efforts of the group, one well-organized person should be chosen to coordinate those efforts and be in charge of communication within the group. Otherwise, deadlines will be missed and potholes will go unfilled.

Appoint a chief editor. This may or may not be the same person as the group manager, but it should be someone who writes well. Without a general editor, collaborative writing becomes writing by committee.

Assign specific tasks to each member. These should include all aspects of research, writing, editing, and distribution. Tasks should be assigned according to the skills and preferences of each member of the group, and everyone should willingly agree to accept his or her assignment. No (heavy) arm-twisting.

Confer regularly and do periodic progress checks. In addition to talking things over throughout the writing process, this is best done by scheduling regular meetings, whether online or in person, and by requiring (and sharing) written samples of everyone's work.

Additional Tips for Collaborating Face to Face

Sit in a circle or around a table. Collaboration is a form of conversation, and most people converse best when speaking face to face—or ear to ear.

Appoint a discussion leader. Someone needs to be in charge of moving the discussion along, while keeping it on point and making sure that everyone participates. Unlike that of group manager or chief editor, however, this job can be assigned to different members of the group at different meetings, or as the topic of discussion changes.

Appoint a scribe. Someone else should take notes and write a summary of the proceedings.

Additional Tips for Collaborating Online

Decide on a method of exchange. For example, you can agree to cut and paste contributions directly into email; or send them as attachments; or post them to an online discussion board inside or outside of your course's learning management system.

Name files clearly and consistently. You need to be able to find each other's work and know what you're looking at.

Be polite; proof before you send. Collaboration should always be synonymous with courtesy. But remember: anything you post to the internet could end up being read by your grandmother.

GENERATING IDEAS

Once you have a topic, purpose, and audience clearly in mind, it's time to start generating ideas. Where do you look for ideas? How do you go from nothing to something in a systematic way?

Over the years, writing teachers have developed a number of techniques to help writers find ideas. Freewriting, looping, listing, and brainstorming are ways to probe what you already know; clustering can help you connect ideas and begin organizing a text around them; questioning can be particularly useful when you're trying to make a topic more specific; and keeping a journal can be helpful at any stage. All of these techniques, in fact, may come in handy at various points in the writing process, not just at the outset.

Freewriting

When you freewrite, you simply put pen to paper (or fingers to keyboard), and force yourself to jot down whatever pops into your head.

1. Write nonstop for a short period of time, say five or ten minutes. If nothing comes to mind at first, just write: "Nothing. I'm getting nothing. The words aren't coming." Eventually, the words *will* come—if you keep writing and don't stop until time runs out.

2. This is freewriting—so skip around freely and don't get bogged down.

3. Circle or underline words and ideas that you might want to revisit, but don't stop freewriting until your time is up. Then go back over what you have written and mark any passages that stand out as promising.

4. Freewrite again, using something you have marked in the previous session as your starting point. Do this over and over until you find an idea you want to explore further.

Here's an example of a five-minute freewriting session by Zoe Shewer, a first-year writing student at Vanderbilt University who was given the assignment "Write about an experience that has taught you something new about yourself."

> Write write write. Five minutes. Okay, something I learned about myself. Yikes, what a question. I'm me. Blond, not too tall—okay, looks really aren't the point here. I'm a pretty good athlete, love riding horses. I have a brother named Max and 2 dogs named Oz and Jazz. I tutor kids in Harlem—I like(volunteering.) I had a great time at Camp Robin Hood last summer. Working with all those different nonprofits was great. But did I learn anything about myself? I learned how to clean gutters, some American Sign Language, how to make spaghetti sauce. I learned that I'm not a good cook. Time.

Freewriting like this is more than a stretching exercise. It can lead to many new ideas if you take something you have just said as the point of departure for more probing. Shewer's freewriting session led her to a possible source for an essay topic: her volunteer work.

Looping

To narrow down the subject you are exploring, try the more directed form of freewriting called *looping*. Looping not only helps you turn up a specific topic, it nudges you into writing sentences about it. Later on, you may want to use some of these sentences in your essay.

1. Freewrite for five or ten minutes, focusing on a single subject or idea and putting down everything about that subject that you can think of.
2. When you've finished that first loop, look over what you've written and summarize the most important part in a sentence: "I learned a lot volunteering last summer."
3. Use this summary sentence as the point of departure for your next loop. Write for another five or ten minutes without stopping. Then reflect on what you've just written, and compose another sentence summing it up: "Volunteering last summer taught me that I have a lot to learn."
4. Do as many loops as necessary until you have a direction in mind. If you already know the final destination of your essay, so much the better; but for now you're mainly looking for ways of refining your topic along the way.

Looping can be especially useful when you are trying to make an abstract subject more concrete. Shewer summed up her freewriting exercise with the sentence "I learned a lot volunteering last summer" and used that sentence as the starting point for a new loop that helped her explore what she learned about herself.

Summary sentence from freewriting: I learned a lot volunteering last summer.

Loop I: I learned a lot volunteering last summer through Camp Robin Hood. At Ready, Willing & Able, Seymour taught me to clean gutters. At ABC, I learned some American Sign Language, and I learned how strong those kids were. Every day, they came in determined to do everything. At the homeless shelter, I learned so much from Elsie about the city and how to survive in it. But did I learn anything about *myself*? At the end of the summer I had more admiration for Seymour, Elsie, and the kids at ABC. They all had so much more experience with life—even the kids. They had a lot of hard knocks and kept getting back up. Maybe I learned just how lucky I've been. But I think I already knew that. Maybe it was mostly that I learned that I really haven't experienced all that much.

Summary sentence: Volunteering taught me that I have a lot to learn.

Loop 2: Volunteering taught me that I have a lot to learn. Seymour told me a lot of stuff that I didn't know before, not just how to drain gutters but what his life was like. Elsie didn't talk much about her personal life, but she did tell me a lot about being homeless. And just being with the kids at ABC gave me insight into what it's like to be disadvantaged. They had to have so much determination. So did Seymour and Elsie. I don't have that kind of determination.

Summary sentence: Volunteering taught me to admire the determination of Seymour, the children at ABC, and Elsie.

As these excerpts show, looping brings ideas into sharper focus. By writing out her thoughts and looping back over them several times, Shewer was able to come up with concrete ideas about what she learned through volunteering.

Listing

Most writing is better and clearer if it is detailed and specific instead of general and abstract. Keeping lists is a good way to generate ideas—and to illustrate those ideas with interesting examples and specific details.

1. A list can be written anywhere: on paper, on a computer, in a notebook, on a napkin. Keep your lists handy so you can add to them at any time.

2. Don't worry about the form of your lists. But if the lists start to get long, group related items into piles, as you would if you were sorting your laundry.

3. Look for relationships not only *within* those piles but *between* them. Later, if you decide to construct a formal outline for your essay, you can build on the loosely arranged lists you already have.

Brainstorming

Brainstorming is a form of listing, but you write down words and ideas in one sitting rather than over time.

1. If you are brainstorming by yourself, first jot down a topic at the top of your page or screen. Then make a list of every idea or word that comes to mind.

2. Brainstorming is often more effective when you do it collaboratively, as part of a team, with everyone throwing out ideas and one person acting as scribe.

3. If you brainstorm with others, make sure everyone contributes. If one person monopolizes the session, the purpose of brainstorming is lost.

Clustering

Clustering helps you to make connections among ideas.

1. Write down your topic in the center of the page, and circle it.

2. Outside this nucleus, jot down related topics and ideas, and circle each one. Draw a line from each of these satellite ideas to the central topic.

3. As you think of additional ideas, phrases, facts, or examples, group them in clusters and connect them to one another.

Zoe Shewer created the following cluster to group her ideas.

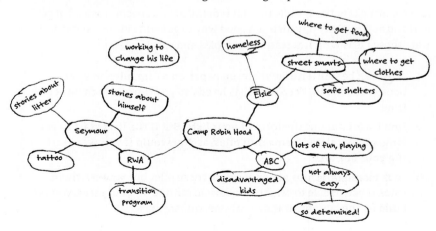

Questioning *Who, What, Where, When, Why,* and *How*

Journalists ask *who, what, where, when, why,* and *how* to uncover the basic information that readers look for in a news story. These standard journalistic questions can be useful for all kinds of writing. Here is how you might use them in an essay about a car accident involving a member of your family:

1. *Who* was involved in the accident? What should I say about my sister (the driver)? About the passengers in the car (including the dog)? The police officer who investigated? The witnesses on the sidewalk?

2. *What* happened? What were the main events leading up to the crash? What did my sister do to avoid hitting the other car head-on? Should I mention that the dog got out of the car first?

3. *Where* did the accident occur? How much of the scene should I describe? The intersection itself? The hill leading up to it?

4. *When* did the accident take place? What time did my sister leave the party? Was it still raining?

5. *Why* did the accident happen? Did the other car swerve into her lane?

6. *How* could it have been avoided? Would my sister have reacted sooner if she hadn't been on her cell phone? Should I write about cellphone usage as a contributing cause in traffic accidents?

Asking key questions like these early in the writing process will help you turn up ideas and figure out which aspects of your subject you want to write about. Later on, the questions you choose to answer will determine, in part, the methods you use to organize your essay. For example, if you decided to explain in detail what happened on the day of your sister's accident, you would draw extensively on the techniques of narration. Or if you decided to focus on the scene of the accident, you would write a largely descriptive essay.

Keeping a Journal

A personal journal can be a great source of raw material for your writing. Here, for example, is part of a journal entry that Annie Dillard kept when she went on a camping trip in Virginia:

Last night moths kept flying into the candle. They would hiss & spatter & recoil, lost upside down & flopping in the shadows among the pans on the table. Or—and this happened often, & again tonight—they'd burn their wings, & then their wings would stick to the next thing they'd touch—the edge of a pan, a lid. . . . These I could free with a quick flip with a spoon or something.

Two years after she made this journal entry, Dillard used some of those same details in an essay entitled "The Death of a Moth." In the published essay, the moth-drawn-to-the-flame becomes a vivid image of the dedicated writer who devotes all her energy to her work. Obviously, however, Dillard did not begin the writing process with a big idea like this in mind, and neither should you. She started with the homely details of pots and pans and ordinary moths as recorded in her journal. If you keep a journal regularly, as many writers do, you will have at your fingertips a world of concrete details to think and write about.

You can learn a lot about keeping a journal from an entry like Dillard's:

1. Write down your observations as close to the time of the event as possible; don't wait until you get home from a camping trip to note what happened while you were camping.

2. The observations in a journal don't have to deal with momentous events; record your everyday experiences.

3. Make each journal entry as detailed and specific as possible; don't just write "the bugs were bad" or "another beautiful day."

4. The entries don't have to be long or formally composed; they are for your eyes alone, so be as informal as you like.

5. You may not know the significance of a particular entry until months, even years, after you've written it.

ORGANIZING AND DRAFTING

Once you accumulate enough facts, details, and other raw material, your next job is to organize that material and develop it into a draft. The method (or methods) of development that you use will be determined by the main point you want your draft to make.

Stating Your Point

As you begin gathering materials for an essay, you probably won't know exactly what your thesis—your main point—is going to be (unless, of course, you've been given a specific one as part of your assignment). Before you begin writing, however, try to state your thesis in one sentence. You may find as you go along that you need to revise it, but you should start with a thesis in mind.

What makes a good thesis statement? First, let's consider what a thesis statement is not. A general announcement of your topic—"in this paper I plan to write about how you can fight climate change"—is *not* a thesis statement. A thesis statement tells the reader what your topic is, and it makes an interesting claim *about* your topic, one that is open to further discussion. This is why statements of fact aren't thesis statements either: "The effects of climate change were first predicted in the 1890s by a little-known Swedish chemist." Historical and scientific facts may help support your thesis, but the thesis itself should say something about your subject that requires further discussion. For example:

> The best way you can fight climate change is by reducing your personal carbon footprint.

> The fight against climate change will be won or lost in developing nations such as India and China.

> The United States is still the biggest energy hog on the planet.

When you draft an essay, make sure you state your thesis clearly, usually near the beginning. Like these examples, your thesis statement should be direct and specific, and it should let readers know what you'll be discussing in your essay.

Making an Outline

An informal outline is simply a list of your main points in the order they might appear in your draft. For example, after grouping her ideas into clusters, Zoe Shewer created this informal outline for her essay on an unexpected lesson:

Volunteering
    three nonprofits
    learned about myself
Ready, Willing & Able
    Seymour
    draining gutters
    telling stories
    his plans
Association to Benefit Children
    disadvantaged kids
    loved to play
    persevered
Homeless shelter
    Elsie
    street smarts
Learned that I have a lot to learn

For longer projects, such as a research paper, you may need a more detailed outline, indicating the order of both the main ideas and the less important ones. When you make a formal outline, you also show—by indenting and using letters and numbers—how all of your ideas fit together to support your thesis.

Thesis statement: Volunteering taught me to admire the determination of Seymour, the children at ABC, and Elsie.

I. Camp Robin Hood
   A. Crash course in volunteering
   B. Ready, Willing & Able
   C. Association to Benefit Children
   D. Homeless shelter
II. Ready, Willing & Able
   A. Seymour
   B. Taught me to drain gutters
   C. Told me about his own life
III. Association to Benefit Children (ABC)
   A. Played with disadvantaged kids
   B. Read to them
   C. Admired their determination
IV. Homeless shelter

A. Elsie
B. Depended on handouts and shelters
C. Had figured out the system
V. Conclusion
A. Wanted to give something back
B. Hope I helped others
C. Sure I learned a lot myself

When you construct a formal outline like this, try to keep items that are at the same level in more or less the same grammatical form. Also, include at least two items for each level, otherwise you don't need to subdivide. Whatever kind of outline you make, however, change it as necessary as you write and revise.

Using the Basic Methods of Development

Once you've accumulated enough material to write about, have narrowed your subject down to a manageable topic, and have a workable thesis, you should choose one or more methods of development.

Zoe Shewer, for example, ultimately chose to develop her topic by writing a narrative that shows what she learned from doing volunteer work over the summer. Within a narrative framework, however, she also incorporated some description and analyzed cause and effect. Whatever you're writing about, you can draw on the following methods, as Shewer did, to help you develop your topic:

- *Tell a story.* Narration is one of the oldest ways of making a point.

- *Help the reader see, hear, feel, smell, or taste* what you're writing about. Good descriptions include specific details that appeal to the senses and help to create some dominant impression in the reader's mind.

- *Give a "for instance."* Giving examples is one of the best ways to make general statements more specific and abstract statements more concrete.

- *Break an activity into steps* in order to figure out and systematically explain how something works or is made. The purpose of a process analysis like this is often to enable the reader to replicate the process, as with a recipe for baking cookies or instructions for using a new app on your phone.

- *Trace similarities and differences.* As a method of development, comparison and contrast tells readers how two subjects are alike or different or both.
- *Divide a subject into types or kinds.* Classification helps to explain a complex subject by breaking it down into basic categories.
- *Identify the main characteristics of your subject.* Definition tells the reader what something is (or is not) by identifying the particular qualities and attributes that set it apart from others like it.
- *Trace causes and effects.* This method of development is a fundamental way of understanding and explaining relationships among actions and events.
- *Make a claim and give evidence to support it.* State a claim, choose the best evidence you can find to support it, and present that evidence in a logical way.

The methods you choose for developing your essay will depend on the nature of your topic and your purpose in writing. If your purpose is simple—to give someone written directions for finding the nearest grocery store, for example—a single method may suffice. Often, however, you will want to use several methods together, as best-selling author Michael Lewis does in *Liar's Poker.*

THE PARTS OF AN ESSAY

No matter what methods of development you use, any essay you write should have a beginning, a middle, and an end. These three basic parts are usually referred to as the introduction, the body, and the conclusion.

In the introduction, you introduce the topic and state your thesis. That is, you tell the reader exactly what you're writing about and what your main point is. In the body—which may run anywhere from a few sentences or paragraphs to many pages—you offer evidence in support of your thesis. In the conclusion, you wrap up what you have to say, often by restating the thesis—but with some variation based on the evidence you have just cited.

For example, here is a brief essay about alligators with its parts indicated in the margins. The author states her thesis in the first two paragraphs. In the middle paragraph—the body of her essay—she cites facts and figures to support her thesis. And in the final paragraph, she concludes by restating that thesis—with a twist.

> At the Congregational Church, Pastor John puts on puppet shows for the children. One of the star characters is Chompers, a crocodile who talks, attends church, and could go to City Hall if he wanted to.
>
> In the real world, however, the alligators on this sanctuary island can't speak for themselves. So maybe it's time for the rest of us to do it for them and ask if we should reevaluate our alligator policy.
>
> *Introduction*
> *States the thesis.*
>
> In 2004, responding to two fatal attacks, the city changed how it deals with alligator complaints. Under that policy, not only nuisance alligators can be destroyed but any alligator in the area that exceeds four feet in length. More than 200 alligators have been killed since the 2004 policy was initiated.
>
> *Body*
> *Supports the thesis with facts, figures, and other evidence.*
>
> Since alligators don't breed until they're about six feet long, we could be on our way to eliminating these reptiles from the island and dramatically altering the natural balance among its wildlife. Fewer alligators mean more raccoons, snakes, and other natural prey left to feed on birds' eggs and hatchlings. Is that what we want?
>
> Now that the alligator population on the island is clearly under control, perhaps even threatened, let's ask City Hall to reconsider its "targeted harvest" policy. Attend Tuesday's Council meeting and speak up for the alligators. Tell 'em Chompers sent you.
>
> *Conclusion*
> *Restates the thesis with a twist.*
>
> —BARBARA JOY WHITE, "Speaking Up for Alligators"

As in this reptilian example, any essay you write should have an introduction and a conclusion that state and restate your main point. In addition, you'll want to include, in the main body of your essay, at least one paragraph for each supporting point you make. If you are writing about how individuals can combat climate change, for example, you might include a body paragraph for each way of reducing carbon consumption that you propose, such as recycling old clothes, eating less red meat, planning a green wedding, and making fewer left turns when driving.

Using Visuals

In addition to giving your essay a clear beginning, middle, and ending, you may want to consider using visuals. Illustrations such as graphs and charts can be especially effective for presenting or comparing data, and photographs can help readers see things you describe in your written text.

This reusable bag lets you avoid using plastic shopping bags, thereby conserving energy and reducing landfill waste. © Doug Steley B / Alamy.

Visuals should never be mere decoration or clip art, however. Any visuals should be directly relevant to your topic and must support your thesis in some way. For example, if you are writing about conserving energy by carrying a reusable shopping bag, you might include an illustration showing the kind of bag you have in mind.

As with a written text, any visual material you include should be appropriate for your audience and purpose. A picture of a raven, for example, would not add much to an essay for a literature class on Edgar Allan Poe's famous poem—but it might be appropriate, if properly labeled, for a biology paper or a field guide to birds.

If you do decide that a visual will genuinely enhance your argument, be sure to refer to it in your text and number it, if necessary, so that readers can find it ("see Fig. 1"). Position the visual as close as you can to the part of your text that it illustrates, and provide a caption that identifies and explains its point. If you found the visual in another source, identify the source and provide documentation in a Works Cited or References list.

REVISING

Revising is a process of re-vision, of looking again at your draft and making necessary changes in content, organization, or emphasis. Occasionally when you revise, you discover only a few minor scrapes and bruises that need your attention. More often, however, revising requires some major surgery: adding new evidence, narrowing a thesis, cutting out paragraphs or entire sections, rewriting the beginning to appeal better to your audience, and so on.

Revising is not generally the time to focus on words or sentences, though you may change some words and smooth out awkward or unclear sentences as you go. Nor is revising a matter of correcting errors, but rather of more general shaping and reshaping. Many writers try to revise far too soon. To avoid this pitfall, put aside your draft for a few hours—or better still, for a few days—before revising.

Reading a Draft with a Critical Eye

Start by reading the draft yourself, and then try to get someone else to look it over—a classmate, a writing tutor, your roommate, your grandmother. Whoever it is, be sure he or she is aware of your intended audience and purpose. Here's what you and the person with fresh eyes should look for as you read:

An effective title. Is the title more than a label? How does it pique the reader's interest? Does it indicate the point of the essay—and if not, should it?

A clear focus. What is the main point? Is it clearly stated in a thesis statement—and if not, should it be? Is the thesis too broad? too narrow?

Sufficient information for your audience. How familiar is the topic likely to be to your readers? Is there sufficient background information? Are there clear definitions for any terms and concepts readers might not know? Will readers find it interesting?

Adequate support for the thesis. What evidence supports the thesis? Is the evidence convincing and the reasoning logical? Could the draft be strengthened by adding more facts or specific details?

Organization. Is the draft well organized? Does it have a clear beginning, middle, and ending? Are paragraphs related to each other by clear transitions? Does each paragraph contribute to the main point, or are some paragraphs off the topic? Does the ending give a sense of closure?

Methods of development. What is the main method of development—is the draft primarily a narrative? a description? an argument? Is this method effective? If not, which other methods might be introduced? For instance, would more examples, or definitions, or a discussion of causes be beneficial?

Sources. Is there material from other sources? If so, how are those sources incorporated—are they quoted? paraphrased? summarized? How are they acknowledged? In other words, is it clear to the reader whose words or ideas are being used? How does the source material support the main point? Have all source materials been properly cited and documented?

Paragraphs. Does each paragraph focus on one main idea and have a clear topic sentence? Does the structure of paragraphs vary, or are they too much alike? If they all begin with a topic sentence, should you consider rewriting some paragraphs to lead up to the topic sentence instead of down from it? Does every sentence in a paragraph support the point that the rest of the paragraph is making? Are there any long or complex paragraphs that should be subdivided?

The more common problem, however, is that paragraphs are too short. Are there paragraphs that should be combined with other paragraphs or developed more fully? How well does the draft flow from one paragraph to the next? If any paragraphs seem to break the flow, look to see if you need to add transitions or to use repetition to help the reader follow the text.

Sentence length and variety. Check the length of your sentences. If they are all approximately the same length, try varying them. A short sentence among long sentences can provide emphasis. On the other hand, too many short sentences, one after another, can sound choppy. Try combining some of them.

Visuals. Does the draft include any visuals? If not, is there any material in the text that would be easier to understand as a chart or table? Any descriptive passages where a photo might help readers see what you're talking about? If there are visuals, are they relevant to the topic? How do they support your thesis?

A Sample Student Essay

Here is Zoe Shewer's first draft of an essay on what she learned about herself from a summer program. It is based on her formal outline.

FIRST DRAFT

How should I spend my summer vacation? Many college students have internships or summer jobs. Some travel. I spent last summer volunteering with three nonprofits through Camp Robin Hood.

Camp Robin Hood is a hands-on summer crash course in New York City nonprofit organizations. Every week, I worked at a different nonprofit: a day care center, a homeless shelter, and a transitional lifestyle program for ex-convicts and former addicts. At every organization, I learned something about working with the underprivileged, but at the end of the summer, I realized that I had also learned something about myself.

I began by working at Ready, Willing & Able, where ex-convicts and former addicts clean streets as part of a transitional lifestyle program. I'll never forget the street cleaning attendant I worked with there. Seymour was tall, tattooed, and a former addict. He was also calm and completely at ease in his RWA jumpsuit, sweeping the sidewalks and wheeling a huge blue trash can through the streets. Seymour taught me how to drain gutters by diverting the flow of water with a rolled-up towel. He also taught me to "read" the back stories in the litter. It was like he saw a story in every piece of trash: a schoolgirl who discarded a bracelet in a temper tantrum, a closet eater who ate Twinkies in the street. He talked about his family, too, and his dreams and plans. I grew to respect him and admire his perseverance and determination, despite all the setbacks in his life.

That respect and admiration was something I would come to feel at each of the nonprofits. At the Association to Benefit Children, an organization that provides services to underprivileged children, I played with and taught children who had many challenges. Like any kids, they loved singing, finger painting, and playing with toys. But there was no escaping the fact that these activities didn't always come easily to them. They worked hard for what they wanted. It was impossible not to admire their determination.

At a homeless shelter, where I handed out clean clothes and tickets for showers, I met people from every walk of life. Some had addiction problems or other illnesses, but many had simply fallen on hard times. The loss of a job or an unexpected medical problem ended up costing them their homes, and they had nowhere else to go. I spent many evenings talking to one woman in particular, Elsie. She had been homeless for several years and knew the streets of New York better than anyone I've ever met. She knew which restaurants would give out their leftover food and when you should appear at their back door for dinner. She knew which churches had the best soup kitchens, and which shelters were safest, and where to find the best cast-off clothing. I never found out how she'd become homeless, but she'd figured out the system and made it work for her. Although I grew up in New York City, her street smarts made me feel like I'd never really known the city.

I volunteered for Camp Robin Hood because I wanted to give something back. I know that my upbringing has been privileged, and I've been lucky to have never gone without. I wanted to do something for those who weren't so lucky. But I discovered that while I may have more tangible goods than those I was volunteering to help, they had a lot to teach me about the intangible: qualities like perseverance, determination, optimism and cheerfulness no matter what the circumstances. They taught me that I have a lot to learn.

Getting Response before Revising

After finishing her first draft, Shewer set it aside for a few hours and then reread it, using the guidelines for reading a draft with a critical eye (pp. 121–22). She also asked a classmate to read it, and he offered her the following comments:

> I really like the topic of your essay, and I think it meets the assignment well. But maybe it would be more effective if you picked one of the three places you worked to focus on, so that you could talk about it more in depth. I'd like to know more about them.
>
> You kind of state a thesis—"At every organization, I learned something about working with the underprivileged, but at the end of the summer, I realized that I had also learned something about myself"—but then you state it more directly at the end of the paper—"They taught me that I have a lot to learn." That works pretty well, and the body paragraphs do support this idea.
>
> You describe the people you meet, but it might be more interesting if there was more of a story.

Shewer agreed with her classmate's suggestions to focus on just one of the places she worked, and to incorporate more narration. She chose to write about her experience at Ready, Willing & Able, and to focus on her day working with Seymour. After some brainstorming about that day, she decided to add a narrative about one incident in particular. She then revised her thesis to reflect her narrower focus on that specific day. She also added a title, which she hadn't included in her first draft.

SECOND DRAFT

Ready, Willing, and Able

July is stifling in New York City, and I was not looking forward to wearing an oversized jumpsuit in ninety-degree heat. I was suited up to clean streets as part of the Camp Robin Hood program. I was at the headquarters of Ready, Willing & Able. Most RWA employees are ex-convicts or former addicts for whom street cleaning is both a job and part of a transitional lifestyle program.

The program coordinator waved me toward a tall man who had apparently been waiting for me. His name was Seymour, and he was the street cleaning attendant I would be working with all day. As he reached out to shake my hand, I noticed that he had a tattoo on his forearm.

We headed out to the street, and while I fidgeted with the broom I carried, Seymour calmly wheeled a bright blue trash can behind him. As we began sweeping the sidewalks, Seymour not only showed me how to drain the gutters, he talked about who might have dropped certain kinds of trash and why and told me about his family and his desire to get his life back on track. Though I had lived in the city my entire life, I began to see things in a new light. I became so absorbed in Seymour's stories that I heard some girls laughing and almost didn't realize they were laughing at me. "I wonder what she did to deserve that!"

I looked up and saw a group of girls about my age laughing at me as they walked past. They obviously thought I was serving a juvenile court sentence. Ordinarily I may have laughed at the idea that I could be mistaken for a juvenile delinquent, but on this day I felt butterflies in my stomach.

What if Seymour thought I was just like those other girls? What if he thought I didn't want to be there and was counting down the minutes until the day would be over? I wanted to tell him that I had a lot of respect for his work and that I knew I couldn't possibly understand what he does just by shadowing him for a day. I wanted to tell him that I was not simply doing a day of community service so I could include it on a résumé.

But Seymour broke the silence, saying, "Put some muscle in it, Goldilocks."

Revising a Second Draft

After setting her revision aside for a day, Shewer came back to her essay and reread it, again following the questions for revision. She liked the story of her day working with Seymour, but she thought that now there was too much narration, and she needed to have more descriptive details. She also decided that she needed to explain more about the incident with the girls—how she felt and how that moment taught her something. Finally, she revised some of her sentences to keep them from being the same length and tried to make some of her language more precise.

FINAL DRAFT

Ready, Willing, and Able

Introduction

Wearing a canvas jumpsuit zipped up to my neck, I must have looked as though I was stepping onto the set of ET: The Extra-Terrestrial, but my actual destination was Madison Avenue, home to some of the fanciest boutiques in New York City. The bright blue jumpsuit I wore was far from high fashion: it was sized for a full-grown man, and it ballooned about my slender frame. My blond hair was pulled back in a ponytail, and the only label I displayed was the bold-lettered logo on my back: Ready, Willing & Able. I was suited up to collect trash from the sidewalks of New York.

Beginning of narrative: the first day

July is stifling in New York City, and I was not looking forward to wearing the oversized jumpsuit in ninety-degree heat. As I made my way through the Ready, Willing & Able (RWA) headquarters, I passed colorfully decorated bulletin boards bearing smiley-faced reminders: "Drug testing is on Monday!" "Curfew is midnight!" Most fulltime employees of RWA are ex-convicts or former addicts for whom street cleaning is the work-for-housing component of a transitional lifestyle program. For me, street cleaning was day one of Camp Robin Hood, a hands-on summer crash course in New York nonprofit organizations. As I selected a broom from the supply closet, I reminded myself that I had volunteered to do this. Feeling like a new kid on the first day of school, I stood nervously next to the program supervisor who would introduce me to the street cleaning attendant I would be helping.

If I was the awkward new kid, the street cleaning attendant to whom I was assigned, a tall man named Seymour, was undoubtedly the

Big Man on Campus. Seymour wore his RWA cap slightly askew, and, as he reached out to shake my hand, I caught a glimpse of a tattoo under his sleeve. We headed out to the street together, and, while I nervously fidgeted with the broom I carried, he calmly wheeled a bright blue trash can behind him. Seymour began sweeping the sidewalks, and I followed his lead. He not only showed me how to drain the gutters by diverting the flow of water with a rolled-up towel, he also taught me how to "read" the back stories in the litter. To Seymour, a torn hemp bracelet on the

Description of key character, with concrete details

Fig. 1. Homeless men get back to work and self-respect with help from the Ready, Willing & Able program sponsored by the DOE Fund.

curb was a schoolgirl's temper tantrum; a Twinkie wrapper in the street was a closet eater's discarded evidence. Though I have lived in New York my entire life, I began to see my surroundings in a new light. The streets that had always felt so familiar seemed full of surprises. As our afternoon continued, Seymour also told me stories about his sister, his desire to get his life back on track after some time on the wrong side of the law, his love of Central Park, and his aspiration to travel across the country.

Dialogue and climax of narrative

After several hours, I had more or less forgotten about my tent-sized RWA jumpsuit when suddenly I heard someone laughing at me: "I wonder what she did to deserve that?!"

Effect of incident

I looked up and saw a group of girls my age looking in my direction and laughing as they walked past. My stomach tightened. They obviously thought I was being punished, perhaps serving a juvenile court sentence. Ordinarily I might have laughed at the idea that I could be mistaken for a juvenile delinquent, but on this day I felt a jumble of feelings—panic, shame, sadness, and admiration for a man whose history is suggested by his jumpsuit and the logo on his back. I will admit that a few hours earlier I was embarrassed about my ill-fitting uniform.

Thesis indicated indirectly

Halfway through the workday, however, the girls' rude comments caused an entirely different kind of shame: What if Seymour thought I was anything like those girls? What if he thought that I was faking a smile and counting down the minutes until the day was over?

Significance of narrative

I suddenly wanted to thank Seymour for this experience. I wanted to tell him that he was probably the best guide through these streets I had ever had, and that I knew I could not possibly understand what he does by shadowing him for a day in a borrowed uniform. I wanted to explain to him that I volunteer regularly in New York: I am committed to working with at-risk children, and have done so for years at an after-school program in Harlem. I wanted to share how much I relate to his closeness with his family, his desire to travel, and his love of Strawberry Fields in Central Park. But the girls' mocking comments and laughter had left us in an uncomfortable silence, and I felt that anything I might say would make us feel even more awkward.

It was Seymour who broke this silence. As I stood next to the trash can and tried to avoid staring off in the direction of the latte-carrying girls, Seymour caught my eye, smiled, and nodded toward my broom with one excellent piece of advice: "Put some muscle in it, Goldilocks."

Conclusion with dialogue

This final draft, Shewer felt, better blended the modes of narration and description, and it fulfilled the assignment to write about an experience that taught her something new about herself. She especially liked the concrete details she included and the dialogue that ended the essay.

EDITING AND PROOFREADING

When you finish revising your essay, you're still not quite done. You've put the icing on the cake, but you need to make sure all the candles are straight and wipe the edge of the plate. That is, you need to edit and proofread your final draft before presenting it to the reader.

When you edit, you add finishing touches and correct errors in grammar, sentence structure, punctuation, and word choice that affect the sense and meaning of your text. When you proofread, you take care of misspellings, typos, problems with your margins and format, and other minor blemishes in the appearance of your document.

Certain types of problems are common to certain types of writing. Here are some tips that can help you check your drafts for some common mistakes.

Tips for Editing Sentences

Check to be sure that each sentence expresses a complete thought—that it has a subject (someone or something) and a verb performing an action or indicating a state of being.

Check capitalization and end punctuation. Be sure that each sentence begins with a capital letter and ends with a period, a question mark, or an exclamation point.

Look for sentences that begin with *it* or *there*. Often such sentences are vague or boring, and they are usually easy to edit. For example, if you've written *There is a doctor on call at every hospital,* you could edit it to read *A doctor is on call at every hospital.*

Check for parallelism. All items in a list or series should have parallel forms—all nouns *(Lincoln, Grant, Lee),* all verbs *(dedicate, consecrate, hallow),* all phrases *(of the people, by the people, for the people).*

Check adjective order. Adjectives usually go in the following order: number, size, shape, age, color, nationality *(a pair of small round hand-me-down navy earrings).*

Tips for Editing Words

There, their. Use *there* to refer to place or direction or to introduce a sentence: *Who was there? There was no answer.* Use *their* as a possessive: *Their intentions were good.*

It's, its. Use *it's* to mean "it is": *It's difficult to say what causes dyslexia.* Use *its* to mean "belonging to it": *Each car has its unique features.*

Lie, lay. Use *lie* when you mean "recline": *She's lying down because she's tired.* Use *lay* when you mean "put" or "place": *Lay the book on the table.*

Tips for Editing Punctuation

Check for commas after introductory elements in a sentence

> The day he disclosed his matrimonial ambitions for me, my uncle sat me at his right during lunch. —SAIRA SHAH, "Longing to Belong"

Check for commas before *and, but, or, nor, so, or yet* in compound sentences

> They divorced when I was in junior high school, and they agreed on little except that I was an impossible child. —RICHARD RUSSO, "Dog"

Check for commas in a series

> A circuit of the courthouse square took you past the grand furniture stores, the two dime stores, the shoe stores, the men's stores, the ladies' stores, the banks, the drugstores.
> —BOBBIE ANN MASON, "Being Country"

When you quote other people's words, be sure to put quotation marks at the beginning and end of the quotation

> Instead of offering an abject apology, Ms. Hegemann insisted, "There's no such thing as originality anyway, just authenticity."
> —TRIP GABRIEL, "Plagiarism Lines Blur for Students in Digital Age"

Check to be sure that you've put commas and periods inside quotation marks

> "Put some muscle in it, Goldilocks." —ZOE SHEWER, "Ready, Willing, and Able"

> "You know," Dave told his grandmother, "I'm responsible for the lives of 40 men." —ANNE BERNAYS, "Warrior Day"

Check your use of apostrophes with possessives. Singular nouns should end in *'s*, whereas plural nouns should end in *s'*. The possessive pronouns *hers, his, its, ours, yours,* and *theirs* should not have apostrophes.

> Robert Bergman's radiant portraits of strangers provoked this medita-
> tion.   —TONI MORRISON, "Strangers"

Morrison's meditation was provoked by the strangers' faces.

> Theirs was the life I dreamt about during my vacations in eastern North
> Carolina.   —DAVID SEDARIS,
>   "Remembering My Childhood on the Continent of Africa"

Proofreading and Final Formatting

Proofreading is the only stage in the writing process where you are *not* primarily concerned with meaning. Of course you should correct any substantive errors you discover, but your main concerns when you proofread are small technicalities and the appearance of your text. Misspellings, margins that are too narrow or too wide, unindented paragraphs, missing page numbers—these are the kinds of imperfections you're looking for as you put the final touch on your document.

Such minor blemishes are especially hard to see when you're looking at your own work. So slow down as you proofread, and view your document more as a picture than as a written text. Use a ruler or piece of paper to guide your eye line by line as you scan the page; or read your entire text backward a sentence at a time; or read it out loud word by word. Use a spellchecker, too, but don't rely on it: a spellchecker doesn't know the difference, for example, between *spackling* and *spacing* or *Greek philosophy* and *Geek philosophy*.

After you've proofread your document word for word, check the overall format to make sure it follows any specific instructions that you may have been given. If your instructor does not have formatting requirements, follow these tips based on the Modern Language Association (MLA) guidelines.

Tips for Formatting an Essay MLA-Style

Heading and title. Put your name, your instructor's name, the name and number of the course, and the date on separate lines in the upper-left-hand corner of your first page. Center your title on the next line, but do not underline it or put it in quotation marks. Begin your first paragraph on the line that follows.

Typeface and size. Use ten-, eleven-, or twelve-point type in an easy-to-read font, such as Times New Roman, Palatino, or Cambria.

Spacing. Double-space your document.

Margins. Set one-inch margins at the top, bottom, and sides of your text.

Paragraph indentation. Indent the first line of each paragraph one-half inch.

Page numbers. Number your pages consecutively in the upper right-hand corner of the page, and include your last name with each page number.

Long quotations. When quoting more than three lines of poetry, more than four lines of prose, or dialogue between characters in a drama, set off the quotation from the rest of your text, indenting it one inch from the left margin. Do not use quotation marks, and put any parenthetical documentation after the final punctuation.

EIGHT

Generating Ideas

MOST COLLEGE ESSAYS succeed or fail at the idea level. Good ideas are likely to produce good essays. A good idea contains within it the seeds of a good argument and an organized essay. Once you have hit upon a good idea, you will find that your essay is easier to organize, easier to write, and easier to revise.

Very few people simply "have" good ideas. The ability to generate good ideas—and good paper topics—is a skill that can be learned. This chapter will introduce some basic strategies—grouped under considering expectations, exploring your topic, and achieving subtlety—that you can use to move beyond your initial thoughts about a topic and generate worthwhile ideas to write about.

CONSIDERING EXPECTATIONS

The writing process cannot be reduced to a precise set of formulas and equations that will produce "correct" essays in every class that requires writing. Different instructors have different preferences and grade written assignments differently. Sometimes, what works well for one instructor will not work at all for another.

Before you start thinking about a writing topic, then, make sure you understand what your instructor expects from you. If you do not meet these expectations, your ideas will not be judged "good"—even if they represent perfectly sound arguments that might be very successful in other contexts. Here are a few strategies that you can use to make sure that your essay ideas will meet your instructor's expectations:

Understand the Assignment

The requirements of an assignment can be very general or very specific. In either case, you must gear your response to the terms of the assignment. Most assignments ask you to perform a certain writing task—to analyze, compare, describe, and so on. It is vital that you understand what this task entails. If you have any questions about the assignment, do not hesitate to ask your instructor to clarify it for you.

Agree/disagree. Assignments that ask you to agree or disagree will usually give you a proposition to consider. Sometimes, this proposition will be an entire reading, as in "Agree or disagree with George Orwell's points in 'Pacifism and the War.'" More often, the proposition will be a single statement or assertion, such as "In 'Pacifism and the War,' George Orwell states that a pacifist position during wartime is necessarily in favor of the enemy. Agree or disagree with this assertion."

A topic of this sort gives you the opportunity to state your opinion. When instructors assign topics such as this one, they are usually not looking for right or wrong answers. Nor do they want you to simply summarize Orwell's essay and state—at the beginning or the end of the essay—whether or not you approve. An assignment to agree or disagree is asking you to state and defend an opinion; it involves both an argument about what you believe *and* valid reasons for that argument. The quality of the reasons that you give, not your opinion, is the most important part of the assignment.

Analyze. "Analyze" is one of the most common directions in college-level writing assignments, but it can have many meanings. Generally speaking, to analyze something is to examine it by comparing how its parts relate to a whole or how certain causes produce an effect. In most (but not all) situations, a textual analysis should focus not on agreeing or disagreeing with the text but on showing how different parts of the text operate toward a particular end. An analysis of a literary text often looks at imagery, symbolism, and other kinds of figurative language. An analysis of an argumentative text usually requires you to look at the argument—to see what it claims and how persuasively it supports those claims.

Apply. One of the best ways to measure how well you understand an argument is to ask you to apply it to a new situation. Consider the following assignment: "Apply George Orwell's reasoning in 'Pacifism and the War' to America's actions in the so-called war on terror." This assignment asks you to consider how the arguments advanced in the original essay—which in this case would include the assertion that refusing to fight an enemy is an act of support for that enemy rather than an act of neutrality—apply to U.S. actions in Afghanistan, in Iraq, and at home. There are, of course, several plausible ways to apply Orwell's argument to this situation. For example, you could argue that, according to Orwell's logic, one could not be a pacifist in the war on terror without being "objectively proterrorist." Or you could argue that, because terrorism is a criminal act rather than a military one, Orwell's argument allows for pacifism (objecting to a military solution to the problem) in the war on terror in a way that it did not allow for pacifism in World War II.

Claim/support. Many writing assignments involve some kind of claim/support structure, but some assignments specifically ask you to construct and support your own argument. In a college class, these assignments usually require you to develop fully your own opinions about things that you read, but they may or may not ask you to cite specific readings. Often, assignments for this kind of writing are phrased as questions: "Is human nature inherently good?" "Is it ever appropriate to disobey the law?" "When is war a justified response to aggression?" "Do people have a moral obligation to help the poor?" These highly debatable questions are all covered in this book, and, at some point, your instructor will probably require you to express and defend your opinions about issues such as these.

An argument about any issue consists of two parts: the claim and the support. You cannot simply make an assertion such as "Everybody has a moral obligation to help the poor" or "War is justified when people are defending their families." You also need to include a statement that gives a reason for your belief: "Everybody has a moral obligation to help the poor because morality is based on our responses to others" or "War is justified when people are defending their families because taking care of one's family is the most important duty that human beings have." The procedure for embedding a claim and a statement of support in a thesis statement is covered in depth in Chapter 9.

Compare/contrast. Strictly speaking, "compare" means to show how things are alike, and "contrast" means to show how they are different. Sometimes, an assignment will ask you to "compare and contrast" two things, such as to "compare and contrast the views of Paley and Darwin on the origins of life on earth." Such an assignment asks you to explain similarities and differences in the two texts. Often, instructors simply use the term "compare" as a way to ask you to look for similarities and differences in two or more texts.

Describe. An assignment to describe something—whether that something is an argument, a painting, or your best friend—asks you to give its essential characteristics without evaluating or taking a position on those characteristics. Though perfect neutrality is rarely possible in a writing assignment (the act of choosing which characteristics to describe conveys an evaluation and a perspective), descriptive writing should present its subject objectively. For example, an assignment that asks you to "describe the situations that led to the emergence of Taoism and Confucianism in ancient China" is asking you to explain a set of historical facts, not to give your opinion about a pair of philosophies.

Respond. Many assignments ask you to respond to another text or to a specific argument in a text. Such assignments may or may not ask you to "agree or disagree" with the argument. They do, however, require something more than mere approval or disapproval. They require you to use the text that you are responding to as the basis for your own arguments or observations.

An assignment asking you to "respond to Machiavelli's assertion that it is better for a ruler to be feared than loved" is asking you to consider this argument and evaluate its appropriateness. Does this argument work better in some political systems than others? Does it rest on defensible assumptions about human nature? Which leaders might have agreed? Which ones might have disagreed? What would a government look like that completely accepted—or completely rejected—Machiavelli's advice? Each of these questions or their answers would be legitimate starting points for an essay asking you to "respond" to Machiavelli's argument.

Summarize/paraphrase. Some writing assignments ask you to summarize or paraphrase other texts. The two words do not mean exactly the same thing. A *summary* is a short encapsulation of a longer argument, cutting out all but the most important details; a *paraphrase* is a restatement of an argument in your own words, containing most of the original text's detail. A paraphrase of a three-page text should take about three pages, while a summary of such a text could consist of a few carefully worded sentences. When writing about other texts, do not summarize extensively or paraphrase unless you are asked to do so. If you merely summarize or paraphrase an argument that you have been asked to analyze or respond to, you will almost certainly fail to meet your instructor's expectations.

Get Responses

To make sure that you have met your instructor's expectations for an assignment, get responses, both to your topic and to your early drafts. You might meet with your instructor to talk about your topic, or you might ask your instructor to comment on drafts. You might also seek out the tutoring resources at your school. Most colleges and universities have a writing center or other tutoring service that can serve as a tremendous resource for improving your writing.

Peer tutors can help writers with every stage of the writing process, not just with the finished product. A good peer tutor will be able to help you think critically about an assignment and brainstorm ideas and essay topics. Occasionally, a tutor will have the expertise to help in areas where you are weak. But sometimes, it just helps to have somebody to bounce ideas off of when you are trying to decide on an essay topic. A peer tutor can also read your essay and point out things that you might miss simply because you are too close to the writing process to view your essay objectively.

Consider Your Audience and Purpose

Before you start writing, ask yourself who you are writing for and what you want to accomplish. The answers to these questions will help you present your ideas appropriately—in a class, this will help you meet your instructor's expectations; outside of school, it will help you effectively reach your intended readers. In both cases, considering your audience and purpose is essential.

Any time that you write for other people, you will be constrained by your audience's expectations. Novelists, journalists, corporate executives, screenwriters, Web designers, and even professors all know that the form, style, and content of their writing must meet certain expectations. "Good writing" in the absolute sense is virtually impossible to define, since writing always occurs in a context of stated or unstated expectations. An effective argument in one context might be totally ineffective in another. Take the following argument as an example: "providing beer in a college dining hall would make the dorms more attractive." This would probably be extremely successful with the student body, much less successful with faculty and administrators, and not successful at all with parents. Part of learning how to be a good writer is learning how to assess these expectations accurately and respond to them effectively.

Just as important as understanding your audience is understanding what you want to accomplish when you write. Different kinds of writing have different purposes. Writing can, among other things, inform, persuade, motivate, express, and entertain. An essay written to persuade your instructor of an argument will be very different from one designed to give an initial impression of a reading. If you begin with a solid understanding of what you want to accomplish when you write, you will be able to incorporate this purpose into every stage of the writing process.

EXPLORING YOUR TOPIC

The strategies listed below are all ways to help you generate ideas. Try them out and see which works best for you. Do not worry about coming up with the perfect topic right away; the process of generating ideas can help you think about different aspects and implications of the topic you finally choose, and you may end up using facets of other ideas in your writing.

Freewriting

The quickest, easiest, and most direct way to fill up an empty piece of paper or blank computer screen is just to start writing. Freewriting is an unconstrained writing exercise in which you simply write down whatever comes to your mind for a set period. The only rule is that you cannot stop writing. A freewriting exercise is designed to tap into the subconscious mind and pull out ideas that may be lurking beneath the surface. To complete such an exercise successfully, you need to override your mind's "editing function" and just write.

Here is a brief example of a freewriting session in response to an assignment to compare the view of liberal education in John Henry Newman's "Knowledge Its Own End" with that in Seneca's "On Liberal and Vocational Studies."

> OK, so I'm supposed to compare what John Henry Newman and Seneca said about education. Both of them talk a lot about liberal education and how it is not supposed to be useful for anything other than itself. When you read them, they sound a lot alike in this way, which is kind of weird since one of them lived in ancient Rome and the other one lived in England like a hundred years ago. Come to think of it, this is probably the biggest difference between them. Seneca lived in a very different kind of society than Newman lived in. Rome was an empire where people owned slaves and were divided into very distinct classes. Newman lived in an industrial country that was pretty much a democracy, at least at the end of his life. Maybe this is why Seneca thought that useful education was a bad thing, and only liberal education was worthwhile, while Newman just thought that they were different things. Most people in Newman's day couldn't afford not to think about how they would earn a living. I guess that's still true today.

This freewriting demonstration follows the usual pattern for such an exercise: it begins with a self-reflective discussion (here I am, doing what I am supposed to be doing), moves to some fairly surface observations about the texts (that both Seneca and Newman talk about liberal education) and then to a statement that, with a lot more refining, could be the basis of a very strong comparison paper: that Newman is more tolerant of practical education than Seneca because Newman lived in a democratic society.

Clustering

Clustering is a good strategy for processing information visually. It consists of drawing some kind of picture that represents the ideas that you are discussing and using that picture to show the relationship between a central, general idea and several more-focused, subordinate ideas. The easiest way to do this is with circles and lines, as in the following diagram, which responds

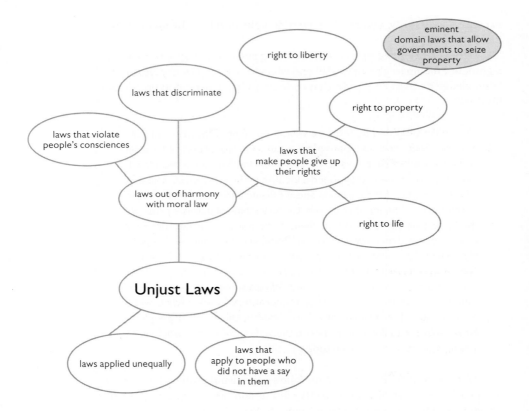

to an assignment to "write a paper that uses Martin Luther King Jr.'s three categories of 'unjust law' to argue that a current law or type of law is unjust." The goal of clustering here is to think of a current law that meets Martin Luther King Jr.'s classification of an unjust law, one that can then be the focus of the essay. Starting simply with "unjust laws," the writer branches out to come up with more-specific kinds of unjust laws. One kind of law, "laws that make people give up their rights," leads the writer to think about different rights, which then leads to the final essay topic: "eminent domain laws," which require people to give up their right to property. In clustering, every idea allows you to jot down several more ideas that are connected to it, so you can continue to refine and develop ideas with increasing layers of specificity. Once you reach an idea that seems workable, you can take it from your cluster and refine it further into an argumentative thesis statement.

Brainstorming

Like freewriting and clustering, brainstorming exercises are meant to get a lot of ideas down on paper without worrying—at least during the exercise—whether they will work for your essay. A brainstorming session can be done alone or in a group, but the ground rules are the same: write down every idea that comes to you, do not try to evaluate the ideas as they come, do not worry about writing complete sentences, and move to the next idea quickly.

Now, imagine staying with the assignment to apply Martin Luther King Jr.'s criteria for unjust laws to a contemporary law and, instead of clustering different kinds of unjust laws, simply throwing out as many ideas as possible. A ten-minute brainstorming session might produce a list like this:

- Slavery
- Segregation laws
- Laws against same-sex marriage
- Laws that give police officers the right to collect information
- Affirmative action laws that treat minorities differently than others
- Prohibition
- Laws that keep women from voting
- Laws that allow countries to attack other countries
- Laws that make it illegal to practice your religion
- Laws against drugs
- Laws that won't let you drink when you are eighteen while others let you be drafted into the army
- Laws that make you wear a helmet or a seat belt
- Laws that don't let you go to the college you want to go to
- Eminent domain laws that allow governments to seize your property
- Laws that don't allow you to defend your house if someone breaks in
- Laws that treat rich people differently than poor people
- Laws that make people homeless
- Laws against people marrying people of other races

Not all the laws on this brainstormed list are suitable for the assignment; some are not current or are not current in the United States, and some are too broad or ill-defined. But a third of these would work very well for the assignment with little or no modification. None of these ideas are thesis statements yet, but they are reasonably good examples of laws that fit the assignment and lend themselves well to good thesis statements and credible essays.

ACHIEVING SUBTLETY

Good writing goes beyond surface issues to explore the deeper meanings and implications of a topic. An argument or idea that digs beneath the surface, that goes beyond the obvious, might be usefully described as "subtle." In a college class, subtle ideas demonstrate to a teacher that you have really thought about an issue, struggled with its complexities, and learned something from an assignment. Once you have come up with a writing topic that meets all the specifications of an assignment, you need to develop and refine your topic to make sure it meets those standards of subtlety—to go beyond the obvious arguments, to do more than just say what you believe about a topic, to *learn* about the topic. This approach turns an acceptable or a good essay topic into a great one.

As you strive for this kind of subtle analysis, keep the following suggestions in mind:

Go Beyond Your First Ideas

The first ideas that will occur to you about a topic will often be the first ideas that occur to everybody else, making the resulting essay "average" by definition. Moreover, the first ideas that occur to you (and everybody else) are rarely very good. Consider an assignment, for example, in which you have been asked to compare the political philosophies of Christine de Pizan and Niccolò Machiavelli. The first thing that someone looking at these two philosophers will notice is that de Pizan is a woman and Machiavelli is a man. From there, many people will conclude that de Pizan's philosophy must be more "feminine" and Machiavelli's more "masculine." The gendered differences between these two authors, however, are by no means the most interesting or significant differences, and they would not lead to the most interesting essay.

Go Beyond the Standard Positions

Issues that are regularly discussed in public forums tend to have easily recognizable "pro" and "con" positions. Sometimes, these standard positions are obvious, knee-jerk reactions to a topic; sometimes, they are well-constructed arguments that have simply been used too often. In most cases, you should steer your own arguments away from these standard arguments, since they are so well known that they will occur to everybody. Even if they are good arguments, they are not *your* arguments, and they do not give you the opportunity to show what kinds of ideas you can come up with on your own.

If the assignment allows it, you might consider staying away entirely from issues that have been discussed so often that few new things are left to say about them. If you do write about such issues, however, approach them with subtlety and avoid the temptation to restate the usual lines of reasoning. Few readers will be persuaded by arguments that simply regurgitate standard lines of thinking.

Consider the following two arguments against legalized abortion, one of the most controversial and often-discussed issues in the modern political landscape:

Argument #1: "Abortion is murder. People who permit or perform abortions are taking innocent human lives, which is the definition of murder, and it doesn't matter how young each life is, since it is a life just the same. A child who has yet to be born is just as valuable as a child who has been born or an adult, so there is no reason why it should be acceptable to kill one if it is not acceptable to kill the other."

Argument #2: "The primary wrong-making feature of a killing is the loss to the victim of the value of its future. . . . The future of a standard fetus includes a set of experiences, projects, activities, and such which are identical with the futures of human beings and are identical with the futures of young children. Since the reason that it is sufficient to explain why it is wrong to kill human beings after the time of birth is a reason that also applies to fetuses, it follows that abortion is . . . seriously morally wrong." (Marquis, Don. "Why Abortion Is Immoral." *Journal of Philosophy* 87 [1990]: 262–77)

These passages are similar in many ways. Both assert that abortion is immoral because of its impact on a human life, and neither uses religious terms or clichés (see below). The first argument, however, simply strings to-gether the standard, predictable arguments that one usually hears in dis-cussions of abortion.

The second argument—which comes from a famous article by a philos-ophy professor—goes well beyond the standard arguments. It frames the is-sue in a way that most people have not considered and adds something new to a very familiar debate. This response is more intellectually challenging than the first and is much more likely to persuade someone who does not already hold an anti-abortion position. It is, in other words, a more subtle approach to the same basic argument.

Avoid Clichés

A cliché is an argument, a phrase, a slogan, or a catchphrase that has been used so often that it no longer conveys its original meaning. Sometimes a cli-ché is simply an overused comparison, such as "dead as a doornail" or "light as a feather," but arguments can also be clichéd. Consider statements such as "When guns are outlawed, only outlaws will have guns," "If you don't like abortion, don't have one," "Make love not war," or "America—love it or leave it." Whatever the original merits of these sentiments may have been, the ar-guments have become clichés that can be invoked by people who have never seriously considered the complicated issues that they raise.

In college writing, clichés often take the place of serious contemplation about an issue. Clichés discourage the development of new ideas. They tend to be short arguments with little support and inflexible conclusions, and they seem (and only seem) to make further thought unnecessary.

Construct a Debatable Position

For a claim to result in an interesting essay, it must be arguable. Consider, for example, the following claim and think of the essay that it would produce: "War kills innocent people." Most people would immediately agree that a lot of innocent people die in wars. Many people, however, would argue that the loss of innocent lives is sometimes necessary, even if it is bad. Others would disagree and say that war is always a bad thing, no matter how necessary it may seem. However, the claim that war kills innocent people would not result in an effective essay because it does not take a position that could be reasonably disputed. A better claim might be: "A commitment to paci-fism on the part of world leaders is the only way to resolve difficult disputes without bloodshed," or "War is ineffective because it deals with the surface political problems that lead to disputes and not the ultimate problems that cause conflict in the first place."

Consider the Implications of an Argument

Most arguments have consequences and implications that are not directly stated but that can be clearly understood when read with a subtle, critical eye. When you develop your ideas, keep in mind what unstated assumptions they rest on and what their consequences might be. For example, if you are writing an essay about responses to poverty and you want to argue that the government should increase welfare to help lift people out of poverty, then you need to consider the implications of such an argument. One unstated as-sumption would be that people are poor because of their circumstances and not because of their behaviors—such as drug use or irresponsible spending—which cannot be controlled by welfare payments. Consider also the possi-ble consequences of increasing welfare payments. Would more people go on welfare? Where would the additional money come from—higher taxes? Or would it be taken from the budgets for other social services, such as Medicare or Head Start (an early-childhood-development program)? Would it mean decreasing spending on other programs the government funds, like the Na-tional Institutes of Health or the National Endowment for the Arts? You need to consider as many aspects like these as possible in your writing. A subtle, persuasive argument addresses both the implications and the consequences of the claim.

This requirement also applies when you analyze or respond to another person's ideas; an analysis or response that addresses unstated implications of an argument is far more effective than one that does not. Take, for exam-ple, Mo Tzu's essay "Against Music." Mo Tzu's stated argument is that music and the pageantry that accompanies it are harmful to society. Rather than focusing on this argument, a deeper reading would analyze the *reason* that Mo Tzu opposed music: music was a luxury that took resources away from society without adding anything to most people's lives. This reasoning has implications for many other things that required or require resources with-out benefiting the majority of people: past examples include the pyramids of Egypt, the Olympics of ancient Greece, the plays of Shakespeare's Globe

Theatre, while present ones include art exhibits, country clubs, and celebrity weddings. A truly subtle analysis of Mo Tzu's argument would account for and examine the implications of his argument that go far beyond what is stated in the text.

Keep Going Until You Have Learned Something

The reason that most instructors give writing assignments is that they believe, with good reason, that the act of writing can teach you something. If you take an assignment seriously, the experience of creating, developing, and structuring a set of ideas can teach you things that just going to class and reading a textbook cannot.

One way to judge whether you have generated a good idea is to consider seriously whether the idea has changed your outlook. Have you learned something that you did not know, considered something that you never have considered before, changed your opinion about a controversial issue, or learned to look at something in a different way? If you have accomplished any of these things, you most likely have produced a solid, fruitful writing topic.

NINE

Structuring Ideas

GOOD IDEAS, EVEN WELL STATED, do not guarantee a good essay. Ideas, no matter how brilliant, must be organized effectively and presented intelligently so they can be understood by a reader. The previous two chapters focused on ways that you interact with both the ideas that you read and the ideas that you generate in response to your reading; both chapters dealt only with you and a text. This chapter will show you how to structure your ideas so that they can be read and appreciated by someone else.

Important structural elements of academic essays include thesis statements, introductions, transitions, and conclusions. This chapter will define these elements and offer techniques to help you use them effectively. Understanding these structural conventions will not only help you produce the kinds of essays that many of your instructors want to receive, it will also help you improve both your thinking and your writing.

In many ways, academic essays that adhere strictly to these guidelines are artificial creations rarely found outside the college classroom—and even in college classes, many teachers will expect you to move beyond these traditional academic writing techniques. But much can be said for the traditional thesis statement and the structural apparatus that supports it. Learning to use them properly can help you stay focused on a single idea and marshal evidence to support a claim, which are essential abilities for every kind of writing: academic, creative, or professional.

However, important as they are, mastering these techniques should not be your goal. They are designed simply to help you reach the ultimate goal of communicating your ideas to someone else. As the ancient Zen masters understood, the methods designed to lead people to enlightenment are not the same thing as enlightenment itself. As you progress as a student and a writer, keep your goal of communication separate from the techniques that you use to achieve it. Intelligent, thoughtful communication is more important than slavish devotion to technique, and these guidelines should be followed only to the extent that they help you reach that goal.

THESIS STATEMENTS

What Is a Thesis?

People can mean two different things when they talk about a "thesis." On the one hand, a thesis is the basic argument that a particular piece of writing makes—the point that an author wants to get across. Most writers, in most circumstances, want to communicate something to an audience; therefore, most writing has a thesis. On the other hand, when writing instructors use the word "thesis," they are usually referring to a thesis statement, a single sentence that summarizes or encapsulates an essay's main argument. Thesis statements of this sort are not required of every kind of writing, nor are they always found in the works of the best professional writers. These writers have learned how to advance a thesis (in the first sense of the word) without creating a single sentence to sum up the argument.

However, composing a thesis statement can be a very useful exercise for developing an argument. It accomplishes several important tasks: (1) it helps you clarify exactly what you are trying to say, which makes the writing process smoother and easier; (2) it serves as a reference point that you can use to eliminate ideas that do not support the main point of the essay; and (3) it tells the reader what kinds of arguments to expect and forecasts what follows.

One common misconception is that a thesis statement should summarize an *essay* rather than an *argument*. The difference is crucial. A thesis statement designed to summarize an essay will usually try to provide a miniature outline and can very quickly become unwieldy. Consider the following example:

There are many differences between Seneca and John Henry Newman: Newman was religious and Seneca was not; Seneca lived in the ancient Roman Empire while Newman lived in Victorian England at a time when it was becoming a modern democracy; and Seneca believed that liberal education was the only good kind of education while Newman believed that both liberal and useful education had their place.

While this sentence may be a good one-sentence summary of a three-to-five-page essay, it does not make a good thesis statement because it does not make an argument. In attempting to summarize everything that the essay says, this sentence does not actually have a point. A better thesis statement would try to summarize less about the essay and more clearly state a major claim:

Newman's view of liberal education is much less restrictive than Seneca's because the society in which Newman lived required most people to acquire enough useful knowledge to earn a living.

This sentence boils down all of the various ideas in the first example into a single, coherent, focused argument that can serve as the main point that the essay will make.

The Thesis Statement as an Argument

Any argument must have two elements: a claim and support for that claim. Because a thesis statement is always, at some level, an argument, it should also include these two elements. The following sentences would not make good thesis statements because they contain only a claim and do not support that claim:

Gandhi had a better understanding of poverty than Malthus.

True objectivity in science can never be achieved.

Liberal general education is a good idea.

To turn these claims into arguments, and therefore thesis statements, you would have to add a "because clause" (which may or may not contain the word "because"), or a brief statement of support that gives the rationale for the claim:

Gandhi's understanding of poverty, which takes into account the spiritual side of human nature, is better than that of Malthus, whose analysis is solely economic.

True objectivity in science requires something that never can be achieved: the presence of a purely unbiased observer.

Liberal general education is a good idea because it prepares people for a variety of different careers rather than for a single job.

Refining Your Thesis Statement

When you view the thesis statement as an argument, with both a claim and support for that claim, you can use it to test whether your essay's argument works. If the thesis statement is a weak argument, then the chances are very good that the essay is also weak. Keep refining your thesis statement until you are reasonably sure that it is a good argument, and then make sure your essay properly addresses the point of your thesis statement.

Revising a thesis statement is really the same thing as revising the *ideas* in your essay. Here are a few things to keep in mind as you revise a thesis statement:

Present an arguable claim. While this requirement is covered at greater length in the previous chapter, it is worth repeating that an essay topic—and therefore a thesis statement, which presents the essay topic—needs to be debatable. A thesis statement should present a claim that a reasonable person could disagree with.

Present a single, focused argument. An essay should have a single argument and a focused thesis statement. Unfortunately, the formula for a "five-paragraph essay," the first kind of essay most people learn to write, can often lead to three (or more) separate ideas that are linked together under a common heading. Consider this example:

> Christianity and Islam are similar to each other in their worship of a single God, their belief in a single holy book, and their strong belief in caring for the poor.

While this might appear at first glance to be a workable thesis statement, it actually offers three arguments instead of one—each similarity between Christianity and Islam could be the focus of an entire essay. Consider how this thesis statement could be broken into three more-specific thesis statements:

> Christianity and Islam are similar to each other because both assert the existence of a single, all-powerful deity who stands outside the natural world.

> The most important similarity between Christianity and Islam is that both religions' followers believe that God has spoken to them through a single book rather than through a long tradition of oral narratives.

> The moral codes of Christianity and Islam are nearly identical in that each religion preaches the spiritually destructive nature of material wealth and the importance of taking care of the poor.

Each of these thesis statements could produce an interesting, focused essay, and each would be more effective and interesting than the essay produced by the first example. This kind of streamlining does not mean that an argument cannot have subpoints, or that different paragraphs should not treat different parts of a general assertion. But you have a responsibility as a writer to make very clear how each assertion supports the main thesis.

Make sure your thesis is open enough to allow for further discussion. Consider the following thesis statement:

> Machiavelli's philosophy could never work because he advocates lying and liars always get caught.

A statement such as this would support only a single paragraph or two of argument after the introduction. The problem, of course, is not with the thesis statement but with the ideas in the essay—the author has not thought of enough to say. Consider the following revision:

> While Machiavelli gave valuable advice to the princes and rulers of his own day, the modern notion of the separation of powers makes it unlikely that any leader of a modern democracy could practice these ideas today.

This statement opens up many more possibilities for analysis, discussion, expansion, and examples of the phenomenon that the writer wants to discuss. This thesis, in fact, will serve as the basis for the full sample essay toward the end of this chapter.

Make sure your thesis can be reasonably supported in the assigned essay. While some theses are too focused to allow for further discussion, others are too expansive to be covered in a short essay. For example:

> Lao Tzu's philosophy in the *Tao Te Ching* is so comprehensive that it encompasses every important aspect of what it means to be human.

This thesis might be defensible in a five-hundred-page book, but no writer could adequately defend such a sweeping statement in a three-to-five-page essay. Narrowing the thesis to a manageable assertion will vastly improve the essay. In the example above, choosing one aspect of human nature and exploring how it is treated in the *Tao Te Ching* creates a much more focused thesis statement, which will lead to a much more manageable and interesting essay:

> In the *Tao Te Ching*, Lao Tzu captures an important paradox of human nature: that inaction is often more productive than action.

The most important thing to remember when you are writing your thesis statement is that the claim that you make in it, and the support that you provide for that claim, set the parameters for the rest of your essay. You must be able to tie every assertion that you make in your essay back to the argument that you articulate in your thesis statement.

INTRODUCTIONS

The Introductory Paragraph

The introductory paragraph is where you make your first impression as a writer, and, just as in relationships, first impressions in reading are very difficult to overcome. This is why many experienced writers spend as much time on the first paragraph of an essay as they do on the rest of the essay. A good introductory paragraph should do three things:

Introduce the purpose of the essay and any important concepts. If your paper is about Newman's and Nussbaum's views on education, your introduction should briefly introduce Newman and Nussbaum and explain, in very basic terms, their views on education. Your goal in the introduction should not be to begin your argument outright, but to clarify all the concepts that you will use in your argument, so that when you use them in the body of your essay, the reader will be familiar with them.

Capture the reader's interest. The introduction should interest the reader in the rest of the essay. It needs to entice the reader to continue reading and convince him or her that something interesting is going to happen in the rest of the essay, that he or she will be educated or entertained or both. (Strategies for doing this are discussed below.)

Provide a platform for any thesis statement. Many writing instructors advise students to place the thesis statement somewhere in the first paragraph, often at or near the end. A thesis statement does not have to go in the introduction, but, if you do choose (or have been instructed) to place it there, it should flow naturally from the introduction. Even if you do not place your thesis statement there, the introduction needs to lay the groundwork for your essential argument, which is summarized in the thesis statement.

Strategies for Beginning.

The strategies below can help make your introductory paragraph more effective. All the examples are based on the thesis statement on Machiavelli in the previous section; the thesis statement is in bold in each example.

Give historical context. An introduction that offers a meaningful discussion of any key concepts can help to orient readers to your argument:

> In the early sixteenth century, a prince had absolute power over his state. When Machiavelli wrote *The Prince* in 1513, therefore, he set out to teach potential leaders how to best utilize the tyrannical power at their disposal. His advice was clear, concise, and very effective for its time; however, much has changed in the past five hundred years. Since the late eighteenth century—when in their new Constitution America's Founding Fathers experimented with a radical idea called the "separation of powers doctrine"—most of the industrialized democracies in the world have adopted some form of power sharing between their executive, legislative, and judicial branches of government. **While Machiavelli gave valuable advice to the princes and rulers of his day, the modern notion of the separation of powers makes it unlikely that any leader of a modern democracy could practice these ideas today.**

Build your introduction around a key definition. Many times, your essay will introduce, or even revolve around, a key definition that actually defines the argument that you are making. In such cases, it is often a good idea to organize your introduction around this definition:

> One of the most innovative features of the American Constitution is the doctrine known as the "separation of powers." According to this doctrine, the various forms of government authority—legislative, executive, and judicial—should never be concentrated in the same hands, and there should be a system of checks and balances to make sure that no single individual or group obtains enough power to exercise control as a dictator. Without the power of a dictatorship, American rulers have had a very difficult time heeding the advice of the Italian philosopher Niccolò Machiavelli, whose political theories are based on the notion of absolute power that he saw as necessary to the effective running of a state. **While Machiavelli gave valuable advice to the princes and rulers of his day, the modern notion of the separation of powers makes it unlikely that any leader of a modern democracy could practice these ideas today.**

Lead directly into the thesis statement. One of the main purposes of the introduction is to set up the thesis statement. If you keep this in mind as you construct your introductory paragraph, you can often write it in such a way that nearly every sentence in it leads directly into the thesis, thus creating the kind of smooth transition that makes readers feel comfortable moving from your introduction to the body of your paper:

> The absolute power that princes had in Niccolò Machiavelli's time was not entirely a bad thing. In a feudal system of government, a strong ruler with great power can be a good thing for a country, while a weak ruler can cause devastating problems. However, in a society that is no longer feudal, a leader with dictatorial power is no longer so desirable. When America's Founding Fathers wrote the Constitution, they realized this and included a requirement that federal powers be separated into different branches of government; since the late eighteenth century, many other nations have adopted similar measures. **While Machiavelli gave valuable advice to the princes and rulers of his day, the modern notion of the separation of powers makes it unlikely that any leader of a modern democracy could practice these ideas today.**

Start with a question or a quote. A good quotation can hook readers into your essay by presenting them with something interesting to read right off the bat. Interesting questions addressed directly to the reader have much the same effect. If used skillfully, such an opening hook can be used as the basis for a very effective introductory paragraph. However, keep in mind that this approach can easily become a cliché; use quotes sparingly in your introduction, and only when they apply directly to your topic.

> "Power tends to corrupt," wrote Lord Acton in 1887, "and absolute power corrupts absolutely." Acton's famous maxim is perhaps nowhere better demonstrated than in sixteenth-century Italy, where political power was the ultimate prize in a deadly game that often involved rebellion, assassination, treason, insurrection, and military conquest. When Niccolò Machiavelli wrote *The Prince* in 1513, he set out to tell political rulers exactly how to get the kind of absolute power that Acton warned of. In the America of today, however, people have learned well the lesson that Acton spent much of his life trying to teach. Since the founding of the American democracy, political power has been separated into three different areas—executive, legislative, and judicial—that are never allowed to fall into the same hands. Thus, while Machiavelli gave valuable advice to the princes and rulers of his day, the modern notion of the separation of powers makes it unlikely that any leader of a modern democracy could practice these ideas today.

Give a contextualizing example. If you are writing about something that may seem distant or be unfamiliar to your readers, consider starting with an example that might be more familiar. The example can then become a point of reference you can use throughout the paper to help explain more difficult concepts.

> In 1974, Richard Nixon became the first president of the United States to resign from office. While it would be difficult to untangle the complicated web of conspiracy and deceit that brought Nixon to this position, most of the scandals known collectively as Watergate share a single motivation: Nixon wanted more power than the Constitution gave him. Being the chief executive officer of the nation was not enough; he also wanted to control legislation and judicial review and to have the power to gather his own intelligence about political enemies. For much of his career, Nixon was a perfect example of a political Machiavellian. However, in 1974 he became a perfect example of the reason that Machiavelli's

approach is no longer valid. **While Machiavelli gave valuable advice to the princes and rulers of his day, the modern notion of the separation of powers makes it unlikely that any leader of a modern democracy could practice these ideas today.**

Avoid clichés. Such formulaic introductory phrases as "Throughout history . . . ," "Since the beginning of time . . . ," and "Webster's Dictionary defines . . . " have been used by so many students, in so many contexts, that they have lost whatever effectiveness they might ever have had as ways to introduce an argument.

TRANSITIONS

One of the most important things you can do to communicate your ideas to a reader is to provide transitions between all of the ideas and support that you use to prove your thesis. An effective transition shows how ideas connect and relate to each other; it also smooths the shift between one idea and another. There are three main kinds of transitions in academic writing:

Transitions within a paragraph. An effective paragraph is organized logically, so that the information at the beginning of the paragraph leads logically to the information at the end of the paragraph. Each sentence in a paragraph should flow from the previous sentence and lead directly into the following one. Otherwise, readers can become confused and alienated from your argument. Consider the following two paragraphs:

> The ideas of Confucius have been responsible for one of the most important religions in the world: Confucianism. It would be more accurate to characterize Confucius as an "ethical philosopher" rather than as a "prophet" or a "religious figure." Confucius said nothing about the kinds of issues that religions usually deal with: divine beings, miracles, revelation, and the afterlife. He was concerned with constructing an ethical system that people could use to determine correct behavior in any situation.

> The ideas of Confucius have been responsible for one of the most important religions in the world: Confucianism. **However,** Confucius himself said nothing about the kinds of issues that religions usually deal with: divine beings, miracles, revelation, and the afterlife. **Instead,** he was con-

cerned with constructing an ethical system that people could use to determine correct behavior in any situation. It would, **therefore**, be more
accurate to characterize Confucius as an "ethical philosopher" rather
than as a "prophet" or a "religious figure."

Even though the ideas presented in the two paragraphs are identical, the
second paragraph is much easier to read. There are two reasons for this. The
first reason is structural: in the first example, the second sentence presents
an unfamiliar claim (that Confucius should be considered a philosopher
rather than a religious figure) that seems to contradict the claim in the first
sentence (that the ideas of Confucius have been responsible for an important world religion). Such abrupt changes of thought tend to take readers
by surprise. The second paragraph, by contrast, gives the evidence first and
proceeds, step by step, to the conclusion, which, by the end of the paragraph,
seems natural, logical, and even inevitable. Arranging ideas in a logical order helps you move smoothly from idea to idea.

The second reason that most readers would prefer the second paragraph
is that it uses transition words such as "however," "instead," and "therefore"
to show how ideas are related to each other within the paragraph. These transition words serve as cues that the reader can use to follow the writer's chain
of reasoning and see logical relationships between different assertions. Good
transition words should reflect the logical relationship between ideas that you
are conveying. Some common transition words and phrases include:

ADDITION	**COMPARISON**
In addition to	Similarly
Also	In comparison
Furthermore	In the same way
Moreover	Compared to

CAUSATION	**CONTRAST**
Consequently	In contrast
Because of	By contrast
Thus	However
Therefore	Nevertheless
As a result of	Conversely
Hence	On the one hand
Then	On the other hand
In effect	Instead

Transitions between paragraphs. A well-written paragraph generally centers on a single idea or claim. It is therefore extremely important to demonstrate how the information in one paragraph relates to the information in the next—otherwise, you end up with interchangeable paragraphs that make good points individually but do not add up to a coherent argument.

Transitions to the overall argument. It is not enough simply to show how the ideas in a paragraph relate to ideas in other paragraphs; you must also show how they relate to your overall argument—the argument encapsulated in your thesis statement. Each time you make a new claim, you should demonstrate how this new information relates to the overall thesis of the essay. A transition can link one claim to the thesis statement, and to the next claim.

For an example of the importance of these last two kinds of transitions, read the following sample essay carefully and try to determine how the ideas in it are connected to each other and to the overall thesis statement (which is the same thesis statement that we used when discussing introductions earlier in this chapter).

Machiavelli: Ideas Whose Time Has Come . . . and Gone

In the early sixteenth century, a prince had absolute power over his state. When Machiavelli wrote *The Prince* in 1513, therefore, he set out to teach potential leaders how to best utilize the tyrannical power at their disposal. His advice was clear, concise, and very effective for its time; however, much has changed in the past five hundred years. Since the late eighteenth century—when in their new Constitution America's Founding Fathers experimented with a radical idea called the "separation of powers doctrine"—most of the industrialized democracies in the world have adopted some form of power sharing between their executive, legislative, and judicial branches of government. **While Machiavelli gave valuable advice to the princes and rulers of his own day, the modern notion of the separation of powers makes it unlikely that any leader of a modern democracy could practice these ideas today.**

Machiavelli argues that a leader must constantly prepare for war. While it is certainly true that a modern head of state must be concerned with the defense of the nation, it is no longer the case that he or she alone can make any final decisions about either war or preparation for war. Thus, when George W. Bush decided to send American troops to Iraq, he had to spend weeks lobbying Congress for permission to commit American troops to a foreign engagement and months attempting to raise the money to support them once they were there.

At the heart of Machiavelli's advice is the assumption that a prince is free to tax the people and spend their money as he or she sees fit. While this was true of all princes in Machiavelli's day, it is very rarely the case for leaders today. Executive officers, such as presidents, do not normally have the power to tax people or to spend their money—both of these powers now rest with legislative bodies, such as the House of Representatives and the Senate. During his first term, for example, President Bill Clinton attempted to violate one of Machiavelli's cardinal rules by taxing people heavily in order to finance a generous health care initiative.

Machiavelli's ideas would not work in most countries today. There are, of course, plenty of exceptions to this rule. Many twentieth-century political leaders managed to seize absolute power over their countries—from Hitler, Stalin, and Mussolini in the early part of the century to Pinochet, Mobutu, and Hussein in our time. These leaders have repeatedly shown that absolute power concentrated in a single person is not in the best interests of the state.

If you had trouble seeing the relationships between the main ideas in this paragraph, do not be alarmed. They are very difficult to see, because the essay does not have any transitions in it. It relies on the reader to be able to recognize the connections. The last three paragraphs in this essay are also completely interchangeable. If you were so inclined, you could take a pair of scissors and cut these paragraphs out, replace them in the essay in any order, and neither the flow nor the logic of the essay would suffer.

Now, read the same essay with all the transitions in place. You will notice that the transitions (in bold) account for about a third of the paper's total word count. Also notice that these transitions are not afterthoughts tacked on to each major idea, but integral parts of the structure of each paragraph.

Machiavelli: Ideas Whose Time Has Come . . . and Gone

In the early sixteenth century, a prince had absolute power over his state. When Machiavelli wrote *The Prince* in 1513, therefore, he set out to teach potential leaders how to best utilize the tyrannical power at their disposal. His advice was clear, concise, and very effective for its time; however, much has changed in the past five hundred years. Since the late eighteenth century—when in their new Constitution America's Founding Fathers experimented with a radical idea called the "separation of powers doctrine"—most of the industrialized democracies in the world have adopted some form of power sharing between their executive, legislative, and judicial branches of government. While Machiavelli gave valuable advice to the princes and rulers of his day, the modern notion of the separation of powers makes it unlikely that any leader of a modern democracy could practice these ideas today.

One of the most important aspects of the separation of powers doctrine is that it eliminates the ability of any president or prime minister to declare or prepare for war without the consent of a legislative body. Machiavelli argues that a leader must constantly prepare for war and study the art of armed conflict. While it is certainly true that a modern head of state must be concerned with the defense of the nation, it is no longer the case that he or she alone can make any final decisions about either war or preparation for war. In nations that observe the separation of powers principle, both war and peacetime military expenditures have much more to do with budgetary committees than with presidential decrees. Thus, when George W. Bush decided to send American troops to Iraq, he had to spend weeks lobbying Congress for permission to commit American troops to a foreign engagement and months attempting to raise the money to support them once they were there. Machiavelli could not have imagined such a division of power in his own day and could hardly have been expected to anticipate it in his advice to princes.

In addition to preventing leaders from going to war whenever they choose, the separation of powers principle also prevents leaders from taking Machiavelli's advice to avoid lavish expenses and to be content to be considered misers rather than spendthrifts (32–33). At the heart of this advice is the assumption that a prince is free to tax the people and spend their money as he or she sees fit. While this was true of all princes in Machiavelli's day, it is very rarely the case for leaders today. Executive officers, such as presidents, do not normally have the power to tax people or to spend their money—both of these powers now rest with legislative bodies, such as the House of Representatives and the Senate. During his first term, for example, President Bill Clinton attempted to violate one of Machiavelli's cardinal rules by taxing people heavily in order to finance a generous health care initiative. He was prevented from doing this by a power that Machiavelli could not have understood: a legislative body that had to approve all new expenditures by the government.

Our experiences with both war and taxation demonstrate that, even though some modern American presidents and European prime ministers have wanted to put Machiavelli's programs into effect, they have rarely had the concentration of power necessary to be completely Machiavellian. There are, of course, plenty of exceptions to this rule. Many twentieth-century political leaders managed to seize absolute power over their countries—from Hitler, Stalin, and Mussolini in the early part of the century to Pinochet, Mobutu, and Hussein in our time. These leaders have repeatedly shown that absolute power concentrated in a single person is not in the best interests of the state, and their examples have caused countries all over the world to incorporate the separation of powers doctrine into their constitutions. This fact makes Machiavelli's advice increasingly less relevant to our day. Almost all of Machiavelli's advice assumed a leader with absolute power; wherever nations follow the doctrine of the separation of powers, such advice will be of little use to modern politicians.

These transitions relate the various ideas in the paper both to each other and to the overall thesis of the essay: that Machiavelli's ideas would not work in a modern democracy because the separation of powers doctrine would prevent anyone from having the power that he ascribes to princes. Each paragraph extends this argument into some realm of contemporary politics and then explicitly explains how it relates back to the overall thesis. As a result, the entire essay comes across as a single, coherent argument about the contemporary relevance of Machiavelli's political theory.

CONCLUSIONS

Conclusions are important. They give readers a sense of closure and writers the opportunity to tie together various threads of argument into focused assertions or to demonstrate the significance of the cases that they have made in their essays. Consider the conclusion to the sample essay about Machiavelli:

Our experiences with both war and taxation demonstrate that, even though some modern American presidents and European prime ministers have wanted to put Machiavelli's programs into effect, they have rarely had the concentration of power necessary to be completely Machiavellian. There are, of course, plenty of exceptions to this rule. Many twentieth-century political leaders managed to seize absolute power over their countries—from Hitler, Stalin, and Mussolini in the early part of the century to Pinochet, Mobutu, and Hussein in our time. These leaders have repeatedly shown that absolute power concentrated in a single person is not in the best interests of the state, and their examples have caused countries all over the world to incorporate the separation of powers doctrine into their constitutions. This fact makes Machiavelli's advice increasingly less relevant to our day. Almost all of Machiavelli's advice assumed a leader with absolute power; wherever nations follow the doctrine of the separation of powers, such advice will be of little use to modern politicians.

This conclusion is designed to take the two major topics (war and taxation) and link them together as different manifestations of the same thing: the limitations imposed on national leaders by the separation of powers doctrine, an idea that goes hand in hand with the overall thesis. But it also has a secondary function, which is to anticipate and correct a potential weakness: the fact that not every government in the world today believes in the separation of powers, and that there are still dictators today who have the kind of absolute power that Machiavelli envisioned in *The Prince*. By bringing up some of these dictators, the writer demonstrates that he or she has considered this issue and that it does not disprove his or her thesis.

Though there are many ways to bring your essay to a close, below are a few strategies you can employ, along with examples of alternate conclusions to the sample paper that we have been working with:

Refer Back to the Introduction

If you started your essay with an introductory quotation, question, or historical situation, you can often return to your introduction as the basis for forming a conclusion. Consider the sample introduction that begins with a discussion of Watergate as a way to explain the separation of powers. Returning to the story of Nixon's resignation would be an excellent way to conclude an essay that began with such an introduction:

> In Machiavelli's society, leaders were often rebelled against, occasionally exiled, and, not infrequently, assassinated. But no Italian prince in the sixteenth century would ever have done what Richard Nixon was forced to do in 1974: resign and leave office because of a Supreme Court deci-

sion forcing him to turn over incriminating evidence to a congressional committee. Supreme Courts and congressional committees simply were not part of the world that Machiavelli inhabited. The fact that they have become such an important part of the world today, and that leaders in democratic countries are prevented from achieving the kind of power that Machiavelli assumed that a prince would have, makes it difficult to see his advice as relevant to American society in the twenty-first century.

Demonstrate the Implications of Your Argument

Sometimes, you can reach the end of an essay only to discover that your argument has some major implications that you have not addressed. The conclusion can be a good place to show how the fairly focused argument that you have been making has broader and more general applications to other kinds of questions and arguments:

> Though America was founded with a separation of powers doctrine designed to prevent any individual from achieving the kind of power that Machiavelli attributed to princes, we have recently been in danger of forgetting what our Founding Fathers did. Recent presidents, from Lyndon Johnson to George W. Bush, have committed troops to long foreign engagements without ever receiving a declaration of war from Congress; congressional committees are famous for attaching spending bills to completely unrelated pieces of legislation; and, in 2000, the Supreme Court divided along partisan political lines to give the presidency of the United States to someone who had not been elected by a majority of the people. The writings of Niccolò Machiavelli do more than show us what life was like during a particularly violent period of the Italian Renaissance. They warn us what our lives will be like should we ever allow our leaders the power to act unilaterally and with impunity.

Close with a Quotation

Just as a quotation can make a good hook for the beginning of an essay, so a quotation can provide an effective way to tie everything together at the end. Furthermore, a well-chosen quotation from someone that the reader recognizes can provide the sense of closure and completeness that should always characterize a concluding paragraph. Beware, however, of using a lengthy quote—another person's words should not make your argument for you but rather sum up what you have already effectively demonstrated:

> Americans often become annoyed at the inefficiency of our political system. Elections are long and drawn out, debates over important issues are held up by political maneuvering, and the courts, Congress, and the president are forever frustrating each other's plans. The media calls this "gridlock," but scholars of the Constitution call it "checks and balances"—and it is this very inefficiency that prevents rulers from being able to follow Machiavelli's advice completely. It is perhaps this element of democratic inefficiency that Winston Churchill had in mind when he reportedly said that "democracy is the worst form of government in the world with the single exception of all the others."

TEN

Supporting Ideas

THOUGH THE TWO TERMS are often used interchangeably, a claim is not the same thing as an argument. For a claim to become an argument, you need to provide some kind of support. You cannot offer support by simply magnifying the intensity of a claim. The claim that "pornography is extremely disgusting and horribly immoral" offers no more support (that is, no support at all) for its position than the simpler claim that "pornography is immoral."

This chapter will show you how to support a claim and thus turn it into an argument. To begin, you must understand how to provide appropriate evidence to support your claim. You must also understand the different ways that people can be persuaded by arguments. According to Aristotle, the three standard elements of persuasion are logos (appeals to logic and reasoning), pathos (appeals to emotion), and ethos (appeals based on the speaker's character). Understanding these building blocks will make you a stronger reader, as you will be able to identify the methods writers use to make their arguments. And it will make you a better writer, as you will be able to employ them intentionally as you craft your own arguments.

SUPPORTING CLAIMS WITH EVIDENCE

Any time you make a claim, you have a responsibility to support it. Support can come in the form of facts, statistics, authorities, examples, or textual citation. The kind of support that you use depends on the claim that you make: for example, the claim that "affirmative action is not a useful educational policy because it has not increased minority graduation rates" would be best supported by statistical evidence, while the claim that "Mencius and Hsün Tzu held opposing views of human nature" would be best supported by quoting their writings (textual citation). When you think about ways to advance your claim, think about all the possible evidence that you can marshal in support of it.

Facts

Most claims benefit from the support of relevant, well-documented facts. Consider, for example, Charles Darwin's argument in *The Origin of Species*. To support his claim that evolution occurs by means of natural selection, Darwin combines several facts, including Charles Lyell's research showing that the earth is extremely old, Thomas Malthus's calculations about the growth rates of populations, and a summary of existing techniques to breed certain characteristics in livestock and domestic animals. Though these facts do not "prove" Darwin's principles, they create a context in which evolution by natural selection is possible and logical.

Sometimes the facts you need to support your claim are straightforward. A claim that "the benefits of organ donation outweigh any potential risks to the recipient" can be supported by facts about organ donation that are readily available in reference books or on the Web. At times, however, other factors can complicate the level of support facts can offer. For example, different definitions of a key term can produce different perceptions of what is factual. The number of people living in poverty in the United States is much lower for those who define "poverty" as "living on the street" than for those who define it as "not owning a house and two cars." When using facts to support your claim, make sure they relate directly to your claim and are clearly defined.

Statistics

Statistics are facts that consist of numerical data. Statistical data can be harnessed in support of most claims about society, culture, or the collective facts of a given country or region. For these claims in particular, statistical evidence about birthrates, marriages, deaths, inheritances, lawsuits, and other matters of public record—the data of everyday life—can be extremely useful in making a historical argument that goes deeper than one based on political, military, and cultural leaders' documents, which usually do not reflect most people's lives. In arguments about contemporary societies, statistics can be found to support and refute arguments about race, gender, crime rates, education, employment, industry, income, political affiliation, public opinion, and dozens of other areas where collective behavior can be tracked and measured. An excellent source for many of these statistics in the United States is the *Statistical Abstract of the United States*, which is published each year by the Census Bureau and made available, free of charge, at www.census.gov.

Authorities

In areas where facts and statistics are unavailable or inconclusive, evidence can be gathered from those with an acknowledged expertise in the field. Though appealing to authority cannot prove a fact definitively—even experts make mistakes!—it can explain what is possible, what is likely, and what is impossible, all of which are extremely important in supporting claims. In many cultures, certain texts or authorities have such high status that their support will virtually guarantee many people's acceptance of a claim. The Bible, the Quran, the Buddha's teachings, and Confucius's words have all had this kind of authority in the cultures that have been built around them. However, these texts are not generally acceptable as authorities in modern academic arguments.

Examples

Examples drawn from history, fiction, personal experience, or even one's imagination can often be used to support a claim. Examples drawn from historical or current events are especially persuasive, as they add factual support. Consider how Margaret Mead uses examples in "Warfare: An Invention—Not a Biological Necessity." She begins by giving examples of "primitive" people who do not have a concept of organized warfare—the Lepchas and the Eskimos. Then, to illustrate the point that warfare does not come with increased social development, she gives examples of what she sees as two equally undeveloped groups of people—the Andamans and the Australian aborigines—who fight wars. Each time that she makes a claim about the development of warfare, she provides an example of a culture somewhere in the world that illustrates her point.

Textual Citation

Writing in response to other texts—such as the ones found in this book—often requires you to write interpretively, or to make claims about what texts mean. Interpretive writing requires you to find support for your claim within the source text. For example, if you claim that Christine de Pizan's *The Treasure of the City of Ladies* gives a more accurate view of human nature than Machiavelli's *The Prince* because it accounts for the human potential to do good, you will need to cite portions of de Pizan's text that refer to this potential.

LOGOS: APPEALS TO LOGIC AND REASON

What Aristotle called *logos*, or appealing to logic and reasoning, is an essential part of supporting an argument. While evidence provides the basis of an argument's support, how we apply logic to that evidence—that is, our reasoning—is part of what makes an argument persuasive.

According to classical theories of argument, our minds move in two different directions to reach conclusions. Sometimes, we reach a conclusion by applying a general fact that we know—or belief that we hold—to a specific situation. This is called deductive reasoning. Most people know, for example, that milk is more expensive at convenience stores than at grocery stores. When someone decides to save money by buying milk at a grocery store rather than at a convenience store, that person is reasoning deductively.

Inductive reasoning works in the opposite direction. We reason inductively when we use firsthand observations to form general conclusions. Sometimes, the process of induction is simply referred to as "generalizing." If, after buying milk at a certain grocery store three times and finding it spoiled each time, someone decided never to buy milk at that store again, that person would be reasoning inductively.

Most of us do not consciously decide to reason deductively or inductively to solve problems. Rather, we constantly employ both forms of reasoning at the same time. We gather facts and observations until we can use them to form general conclusions (inductive reasoning), and we use those general conclusions to make judgments about specific situations (deductive reasoning). When we do not have a good understanding of how deductive and inductive reasoning work, however, we can be more easily persuaded by arguments that are weak or misleading. This section will explain how both kinds of reasoning can support claims.

Deductive Reasoning

The basic unit of deductive reasoning is called a syllogism, which can be thought of as a kind of mathematical formula that works with words rather than numbers. In its most basic form, a syllogism contains two premises and a conclusion drawn from those premises:

Major premise (dealing with a category): All dogs have four legs.

Minor premise (dealing with an individual): Rover is a dog.

Conclusion: Rover has four legs.

The major premise asserts that all members of a category share a certain characteristic. In the example above, everyone who belongs to the category of "dogs" shares the characteristic of "four legs." However, the characteristic can apply to other categories, too—for example, cats also have four legs. If we were to represent the major premise above graphically, it would look like this:

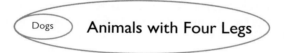

The three simple statements in the syllogism above do not include evidence that Rover is actually a dog; thus, we cannot be sure that the syllogism is true. We can say, though, that *if* all dogs have four legs *and* Rover is a dog, *then* Rover must have four legs. This is because the syllogism is sound, meaning that the premises lead infallibly to the conclusion. A syllogism can be completely true yet unsound. It can also be sound yet demonstrably untrue. Consider the following two arguments:

Major premise: Dogs have purple teeth and green fangs.

Minor premise: Rover is a dog.

Conclusion: Rover has purple teeth and green fangs. (Sound but untrue: the major premise is false.)

Major premise: Basketball players are tall.

Minor premise: Shaquille O'Neal is tall.

Conclusion: Shaquille O'Neal is a basketball player. (True but unsound: simply being tall does not make Shaquille O'Neal a basketball player; plenty of tall people are not basketball players.)

To see why the example above that uses basketball players and Shaquille O'Neal is unsound, consider how the major premise would look if represented graphically:

Because the category of "Basketball Players" is contained entirely within the characteristic of "Tall People," it is logical to assert that all basketball players are tall. It is also logical to assert that someone who is not tall cannot be a basketball player. However, since a large part of the circle representing "Tall People" lies outside the category "Basketball Players," it is not logical to assert that someone who is tall is also a basketball player. If we substitute a different name for "Shaquille O'Neal," it becomes clear why the syllogism is unsound:

Major premise: Basketball players are tall.

Minor premise: Barack Obama is tall.

Conclusion: Barack Obama is a basketball player. (Unsound and untrue)

The following syllogism would also be unsound, because it asserts that if an individual is not in the category named in the major premise (basketball players), he must not have the characteristic in the major premise (tallness):

Major premise: Basketball players are tall.

Minor premise: Barack Obama is not a basketball player.

Conclusion: Barack Obama is not tall. (Unsound and untrue)

To turn the original syllogism into a sound one that asserts that an individual fits the category of the major premise and therefore shares its characteristics, we would need to rewrite it like this:

Major premise: Basketball players are tall.

Minor premise: Shaquille O'Neal is a basketball player.

Conclusion: Shaquille O'Neal is tall. (Sound and true)

A sound syllogism can also assert that an individual who does not share the characteristic in the major premise (in this example, tallness) cannot be part of the category named in the major premise (in this example, basketball players):

Major premise: Basketball players are tall.

Minor premise: George Stephanopoulos is not tall.

Conclusion: George Stephanopoulos is not a basketball player. (Sound and true)

Understanding the structure of syllogisms can be helpful in understanding real-world claims. Consider the following hypothetical statement:

When America was attacked, those who sympathized with these attacks and wished our attackers well opposed going to war in Iraq. At the very moment that terrorists were hoping that we would not go to war, Senator Jones gave a speech on the Senate floor opposing the war. It is important that Americans understand that, in these crucial moments, Senator Jones's sympathies lay with the enemy.

Once we eliminate the political hyperbole in this statement, we are left with a fairly straightforward syllogism:

Major premise: People who support terrorism opposed going to war in Iraq.

Minor premise: Senator Jones opposed going to war in Iraq.

Conclusion: Senator Jones supports terrorism.

Whether or not one considers the premises of this argument to be true, the conclusion is unsound: it states that because the minor premise asserts that an individual shares the characteristic in the major premise (opposing going to war), he must therefore belong to the category in the major premise (people who support terrorism).

When you examine an argument, such as the example above or the ones in this book, think critically about its logic and reasoning. If you were to state the argument in a syllogism, would the syllogism be sound? For example, consider this thesis statement offered earlier in the chapter: "Affirmative action is not a useful educational policy because it has not increased minority graduation rates." Arranged in a syllogism, it would look like this:

Major premise: Useful educational policies increase graduation rates.

Minor premise: Affirmative action has not increased minority graduation rates.

Conclusion: Affirmative action is not a useful educational policy.

Since the minor premise claims that an individual (in this case, a specific instance of educational policy, affirmative action) does not share the characteristic in the major premise, the conclusion that it does not belong to the category in the major premise is sound—and, therefore, the argument is sound (which does not necessarily make it true). Applying this logic to your own arguments can help you ensure that your arguments are sound.

Inductive Reasoning

Inductive reasoning does not produce the kind of mathematical certainty that deductive reasoning does, but it can produce conclusions with a very high likelihood of being true. We engage in induction when we gather together bits of specific information and use our own knowledge and experience to make an observation about what must be true. Inductive reasoning uses observations and prior experiences, rather than syllogisms, to reach conclusions. Consider the following chains of observations:

Observation: John came to class late this morning.

Observation: John's hair was uncombed.

Prior experience: John is very fussy about his hair.

Conclusion: John overslept.

The reasoning process here is directly opposite to that used in deductive syllogisms. Rather than beginning with a general principle (people who comb their hair wake up on time), the chain of evidence begins with an observation and then combines it with other observations and past experience to arrive at a conclusion.

There are three basic kinds of inductive reasoning: generalization, analogy, and statistical inference.

Generalization

This is the most basic kind of inductive reasoning. You generalize whenever you make a general statement (all salesmen are pushy) based on observations (the last three salesmen who came to my door were pushy). When you use specific observations as the basis of a general conclusion, you are said to be making an inductive leap.

Generally speaking, the amount of support needed to justify an inductive leap is based on two things: the plausibility of the generalization and the risk factor involved in rejecting a generalization.

Implausible inductive leaps require more evidence than plausible ones do. More evidence is required, for example, to support the notion that a strange light in the sky is an invasion force from the planet Xacron than to support the notion that it is a low-flying plane. Since induction requires us to combine what we observe with prior experience, and most of us have more prior experience with low-flying planes than with extraterrestrial invaders, it will take more evidence of an alien invasion force to overcome our prior experience of low-flying planes.

An inductive leap is more easily justified—that is, you can supply less support for it—when rejecting it carries a great risk. Consider the following two arguments:

1. I drank milk last night and got a minor stomachache. I can probably conclude that the milk was a little bit sour, and I should probably not drink that milk again.

2. I ate a mushroom out of my backyard last night, and I became violently ill. I had to be rushed to the hospital to have my stomach pumped. I can probably conclude that the mushroom was poisonous, and I should probably not eat mushrooms from my backyard again.

Technically, the evidence for these two arguments is the same. They both generalize from a single instance, and they both reach conclusions that could be accounted for by other factors. However, most people would

take the second argument much more seriously, simply because the consequences for not doing so are much more serious.

There are two common errors in generalization: hasty generalization
and exclusion.

Hasty generalization. Inductive fallacies tend to be judgment calls—different people have different opinions about the line between correct and incorrect induction. You commit a hasty generalization, the fallacy most often
associated with generalization, when you make an inductive leap that is
not based on sufficient information. Another term for this is "jumping to
conclusions." Look at the following three statements and try to determine
which generalizations are valid and which are hasty.

1. General Widgets is a sexist company. It has over five thousand employees,
   and not a single one of them is female.

2. General Widgets is a sexist company. My friend Jane, who has a degree in
   computer science, applied for a job there, and it went to a man who majored in history.

3. General Widgets is a sexist company. My friend Jane applied there, and she
   didn't get the job.

Because different people can be convinced by different levels of evidence, it
can be surprisingly difficult to identify a hasty generalization.

Exclusion. A second fallacy that is often associated with generalization,
exclusion occurs when you omit an important piece of evidence from the
chain of reasoning that is used as the basis for the conclusion. If I generalize that my milk is bad based on a minor stomachache and fail to take into
account the seven hamburgers I ate after drinking the milk, I have excluded
the hamburgers from the chain of reasoning and am guilty of exclusion,
which can lead to an invalid conclusion.

Analogy

To make an argument using an analogy is to draw a conclusion about one
thing based on its similarities to another thing. Consider, for example, the following argument against a hypothetical military action in the Philippines.

In the 1960s, America was drawn into a war in an Asian country, with a terrain largely comprising jungles, against enemies that we could not recognize and accompanied by friends that we could not count on. That war began slowly, by sending a few "advisors" to help survey the situation and offer military advice, and it became the greatest military disgrace that our country has ever known. We all know what happened in Vietnam. Do we really want a repeat performance in the Philippines?

In other words, this argument is saying the following: A war in the Philippines would be disastrous. Our soldiers had a terrible time fighting in the jungles in Vietnam, and the terrain around Manila is even worse. An argument like this is an example of a valid analogy. It takes an observation (we had a hard time fighting in the jungles of Vietnam), makes a generalization (it is hard to fight modern warfare in a jungle terrain), and then applies it to another instance (we would have a hard time fighting in the jungles of the Philippines).

Analogies can be useful in illustrating key points (such as the inability of modern militaries to contain rebellions based in jungle terrains), but they do not prove their points simply by being analogies. The most common error found in arguments that use analogies is the false analogy. In a false analogy the characteristics considered are irrelevant, inaccurate, or insufficient.

If we decide to attack the Philippines, we should probably do it in January.
In 1991, we attacked Iraq in January, and look how well that turned out.

Though it goes through the same process, this analogy is based on irrelevant information (the time of year we attacked Iraq).

Statistical inference

We employ this third variety of inductive reasoning whenever we assume that something is true of a population as a whole because it is true of a certain portion of the population. Politicians and corporations spend millions of dollars a year gathering opinions from relatively small groups of people to form bases for statistical inferences, upon which they base most of their major decisions. Inductions based on statistics have proven to be extremely accurate as long as the sample sizes are large enough to avoid large margins of error. Political exit polls, for example, often predict results extremely accurately based on small voter samples, and the Nielsen ratings report the television viewing habits of over a hundred million households based on sample sizes of about a thousand American families. However, using statistical inference carries the risk of using an unrepresentative sample.

Unrepresentative sample. This is a statistical group that does not adequately represent the larger group that it is considered a part of. Any sample of opinions in the United States must take into account the differences in race, age, gender, religion, and geographic location that exist in this country. Thus, a sample of one thousand people chosen to represent all of these factors would tell us a great deal about the opinions of the electorate. A sample of one thousand white, thirty-year-old, Lutheran women from Nebraska would tell us nothing at all about the opinions of the electorate as a whole. Because samples must be representative to be accurate, it is a fallacy to rely on straw polls, informal surveys, and self-selecting questionnaires to gather statistical evidence.

PATHOS: APPEALS TO EMOTION

Aristotle called his second element of persuasion *pathos*, or appeals to emotion. Most people are at least as governed by their emotions as they are by reason, and they are even more likely to be motivated to adopt an opinion or course of action when logical appeals are combined with appeals that work on an emotional level. Advertisers and political campaigns have become extremely good at making these kinds of appeals— often to the point that they exclude logical arguments altogether and appeal only to emotions. They know that emotional appeals work. However, emotional appeals do not have to be manipulative; when used effectively and judiciously, they can help you connect with your reader or illustrate the emotional aspects of an issue.

Below are some of the most common kinds of emotional appeals. All of them can be used in manipulative ways, but they can also all be used in conjunction with other kinds of support to produce extremely compelling and effective arguments.

Sympathy

Most people are moved by the misfortunes of others. When we see victims of injustice, economic hardship, crime, war, or disaster, we sympathize and want to help. Appeals to sympathy or pity tend to be most persuasive when they describe the plights of individuals, and are paired with facts, statistics, and an analysis of large-scale phenomena. For example, in a piece of writing about poverty in less-developed countries, the story of a single child dying of starvation would provide a more effective emotional appeal than would a well-reasoned statistical analysis of childhood death rates in twenty-six nations, but the combination of the two would make for the best argument—it would appeal to both emotion and reason.

Fear

When people do not feel safe, or when they feel that their security (physical or economic) is in jeopardy, they become susceptible to appeals to fear. This is why automakers list safety as a major component of new cars and why politicians foreground their commitment to creating jobs and a healthy economy. An appeal to fear creates a sense of fear in the audience and connects its argument to resolving the fear. In the above example of automakers, emphasizing the safety of their cars both puts forth the possibility of being in an auto accident and offers the reassurance that if you buy one of their cars, you will be safe. Politicians who emphasize their commitment to creating new jobs and a healthy economy tap into fears of financial struggles and simultaneously offer the reassurance that if they are elected, they will put those fears to rest.

Anger

When writers appeal to anger, they frame an issue in a way that angers an audience and then use that anger to reinforce their claim. Usually, this means telling the audience something that they did not previously know and that, once known, elicits anger.

Most people are moved to a sense of anger by injustice, unfairness, and cruelty. Exposing unfairness can be an effective way to appeal to this sense of anger. Consider, for example, the following argument:

> Shopping at Cheap Stuff is immoral. In order to keep their prices low, they pay subminimum wages with no benefits, and they subject their employees to dangerous working conditions. They have been cited

more times than any other corporation for unfair labor practices, and twelve employees during the past year have been killed on the job in unnecessary accidents. The money I save just isn't worth supporting this corporation.

Belonging

Many successful arguments appeal to people's desire to be part of something larger than themselves. An obvious example of this kind of appeal is the appeal to patriotism, or the sense of belonging to a nation. People are often willing to risk their lives for what they believe to be their duty to their country. Appeals to belonging also connect claims to other groups: religious organizations, states, cities, schools, labor unions, fraternities, and so on.

Successful appeals to belonging create a sense in the reader of being part of a larger group. This approach can be very similar to the fallacy of bandwagoning. The difference is that an effective appeal does not offer itself as proof of a claim; it simply frames the argument in a way that creates a sense of belonging in the reader. Consider the following argument against censorship:

> The current efforts to censor language and content in popular music and television programs are fundamentally un-American. This nation was founded on ideas of freedom of speech and expression that were considered heretical in Europe but which became the fabric of the Constitution of the United States of America. This principle was enshrined in the First Amendment and is the reason that America has remained a strong country for two hundred years. Those who censor our entertainers destroy part of what makes America a great nation.

The writer here is making an argument by appealing to the larger concept of "America" to which (we assume) the audience belongs. The appeal is grounded in the audience's desire to be part of this larger entity and the values that it espouses.

Pride/Vanity

Appeals to pride and vanity sometimes take the form of simple flattery, but they also include appeals to people's desire to be attractive, professional, and well-thought-of by their peers. As you might expect, this kind of appeal is common in advertising for clothing and cosmetics, as well as for alcohol and cars.

ETHOS: THE WRITER'S APPEAL

According to Aristotle, the most powerful element of persuasion is neither logos (logic) nor pathos (emotion), but ethos, which is also the most difficult of the three terms to define. Although the Greek word *ethos* is the root of our word "ethical," "ethos" does not quite mean "persuasion by appeals to ethics." Rather, it refers to the persuasion through the audience's perception of the speaker. At the heart of Aristotle's notion of ethos is the somewhat circular fact that most people are persuaded by arguments that are made by people that they find persuasive.

A writer's or speaker's ethos, then, is composed of everything that makes an audience consider him or her persuasive. You project a persuasive ethos when you communicate to your audience that you are the sort of person who should be believed: intelligent, well-qualified, and assertive, but also kind, moderate, and sympathetic to their points of view. The ethos of a speaker may include things like tone of voice, level of comfort in speaking, and physical attractiveness. The ethos of a writer may be harder to see, but it is no less important.

Reading someone's writing for the first time is like meeting someone new. We come to the text with certain expectations, which can be met, exceeded, or disappointed. In just a few minutes, we form an impression of the writer that, fair or not, colors the rest of our experience with the work and affects how persuaded we are by its argument. Here are a few things to consider as you work to create a good ethos in your writing:

Establish Your Credibility

In many kinds of writing, you can appropriately introduce yourself to an audience and explain why you are qualified to give the opinions you are about to give. For example, a very persuasive editorial on the problems faced by single mothers might begin with a paragraph such as this:

> Every time I hear some politician talk about the "single mother" prob-
> lem, I cringe. To them, single motherhood is a problem to be solved; to
> me, it is a life to be lived. Five years ago, my husband died, leaving me
> with three daughters—twelve, nine, and four—to raise by myself. We
> were not rich, and my husband did not have life insurance. Since then,
> I have always had a job, sometimes two, and have at times paid more
> than half of my take-home pay in child care. And yes, I have also been
> on welfare—not because I am lazy or because I want the government to
> subsidize my "promiscuous lifestyle," but because I had no other way to
> feed and house my children.

The writer of this piece not only lays the groundwork for an argument about single mothers but also establishes that her own experience has qualified her to give an informed, thoughtful opinion.

Be Generous to Other Points of View

People want to know that you respect them. When you are writing to a general audience—one in which every reader may have a different opinion on a given issue—be careful to avoid dismissing or disrespecting the people you are trying to persuade. Not only are people much more likely to be persuaded by someone who respects them, but writing that exhibits contempt for others often offends even those who share the opinion being expressed. Look at the following two examples and determine which one projects a more persuasive ethos:

1. There is something rotten in this country: fur. Can you imagine anything more inhumane and immoral than killing an animal just to wear its fur as an expensive coat? The rich women and middle-class posers who participate in the fur trade are probably too dumb to realize that they are wearing the remains of a living creature that was killed just to make their coats fit with this year's fashion trends. If they do know they're contributing to the deaths of innocent animals, then they're just cruel, violent, trend-followers.

2. Society has come a long way since the days when people had to wear the skins of mammoths and saber-toothed tigers to keep warm during the cold winters. Now, synthetic materials can keep us much warmer than the skin of any animal. However, each year, forty million animals are killed to produce commercial fur. Many of these animals are still caught in the wild using painful traps. Millions of decent people who would never treat an animal with wanton cruelty unknowingly participate in just such cruelty when they buy coats, gloves, and other items of clothing made with animal fur.

In the first example, the writer displays contempt and anger for those who wear fur. In the second example, however, the writer maintains a calm, respectful tone and offers those who do wear fur the benefit of the doubt.

Do Not Show Off

Whatever your topic, it is important to show the reader that you know what you are talking about. Carefully research key concepts and make sure to point out relevant facts. But at the same time, avoid being overbearing. Beating people over the head with big words and unnecessary facts is rarely persuasive. The line between competence and arrogance is a fine one, but no distinction is more important to the construction of a persuasive ethos.

Make Only Claims That You Can Support

The best way to ruin a good case is to try to make it sound like a great case. If you have evidence to support the claim that affirmative action has had a minimal impact on minority graduate rates, then say so. Do not say "affirmative action has not helped a single person get through school" or "affirmative action has been completely useless over the last twenty years with regard to minority graduation rates." Sometimes, it can even be effective to understate your case a little bit in your introduction and let the evidence speak for itself, as in the following statement:

> In the twenty years that affirmative action programs have been in effect at institutions of higher learning, their actual impact has been difficult to ascertain, but they do not appear to have been a decisive factor in minority graduation rates.

Proofread Your Writing Carefully

When a piece of writing includes shifts in verb tense, sentence fragments, and careless errors in spelling, grammar, and punctuation, readers make certain assumptions about the writer. They might assume that he or she is ignorant, careless, and uneducated. These assumptions may not be true, but they are nonetheless part of the ethos that the writer projects. Careful proof-reading can eliminate basic grammatical errors that could seriously injure your ability to be persuasive.

ANTICIPATING COUNTERARGUMENTS

As you build support for your claims, try to anticipate the arguments that might be made against them. This will help you eliminate weaknesses in your argument that might prevent people from being persuaded by your claims. It will also demonstrate to your readers that you are aware of and have considered other positions.

To identify a counterargument, imagine that you were given an assign-ment to rebut your own argument. What weaknesses do you see that could become the basis for a rebuttal essay? If you know somebody else who can read what you have written with an objective eye and rebut it, ask that per-son to do so. Conducting research can also help you identify the kinds of arguments that have been made or are currently being made against the position that you are taking.

Once you have identified a counterargument, acknowledge it in your essay and respond to it directly. For example, if you are writing an essay about the importance of liberal education, one counterargument might be that colleges should teach useful job skills instead of a broad range of sub-jects. You could incorporate this into your essay by saying something like this:

> Some people may object to the argument that colleges and universities should focus on liberal education on the grounds that they would better serve students by providing them with the job skills they will need after college. However, there are plenty of ways that someone can learn how to weld or enter data into a spreadsheet—internships, part-time jobs, seminars, classes at a trade or vocational school. There is no other way to get the kind of liberal education that a university provides.

The best way to thwart a counterargument is to qualify your own claims—that is, to eliminate absolute claims from your essay, such as "every student can benefit from courses in philosophy" or "nobody learns everything that they need to know for a job in their undergraduate education." When you make claims such as these, they can be refuted with a single counterexample—for example, "the philosophy course I took never benefited me at all" or "as an undergraduate my sister learned everything she needed to know for her job." It is better to avoid such absolutes and say instead that "most students can benefit from courses in philosophy" or "as undergraduates the overwhelming majority of people do not learn everything they need to know for their jobs."

Finally, do not be afraid to cut out any claim that you cannot support. If you have several strong claims and one or two that are weaker or more difficult to support, cut the weakest claims so that they do not give people reasons to reject your entire argument.

ELEVEN

Synthesizing and Incorporating Ideas

WHILE AN ISOLATED IDEA can occur to someone, more-interesting ideas—and, usually, changes in society, science, and scholastic thought—come from connecting several ideas. One name for this kind of connection is "synthesis." As the word *thesis* means a proposition, an argument, or a point of view, synthesis means a combination of different propositions, arguments, or points of view. One hallmark of a strong writer is the ability to synthesize ideas from multiple sources to form his or her own opinions.

Synthesizing ideas requires you to use all of the skills discussed in other chapters of this guide. You must read and understand multiple sources and be able to summarize them quickly and efficiently; discover how to discuss different texts in ways that are meaningful without being clichéd; construct a claim—and in many cases a thesis statement—that asserts an interesting, arguable relationship between different ideas; and locate the evidence necessary to support that claim. This chapter will discuss some of the most common ways to synthesize ideas: summarizing multiple sources, comparing and contrasting, finding themes and patterns, and synthesizing ideas to form your own argument.

SUMMARIZING MULTIPLE SOURCES

Writers often need to summarize, as quickly as possible, what others have said before they can present their own thoughts on an issue. Most often, this kind of writing forms part of a response essay or a research essay.

Writing a literature review, or any other summary of multiple texts, is somewhat different from writing a summary of a single text. It simultaneously requires you to tighten your focus and to make connections between different texts. As you summarize multiple texts in your own writing, keep these suggestions in mind:

Be Succinct and Selective

The more you have to summarize, the less space you can devote to any one source. While a three-page summary of a single text will include quite a bit of detail about the main and supporting arguments, a three-page summary of ten texts can devote only a few sentences to each text. Choose the points that you want to include carefully, and make sure your wording is as concise as possible. Include only those elements of the text that relate to your overall purpose.

Construct a Framework That Leads to Your Ideas

Rather than simply stating the main idea of each text, construct a framework in which you can relate the ideas from multiple texts to each other, so that they all lead directly into your main idea. For example, imagine that you have been given an assignment to write your own definition of "human nature" based on selections by Thomas Hobbes, Ruth Benedict, and Edward O. Wilson. While simply summarizing each of these texts would adequately convey their major points, framing them so that they relate to each other makes the summary much more focused and concise, and allows you to synthesize them to form your own argument.

> Those who study human nature frequently focus on the interaction between human nature and culture, questioning how much our inherent nature forms our culture—and how much our culture can affect our basic nature. For Thomas Hobbes, human beings are inherently selfish and aggressive, but our own self-interest can compel us to form cooperative

societies and develop cultures. Edward Wilson, working from a modern Darwinian framework unavailable to Hobbes, makes a very similar argument. According to Wilson, evolution-shaped attributes very similar to those that Hobbes perceived in human nature—such as the desire to mate and the urge to defend territory—determine the way that we interact with others in society, which forms the basis of culture.

Ruth Benedict places a much stronger emphasis on the way that culture shapes human nature, but she also starts out with inherent (and presumably inherited) human characteristics. Like Hobbes and Wilson, Benedict believes that human beings across cultures have the same set of inherent traits. Unlike the other two, however, Benedict focuses on the differences among human beings. According to Benedict, human beings in all cultures are born with the same spectrum of characteristics, but those characteristics are encouraged or discouraged to different extents by the cultures in which people live. This view is perfectly compatible with the views of both Hobbes and Wilson; it simply emphasizes the other half of the nature/culture equation.

The framework for this discussion revolves around a single question: how does each author view the interaction between human nature and culture? Once this question has been answered by the three authors whose works are summarized, the writer is free to propose his or her own answer to the question, thus synthesizing the ideas in the summary portion.

COMPARING AND CONTRASTING

One of the most common assignments in college courses is to compare or contrast different texts, concepts, or phenomena. To *compare* things means to discuss how they are similar, while to *contrast* things means to show how they are different. However, in general usage, the term "compare" can be used for either operation.

A comparison/contrast assignment involving texts (including visual texts such as paintings or photographs) requires you to make connections between two or more opinions, arguments, theories, or sets of facts. A good comparison/contrast essay, however, does more than just list similarities and differences—when done well, it can become a vehicle for generating a unique and creative synthesis of different ideas.

As with any writing assignment, the key to good comparison and contrast essays is to generate an interesting, subtle topic to write about. Look beyond surface similarities or differences and try to invent, rather than simply discover, a compelling basis for viewing two (or more) texts in relation to each other. Here are a few suggestions to keep in mind:

Choose a Single Point for Comparison

Consider the following thesis statement:

> Plato and Machiavelli are very different in their nationalities and their cultures; however, they are similar in the way that they present their ideas. They both emphasize the importance of knowledge, and believe that certain people are superior to others.

This kind of listing is appropriate for prewriting, but it lacks the focus and organization necessary for a good essay. Instead of simply listing similarities and differences, you need to create a framework in which the comparison makes sense. Doing so will often mean choosing a single area of similarity or difference and focusing entirely on that area, as in the following revision of the above statement:

> The crucial difference between Plato and Machiavelli is that Plato sees ultimate truth as existing beyond the material world while Machiavelli believes that material reality is the only truth that matters.

This framework, of course, cannot account for all the differences between Plato and Machiavelli, but it does not have to. A comparison/contrast paper does not need to be exhaustive nearly as much as it needs to be focused. By looking only at Plato's and Machiavelli's views of material reality, you will be able to develop a significant, interesting approach to reading the two texts together.

Do Not Try to Compare Everything

Any two things can be compared or contrasted in hundreds of different ways, most of which will not be relevant to your main point. Stick closely to the focus of that essay and be ruthless in cutting out details that do not support your primary claim.

Avoid Stating the Obvious

Many comparison/contrast assignments deal with pairs of things whose surface similarities or differences are easy to see. When this is the case, consider working against the obvious. Look for ways that clearly similar things are different or that clearly different things are the same. An apple is different from a monster truck, for example, in many ways—so many, in fact, that there is little value in pointing them out. If you can come up with a compelling argument, though, about how an apple is *like* a monster truck (perhaps that they have both become much bigger than they need to be to fulfill their natural functions), you will have a very interesting essay indeed.

The same principle applies when you are comparing ideas. Imagine that you have been asked to compare or contrast a pair of essays whose main points obviously contradict—such as Mencius's chapter on the inherent goodness of human nature and Hsün Tzu's rebuttal essay, "Man's Nature Is Evil." The essays clearly oppose each other, but they also share a number of assumptions about what kinds of behavior constitute "good" and "evil." Finding those assumptions and making them the basis of a comparison paper will be much more interesting than simply repeating the obvious fact that Mencius thought that people were good, while Hsün Tzu thought that they were bad.

Compare Underlying Assumptions

Beneath every claim is an assumption, a presumption that makes it possible for a claim to be true. The claim that "higher education is a good thing because it helps people get good jobs and earn more money throughout their lives" only holds fast if earning more money is considered to be a good thing. The most obvious—and therefore the least subtle—connections between two works will usually be found in what the authors explicitly state. More sophisticated connections can be found in the underlying principles and premises that are necessary for an argument to make sense.

For example, consider this comparison, based on an underlying assumption shared by Plato's "Speech of Aristophanes" and Vandana Shiva's *Soil, Not Oil*:

> On the surface, Plato's philosophical "Speech of Aristophanes" and Vandana Shiva's environmentalist essay *Soil, Not Oil* seem to have nothing in common. One is a whimsical parable about the creation of the human

species, and the other is an impassioned plea for a just distribution of resources among the people of the earth. Underneath the surface, however, both selections make the argument that human nature is incomplete and fractured. Plato believes that human beings are partial beings until they find a romantic partner who can complete them. Shiva sees human nature as something that cannot survive long without a connection to nature and the environment. In sum, Plato and Shiva believe that human beings cannot ever be self-sufficient enough to meet all of their own needs.

Neither Plato nor Shiva attempts to prove that people are incomplete; this assumption lies behind the arguments that both make. Keep in mind that an underlying assumption may not be referred to in a text. It is not a major point of an argument, but it is the underlying value or idea that makes the argument possible.

FINDING THEMES AND PATTERNS

Some ideas—particularly those featured in this book, such as the role of law and government or the essence of human nature and the mind—have been explored throughout history in societies that otherwise have little in common. Showing how these ideas influence one another and how they appear in different societies and contexts throughout history can help you synthesize multiple arguments.

Show How Ideas Interact

One very important way to synthesize arguments is to demonstrate how ideas interact with each other. Ideas can influence other ideas in a number of different ways:

- *One idea can be based directly on another idea.* For example, William Blake's poem "The Tyger" is based directly on the idea of the sublime articulated by Edmund Burke in *The Sublime and Beautiful.*
- *An idea can be based indirectly on another idea.* Garrett Hardin's "Lifeboat Ethics," for instance, draws much of its inspiration from Thomas Malthus's *Essay on the Principle of Population.*

- *An idea can be influenced by a combination of other ideas.* For example, Charles Darwin's *The Origin of Species* was influenced by Charles Lyell's *Principles of Geology*, which established that the earth was much older than people had previously thought, and Thomas Malthus's *Essay on the Principle of Population*, which showed how the competition for resources changed certain aspects of human society.

- *An idea can be based on a general perception created by another influential text.* For example, Edward Wilson's argument in "The Fitness of Human Nature" draws largely on the framework for understanding nature created by Charles Darwin.

- *An idea can synthesize a number of other ideas.* For example, Martin Luther King Jr.'s "Letter from Birmingham Jail" cites the work of, among others, Jesus, Gandhi, Henry David Thoreau, and Thomas Aquinas.

- *An idea can be formulated as a rebuttal to another idea.* For example, Hsün Tzu's "Man's Nature Is Evil" was written in direct rebuttal to Mencius's views in "Man's Nature Is Good."

- *An idea can be formulated in general opposition to another system of thought.* For example, George Orwell's "Pacifism and the War" opposes the entire ethical position of pacifism.

To demonstrate a pattern of influence among two or more texts, you must first establish that such influence is theoretically possible. You do not have to prove that one author knew another author's work directly. People can be very influenced by ideas whose sources they do not know. However, no idea has been universally influential at every moment in history. It would be difficult to assert, for example, that Plato was influenced by the Buddha's teachings, which were written down thousands of miles away in a culture that had no known contact with Plato's Athens. And it would be impossible to argue persuasively that Plato was influenced by the ideas of Richard Feynman, who lived and wrote more than two thousand years after Plato died.

Once the possibility of influence has been established, the case for influence must be made through very close readings of the relevant texts. Consider an assignment to explore the possible influences of Taoism on Sun Tzu's military theories in *The Art of War*. For the most part, Sun Tzu's ideas could not be further removed from Lao Tzu's. Lao Tzu was a pacifist who abhorred war and believed that it is wrong to try to force people to do anything. Sun Tzu was a military commander who believed that, with the right tools, it is always possible to impose one's will on another. However, both texts came out of China's Period of Warring States, and Lao Tzu's *Tao Te Ching* is unquestionably the older of the two works. Under these circumstances, it is entirely possible that Sun Tzu's work was influenced by the *Tao Te Ching*.

But the fact that Sun Tzu does not directly quote or refer to Lao Tzu means that the case for influence must be made through close reading. To create a persuasive case for influence, begin by listing each text's main points:

Tao te Ching	The Art of War
• Exertion is unnecessary.	• The best way to win a battle is not to fight it.
• Leaders should allow things to happen naturally.	• An enemy should be taken intact, without destroying cities.
• Distinctions between people are counterproductive.	• Understanding military strategy is important.
• Genuine power is achieved by allowing others to come to you.	• Politicians should not interfere with generals.
• The best way to govern people is not to govern them.	• Harmonious human relations are important to victory.
• It is impossible to influence the course of events.	• Commanders should know themselves.
• War is senseless.	• Commanders should know their enemies.
• Leaders should always follow "the Way."	

Lurking amid all of the different assertions in these two texts is one undeniable similarity: Sun Tzu, like Lao Tzu, believes that winning through inaction (that is, never having to fight) is superior to winning through action (that is, superior numbers or strategies). Given the prevalence of Taoist ideas during the time in which Sun Tzu wrote, this similarity is not likely coincidental; rather, it is strong evidence of a pattern of influence.

Locate a Larger Theme

Another way to synthesize ideas is to show how a text fits into a larger theme, or big idea. Many of the selections in this book attest to the fact that human beings struggling with similar questions often come up with similar—or at least partially similar—answers. Cultures and individuals with no connections to each other have arrived at strikingly similar responses to questions such as "Is human nature good or evil?", "Is war ever justified?", and "Do we have a responsibility to those less fortunate than ourselves?"

To see how individual ideas fit into larger themes or patterns, consider the following five images:

- Dorothea Lange: *Migrant Mother*
- Pablo Picasso: *Guernica*
- William Hogarth: *Gin Lane*
- Joseph Wright of Derby: *An Experiment on a Bird in the Air Pump*
- Lisa Yuskavage: *Babie I*

The following chart attempts to describe the mother-and-child theme of each work as it relates to the work's larger theme.

Work	Description of Mother-And-Child Scene	Overall Theme
Dorothea Lange: *Migrant Mother*	The mother holds a baby to her breast, shelters it from the camera and the squalor of the lean-to.	The determination of a mother to protect her children
Pablo Picasso: *Guernica*	An anguished mother holds the twisted body of a dead child.	The anguish of war
William Hogarth: *Gin Lane*	A drunken mother reaches for a dip of snuff while her infant child falls to its death.	The negative consequences of alcoholism
Joseph Wright of Derby: *An Experiment on a Bird in the Air Pump*	A terrified mother turns away from the experiment while holding her daughter, who looks on with a mix of terror and curiosity.	The mixed reaction to scientific progress during the Enlightenment
Lisa Yuskavage: *Babie I*	A woman who does not appear to be a wife or a mother holds a wilting bouquet of flowers.	The ambiguous position of a woman who does not have a child in a society that values women primarily as wives and mothers

As this chart shows, the connection between the works goes beyond simply the existence of a mother-and-child pair: in each case the relationship between the mother and the child reflects the argument of the overall work. In the painting about anguish, the mother is in anguish over the child; in the painting about alcoholism, the mother's alcoholism causes the child's death. A connection of this kind could lead to a very strong synthesis essay that could go beyond the five works here and draw conclusions about the overall theme of mothers and children in art. The introduction to such an essay might look like this:

Mothers and Children in Art

The bond between a mother and her children goes deeper than the patterns of any particular culture; the mother-child bond has a sound basis in evolution and forms one of the few truly universal elements of the human experience. For this reason, strong connections between mothers and children can be found in almost every human society, and depictions of mothers and children can be found in almost every kind of art. This does not mean, however, that the depictions are all the same. Different cultures value different things at different times, and artistic production usually follows along. However, because the connection between mothers and children is universally strong in human societies, artists from a variety of cultures have been able to use this connection as the basis for a variety of different arguments about the human condition.

SYNTHESIZING IDEAS
TO FORM YOUR OWN ARGUMENT

One mark of a strong writer is his or her ability to form ideas that draw upon other sources but are neither slavish imitations of, nor uncritical reactions to, other people's opinions. This synthesis process lies at the very heart of critical analysis.

Synthesizing Ideas:
A Model from Classical Rhetoric

When you encounter a new idea, you need not accept it as absolute truth *or* reject it out of hand. In their discussions of invention, ancient rhetoricians identified five different ways that an idea could affect a reader or a listener. One reaction from a reader or a listener is absolute and uncritical agreement, while another is complete disagreement. Ancient rhetoricians recognized that most reactions fall somewhere in between. The other three cases, explored below, illustrate how your reaction to an idea can lead you to synthesize ideas to form your own.

You can simply become informed about an issue. Often, the process of coming up with your own idea requires nothing more than the knowledge that an issue exists and an understanding of the arguments that compose it. Once you understand how an issue has been defined, you can apply your own experience to make informed judgments about it. It is often valuable to read other people's ideas simply to become informed about the issues that they discuss.

If, for example, you are unaware of the debate among scientists trying to describe human nature as either a biological or a sociological phenomenon ("nature vs. nature"), Edward Wilson's "The Fitness of Human Nature" is probably not going to convince you one way or the other. However, it is enough to give non-specialists a vocabulary for discussing the issues, thereby paving the way for future discussions and arguments.

You can become convinced that an issue is important. Very often people recognize an issue without really understanding its importance or its consequences. This was the case in 1798 when Thomas Malthus wrote *An Essay on the Principle of Population*. People at the time understood that populations were increasing, but they saw this as a good thing because it increased available labor and kept the price of goods down. Malthus, however, demonstrated with compelling arguments that increases in population would eventually outstrip increases in food supply and cause serious catastrophes for societies that did not control their growth rates.

Malthus's arguments awakened people to the dangers of unchecked population growth and opened a door for people to generate their own ideas about how best to deal with the problem. As it turns out, most modern thinkers who label themselves "Malthusian" advocate solutions to the problem of overpopulation that Malthus rejected—they have taken his ideas and synthesized them with other facts, policies, and values to create their own ideas. Malthus was a devout Anglican minister who believed that contraception was a sin and abortion an unspeakable evil. These beliefs, however, have not stopped Malthus's ideas from becoming the cornerstone of modern arguments favoring wide distribution of birth control and universal access to abortion. Those who hold such views are not being inconsistent; they are simply synthesizing Malthus's ideas about the importance of a problem with their own opinions of how best to solve it.

You can agree with only some points of an argument. Though writers often present their ideas as all-or-nothing propositions, you do not have to accept them as such. Most arguments are composed of different elements that often can be separated from each other and accepted on their own. It is perfectly valid to reject some elements of an argument and accept others.

For example, Garrett Hardin's "Lifeboat Ethics: The Case against Helping the Poor" includes the following assertions:

1. Overpopulation is a threat to human civilization.
2. Third-world countries are increasing in population at a rate much faster than first-world countries.
3. Giving food and other kinds of aid to overpopulated countries simply allows them to continue to increase their populations without paying a price.
4. Allowing immigration from overpopulated countries into other countries has the same effect as giving food aid to those countries.
5. Developed nations should therefore close their borders to immigration and stop the policy of giving food or other kinds of aid to overpopulated, under-developed countries.

It is possible to accept some of these assertions while rejecting others, and even to agree with Hardin's premises and disagree with his conclusions. One might argue, for example, that food aid is a way to persuade other countries to adopt population control strategies. Or one could present evidence that population decreases when standards of living increase, and that it is in our best interest to raise the standards of living of people in "developing countries" so that they will decrease their own populations naturally. You can combine some of his arguments with your own observations to construct a synthesis that is uniquely your own.

Synthesizing Ideas: A Model from Philosophy

In the early part of the nineteenth century, the German philosopher Georg Wilhelm Friedrich Hegel (1770–1831) developed a system for synthesizing ideas that has become known as "Hegelian dialectic." Hegelian dialectic involves three steps, known to Hegel's students as the thesis, the antithesis, and the synthesis. In Hegel's sense of the word, a thesis is a proposition, an antithesis is an opposite proposition, and a synthesis is a third proposition that resolves the apparent contradiction between the two. Here is an example using the works of Mencius and Hsün Tzu that were discussed earlier in this chapter:

Thesis: Human nature is inherently good (Mencius).

Antithesis: Human nature is inherently evil (Hsün Tzu).

Synthesis: *Neither inherently good nor inherently evil, human nature is inherently self-interested, which can be "good" in some circumstances and "evil" in others.*

In the Hegelian model, the interplay between opposites, which is referred to as a "dialectic," occurs constantly, with each synthesis becoming a new thesis that provokes an antithesis and requires a new synthesis. For example, the "synthesis" statement above can become a new thesis:

Thesis: Human nature is self-interested.

Antithesis: Human nature is altruistic.

Synthesis: *There is no real opposition between selfishness and altruism, since human beings often perceive their own self-interest in helping others in their family and their society.*

And, of course, this synthesis can produce yet another trio of arguments:

Thesis: People help others because they perceive it to be in their own best interest.

Antithesis: People often act altruistically when there is no hope of self-interest, as when soldiers sacrifice their lives to save others.

Synthesis: *Even the utmost altruistic acts can be based on a form of self-interest, as when people who sacrifice their lives to help others derive pleasure from the knowledge that they are doing so.*

At this point, the exercise of resolving antitheses has led us to formulate an idea that is solidly based on the ideas of Mencius and Hsün Tzu without duplicating either of their opinions exactly. Any of the three "synthesis" propositions in this exercise could be refined to make an original and creative thesis. Taken together, they form the basis for the following sample paper, which also draws on ideas from Ruth Benedict and Thomas Hobbes to achieve a synthesis that does not completely accept or reject any of its source materials.

Human Nature, Morality, and Altruism:
Are People Good, or What?

As Confucianism became more and more influential in ancient China, even the major Confucians could not agree on one key issue: is human nature essentially good or essentially evil? Mencius, the most influential Confucian besides Confucius himself, weighed in strongly on the side of inherent human virtue. His fellow Confucian, Hsün Tzu, believed the opposite—he felt that people are inherently evil. Though this same debate has been replicated in most of the great religions and philosophies of the world, the terms that it incorporates are problematic. *Human nature can be neither inherently good nor inherently evil, since "good" and "evil" are constructed differently by different cultures.*

In "The Individual and the Pattern of Culture," Ruth Benedict explains how different behaviors can be seen in different moral lights by different cultures. Eating a relative's dead body would be seen as a horribly evil act by someone in New York. Not eating a relative's dead body, on the other hand, would be seen as an unforgivable moral lapse in some parts of New Guinea. With these variations in what constitutes good and evil, it is impossible to ascribe either character trait to humanity in the abstract. The most that can be said is that human beings are inherently disposed or inherently not disposed to act according to the dictates of their home cultures.

One could argue with much more conviction, however, that human beings are inherently self-interested. In certain states, such as the Hobbesian "state of nature," this self-interest leads to a state of "war of all against all." However, Hobbes also argues that human beings, recognizing their self-interest, come together and form societies and act—often altruistically—to preserve those societies. When this is the case, self-interest is at the heart of behavior that both Mencius and Hsün Tzu would undoubtedly have seen as "good." *There is, therefore, no real opposition between selfishness and altruism, since human beings often perceive their own self-interest in helping others in their family and their society.*

Yet there are some occasions—especially in times of war, plague, famine, or great oppression—in which people act altruistically when there is no possibility of this act working in their own favor. A young marine throwing himself on a hand grenade to save his companions, a mother giving the last bit of food to her family and starving to death, a political dissident taking on a totalitarian regime knowing that it will mean death—actions of these sorts can be documented in cultures throughout the world, and yet they do not seem to be accounted for by a theory of human nature as inherently selfish.

However, *even the utmost altruistic acts can be based on a form of self-interest, as when people who sacrifice their lives to help others derive pleasure from the knowledge that they are doing so.* Nothing is wrong with such a feeling. It would be foolish to suggest that people who derived pleasure in helping others were acting "selfishly" in the normal, pejorative sense of the word. It is reasonable, however, to assume that they would not act in this way unless they derived satisfaction from doing so—and satisfaction, even when earned through acts of great self-sacrifice, is "selfish" in the broadest sense of the word.

To return to the debate between Mencius and Hsün Tzu, it is fair to say that the two great Chinese thinkers used the terms "good" and "evil" when they really meant "selfish" and "unselfish." A close examination of human societies, however, supports the argument that no ironclad distinction exists between selfish and unselfish action, since both are, in some way or another, in the perceived self-interest of the people who act. The most that can be said about the "inherent" properties of human nature is that human nature is inherently self-interested—and that this is not necessarily a bad thing.

QUOTING, PARAPHRASING, AND SUMMARIZING

Here are a few suggestions for working with quotations, paraphrases, and summaries. More specific suggestions on each kind of citation follow. As a general rule, these three methods help you to illustrate, establish, or support your own argument, but you should not allow quotations, paraphrases, and summaries to speak for you. Whenever you cite—that is, refer to—other people's ideas, your reader must be able to differentiate between those ideas and your own.

Quoting

When you quote a source, you reproduce the language of that source exactly. Quoting is the best choice when the original wording is so eloquent or focused that something would be lost in changing it.

Select quotations carefully. Select a few quotations that express important points within your argument. Make sure that every word of quoted material is relevant to your argument—quotations that are unnecessarily long distract the reader from your ideas.

Introduce the context for a quotation. Let your readers know where your citation originated—who said or wrote it, why he or she is an authority, and where the citation can be found. Establishing that context clarifies the importance of the citation for the reader and, more often than not, will make the cited material more interesting and persuasive.

> Awkward: Princes cannot always be moral. "And you have to understand this, that a prince, especially a new one, cannot observe all those things for which men are esteemed, being often forced, in order to maintain the state, to act contrary to faith, friendship, humanity, and religion" (Machiavelli 405) .

> Revised: Machiavelli writes that, while leaders should try to be moral when possible, they are often required by circumstances to act in ways that are contrary to "faith, friendship, humanity, and religion" (Machiavelli 405).

Maintain control of the verb tense and sentence structure. If you quote someone else's words within your writing, you need to control the verb tense and sentence structure of your writing while still using the exact words of your source. Pay close attention to the verb tenses, subject-verb agreement, and noun-pronoun agreement when you incorporate a quote into your writing. If you need to, rewrite your sentence or use ellipses or brackets to alter the quotation.

> Awkward: Machiavelli believed about princes, "and you have to understand this, that a prince, especially a new one, cannot observe all those things for which men are esteemed" (405).

> Revised: Machiavelli did not believe that rulers should be immoral simply for the sake of immorality, but he did believe that practically minded political leaders did not have the luxury of observing "all those things for which men are esteemed" (405).

Use block style for long quotations. Block quotations are a good strategy for analyzing long passages from a text or for citing passages that are difficult to summarize and extremely important for your argument. However, you should use this strategy sparingly—only when the material is extremely important and there is no better way to incorporate it into your essay.

If you use a block quotation, introduce it clearly and then present the quotation indented (in MLA style, it should be ten spaces from the left margin; in APA style, five spaces). Here is an example of how a block quotation looks within an essay:

> One of Machiavelli's most controversial points is that leaders must be willing to act in immoral ways when doing so will preserve the stability of their government:
>
>> A prince, especially a new one, cannot observe all those things for which men are esteemed, being often forced, in order to maintain the state, to act contrary to faith, friendship, humanity, and religion. Therefore it is necessary for him to have a mind ready to turn itself accordingly as the winds and variations of fortune force it, yet, as I have said above, not to diverge from the good if he can avoid doing so, but, if compelled, then to know how to set about it. (405)

Use ellipses (...) and brackets ([ ]) to indicate changes in a quotation. Occasionally, you will be able to create a very poignant short quote by using just the beginning phrases and ending phrases from a long paragraph. Or you might find that a word or two in the middle of a sentence would confuse your reader by referencing material in a section of the text that you are not quoting. In instances such as these, you may use ellipsis marks (...) to indicate the omission of words in quoted material.

If you need to change the text of a quotation, use brackets ([ ]) to indicate the altered text. You most commonly will use brackets to change the verb tense to make the quoted material compatible with your own syntax, so that you can use the quote in the middle of your sentence. Adding a phrase in brackets can also allow you to clarify a confusing term or substitute a noun for a pronoun.

For example, the extended block quote above from Machiavelli's *The Prince* could be effectively altered within an essay like this:

> Machiavelli argued that it was "necessary for [a prince] to have a mind ready to turn itself accordingly as the winds and variations of fortune force it . . . not to diverge from the good if he can avoid doing so, but, if compelled, then to know how to set about it" (405).

Ellipses and brackets are acceptable when used to focus an argument or to clarify meaning, but they should never be used to change the meaning of the quotation or misrepresent the author's intent.

Paraphrasing

Paraphrase if you do not need to reproduce the exact wording of a source, but wish to restate its information. A paraphrase uses your own words and sentence structure, includes the source's main points and details, and is usually the same length as the original.

Indicate source. Whenever you use someone else's ideas, you need to credit them—even if the wording is entirely your own (as it must be in a paraphrase). For guidelines on documenting your sources in MLA and APA styles, see p. 210.

Use your own words and your own sentence structure. By definition, a paraphrase must be in your own words and your own structure. One common way of trying to get around this rule is the "half-baked paraphrase," which attempts to use slightly different words to reproduce the ideas in a source. The first paragraph below comes from Margaret Mead's essay "Warfare: An Invention—Not a Biological Necessity"; the second is an example of a half-baked paraphrase of the same passage:

> Source: Warfare is just an invention known to the majority of human societies by which they permit their young men either to accumulate prestige or avenge their honor or acquire loot or wives or slaves or sago lands or cattle or appease the blood lust of their gods or the restless souls of the recently dead. It is just an invention, older and more widespread than the jury system, but none the less an invention. (500)

> Improper paraphrase: According to Margaret Mead, war is only a discovery that most human cultures have in common, one that enables them to allow their youth to acquire honor or revenge or to get money, women, servants, property, or livestock or to placate their deities' desire for blood or the souls of those who have died recently. War is simply a discovery, one that has been around longer than trial by jury, but still a discovery. (500)

The second paragraph is far too close in sentence structure and wording to be a true paraphrase; the writer has not really used his own words. Here is an example of a proper paraphrase of the same passage:

> **Proper paraphrase:** Margaret Mead argues persuasively that warfare is not an inevitable product of human nature. Rather, it was invented in most (not all) societies as an economic or religious tool, to permit young men in that society to become wealthy or worship appropriately. Although it is older and more common than many other inventions, like the jury system, it too was created for a purpose. (500)

Enclose in quotation marks any wording that is not your own. If you find in writing a paraphrase that you want to use wording from the original source, make sure that you enclose it in quotation marks. It should be clearly distinguished from your own wording and be properly documented. (See p. 210 for information on how to document sources.)

Summarizing

If you want to highlight only the most important details of a passage, summarize. Unlike quotations or paraphrases, summaries should not include details. Instead, summaries highlight the aspects of a source that are most important or most relevant to your argument. Keep your summaries short and focused, trim away any extraneous detail, and concentrate on what's most important. See, for example, how the following passage uses summaries to highlight and compare the main ideas from two texts:

> Even liberal modern philosophers cannot agree with each other about our moral responsibility to the poor. On the one hand, in "Two Principles of Justice," John Rawls insists that a basic understanding of fairness requires us to distribute our resources in a way that everybody would see as fair if they viewed it from a neutral perspective (354). Garrett Hardin, on the other hand, believed that giving food, money, or other resources to poor people, especially those in less developed countries, is actually an immoral action. In "Lifeboat Ethics: The Case against Helping the Poor," Hardin argues that the earth's carrying capacity is limited and that it is unfair to allow people to exceed this capacity by having more children than the planet can support—thus placing everyone in danger (360).

Use your own words. Like a paraphrase, a summary by definition must be in your own words. Avoid using words and phrases similar to those in the source.

Indicate the source. Whenever you use or cite someone else's ideas, you need to credit them—even if the wording is entirely your own. For guidelines on documenting your sources in MLA and APA styles, see p. 210.

DOCUMENTING SOURCES

Whenever you use another's ideas or refer to a source in your writing, you need to provide documentation—identifying information—for your source. Plagiarism is any use of another person's idea without proper documentation. Whether it's intentional or not, plagiarism is an act of academic dishonesty that can have serious repercussions. Plagiarism includes (1) using the exact words of a writer without quotation marks, (2) using a writer's words, ideas, or both without an in-text citation or other form of documentation, and (3) paraphrasing or summarizing another writer's ideas by using the language or sentence structure of the original source. All of the following elements must be documented:

Ideas You Have Summarized or Paraphrased from a Source

It is plagiarism to summarize, paraphrase, or just use someone's ideas without attributing those ideas to their source.

In the example from "Warfare: An Invention—Not a Biological Necessity," it would have been dishonest for the writer of the paraphrase to take credit in any way for the basic idea of Mead's essay: that warfare is an invention that spread from culture to culture rather than an inherent element of the human condition. Any idea that you borrow from another source must be attributed to that source, even if all the writing is your own.

Visuals that you did not create—photographs, tables, charts, graphs, and so on—must also be cited. If the visuals are ones you created, make sure that you acknowledge the work as your own.

Facts That Are Not Considered Common Knowledge

In the middle of "Warfare: An Invention—Not a Biological Necessity," Margaret Mead writes that the Andaman pygmies living in the Bay of Bengal had a knowledge of organized warfare long before they ever encountered Europeans or other more technologically sophisticated societies. Even if you use this fact in another context (say in an essay about the organization of pygmy tribes), you must still cite Mead as the basis for this information, because it is not what scholars call "common knowledge."

In this context, "common knowledge" refers to the kind of information that is generally known or that is easily available in reference works. For example, the facts that the Andaman Islands are in the Bay of Bengal and that the native inhabitants of these islands are pygmies can be readily found in reference books and online, making them part of the pool of general knowledge. You would not need to cite Mead (or anyone else) as your source for these facts.

Approaches or Organizational Strategies Borrowed from a Source

Creating interesting, subtle frameworks for discussing ideas is one of a writer's most important skills. If, in searching for such a framework, you borrow from someone else's work, you must acknowledge it. Imagine, for example, that, in searching for a way to compare Machiavelli's *The Prince* and de Pizan's *Treasure of the City of Ladies*, you came across a website comparing them as "political theories," "cultural theories," and "theories of history." If you used these three categories in your own essay, you would need to acknowledge the website as your source—even if your actual comparisons did not borrow at all from the original source.

Anyone Who Has Helped You Develop Your Ideas

Whenever you collaborate with other people on your writing, make sure you give them proper credit. (Keep in mind that your instructor might not allow collaboration of any kind, in which case the ideas that you come up with must be entirely your own.) Contributions from other students, professors, colleagues, friends, and family should be acknowledged either in the body of the text or in a footnote or an endnote that explicitly gives credit where it is due. A note such as "Thanks to Dr. Mary Johnson of the Department of Psychology for her contribution to my understanding of Freud's concept of the ego" can be placed either at the end of an essay or at the point in your argument where the relevant discussion occurs.

DOCUMENTATION STYLES

Different academic disciplines use several different styles to document sources. Two common styles for undergraduate writing are the Modern Language Association (MLA) style and the American Psychological Association (APA) style. Before writing an essay, determine which style your instructor prefers and refer to an official style guide for detailed instructions on using that style. The guidelines that follow are not a replacement for a style manual, which provides much more detail on different kinds of documentation.

MLA Style

This style originated for the discussion of literature and is currently used in many humanities disciplines. MLA format places a minimal amount of information in an in-text citation and puts full bibliographical citations at the end on a Works Cited page.

In-text documentation

When you cite another source in your own writing, place enough information in parentheses for the reader to locate the source on your Works Cited page. If you have already identified your source, put the page number in parentheses immediately after the citation. Place the parentheses after the closing quotation marks but before the period:

> According to civil rights leader Martin Luther King, a law is unjust if it "is a code that a majority inflicts on a minority that is not binding on itself" (435).

If you're citing a source that doesn't have page numbers, such as a website, include the paragraph or section number in parentheses:

> According to the Nobel Prize organization, King "led a massive protest in Birmingham, Alabama, that caught the attention of the entire world, providing what he called a coalition of conscience, and inspiring his 'Letter from a Birmingham Jail'" (par. 3).

Quotations that run for more than four lines should be set off in blocks, without quotation marks. In the block-quote format, the parenthetical citation comes after the period:

> King criticized the view that laws should always be obeyed by citing the example of Nazi Germany's laws against helping Jews:
>> We should never forget that everything Adolf Hitler did in Germany was "legal" and everything the Hungarian freedom fighters did in Hungary was "illegal." It was "illegal" to aid and comfort a Jew in Hitler's Germany. Even so, I am sure that, had I lived in Germany at the time, I would have aided and comforted my Jewish brothers. (436)

If a paragraph does not give enough information to identify a citation, then include the author's name parenthetically:

> Many people believe that disobeying laws that are unjust is actually an expression of "the very highest respect for the law" (King 435).

If you have two works by the same author, add a word or phrase from the title to identify the work:

> King draws three different distinctions between "just laws" and "unjust laws" ("Letter" 434–35).

Bibliographical citations

Full bibliographical citations are given at the end of an essay on a separate page titled "Works Cited." The Works Cited page lists sources alphabetically by author, or, if an author is unavailable, by title. When an author is listed multiple times, the listings are arranged alphabetically by title. Below are the formats for some of the most common kinds of citations that you will need on your Works Cited page.

Single-Author Book

Elshtain, Jean Bethke. *Just War against Terror: The Burden of American Power in a Violent World.* New York: Basic, 2003. Print.

Multiple-Author Book (Fewer than Four Authors)

Malless, Stanley, and Jeffrey McQuain. *Coined by God: Words and Phrases That First Appear in the English Translations of the Bible.* New York: Norton, 2003. Print.

Works in an Anthology

Weil, Simone. "Equal." *Reading the World: Ideas That Matter.* 3rd ed. Ed. Michael Austin. New York: Norton, 2015. 571. Print.

Single-Author Journal Article (Paginated by Volume)

Weinberger, Jerry. "Pious Princes and Red-Hot Lovers: The Politics of Shakespeare's *Romeo and Juliet.*" *Journal of Politics* 65 (2003): 370–75. Print.

Multiple-Author Journal Article (Paginated by Issue)

Weaver, Constance, Carol McNally, and Sharon Moerman. "To Grammar or Not to Grammar: That Is *Not* the Question!" *Voices from the Middle* 8.3 (2001): 17–33. Print.

Scholarly Edition

Austen, Jane. *Sense and Sensibility.* Ed. Claudia Johnson. New York: Norton, 2001. Print.

Magazine Article—Monthly

Hawass, Zahi. "Egypt's Forgotten Treasures." *National Geographic* Jan. 2003: 74–87. Print.

Magazine Article—Weekly

Samuelson, Robert J. "The Changing Face of Poverty." *Newsweek* 18 Oct. 2004: 50. Print.

Newspaper Article

> Farenthold, David. "Town Shaken by Lobster Theft." *Washington Post*
>   9 Oct. 2005: A3. Print.

Article from an Electronic Database

> Moore, Kathleen D. "The Truth of the Barnacles: Rachel Carson and
>   the Moral Significance of Wonder." *Environmental Ethics* 27.3 (Fall
>   2005): 265–77. *Academic Search Premier*. Web. 9 Oct. 2005.

Work That Appears Only Online

> Nasr, Seyyed Hossein. "The Meaning and Concept of Philosophy in
>   Islam." *Islamic Philosophy Online*. Ed. Muhammed Hozien. Islamic
>   Philosophy Online, Inc., 5 May 2007. Web. 23 Apr. 2009.
> Gross, Daniel. "The Quitter Economy." *Slate*. Slate, 24 Jan. 2009. Web.
>   26 April 2009.

Online Work also in Print

> Dowd, Maureen. "Sacred Cruelties." *New York Times*, 7 April 2002.
>   Web. 9 Oct. 2005.

APA Style

APA style is used in most social sciences, including education, nursing, and social work. In-text citations in the APA style give a publication date as well as a name, with full bibliographic information provided on a References page.

Before writing an essay, determine which style your instructor prefers and refer to an official style guide for detailed instructions on using that style. The following table gives brief guidelines in MLA and APA styles for some of the most common documentation tasks. This table is not a replacement for a style manual, which provides much more detail on different kinds of documentation.

In-text documentation

When you summarize the contents of an article, document the source by placing the date immediately after the author's name:

> King (1963) discusses the role of civil disobedience in trying to change unjust laws.

APA guidelines require page numbers at the end of quotations. This is also true if you paraphrase a passage or cite a fact that can be found on a specific page:

> King (1963) defined an unjust law as one "not rooted in eternal and natural law" (p. 434).

> King (1963) argued that moral laws take precedence over human laws (p. 434).

In APA articles, it is not unusual to have two sources by the same author (since someone working on a given topic in the social sciences will often contribute to several papers as part of an overall study). If the texts are from the same year, use lowercase letters to distinguish between different articles:

> King (1963b) asserted that people have a moral obligation to disobey unjust laws.

If your text does not contain enough information to identify a source that you are citing, give the name, date, and, if necessary, page number of that source in the parenthetical citation:

> Many in the civil rights movement argued that civil disobedience was a moral duty (King, 1963, p. 434).

If you need to quote more than forty words, set the quotation off in a block. For block quotes, indent five spaces from the left margin and type the quoted text without quotation marks. The parenthetical citation comes after the period:

> King (1963) also believed that laws that were not unjust in their nature could be applied in unjust ways:
>
> > Sometimes a law is just on its face and unjust in its application. For instance, I have been arrested on a charge of parading without a permit. Now, there is nothing wrong in having an ordinance which requires a permit for a parade. But such an ordinance becomes

unjust when it is used to maintain segregation and to deny citizens
the First Amendment privilege of peaceful assembly and protest.
(p. 435)

If you are citing a source that does not have a page number—such as a
webpage—include instead the number of the paragraph where the information can be found, using either the ¶ symbol or the abbreviation "para."

According to the Nobel Prize organization, King "led a massive protest
in Birmingham, Alabama, that caught the attention of the entire world,
providing what he called a coalition of conscience, and inspiring his 'Letter from a Birmingham Jail'" (para. 3).

Bibliographical citations

Full bibliographical citations are given at the end of an essay on a separate
page titled "References." The References page lists works alphabetically by author, or, if an author is unavailable, by title. When an author is listed multiple
times, the listings are arranged by date. Below are the formats for some of the
most common kinds of citations that you will need on your References page.

Single-Author Book

Elshtain, J. B. (2003). *Just war against terror: The burden of American power
in a violent world.* New York, NY: Basic Books.

Multiple-Author Book (Fewer than Four Authors)

Malless, S., & McQuain, J. (2003). *Coined by God: Words and phrases that
first appear in the English translations of the Bible.* New York, NY:
Norton.

Works in an Anthology

Weil, S. (2015). Equality. In M. Austin (Ed.), *Reading the world: Ideas that
matter* (pp. 575–78). New York, NY: Norton. (Original work
published 1940)

Single-Author Journal Article (Paginated by Volume)

Weinberger, J, (2003). Pious princes and red-hot lovers: The politics of
Shakespeare's *Romeo and Juliet. Journal of Politics, 65,* 370–375.

Multiple-Author Journal Article (Paginated by Issue)

Weaver, C., McNally, C., & Moerman, S. (2001). To grammar or not to grammar: That is *not* the question! *Voices from the Middle.* 8(3), 17–33.

Scholarly Edition

Austen, J. (2001). *Sense and sensibility* (C. Johnson, Ed.). New York, NY: Norton.

Magazine Article—Monthly

Hawass, Z. (2003, January). Egypt's forgotten treasures. *National Geographic, 203.* 74–87.

Magazine Article—Weekly

Samuelson, R. J. (2004, October 18). The changing face of poverty, *Newsweek, 144,* 50.

Newspaper Article

Farenthold, D. (2005, October 9). Town shaken by lobster theft. *The Washington Post,* p. A3.

Article from an Electronic Database

Moore, K. D. (2005). The truth of the barnacles: Rachel Carson and the moral significance of wonder. *Environmental Ethics,* 27(3), 265–277. Retrieved from Academic Search Premier database.

Work that Appears Only Online

Nasr, S. H. (2007, May 5). The meaning and concept of philosophy in Islam. Retrieved April 23, 2009, from http://www.muslimphilosophy.com/ip/nasr-ipi.htm

Gross, D. (2009, 24 January). The quitter economy. *Slate.* Retrieved from http://www.slate.com/id/2209617

Online Work also in Print

Dowd, M. (2002, April 7). Sacred cruelties (Electronic version). *New York Times.* Retrieved from http://www.nytimes.com/2002/04/07/opinion/07DOWD.html

Clarissa Porter

Professor Croft

English 101, Section 10

February 13, 2015

Human Nature in Mencius and Hsün Tzu

Mencius and Hsün Tzu were both Chinese scholars living during the Period of Warring States. They were both self-professed Confucians, and they both believed that rites and rituals were necessary in order to perfect human beings. Both Mencius and Hsün Tzu gave a lot of thought to questions of human nature, but, as many writers and scholars have pointed out, they came to very different conclusions. Mencius believed that human beings were inherently good, and that they only act in evil ways when their natural goodness is perverted. Hsün Tzu, on the other hand, believed that human nature is inherently evil and must be corrected by strict religious observances. These differences, however, have often been exaggerated. Mencius and Hsün Tzu have certain theoretical differences about the abstract concept of human nature, but their view of what humans should do is nearly identical.

The differences between Mencius and Hsün Tzu have been the subject of substantial commentary. In *China's Imperial Past*, for example, Charles O. Hucker asserts that

> Whereas Mencius's conception of the essential goodness of
> human nature has led some specialists to characterize him
> as a tenderhearted idealist, it is universally agreed that the

> last great Confucian thinker of the formative age, Hsün Tzu,
> was an unsentimental, ruthlessly tough-minded rationalist.
> His characteristic intellectual approach was "Humbug! Let's
> consider the facts." (82)

Hucker's characterization here is backed up by the authors themselves. Mencius argues that "human nature is inherently good, just like water inherently flows downhill. There is no such thing as a person who isn't good, just as there's no water that doesn't flow downhill" (79). Hsün Tzu directly contradicts this. "Mencius," Hsün Tzu says, "states that man's nature is good, and that all evil arises because he loses his original nature. Such a view, I believe, is erroneous" (86). Even the title of Hsün Tzu's essay, "Man's Nature Is Evil," betrays his fundamental difference with Mencius.

The difference between the two Confucian scholars is fundamental, but is it important? Some scholars believe that the differences between them stem from different views of morality but that, in the words of David E. Soles, "they are in substantial agreement as to the empirical facts of human nature" (123). Soles believes that the differences between Mencius and Hsün Tzu are real, but that these differences are not the result of the two considering sets of facts about human behavior. Both philosophers acknowledge that human beings sometimes act morally and sometimes immorally. They differ drastically in what they see as the root cause for this behavior—Mencius believes that people are immoral when they deny their natures and Hsün Tzu believes that they are immoral when they do not. Amazingly, though, these differences do not result in any practical differences in the behavior that they recommend.

Like Confucius, Hsün Tzu believes that we must all shape our characters through an elaborate series of purifying rituals. These rituals, he believes, turn inherently evil people into moral beings:

> Mencius states that man is capable of learning because his nature is good, but I say that this is wrong. It indicates that he has not really understood man's nature nor distinguished properly between the basic nature and conscious activity. The nature is that which is given by Heaven; you cannot learn it, you cannot acquire it by effort. Ritual principles, on the other hand, are created by sages; you can learn to apply them, you can work to bring them to completion. That part of man which cannot be learned or acquired by effort is called the nature; that part of him which can be acquired by learning and brought to completion by effort is called conscious activity. This is the difference between nature and conscious activity. (85)

Conscious activity is just as important to Mencius, who, according to the online edition of the *Stanford Encyclopedia*, "regarded the transformative power of a cultivated person as the ideal basis for government. In addition, he spelled out more explicitly the idea that order in society depends on proper attitudes within the family, which in turn depends on cultivating oneself." Mencius believed that people should engage in ritual self-cultivation through the very same Confucian rituals advocated by Hsün Tzu.

For Hsün Tzu, Confucian rituals are necessary to change human nature into something good. For Mencius, they are necessary to cultivate raw human nature, which is already good, into the polished attributes of a gentleman. Their philosophical views could not be farther apart, but in the end, the behavioral norms that they expound are very similar, and their dedication to Confucian rituals is identical. Their enmity is limited to the realm of the abstract. In practice, they would have us do the same things, albeit for very different reasons.

Porter   5

Works Cited

Hsün Tzu. "Man's Nature Is Evil." *Reading the World: Ideas That Matter.*
    3rd ed. Ed. Michael Austin. New York: Norton, 2015. 84–92. Print.

Hucker, Charles O. *China's Imperial Past: An Introduction to Chinese
    History and Culture.* Stanford, CA: Stanford UP, 1975. Print.

Mencius. "Man's Nature Is Good." *Reading the World: Ideas That Matter.*
    3rd ed. Ed. Michael Austin. New York: Norton, 2015. 78–82. Print.

Shun, Kwong Loi. "Mencius." 2004. *Stanford Encyclopedia of Philosophy.*
    Web. 11 Feb. 2009.

Soles, David E. "The Nature and Grounds of Xunzi's Disagreement with
    Mencius." *Asian Philosophy* 9.2 (1999): 123–33. Print.

Revising and Editing

WRITING IS NOT A PRODUCT but a process—a draft can always be revised, reshaped, reformed, and improved. Once you've finished a draft of an essay, it's best to put it aside for a day or two and then approach it with a fresh eye—a "re-vision."

Revising a draft often means reimagining it from the ground up. During revision you'll want to rethink the basic ideas of your essay and rewrite the text as needed. You may revisit several stages of the writing process, perhaps doing more research, revising your thesis, and reorganizing your draft. Just as a renovated building often looks nothing like it did before renovations, it is not uncommon for writers to find that, after two or three revisions, almost nothing remains of the drafts that they started with.

Once you've completed rethinking and rewriting—a process you may go through several times—it's time to edit. This is the time to correct errors in spelling, punctuation, and grammar, and check for other mechanical issues.

In the following pages are guidelines and suggestions for the revision process—for rethinking, rewriting, and editing your essays.

Rethinking

Give yourself plenty of time. Good writing takes time. You cannot create and revise multiple drafts the night before an essay is due. Your best essays will be the ones that you start well in advance of their due date and keep thinking about until they are done. This does not necessarily mean that you must spend more time on a paper than do those who procrastinate until the very end. Six hours spread over a week will almost always produce a better paper than six hours spent the night before it is due.

Ask other people to read your draft and provide feedback. The very act of writing suggests an audience, and, to be sure, your instructor will generally be the final audience for your efforts. But it is usually a good idea to get feedback on a draft during the revision process. A friend, a classmate, or a writing tutor can let you know if you have effectively translated your ideas into written words—and even if the ideas were worth translating in the first place.

Reread the assignment and make sure that you have followed it correctly. Good writing meets the expectations of its audience. When the audience is a teacher who has given you an assignment, you must make absolutely certain that you have followed the instructions as closely as possible. Refer to the assignment guidelines when you have finished a draft and again when you're revising—just to make sure that, in the process of crafting your essay, you have not strayed away from the assignment or failed to answer a critical question asked by the instructor.

Identify your thesis and consider how each part of the essay supports it. It's not unusual to discover what you are trying to say while you are writing your first draft. If you find that, by the end of your draft, you're focusing on a different thesis from the one you started with, you'll want to revise your original thesis statement or revise other parts of your essay. In either case, make sure that your entire essay, all your evidence, develops and supports the same thesis—and make sure that that thesis is clearly indicated.

Don't be afraid to throw out ideas that don't work. One of the hardest things for any writer to do is to cut out words, sentences, or whole paragraphs that he or she has spent a substantial amount of time creating. After we labor over a piece of writing, we feel an ownership of, and even a responsibility to, the words that we have brought into being. But nobody has good ideas all of the time, and even good ideas can be extraneous if they don't support the thesis. If you decide that an idea is not worth pursuing, or that it doesn't support or develop your thesis, you must be willing to cut it—even if it means scrapping the entire paper and starting over from scratch.

Rewriting

Make sure that your introduction and conclusion are consistent with each other. In the same way that ideas can drift away from the thesis during the course of writing a paper, conclusions can drift away from introductions. Use the revision process as an opportunity to revisit these two crucial paragraphs and make sure that they are working together. You might revise your introduction so that it anticipates your conclusion or revise your conclusion so that it refers to or extends your introduction—just make sure that the two paragraphs tie your essay together. This will encourage readers to view your essay as a self-contained, coherent argument.

Make sure that you have clear transitions between all major ideas. Transitions between ideas are an important part of orienting a reader to your paper. They can also be difficult to include in a first draft, since you are so often discovering ideas through the process of writing. You should therefore check the beginning and end of each paragraph and revise as needed to include transitions that move readers gracefully and seamlessly from one idea to the next.

Look for ways to eliminate useless words and phrases. It's easy to fall into the trap of using more words than are needed to convey an idea. But fewer words often mean clearer, more elegant prose. If you look carefully at your first draft, you will probably find it full of "deadwood": "there is" or "there are" at the beginnings of sentences; wordy constructions such as "because of the fact that"; and unnecessary additions and qualifications of all kinds. As you rewrite, look for ways to eliminate extra words that do not add meaning.

Pay attention to your ethos. Readers usually judge writers by the ethos—the overall persona—projected in a piece of writing. During the revision process, pay special attention to the ethos that you are projecting. This is the time to build rapport and establish credibility with your readers by striking the right tone and making sound arguments.

Editing

Make sure that you have documented every source. The line between accidentally omitting documentation of a quotation and plagiarizing a paper is very thin. As you prepare your final draft for submission, make sure that you have properly documented every outside source that you used in any way.

Refer to a handbook or other source for grammar and usage questions. Many instructors require or recommend a handbook for composition courses. Handbooks contain a wealth of information about grammar rules, punctuation conventions, documentation styles, and other nuts-and-bolts elements of writing. If your instructor has chosen a specific handbook, use it faithfully. If not, select one in your library or bookstore and refer to it when revising your papers.

Read your entire essay out loud to catch any errors you might have missed. Just as reading sentences out loud can help you catch awkward passages, reading an entire essay out loud, carefully and slowly, can help you see missing words, extra characters, spelling errors not caught by spellcheckers, and other problems with your paper that can result from carelessness.

Revising and Editing Checklist

During the revision process, keep the following questions in mind.

Ideas

- Have you met the guidelines for the assignment?
- Have you generated an idea that is original enough to make an impact on the reader?
- Is the idea sufficiently focused?

Structure

- Is there an arguable, well-written thesis?
- Does the introductory paragraph set up the thesis and define key terms in the essay?

- Are there solid, well-constructed transitions between all major ideas?
- Does the concluding paragraph tie together major arguments in the essay and bring the whole to a definite conclusion?

Argument

- Have you considered how your audience will respond to your arguments? How have you appealed to your audience?
- Have you constructed a persuasive ethos? Is it reasonable and knowledgeable?
- Are all of your major claims supported with appropriate evidence?
- Do all of the supporting arguments in the essay support the main thesis? That is, are they relevant and focused?

Correctness

- Have you integrated all quotations, paraphrases, and summaries smoothly into your own writing?
- Have you properly documented all outside sources according to the style guide required by the assignment?
- Have you read your essay out loud to check for awkward phrasing and to catch errors that you might miss reading silently?
- Have you proofread carefully and corrected any errors in grammar, spelling, or punctuation?

THIRTEEN

How to Write Good Sentences

WHEN A COLLEGE STUDENT asked author Annie Dillard, "Do you think I could become a writer?" Dillard replied with a question of her own: "Do you like sentences?" French novelist Gustave Flaubert certainly did, once saying that he "itched with sentences." We'll bet itching with sentences is not something you've experienced—and that liking or not liking sentences is not something you've ever thought about—but we'll also bet that you know something about how important sentences are. Anyone who has ever tried to write the perfect tweet or, better yet, the perfect love letter knows about choosing just the right words for each sentence and about the power of the three-word sentence "I love you"—or the even shorter sentence that sometimes follows from such declarations: "I do."

In his book *How to Write a Sentence,* English professor Stanley Fish declares himself to be a "connoisseur of sentences" and offers some particularly noteworthy examples. Here's one, written by a fourth grader in response to an assignment to write something about a mysterious large box that had been delivered to a school:

▶ I was already on the second floor when I heard about the box.

This reminded us of a favorite sentence of our own, this one the beginning of a story written by a third grader:

▶ Today, the monster goes where no monster has gone before: Cincinnati.

Here the student manages to allude to the famous line from *Star Trek*—"to boldly go where no man has gone before"—while suggesting that Cincinnati is the most exotic place on earth, and even using a colon effectively. It's quite a sentence.

Finally, here's a sentence that opens a chapter from a PhD dissertation on literacy among young people today:

▶ Hazel Hernandez struck me as an honest thief.

Such sentences are memorable: They startle us a bit and demand attention. They make us want to read more. Who's Hazel Hernandez? What's an honest thief, and what makes her one?

As these examples suggest, you don't have to be a famous author to write a great sentence. In fact, crafting effective and memorable sentences is a skill everyone can master with careful attention and practice. You may not come up with a zinger like the famous sentence John Updike wrote about Ted Williams' fabled home run in his last at bat at Fenway Park—"It was in the books while it was still in the sky"—but you can come close.

Just as certain effects in film—music, close-ups—enhance the story, a well-crafted sentence can bring power to a piece of writing. So think about the kind of effect you want to create in what you're writing—and then look for the type of sentence that will fit the bill. Though much of the power of the examples above comes from being short and simple, remember that some rhetorical situations call for longer, complex sentences—and that the kind of sentence you write also depends on its context, such as whether it's opening an essay, summing up what's already been said, or something else. This chapter looks at some common English sentence patterns and provides some good examples for producing them in your own work.

FOUR COMMON SENTENCE PATTERNS

We make sentences with words—and we arrange those words into patterns. If a sentence is defined as a group of words that expresses a complete thought, then we can identify four basic sentence structures: a simple sentence (expressing one idea); a compound sentence (expressing more than one idea, with the ideas being of equal importance); a complex sentence (expressing more than one idea, with one of the ideas more important than the others); and a compound-complex sentence (with more than one idea of equal importance and at least one idea of less importance).

Simple Sentences: One Main Idea

Let's take a look at some simple sentences:

- ▶ Resist!
- ▶ Consumers revolted.
- ▶ Angry consumers revolted against new debit-card fees.
- ▶ A wave of protest from angry consumers forced banks to rescind the new fees.
- ▶ The growth of the internet and its capacity to mobilize people instantly all over the world have done everything from forcing companies to rescind debit-card fees in the United States to bringing down oppressive governments in the Middle East.

As these examples illustrate, simple sentences can be as short as a single word—or they can be much longer. Each is a simple sentence, however, because it contains a single main idea or thought; in grammatical terms, each contains one and only one main clause. As the name suggests, a simple sentence is often the simplest, most direct way of saying what you want to say—but not always. And often you want a sentence to include more than one idea. In that case, you need to use a compound sentence, a complex sentence, or a compound-complex sentence.

Compound Sentences: Joining Ideas That Are Equally Important

Sometimes you'll want to write a sentence that joins two or more ideas that are equally important, like this one attributed to former President Bill Clinton:

- ▶ You can put wings on a pig, but you don't make it an eagle.

In grammatical terms, this is a compound sentence with two main clauses, each of which expresses one of two equally important ideas. In this case,

Clinton joined the ideas with a comma and the coordinating conjunction *but*. But he had several other options for joining these ideas. For example, he could have joined them with only a semicolon:

▶ You can put wings on a pig; you don't make it an eagle.

Or he could have joined them with a semicolon, a conjunctive adverb like *however*, and a comma:

▶ You can put wings on a pig; however, you don't make it an eagle.

All of these compound sentences are perfectly acceptable—but which seems most effective? In this case, we think Clinton's choice is: It is clear and very direct, and if you read it aloud you'll hear that the words on each side of *but* have the same number of syllables, creating a pleasing, balanced rhythm— and one that balances the two equally important ideas. It also makes the logical relationship between the two ideas explicit; the version with only a semicolon, by contrast, indicates that the ideas are somehow related but doesn't show how.

Using *and*, *but*, and other coordinating conjunctions. In writing a compound sentence, remember that different coordinating conjunctions carry different meanings that signal different logical relationships between the main ideas in the sentence. There are only seven coordinating conjunctions.

COORDINATING CONJUNCTIONS

and	or	yet	nor
but	so	for	

▶ China's one-child policy has slowed population growth, *but* it has helped create a serious gender imbalance in the country's population.

▶ Most of us bike to work, *so* many of us stop off at the gym for a shower first.

▶ The champagne bottle crashed, the crowd cheered, *and* the ship slid down the ramp into the water.

See how the following sentences express different meanings depending on which coordinating conjunction is used:

▶ You could apply to graduate school, *or* you could start looking for a job.

▶ You could apply to graduate school, *and* you could start looking for a job.

Using a semicolon. Joining clauses with a semicolon only is a way of signaling that they are closely related without saying explicitly how. Often the second clause will expand on an idea expressed in the first clause.

▶ My first year of college was a little bumpy; it took me a few months to get comfortable at a large university far from home.

▶ The Wassaic Project is a multidisciplinary arts organization in Dutchess County, New York; artists go there to engage in "art, music, and everything else."

Adding a conjunctive adverb can make the relationship between the ideas more explicit:

▶ My first year of college was a little bumpy; *indeed,* it took me a few months to get comfortable at a large university far from home.

Note that the conjunctive adverb in this sentence, *indeed,* cannot join the two main clauses on its own—it requires a semicolon before it. If you use a conjunctive adverb with only a comma before it, you've made a mistake called a comma splice.

SOME CONJUNCTIVE ADVERBS

also	indeed	otherwise
certainly	likewise	similarly
furthermore	nevertheless	therefore
however	next	thus

READ THROUGH something you've written recently and identify compound sentences joined with and. *When you find one, ask yourself whether it is the best word to use: Does it express the logical relationship between the two parts of the sentence that you intend? Would* but, or, so, for, nor, *or* yet *work better?*

Complex Sentences:
When One Idea Is More Important than Another

Many of the sentences you write will contain two or more ideas, with one more important than the other(s). So you need ways to indicate this difference: In grammatical terms, you want to show that a less important idea is subordinate to a more important one. Instead of putting the less significant idea in a main clause, then, you put it in one of several kinds of subordinate clauses:

▶ Most scientists believe *that global warming is caused by humans.*

▶ Those *who disagree* are a small minority of the scientific community.

▶ *If ocean levels rise significantly,* many cities *that are built at sea level* will be threatened.

As these examples show, the less important ideas—the ones in the subordinate clauses (italicized here)—can't stand alone as sentences: When we read "that global warming is caused by humans" or "who disagree," we know that something's missing. Subordinate clauses begin with words such as *if* or *because*—subordinating conjunctions, words that signal the logical relationship between the subordinate clause and the rest of the sentence.

SOME SUBORDINATING CONJUNCTIONS

after	even though	until
although	if	when
as	since	where
because	that	while
before	though	who

Note that a subordinate clause can come at the end of a sentence, in the middle, or at the beginning. When it comes at the beginning, it is usually followed by a comma, as in the third example. If the opening clause in that sentence is moved to the end, there's no need for a comma: "Many cities that are built at sea level will be threatened if ocean levels rise significantly."

Grammatically, each of the three examples above is a complex sentence: It has one main idea and one or more ideas of less importance. In writing, you will often have to decide whether to combine ideas in a compound sentence, which gives the ideas equal importance, or in a complex one, which makes one idea more important than the other(s). Looking again at our sentence about the pig and the eagle, Bill Clinton could have written it as a complex sentence:

▶ Even though you can put wings on a pig, you don't make it an eagle.

Again, though, we think Clinton made a good choice in giving the two ideas in the sentence equal weight because doing so balances the sentence perfectly, telling us that both parts of the sentence are equally important. In fact, either part of this sentence isn't interesting in itself: It's the balancing and the contrast that make it interesting—and memorable.

Compound-Complex Sentences:
Multiple Ideas—Some Less Important, Some More

When you are expressing three or more ideas in a single sentence, you'll sometimes want to use a compound-complex sentence, which gives some of the ideas equal importance and others less importance. Grammatically, such sentences have at least two main clauses and one subordinate clause.

▶ ────── MAIN CLAUSE ──────┐┌─ SUBORDINATE CLAUSE
We have experienced unparalleled natural disasters that have devastated

──────────┐┌────── MAIN CLAUSE ──────
entire countries, yet identifying global warming as the cause of these

──────────┐
disasters is difficult.

▶ ────── SUBORDINATE CLAUSE ──────┐┌─MAIN
Even after distinguished scientists issued a series of reports, critics

CLAUSE ──────────┐┌────── SUBORDINATE CLAUSE──────┐
continued to question the findings because they claimed results were falsified;

┌────── MAIN CLAUSE ──────┐
nothing would convince them.

As these examples show, English sentence structure is flexible, allowing you to combine groups of words in different ways in order to get your ideas across to your audience most appropriately and effectively. There's seldom only one way to write a sentence to get an idea across: As the author, you must decide which way works best for your rhetorical situation.

WAYS OF EMPHASIZING
THE MAIN IDEA IN A SENTENCE

Sometimes you will want to lead off a sentence with the main point; other times, you might want to hold it in reserve until the end. Cumulative sentences start with a main clause and then add on to it, "accumulating" details. Periodic sentences start with a series of phrases or subordinate clauses and save the main clause for last.

Cumulative Sentences: Starting with the Main Point

In this kind of sentence, the writer starts off with a main clause and then adds details in phrases and subordinate clauses, extending or explaining the thought. Cumulative sentences can be especially useful for describing a place or an event, operating almost like a camera panning across a room or landscape. The sentences below create such an effect:

▶ The San Bernardino Valley lies only an hour east of Los Angeles by the San Bernardino Freeway but is in certain ways an alien place: not the coastal California of the subtropical twilights and the soft westerlies off the Pacific but a harsher California, haunted by the Mojave just beyond the mountains, devastated by the hot dry Santa Ana wind that comes down through the passes at 100 miles an hour and whines through the eucalyptus windbreaks and works on the nerves.
　　　　　　　　　—JOAN DIDION, "Some Dreamers of the Golden Dream"

▶ Public transportation in Cebu City was all about jeepneys: refurbished military jeeps with metal roofs for shade, decorated with horns and mirrors and fenders and flaps; painted with names, dedications, quotations, religious icons, logos—and much, much more.

▶ She hit the brakes, swearing fiercely, as the deer leapt over the hood and crashed into the dark woods beyond.

▶ The celebrated Russian pianist gave his hands a shake, a quick shake, fingers pointed down at his sides, before taking his seat and lifting them imperiously above the keys.

These cumulative sentences add details in a way that makes each sentence more emphatic. Keep this principle in mind as you write—and also when you revise. See if there are times when you might revise a sentence or sentences to add emphasis in the same way. Take a look at the following sentences, for instance:

▶ China has initiated free-market reforms that transformed its economy from a struggling one to an industrial powerhouse. It has become the world's fastest-growing major economy. Growth rates have been averaging 10 percent over the last decade.

These three sentences are clearly related, with each one adding detail about the growth of China's economy. Now look what happens when the writer eliminates a little bit of repetition, adds a memorable metaphor, and combines them as a cumulative—and more emphatic—sentence:

▶ China's free-market reforms have led to 10 percent average growth over the last decade, transforming it from a paper tiger into an industrial dragon that is now the world's fastest-growing major economy.

Periodic Sentences: Delaying the Main Point until the End

In contrast to sentences that open with the main idea, periodic sentences delay the main idea until the very end. Periodic sentences are sometimes fairly long, and withholding the main point until the end is a way of adding emphasis. It can also help create suspense or build up to a surprise or inspirational ending.

▶ In spite of everything, in spite of the dark and twisting path he saw stretching ahead for himself, in spite of the final meeting with Voldemort he knew must come, whether in a month, in a year, or in ten, he felt his heart lift at the thought that there was still one last golden day of peace left to enjoy with Ron and Hermione.   —J. K. ROWLING, *Harry Potter and the Half-Blood Prince*

▶ Unprovided with original learning, uninformed in the habits of thinking, unskilled in the arts of composition, I resolved to write a book.
                    —EDWARD GIBBON, *Memoirs of My Life*

▶ In the week before finals, when my studying and memorizing reached a fever pitch, came a sudden, comforting thought: I have never failed.

Here are three periodic sentences in a row about Whitney Houston, each of which withholds the main point until the end:

▶ When her smiling brown face, complete with a close-cropped Afro, appeared on the cover of *Seventeen* in 1981, she was one of the first African-Americans to grace the cover, and the industry took notice. When she belted out a chilling and soulful version of the "Star-Spangled Banner" at the 1991 Super Bowl, the world sat back in awe of her poise and calm. And in an era when African-American actresses are often given film roles portraying

them as destitute, unloving, unlovable, or just "the help," Houston played
the love interest of Kevin Costner, a white Hollywood superstar.

—ALLISON SAMUELS, "A Hard Climb for the Girl Next Door"

These three periodic sentences create a drumlike effect that builds in intensity as they move through the stages in Houston's career; in all, they suggest
that Houston was, even more than Kevin Costner, a "superstar."

Samuels takes a chance when she uses three sentences in a row that
withhold the main point until the end: Readers may get tired of waiting for
that point. And readers may also find the use of too many such sentences to
be, well, too much. But as the example above shows, when used carefully
a sentence that puts off the main idea just long enough can keep readers'
interest, making them want to reach the ending, with its payoff.

You may find times in your own writing when revising to create a periodic sentence can make your writing more emphatic. Take a look at the
following sentence from an essay on the use of animals in circuses:

▶ The big cat took him down with one swat, just as the trainer, dressed in
khakis and boots, his whip raised and his other arm extended in welcome to
the cheering crowd, stepped into the ring.

This sentence paints a vivid picture, but it gives away all the action in the
first six words. By withholding that action until the end, the writer builds
anticipation and adds emphasis:

▶ Just as the trainer stepped into the ring, dressed in khakis and boots, his
whip raised and his other arm extended in welcome to the cheering crowd,
the big cat took him down with one swat.

OPENING SENTENCES

The opening sentences in your writing carry big responsibilities, setting the
tone and often the scene—and helping draw your readers in by arousing
their interest and curiosity. Authors often spend quite a lot of time on opening sentences for this very reason: Whether it's a business report or a college
essay or a blog posting, the way it begins has a lot to do with whether your
audience will stay with you and whether you'll get the kind of response you
want from them. Here are three famous opening sentences:

▶ I am an invisible man.   —RALPH ELLISON, *Invisible Man*

▶ The sky above the port was the color of television, tuned to a dead channel.

—WILLIAM GIBSON, *Neuromancer*

▶ They shoot the white girl first.   —TONI MORRISON, *Paradise*

Each of these sentences is startling, making us read on in order to find out more. Each is brief, leaving us waiting anxiously for what's to come. In addition, each makes a powerful statement and creates some kind of image in readers' minds: an "invisible" person, a sky the color of a "dead" TV channel, someone being shot. These sentences all come from novels, but they use strategies that work in many kinds of writing.

It usually takes more than a single sentence to open an essay. Consider, for example, how Michael Pollan begins a lengthy essay on animal liberation:

▶ The first time I opened Peter Singer's *Animal Liberation*, I was dining alone at the Palm, trying to enjoy a rib-eye steak cooked medium-rare. If this sounds like a good recipe for cognitive dissonance (if not indigestion), that was sort of the idea. Preposterous as it might seem to supporters of animal rights, what I was doing was tantamount to reading *Uncle Tom's Cabin* on a plantation in the Deep South in 1852.

—MICHAEL POLLAN, "An Animal's Place"

The first sentence presents an incongruous image that holds our attention (he's eating a steak while reading about animal liberation). Then the rest of the paragraph makes this incongruity even more pronounced, even comparing the situation to someone reading the antislavery novel *Uncle Tom's Cabin* while on a slave-owning plantation. It's an opening that makes us read on.

Here is the opening of a blog posting that begins with a provocative question:

▶ Have you ever thought about whether to have a child? If so, what factors entered into your decision? Was it whether having children would be good for you, your partner and others close to the possible child, such as children you may already have, or perhaps your parents? For most people contemplating reproduction, those are the dominant questions. Some may also think about the desirability of adding to the strain that the nearly seven billion people already here are putting on our planet's environment. But very few ask whether coming into existence is a good thing for the child itself.

—PETER SINGER, "Should This Be the Last Generation?"

Singer's question is designed to get the reader's attention, and he follows it up with two additional questions that ask readers to probe more deeply into their reasons for considering whether or not to reproduce. In the fifth sentence, he suggests that the answers people give to these questions may not be adequate ones, and in the last sentence he lays down a challenge: Perhaps coming into existence is not always good for "the child itself."

Here's another example of an opening that uses several sentences, this one from a student essay about graphic memoirs:

> ▶ In 1974, before the Fall of Saigon, my 14-year-old father, alone, boarded a boat out of Vietnam in search of America. This is a fact. But this one fact can spawn multiple understandings: I could ask a group of students to take a week and write me a story from just this one fact, and I have no doubt that they would bring back a full range of interpretations.
> —BRANDON LY, "Leaving Home, Coming Home"

This opening passage begins with a vivid image of a very young man fleeing Vietnam alone, followed by a very short sentence that makes a statement and then a longer one that challenges that statement. This student writer is moving readers toward what will become his thesis: that memoirs can never tell "the whole truth, and nothing but the truth."

Finally, take a look at the opening of the speech Toni Morrison gave when she won the Nobel Prize for Literature:

> ▶ Members of the Swedish Academy, Ladies and Gentlemen:
> Narrative has never been mere entertainment for me. It is, I believe, one of the principal ways in which we absorb knowledge. I hope you will understand, then, why I begin these remarks with the opening phrase of what must be the oldest sentence in the world, and the earliest one we remember from childhood: "Once upon a time . . ."

Here Morrison begins with a deceptively simple statement, that narrative is for her not just entertainment. In the next two sentences, she complicates that statement and broadens her claim that narrative is the way we understand the world, concluding with what she calls "the oldest sentence in the world."

You can use strategies similar to the ones shown here in opening your college essays. Here are just some of the ways you might begin:

- With a strong, dramatic—or deceptively simple—statement
- With a vivid image

- With a provocative question
- With an anecdote
- With a startling claim

Opening sentences online. If the internet lets us send messages to people all over the world, it also challenges us to get and keep their attention. And with limited space and attention (small screens; readers in a hurry, scanning for what they need), writers need to take care to craft opening sentences of any text posted online to be as attention getting and informative as possible.

In email, for instance, first sentences often show up in auto-preview lines, so it's a good idea to write them carefully. Here's the first line of an email sent recently to everyone at W. W. Norton:

▶ A Ping-Pong table has been set up on the 4th floor in loving memory of Diane O'Connor.

This email was sent by O'Connor's colleagues, honoring her efforts to persuade Norton to have an annual company Ping-Pong tournament. It might have said less ("Ping-Pong on 4," "Remembering Diane"), as email usually does—but there was more that they wanted to say.

And then there's *Twitter.* As if it weren't enough of a challenge to say what you want to say in 140 characters, you'd better begin with a sentence that will catch readers' attention. Here are two tweets that got ours:

▶ Steve Jobs was born out of wedlock, put up for adoption at birth, dropped out of college, then changed the world. What's your excuse?   —@JWMOSS

▶ It's so weird because Rush Limbaugh has been such an awesome human being until now.   —@BUCK4ITT

You'll want to think carefully about how you open any text that you post to the web—and to craft opening sentences that will make sense in a *Google* search list. Here are two that we like:

▶ Smith Women Redefine "Pearls and Cashmere."

This is the headline for an article in *Inside Higher Ed,* an online magazine read by educators, but it's also the line that comes up in a *Google* search. The article is about a controversy at Smith College—and we think you'll agree that the headline surely got the attention of those scanning the magazine's list of articles or searching *Google.*

▶ **The Art of Fielding** is a 2011 novel by former *n+1* editor <u>Chad Harbach</u>. It centers on the fortunes of <u>shortstop</u> Henry Skrimshander, and his career playing <u>college baseball</u> with the Westish College Harpooners, a <u>Division III</u> <u>(NCAA)</u> team.

This is the start of the *Wikipedia* entry for a novel, which comes up in a *Google* search. As you can see, it identifies the book, says who wrote it, and gives a one-sentence description of the story. Safe to say, the authors of this entry were careful to provide this information in the very first sentences.

CLOSING SENTENCES

Sentences that conclude a piece of writing are where you have a chance to make a lasting impact: to reiterate your point, tell readers why it matters, echo something you say in your opening, make a provocative statement, issue a call for action.

Here's Joe Posnanski, wrapping up an essay on his blog arguing that college athletes should not be paid:

▶ College football is not popular because of the stars. College football is popular because of that first word. Take away the college part, add in money, and you are left with professional minor league football . . . . See how many people watch that.   —JOE POSNANSKI, "The College Connection"

These four sentences summarize his argument—and the last one's the zinger, one that leaves readers thinking.

Now take a look at the conclusion to a scholarly book on current neurological studies of human attention, the brain science of attention:

▶ Right now, our classrooms and workplaces are structured for success in the last century, not this one. We can change that. By maximizing opportunities for collaboration, by rethinking everything from our approach to work to how we measure progress, we can begin to see the things we've been missing and catch hold of what's passing us by.

　If you change the context, if you change the questions you ask, if you change the structure, the test, and the task, then you stop gazing one way and begin to look in a different way and in a different direction. You know what happens next:

　Now you see it. —CATHY DAVIDSON, *Now You See It: How the Brain Science of Attention Will Transform the Way We Live, Work, and Learn*

Cathy Davidson uses two short paragraphs to sum up her argument and then concludes with a final paragraph that consists of just one very short four-word sentence. With this last sentence, she uses a tried-and-true strategy of coming full circle to echo the main idea of her book and, in fact, to reiterate its title. Readers who have worked their way through the book will take pleasure in that last sentence: *Now* they do see her point.

For another example, note how in the ending to a speech about language and about being able to use "all the Englishes" she grew up with, author Amy Tan closes with a one-sentence paragraph that quotes her mother:

▶ Apart from what any critic had to say about my writing, I knew I had succeeded where it counted when my mother finished reading my book and gave me her verdict: "So easy to read."   —AMY TAN, "Mother Tongue"

Tan's ending sums up one of her main goals as an author: to write so that readers who speak different kinds of English will find her work accessible, especially her mother.

Finally, take a look at how Toni Morrison chose to close her Nobel Prize acceptance speech:

▶ It is, therefore, mindful of the gifts of my predecessors, the blessing of my sisters, in joyful anticipation of writers to come that I accept the honor the Swedish Academy has done me, and ask you to share what is for me a moment of grace.   —TONI MORRISON, Nobel Prize acceptance speech

In this one-sentence conclusion, Morrison speaks to the past, present, and future when she says she is grateful for those writers who came before her, for those who are writing now (her sisters), and for those yet to come. She ends the sentence by asking her audience to share this "moment of grace" with her and, implicitly, with all other writers so honored.

You may not be accepting a Nobel Prize soon, but in your college writing you can use all the strategies presented here to compose strong closings:

- By reiterating your point
- By discussing the implications of your argument
- By asking a question
- By referring back to your beginning
- By recommending or proposing some kind of action

IDENTIFY two memorable openings and closings from a favorite novel, comic book, film, or blog. What makes them so good? Do they follow one of the strategies presented here?

VARYING YOUR SENTENCES

Read a paragraph or two of your writing out loud and listen for its rhythm. Is it quick and abrupt? slow and leisurely? singsong? stately? rolling? Whatever it is, does the rhythm you hear match what you had in mind when you were writing? And does it put the emphasis where you want it? One way to establish the emphasis you intend and a rhythm that will keep readers reading is by varying the length of your sentences and the way those sentences flow from one to the other.

A string of sentences that are too much alike is almost certain to be boring. While you can create effective rhythms in many ways, one of the simplest and most effective is by breaking up a series of long sentences with a shorter one that gives your readers a chance to pause and absorb what you've written.

Take a look at the following passage, from an article in the *Atlantic* about the finale of the *Oprah Winfrey Show*. See how the author uses a mix of long and short sentences to describe one of the tributes to Oprah, this one highlighting her support of black men:

▶ [Oprah's] friend Tyler Perry announced that some of the "Morehouse Men," each a beneficiary of the $12 million endowment she has established at their university, had come to honor her for the scholarships she gave them. The lights were lowered, a Broadway star began singing an inspirational song, and a dozen or so black men began to walk slowly to the front of the stage. Then more came, and soon there were a score, then 100, then the huge stage was filled with men, 300 of them. They stood there, solemnly, in a tableau stage-managed in such a way that it might have robbed them of their dignity—the person serenading them (or, rather, serenading Oprah on their behalf) was Kristin Chenoweth, tiniest and whitest of all tiny white women; the song was from *Wicked*, most feminine of all musicals; and each man carried a white candle, an emblem that lent them the aspect of Norman Rockwell Christmas carolers. But they were not robbed of their dignity. They looked,

The Morehouse Men surprise Oprah.

all together, like a miracle. A video shown before the procession revealed that some of these men had been in gangs before going to Morehouse, some had fathers in prison, many had been living in poverty. Now they were doctors, lawyers, bankers, a Rhodes Scholar—and philanthropists, establishing their own Morehouse endowment.

—CAITLIN FLANAGAN, "The Glory of Oprah"

The passage begins with three medium-length sentences—and then one very long one (seventy-two words!) that points up the strong contrast between the 300 black men filling the stage and the "whitest of white" singer performing a song from the "most feminine" of musicals. Then come two little sentences (the first one eight words long and the second one, seven) that give readers a chance to pause and absorb what has been said while also making an important point: that the men "looked, all together, like a miracle." The remainder of the passage moves back toward longer sentences, each of which explains just what this "miracle" is. Try reading this passage aloud and listen for how the variation in sentences creates both emphasis and a pleasing and effective rhythm.

In addition to varying the lengths of your sentences, you can also improve your writing by making sure that they don't all use the same structure or begin in the same way. You can be pretty sure, for example, that a passage in which every sentence is a simple sentence that opens with the subject of a main clause will not read smoothly at all but rather will move along awkwardly. Take a look at this passage, for example:

> ▶ The sunset was especially beautiful today. I was on top of Table Mountain in Cape Town. I looked down and saw the sun touch the sea and sink into it. The evening shadows crept up the mountain. I got my backpack and walked over to the rest of my group. We started on the long hike down the mountain and back to the city.

There's nothing wrong with these sentences as such. Each one is grammatically correct. But if you read the passage aloud, you'll hear how it moves abruptly from sentence to sentence, lurching along rather than flowing smoothly. The problem is that the sentences are all the same: Each one is a simple sentence that begins with the subject of a main clause (*sunset, I, I, evening shadows, I, we*). In addition, the use of personal pronouns at the beginning of the sentences (three *I*'s in only six sentences!) makes for dull reading. Finally, these are all fairly short sentences, and the sameness of the sentence length adds to the abrupt rhythm of the passage—and doesn't keep readers reading. Now look at how this passage can be revised by working on sentence variation:

> ▶ From the top of Cape Town's Table Mountain, the sunset was especially beautiful. I looked down just as the fiery orb touched and then sank into the sea; shadows began to creep slowly up the mountain. Picking up my backpack, I joined the rest of my group, and we started the long hike down the mountain.

This revision reduces the number of sentences in the passage from six to three (the first simple, the second compound-complex, the third compound) and varies the length of the sentences. Equally important, the revision eliminates all but one of the subject openings. The first sentence now begins with the prepositional phrase ("From the top"); the second with the subject of a main clause ("I"); and the third with a participial phrase ("Picking up my backpack"). Finally the revision varies the diction a bit, replacing the repeated word "sun" with a vivid image ("fiery orb"). Read the revised passage aloud and you'll hear how varying the sentences creates a stronger rhythm that makes it easier to read.

This brief chapter has only scratched the surface of sentence style. But we hope we've said enough to show how good sentences can be your allies, helping you get your ideas out there and connect with audiences as successfully as possible. Remember: Authors are only as good as the sentences they write!

TAKE A LOOK at a writing assignment you've recently completed. Read it aloud, listening for rhythm and emphasis. If you find a passage that doesn't read well or provide the emphasis you want, analyze its sentences for length (count the words) and structure (how does each sentence begin?). Revise the passage using the strategies presented above.

FOURTEEN

Designing What You Write

DESIGN. IT'S A WORD YOU HEAR ALL THE TIME, one you use without thinking about it. "Kate Middleton's wedding dress was designed by Sarah Burton for Alexander McQueen." "Have you seen Apple's design for the new Nano?" "Frank Gehry's design of the Disney Concert Hall astonished critics with its waves of gleaming stainless steel." "My essay was designed to get the attention of the college admissions committee."

Fashion, technology, architecture, toys: Everything is designed, including writing. Whenever you write something—a slide presentation for a report, a blog post, an essay—you design it, whether you are conscious of doing so or not. You select a medium and tools: a lined notebook and a pencil, a text message and a smartphone, white paper and a laser printer. You choose fonts and colors: big red capital letters for a poster, 12-point black Times New Roman for an essay. You think about including visuals: a bar graph on a slide, a cartoon in a blog, a photo in an essay. You consider whether to use multiple columns and where to leave some white space. You decide what you want readers to notice first and put that in a prominent position.

This chapter discusses several key design elements: typography, color, visuals, and layout. Whatever fonts or images you use, though, remember that they are not mere decoration. However you design a text, you need to be guided by your purpose, your audience, and the rest of your rhetorical situation.

THINKING RHETORICALLY ABOUT DESIGN

Your design choices play a role in the way your audience receives your message and whether your text achieves its purpose. Look, for example, at the different ways that Coca-Cola was advertised in 1913 and 2010. In 1913, Coke was relatively new, and its ads relied on words to introduce it to an audience that was not yet familiar with it, telling them it had "character" and was "delicious," "refreshing," and "thirst-quenching." The ad shown here was designed so that these words would pop and be easy to read. To reach today's audiences, advertisers use today's media—in the case of the 2010 ad here, a video—to reach a mass audience. The cartoon characters Stewie Griffin and Underdog vie for control of the Coke bottle balloon, and the only word is the one on the bottle: "Coca-Cola." One thing the two ads have in common, though, is the logo: Whether it's in black ink on white paper or red and white pixels on a screen, the Coca-Cola logo was *designed* to be recognizable—and thus to get our attention.

In designing what we write, we need always to think about how we can best reach our audience and achieve our purpose. Given the deluge of words, images, and other data, readers today are less likely than they once were to read anything start to finish. Instead, they may scan for just the information they need. As an author, then, you need to design your documents to be user-friendly: easy to access, to navigate, to read—and to remember.

Remember as well that your design can shape your audience's reaction before they read a word, so you'll want to start by thinking about that audience, your purpose, and your entire rhetorical situation.

A print ad for Coca-Cola in Georgia Tech's 1913 yearbook and a video ad presented during the telecast of the 2010 Super Bowl.

- *What's your genre?* Does it call for certain design elements—a style or size of type, perhaps, or tables and graphs?

- *Who is your audience,* and what design elements will appeal to them? Are there any elements that might *not* appeal to them—or cause them to question your authority as author?

- *What is your purpose?* To provide information? To entertain? To persuade readers to take some kind of action? What design elements might help you achieve that purpose? Is there anything that would work against it—using a playful typeface in a business letter, for example?

- *What's your stance as an author,* and how do you want to come across to your audience? Do you want to seem businesslike? serious? ironic? practical and matter-of-fact? How can your design—fonts, color, images—reflect that stance?

- *Consider the larger context.* Do you have any time constraints? What technology do you have available? Does your assignment have any design requirements?

- *What's your medium*—print? digital? spoken?—and what kinds of design elements are appropriate (or possible)? A print essay, for example, could include photographs but not video.

CHOOSING FONTS

We have hundreds of fonts to choose from today. The ones we use affect our message—what it looks like, and how it is received—so it's important to think carefully about what's appropriate for our medium, genre, and the rest of our rhetorical situation.

Serif fonts such as Times New Roman or Bodoni have a traditional look, whereas sans serif fonts such as Arial or Futura give a more modern look. Your instructors may require you to use a specific font, but if you get to choose, you'll want to think about what look you want for your text—and what will be most readable. Some readers find serif fonts easier to read in longer pieces of writing. Sans serif, on the other hand, tends to be easier to read in slide presentations. Save novelty or decorative fonts such as **Impact** or *Allegro Script* for your nonacademic writing—and even there, use them sparingly, since they can be difficult (or annoying!) to read.

Most fonts include **bold**, *italics,* and underlining options, which you can use to highlight parts of a text. In academic writing, bold is generally used for headings, whereas italics or underlining is used for titles of books, films, and other long works. If you're following MLA, APA, or another academic style, be careful that your use of fonts conforms to their requirements.

Readability matters. For most academic and workplace writing, you'll want to use 10-to-12-point type, and at least 18-point type for most presentation slides. Academic writing is usually double-spaced; letters and résumés are single-spaced.

Headings

Brief texts may need no headings at all, but for longer texts, headings can help readers follow the text and find specific information. Some kinds of writing have set headings that authors are required to use—IMRAD reports, for instance, require introduction, methods, research, and discussion headings. When you include headings, you need to decide on wording, fonts, and placement.

Wording. Make headings succinct and parallel. You could make them all nouns ("Energy Drinks," "Snack Foods"), all gerund phrases ("Analyzing the Contents of Energy Drinks," "Resisting Snack Foods"), or all questions ("What's in Energy Drinks?" or "Why Are Snack Foods So Hard to Resist?").

Fonts. If you're using more than one level of heading, distinguish them from one another typographically by using bold, italic, underlining, and capitalization. For example:

FIRST-LEVEL HEADING
Second-Level Heading
Third-Level Heading

When you get to choose, you may want to make headings larger than the main text or to put them in a different font or color (as we do throughout this book). But if you're following mla or apa styles, be aware that they require headings to be in the same font as the main text.

Placement. You can center headings or set them flush left above the text or place them to the left of the text; but whatever you do, treat each level of heading consistently throughout the text. If you're following MLA or APA styles, be aware that first-level headings must be centered.

USING COLOR

Sometimes you'll be required to write in black type on a white background, but many times you'll have reason to use colors. In some media, color will be expected or necessary—on websites or presentation slides, for instance. Other times it may be inappropriate—in a thank-you note following a job interview at a law firm, or in an application essay to business school. As with any design element, color should be used to help you get a message across to an audience, never just to decorate your text.

Be aware that certain colors evoke specific emotional reactions: blue, like the sky and sea, suggests spaciousness and tranquility; red invokes fire and suggests intense energy and emotions; yellow, the color of our sun, generates warmth and optimism. Also remember that certain colors carry different associations across cultures—to Westerners, white suggests innocence and youth, but in China white is traditionally associated with death (which is why Chinese brides wear red).

Especially if you use more than one color in a text, you'll want to consider how certain colors work together. Look at the color wheel on p. 254 to see how the colors are related. *Primary colors* (red, blue, and yellow) create an effect of simplicity and directness. The more *secondary and tertiary colors* you use, the more sophisticated the design. *Complementary colors*, located opposite each other on the color wheel, look brighter when placed next to each other. (Black and white are also considered complementary colors.) *Cool and dark colors* appear to recede, whereas *warm and bright colors* seem to advance. So using both cool and warm colors can create a feeling of movement and energy.

Remember that any color scheme includes the type, the background, and any images or graphics that you use. If colorful photos are an important part of your website, they'll stand out most strongly on a white background and with black type—both of which you may want to use for that reason alone. If you're writing a report that includes multicolored pie charts and want to have color headings, you wouldn't want to use primary colors in the headings and pastels in the charts. In short, if you use colors, make sure they work well with all the other design elements in the text.

Using color to guide readers. Like bold or italic type, color can help guide readers through a text. Color is an important navigational element on websites, sometimes used to indicate links and to highlight headings. For such uses of color, though, it's important to choose colors that are easy to see.

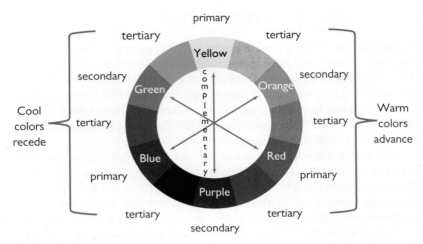

A color wheel.

Considering legibility. Using color can make your writing easier—or harder—to read. Use type and background colors that are compatible. Dark type on a light background works best for lengthy pieces of writing, while less text-heavy projects can use a light text on a dark background. In either case, be sure that the contrast is dramatic enough to be legible. Keep in mind many people, largely males, can't see or distinguish certain colors (notably, red and green) so be sure to have a good reason if you use these colors together.

USING VISUALS

Authors today write with more than just words. Photos, charts, tables, and videos are just some of the visual elements you can use to emphasize important information, and sometimes to make your writing easier or more interesting to read. Would a photo help readers see a scene you're describing? Would readers be able to compare data better in a table or chart than in a paragraph? Would a map help readers see where an event you're describing takes place? Would an image help an audience at an oral presentation see what you're talking about? These are questions you should be asking yourself as you write.

Be sure that any visuals you use are relevant to what you have to say—that you use them to support your point, not just to decorate your text. And remember that even the most spectacular images do not speak for themselves: You need to refer to them in your text and to explain to readers what they are and how they support what you're saying.

Kinds of Visuals

You may be assigned to include visuals—but if not, a good way to think about what kinds of visuals to use (or not) is by considering your rhetorical situation. What visuals would be useful or necessary for your topic and purpose? What visuals would help you reach your audience? What kinds of visuals are possible in your medium—or expected in your genre?

Photographs can help an audience envision something that's difficult to describe or to explain in words. A good photo can provide powerful visual evidence for an argument, and can sometimes move readers in a way that words alone might not. Think of how ads for various charities use photos of hungry children to appeal to readers to donate.

Photos can be useful for many writing purposes, letting readers see something you're describing or analyzing, for instance, or even something you're reporting on. You can take your own photos, or use ones that you find in other sources. Remember, however, to provide full documentation for any photos that you don't take yourself.

A photo of street art in a Texas parking lot demonstrates the layering effect of graffiti in a way that would be difficult to do with words alone.

A video of a public service announcement about the dangers of texting while driving created by the South Dakota Office of Highway Safety can be used as an example of the ways different states approach the issue.

Videos are useful for demonstrating physical processes or actions and for showing sequences. Your medium will dictate whether you can include videos in a text. The print version of a newspaper article about aerialist skiers, for instance, includes a still photo of a skier in mid-jump, whereas the same article on the newspaper's website and on a TV news report features videos showing the skier in action. Your topic and genre will affect whether or not you have reason to include video: If you were writing a process analysis to teach a skier how to perform a double-full-full-full, a video would be far more useful than a still photo.

Graphs, charts, and tables. Numerical and statistical data can be easier both to describe and understand when they are presented visually. You'll often have occasion to present data in bar graphs, pie charts, and the like, especially in reports and analyses. In many cases, you'll be able to find tables and graphs in your research and then to incorporate ones you find into your own writing. You can also use templates found in *Excel*, *Word*, *PowerPoint*, and other programs to create charts and tables yourself. Whether you find or create them, be sure to indicate in your text how they support your argument.

Line graphs are useful for illustrating trends and changes over time—how unemployment fluctuates over a period of time, for instance. By using more than one line, you can compare changes in different variables, such as unemployment for those with a college education and those with only

Fantasy sports at a glance

The typical player is a 34-year-old male with a college degree who spends almost nine hours each week consuming fantasy sports.

Fantasy sports players in the U.S.

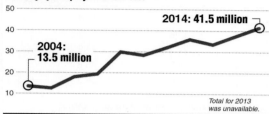

2014: 41.5 million

2004:
13.5 million

Total for 2013 was unavailable.

2004 2005 2006 2007 2008 2009 2010 2011 2012 2013 2014

Average daily winnings
For daily players

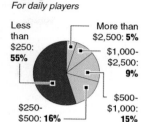

Less than $250: 55%

More than $2,500: 5%

$1,000-$2,500: 9%

$500-$1,000: 15%

$250-$500: 16%

A line graph shows the number of fantasy sports players in the U.S. over a period of ten years. (*left*); a pie chart and a bar chart show the amount of money that fantasy sports players win, and the fees they pay.

Amount spent on entry fees in a year
For daily players

$1-$50	65%
$51-$100	17%
$101-$300	9%
$301+	9%

Source: Fantasy Sports Trade Association, Eilers Research

Graphic: Chicago Tribune/TNS

a high school education. When comparing more than one variable, the lines should be in two different colors so that readers can easily see the comparison.

Bar graphs are useful for comparing quantitative data in different categories, such as for different age groups or different years. In the example shown on this page, see how the bars make it easy to compare sales of Apple products over the course of several months. It would be easy enough to convey this same information in words alone—but more work to read and harder to remember.

Pie charts give an overview of the relative sizes of parts to a whole, such as what share of a family budget is devoted to food, housing, entertainment, and so on. Pie charts are useful for showing which parts of a whole are more or less significant, but they are less precise (and less easy to read) than bar graphs. It's best to limit a pie chart to six or seven slices, since when the slices become too small, it's difficult to see how they compare in size.

Tables are efficient ways of organizing and presenting a lot of information concisely, in horizontal rows and vertical columns. Table 1 on the next page presents data about home internet access in the United States, information that is made easy to scan in a table.

Table I
US Home Internet Access by Age Group, 2009

Age of Householder	No In-Home Internet (%)	In-Home Internet (%)
Under 25 years	33.0	67.0
25-34 years	25.8	74.2
35-44 years	22.2	77.8
45-55 years	24.2	75.8
55 years and older	41.8	58.2

Source: United States, Dept. of Commerce, Census Bureau; "Internet
Use in the United States: October 2009," Current Population Survey; US
Dept. of Commerce, Oct. 2009; Web; 11 June 2012; table 1.

Maps can provide geographic context, helping to orient your audience to places mentioned in your text. A report on the 2011 earthquake in New Zealand, for example, includes maps of the city of Christchurch showing where the earthquake was centered. Include a map when seeing a location is important to your point.

Diagrams are useful for illustrating details that cannot be shown in a photograph. A carefully drawn diagram can deliver a lot of information in a small amount of space.

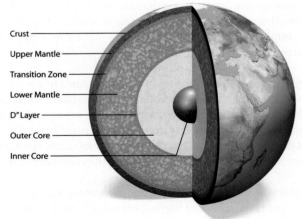

A diagram of the earth's internal structure shows the various layers.

CHRISTCHURCH BUILDINGS DAMAGE

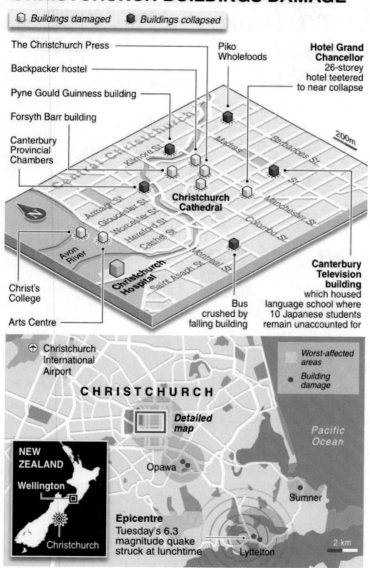

Buildings damaged   Buildings collapsed

The Christchurch Press

Backpacker hostel

Pyne Gould Guinness building

Forsyth Barr building

Canterbury Provincial Chambers

Piko Wholefoods

Hotel Grand Chancellor
26-storey hotel teetered to near collapse

Central Christchurch

Kilmore St.

Madras

Barbadoes St.

200m

Christchurch Cathedral

Manchester St.

Armagh St.

Gloucester St.

Worcester St.

Hereford St.

Cashel St.

Colombo St.

Avon River

Montreal St.

Christchurch Hospital

Saint Asaph St.

Christ's College

Arts Centre

Bus crushed by falling building

Canterbury Television building
which housed language school where 10 Japanese students remain unaccounted for

⊕ Christchurch International Airport

Worst-affected areas

● *Building damage*

CHRISTCHURCH

Detailed map

NEW ZEALAND

Wellington

Opawa

Pacific Ocean

Sumner

Christchurch

Epicentre
Tuesday's 6.3 magnitude quake struck at lunchtime

Lyttelton

2 km

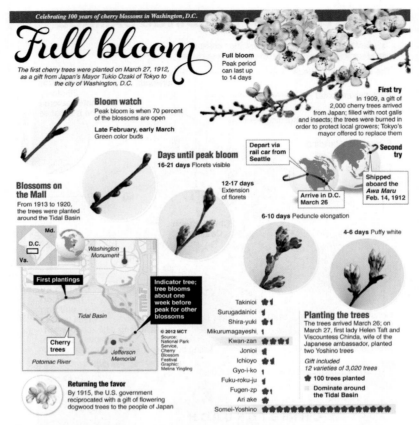

This infographic on the cherry blossom season in Washington, D.C., includes photos, diagrams, maps, and a bar chart.

Infographics incorporate several different types of visuals—charts, tables, photos—on a single topic to give detailed information about a topic. Because infographics can be so densely packed with information, make sure you can display them large enough for your audience to be able to read.

Creating Visuals

You can find visuals online, scan them from print sources, or create them yourself using basic software or a digital camera. If you come across an illustration you think would be useful, make a copy. Scan or photocopy visuals from print sources; for a digital source, import a link or make a screen grab from digital sources. Label everything clearly. Be aware that visuals—and any data you use to compile them—need to be documented in a caption or source note, so keep track of where you found everything as you go.

- *Photographs and videos.* If you plan to print an image, save each file in as high a resolution as possible. If a photo is only available in a very small size or low resolution, try to find a more legible option. Be careful about cropping, adjusting color, and altering images in other ways that could change the meaning; straying too far from the original is considered unethical.

- *Graphs, charts, and tables.* Be consistent in your use of fonts and colors, especially if you include more than one graph, chart, or table. Be sure that the horizontal (x) and vertical (y) axes are labeled clearly. If you use more than one color, add labels for what each color represents. When you have many rows or columns, alternating colors can make categories easier to distinguish.

- *Maps.* Provide a title and a key explaining any symbols, colors, or other details. If the original is missing these elements, add them. If you create the map yourself, include a key with different colors or other symbols to highlight notable locations or other important information.

- *Diagrams.* Use a single font for all labels, and be sure to make the diagram large enough to include all of the necessary detail.

Introducing and Labeling Visuals

Introduce visuals as you would any other source materials, explaining what they show and how they support your point. Don't leave your audience wondering how a photo or chart pertains to your project—spell it out, and be sure to do so *before* the visual appears ("As shown in fig. 3, population growth has been especially rapid in the Southwest.") Number visuals sequentially, numbering tables and figures separately. If you're following MLA, APA, or another academic style, be sure to follow their guidelines for how to label tables and figures.

MLA style. For tables, provide a number ("Table 1") and a descriptive title ("Population Growth by Region, 1990–2010") on separate lines above the table; below the table, add a caption explaining what the table shows and including any source information. For graphs, charts, photos, and diagrams, provide a figure number ("Fig.1"), caption, and source information below the figure. If you give only brief source information in a parenthetical citation, include the source in your list of works cited.

APA style. For tables, provide a number ("Table 1") and a descriptive title on separate lines above the table; below the table, include a note with informa-tion about the source. For charts, diagrams, graphs, and photos, include a fig-ure number ("Figure 1") and source information in a note below the figure.

PUTTING IT ALL TOGETHER

Once you've chosen fonts, colors, and visuals, you need to think about how they all come together as a text. Look, for instance, at the homepage of TED, a nonprofit group devoted to disseminating "ideas worth spreading." It's easy to read with a sans-serif font and minimal text. The logo draws your eye because it's large, red, capitalized, and positioned in the upper left corner of the screen. The soft gray "ideas worth spreading" complements the red and leads your eye to the bold black text below—"Riveting talks by remarkable people, free to the world"—which defines the site's purpose and audience. Each of the cascading images is a link to a specific TED talk, and when you mouse over each image, a short summary pops up. Note how white space separates the parts and makes the page easy to read. No surprise that this site won a Webby Award, the online equivalent of an Oscar.

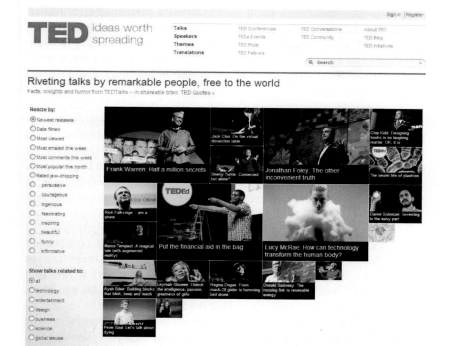

You may not have occasion to design anything as large or complex as a TED site, but the same design principles will apply for all the writing you do. Whether you're designing a report, a photo essay, or a slide presentation, chances are you'll be working with some combination of words, images, and graphs or charts, which you'll need to put on paper or screen in order to reach a certain audience for some purpose.

Look beyond the details and think about what you want your design to accomplish. To help your audience grasp a simple message as fast as possible? convey your identity as a hip and creative author? conform to the requirements of a certain academic style? be simple enough to implement by an approaching deadline? Taking such a perspective can help you determine how to "put it all together" in a way that achieves what you intend.

Keep it simple. Sometimes you'll need to follow a prescribed organization and layout, but if you get to decide how to design your document, take this advice: Don't make your design any more complex than you have to. Readers want to be able to find information they need—and they won't want to spend time deciphering a complex hierarchy of headings or an intricate navigational system.

Think about how to format your written text. Should it all be in the form of paragraphs, or is there anything that should be set off as a list? If so, should it be a bulleted list to make it stand out, or a numbered list to put items in a sequence? If your text includes numerical data, should any of it be presented in a graph, chart, or table? Would that make it easier for readers to grasp? Is there anything else that's especially important that you'd like to highlight in some way?

Position visuals carefully. Keep in mind how they will look on a page or screen. Placing them at the top or bottom of a print page will make it easier to lay out pages and will cause less interruption to your text. If your text will be online, you have more freedom to put them wherever you wish. Reproduce visuals large enough so that readers will be able to see all the pertinent detail; if you're using a file, be aware that digital images become fuzzier when they are enlarged. Downsave images to reduce file sizes; you don't want readers to have problems loading the image. Look over your text carefully to be sure that nothing is too small or blurry to read.

Use white space to separate the various parts of your text. Add some extra space above headings and around lists, images, graphs, charts, and tables.

Organize the text. Whether your text is a simple five-page report or a full website, readers will need to know how it's organized. In a brief essay, you might simply indicate that in a sentence in your introduction, but in lengthier pieces, you may need headings, both to structure your text and to make it easy for readers to navigate.

If you're creating a website, you'll need to figure out how you're dividing materials into pages and to make that clear on the site's homepage. Most homepages have a horizontal navigation bar across the top indicating and linking to the main parts, and often another navigation menu going down the left side of the screen, with links to specific materials on the site. The same navigation menus should appear in the same position on all the other pages of the site—and make sure that every page includes a link to take readers back to the homepage. Look at these examples from *National Geographic*. You can see the consistency from the homepage through the subsequent pages; note the elements that help readers navigate between pages: Colors, fonts, and navigational information are the same on all pages.

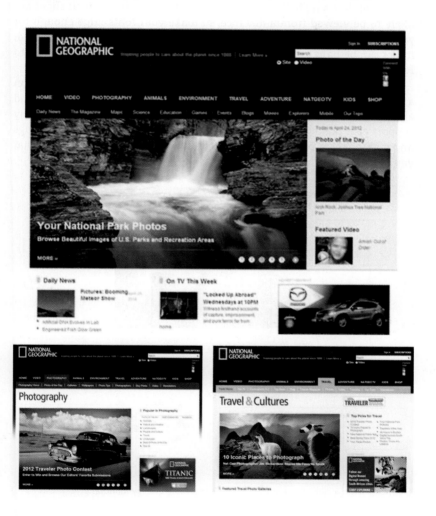

Creating Slide Presentations

When you give an oral report, slides can help make your main points clear and memorable. Presentation software such as *PowerPoint* or *Keynote* makes it fairly easy to design slides, providing templates and layouts to guide you.

Three principles to keep in mind when you're designing slide presentations: legibility, simplicity, and consistency. Remember that your slides are likely to be viewed from a distance, so make your fonts large enough for your audience to read, at least 18 points. Simple bold fonts are easiest to read; italics can be hard to read and are best avoided. Bulleted lists are easier to read than paragraphs.

Keep slides as simple as you can. Don't put too much information on a slide, and keep points in bulleted lists brief. Decorative backgrounds and animations can be distracting; don't include them unless they in some way support your points. And be consistent. Using one font or color for headings and making them parallel in structure will help your audience follow what you're saying.

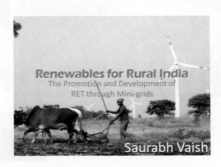

Examples from a slide presentation about renewable energy in India.

FIFTEEN

Checking for Common Mistakes

POET NIKKI GIOVANNI ONCE SAID, "Mistakes are a fact of life. It is the response to the error that counts." Albert Einstein put a little different spin on the issue when he said, "Anyone who has never made a mistake has never tried anything new." We agree. Anyone who writes is going to make mistakes: That's a given. What matters is to know when something *is* a mistake, to learn from any mistakes we make, and sometimes even to use them, as Einstein might say, to try something new.

Most of all, it means understanding that what may be a mistake in one context may be perfectly appropriate in another, depending—as always—on your purpose, your audience, and the rest of your rhetorical situation. So when you're editing your writing, you need to think about what's appropriate for your particular rhetorical context.

As a college writer, you may sometimes decide to use a sentence fragment or something else that's typically seen as an error for special effect. In most of your academic writing, however, it's wise to play it safe and avoid anything that might be considered a mistake. This chapter offers tips and examples for checking and editing your writing for some common mistakes, arranged alphabetically from articles to verbs.

WHAT'S THE DIFFERENCE between *a dog* and *the dog?* "A" dog could be any dog; it does not matter which one. "The" dog, by comparison, refers to one specific dog. *A, an,* and *the* are articles. Use *a* or *an* with nouns when their specific identity isn't known or doesn't matter: *I want a golden retriever.* Use *the* with nouns whose specific identity is known or has been mentioned: *I want the golden retriever I told you about last week.*

When to Use *A* or *An*

Use *a* or *an* with singular count nouns that cannot be identified specifically. Count nouns are those referring to things you can count: *one egg, two chairs, three facts.* Use *a* before words beginning with a consonant sound: *a baby;* use *an* before words beginning with a vowel sound: *an apple.* (And be careful to consider sound rather than spelling: *a uniform, an uncle.*)

Do not use *a* or *an* before a noncount noun, one that refers to an abstract concept or something that cannot be counted or made plural such as *loyalty, knowledge,* or *gasoline.*

▶ The vacant apartment looked much better with *furniture* in it.

When to Use *The*

Use *the* with nouns that can be identified specifically—singular and plural, count and noncount.

▶ Many cities have passed laws that require restaurants to provide information about *the ingredients* in their food.

▶ Tyler Cowen criticizes *the eat-local movement* as expensive and snobbish.

When to Use No Article

When you're making a generalization, no article is needed with noncount or count nouns.

▶ Large *corporations* generally offer *health insurance* to *employees.*

▶ Most *Americans* like *ice* in their *drinks.*

WHEN TO USE *A* OR *AN*

▶ My parents see attending college as *an honor* and *a privilege*.

▶ Studying in another country can give you *a new perspective* on your home country.

▶ The chef added *a little water* to the stew because it was too thick.

▶ When I'm 16, I'm getting ~~the~~ ^a Chrysler because of their Super Bowl ads.

There's more than one kind of Chrysler, and the writer doesn't indicate which one he plans to get.

WHEN TO USE *THE*

▶ *The U.S. Supreme Court* has nine members, who are appointed by *the president*.

▶ After *the attacks* of September 11, 2001, on *the World Trade Center* and *the Pentagon*, Americans recognized *the need* for better security at airports.

▶ Bobby Thomson's home run against *the Brooklyn Dodgers* became known as "*the shot* heard 'round *the world*." Russ Hodges captured *the excitement* in his radio broadcast, shouting out, "*The Giants* win *the pennant! The Giants* win *the pennant! The Giants* win *the pennant!*"

WHEN TO USE NO ARTICLE

▶ *People* whose bodies are intolerant of *lactose* cannot digest *milk* easily.

▶ Many *people* have found that winning a lottery does not bring them *happiness*.

▶ Airline *passengers* now often have to pay fees to check *luggage*.

TO SEE HOW IMPORTANT COMMAS ARE, read the following sentence: *Let's eat Grandma!* Now see what a difference a comma can make:

► Let's eat, Grandma!

We found this sentence on *Facebook,* followed by this excellent advice: "Punctuation saves lives."

This section focuses on some of the ways that commas help authors and readers, from setting off introductory words to separating items in a series to making sure that Grandma gets to eat rather than being eaten.

To Set Off Introductory Words

Put a comma after any word, phrase, or clause that comes before the subject of the sentence. Some authors omit a comma after very short introductory elements, but you'll never be wrong to so include it.

► In 2012, the New York Giants defeated the New England Patriots in the Super Bowl.

► Gleefully, New Yorkers celebrated.

► Holding up the Vince Lombardi trophy, MVP Eli Manning waved to the fans.

► To honor the team, Mayor Bloomberg gave each player a key to the city.

► As he accepted his key, Victor Cruz did his signature salsa moves.

Be careful of sentences with inverted word order, where the subject comes after the verb; do not put a comma after a phrase that begins such a sentence.

► On the horizon appeared a plane.

► In the package were a box of chocolate-chip cookies and various salty snacks.

TO SET OFF INTRODUCTORY WORDS

▶ The marathon completed, the runners greeted their friends and family members.

▶ At the candidate's rally, her supporters waved signs and shouted encouragement.

▶ Because they are dissatisfied with both public and private schools, some parents homeschool their children.

▶ Joyfully, the Heat celebrated after defeating the Thunder in the NBA Finals.

▶ Distracted by a text message, the driver failed to see the stop sign.

▶ Frantically stacking sandbags, the volunteers tried to hold back the rising floodwaters.

▶ To write well, seek out responses to your draft and allow time to revise.

▶ Although many texters enjoy breaking linguistic rules, they also know they need to be understood.

To celebrate World Poetry day in 2007, T-Mobile tried to find the UK's first "Txt laureate" in a competition for the best romantic poem in SMS.

The most important finding is that texting does not erode children's ability to read and write. On the contrary, literacy improves.

In short, it's fun.

—DAVID CRYSTAL, "2b or Not 2b"

To Join Clauses in Compound Sentences

Put a comma before the coordinating conjunction (*and, but, for, nor, or, so,* or *yet*) that connects the main clauses in a compound sentence.

▶ A balanced budget amendment to the Constitution sounds like a good way to reduce spending, but the government needs more budgetary flexibility for varying economic conditions.

To Set Off Nonessential Elements

Parts of a sentence that are not essential to its meaning should be set off with commas. Parts that are essential to a sentence's meaning should not be set off with commas.

NONESSENTIAL CLAUSE   Opera fans, who are notoriously fickle, loved Luciano Pavarotti throughout his long career.

ESSENTIAL CLAUSE   Opera fans who love *The Magic Flute* would especially appreciate Ingmar Bergman's film version.

NONESSENTIAL PHRASE   The wood, cut just yesterday, needs to cure before it can be burned in the fireplace.

ESSENTIAL PHRASE   Wood cut from hardwood trees burns longer and hotter than wood cut from softwood trees.

NONESSENTIAL WORDS   My sister, Laura, loves to make the cranberry sauce for Thanksgiving.

ESSENTIAL WORDS   My sister Susan always brings her special mashed potatoes for Thanksgiving, while my sister Betty brings pumpkin pie.

In the first sentence, the author has only one sister, so her name is not essential to the meaning—and is thus enclosed in commas. In the second, the names of the sisters are essential to the meaning because there is more than one sister.

TO JOIN CLAUSES IN COMPOUND SENTENCES

▶ The tornado severely damaged the apartment building, but the residents all survived.

▶ Several residents were trapped for hours in the wreckage, and one was not rescued until two days later.

▶ I grew up in Kansas, so I take tornado warning sirens seriously.

TO SET OFF NONESSENTIAL ELEMENTS

▶ Members of the baby boom generation, who were born between World War II and the early 1960s, have started to become eligible for Medicare.

▶ The dramatic increase in childhood obesity in the United States, which public health officials have described as a crisis, has many possible contributing causes.

▶ Fast-food chains, blamed for encouraging fattening food, are trying to offer lower-calorie options.

▶ Daniel Radcliffe, famous for his lead role in the Harry Potter movies, starred on Broadway in *Equus* and *How to Succeed in Business without Really Trying*.

▶ *Glee*, the hit TV show about a high school glee club, has made many of its cast members into celebrities.

▶ Congress should increase access to medical and health savings accounts, which give consumers the option of rolling money reserved for health care into a retirement account.
                                        —RADLEY BALKO, "What You Eat Is Your Own Business"

▶ Growing corn, which from a biological perspective had always been a process of capturing sunlight to turn it into food, has in no small measure become a process of converting fossil fuels into food.
                                        —MICHAEL POLLAN, "What's Eating America"

To Separate Items in a Series

Use a comma to separate items in a series. Some authors omit the comma before the final item in the series, but you'll never be wrong to include it—and sometimes omitting the comma can confuse your readers.

▶ We're celebrating Cinco de Mayo with a special menu: tamales, refried beans, chicken and beef tacos, fresh salsa, and corn.

The final comma makes it clear that fresh salsa and corn are two separate items.

To Set Off Interjections, Direct Address, Tag Questions, and Contrasting Elements

INTERJECTIONS	Wow, that was a great film!
DIRECT ADDRESS	"Corporations are people, my friend." —MITT ROMNEY
TAG QUESTIONS	You're kidding, aren't you?
CONTRASTING ELEMENTS	Tai chi, unlike yoga, is practiced for its martial training as well as for its health benefits.

To Set Off Parenthetical and Transitional Expressions

▶ Umami, by the way, has recently been recognized as a fifth taste, along with sweet, bitter, sour, and salty.

▶ Homemade applesauce, in fact, is both tastier and healthier than store-bought applesauce.

▶ In other words, we're arguing that it makes no sense to build a large waste transfer station in a densely populated residential neighborhood.

TO SEPARATE ITEMS IN A SERIES

▶ My father told me I was going to college even if he had to beg, borrow, or steal the money.

▶ Americans today can eat pears in the spring in Minnesota, oranges in the summer in Montana, asparagus in the fall in Maine, and cranberries in the winter in Florida. —KATHERINE SPRIGGS, "On Buying Local"

▶ Students came to class in cars, on bicycles, on foot, and even on skateboards.

▶ The cat ran out the door, across the road, and into the woods.

TO SET OFF INTERJECTIONS, DIRECT ADDRESS, TAG QUESTIONS, AND CONTRASTING ELEMENTS

▶ "Oh, I think you know what I'm talking about," Samantha said.

▶ Mike laughed and said, "Dude, you need some help."

▶ Members of Congress have to file financial disclosure forms, don't they?

▶ The queen, not the king, is the most powerful piece in chess.

▶ The Penn State football program, unlike the programs of many other top-ranked schools, is known for the high graduation rate of its players.

TO SET OFF PARENTHETICAL AND TRANSITIONAL EXPRESSIONS

▶ Investment income, on the other hand, is taxed at a lower rate.

▶ Wind power, however, has environmental disadvantages as well as benefits.

▶ Ultimately, what's at stake is the health of everyone who lives or works in this neighborhood.

With Addresses, Place Names, and Dates

▶ Please send any contributions to The Oregon Cultural Trust, 775 Summer St. NE, Ste. 200, Salem, OR 97301-1280.

▶ Strasbourg, France, is the site of the European Parliament.

▶ No one who experienced the events of September 11, 2011, will ever forget that day.

To Set Off Quotations

▶ "In my view," said Junot Díaz, "a writer is a writer because even when there is no hope, even when nothing you do shows any sign of promise, you keep writing anyway."

▶ "Poetry is not a healing lotion, an emotional massage, a kind of linguistic aromatherapy," said Adrienne Rich in a speech to the National Book Foundation in 2006.

▶ "Don't compromise yourself," Janis Joplin advised. "You are all you've got."

Do not use a comma before quotations that are introduced with *that*.

▶ It was Virginia Woolf who said that "A woman must have money and a room of her own if she is to write fiction."

Do not use a comma to set off an indirect quotation, one that does not quote someone's exact words.

▶ In a commencement address at Harvard in 2008, J. K. Rowling spoke about failure, saying that failure teaches you who you are and who you can be.

▶ Tallulah Bankhead once said that if she had her life to live over again, she'd make the same mistakes, only sooner.

WITH ADDRESSES, PLACE NAMES, AND DATES

▶ The company's address is 500 Fifth Ave., New York, NY 10110.

▶ The performance venues in Branson, Missouri, have become popular tourist destinations.

▶ The movie director Ang Lee was born in Chaochou, Taiwan, and came to the United States to attend college.

▶ President Franklin Roosevelt said that December 7, 1941, was "a day that will live in infamy."

TO SET OFF QUOTATIONS

▶ The King James Bible warns, "Pride goeth before destruction."

▶ "Life can only be understood backward, but it has to be lived forward," wrote Søren Kierkegaard.

▶ "There have been only two geniuses in the world," insisted Tallulah Bankhead, "Willie Mays and Willie Shakespeare."

▶ When he was asked if Major League Baseball was ready for an openly gay player, Willie Mays was quick to respond, asking, "Can he hit?"

▶ Humphrey Bogart once declared that he'd "rather have a hot dog at the ballpark than a steak at the Ritz."

▶ Lauren Bacall was once quoted as saying that "Imagination is the highest kite that one can fly."

Unnecessary Commas

Do not put commas around essential elements

▶ The Galápagos Islands are home to many species of plants and animals, that are found nowhere else.

▶ Shirley Brice Heath's book, *Ways with Words,* is a study of children learning to use language in two communities in the Carolinas.

Since Heath has written more than one book, the title is essential information and should not be set off by commas.

Do not put commas between subjects and verbs

▶ What the original Occupy Wall Street protesters could not have anticipated, was the speed with which their movement would spread throughout the country.

▶ The only reason that the committee gave for its decision to end the program, was lack of funds.

Do not put commas between compound subjects or verbs

▶ People who live in "red" states, and those who live in "blue" states hold many mistaken beliefs about each other.

▶ The chef whisked the eggs and milk together in a bowl, and poured the mixture into the omelet pan.

Do not add a comma after a question mark or an exclamation point

▶ "Hi, may I help you?," shouted the manager at Gates Bar-B-Q.

▶ "Everybody out of the water!," yelled the lifeguard.

UNNECESSARY COMMAS

Around essential elements

▶ The painting, that was found in the abandoned house, sold for ten thousand dollars.

▶ The novelist, Jonathan Franzen, has been invited to speak at a campus writers' seminar next month.

▶ The article argues that children, raised in conditions of poverty, often suffer long-term damage to their cognitive development.

Between subjects and verbs

▶ One of the factors that make the health-care system in the United States so expensive, is the amount spent to extend the last few months of patients' lives.

In compound subjects or verbs

▶ Families looking for more affordable space, and hipsters looking for a cool cultural scene all flocked to Brooklyn.

▶ The earthquake and tsunami devastated the northeastern coast of Honshu, but mostly spared the densely populated Tokyo and Osaka areas.

After a question mark or an exclamation point

▶ "What can I possibly do about global warming?," ask many of my friends.

▶ "I want my money back!," the angry customer yelled.

A COMMA SPLICE OCCURS when you join two main clauses with only a comma. Leave out the comma, and it's a fused sentence. Writing like this might be perfectly appropriate in a tweet or a comment on a blog, but it's likely to be seen as a mistake in academic writing. This section shows four ways to edit comma splices and fused sentences.

COMMA SPLICE   Why build a new stadium, the existing one is just fine.

FUSED SENTENCE   She shoots she scores we win!

Make the Clauses into Two Separate Sentences

▶ Tropical Storm Irene caused major flooding in the Northeast ~~hundreds~~ of roads and bridges were damaged or destroyed. *. Hundreds*

Link Clauses with Comma + *And, But, Or, Nor, For, So,* or *Yet*

▶ Tropical Storm Irene caused major flooding in the Northeast *,and* hundreds of roads and bridges were damaged or destroyed.

Link the Clauses with a Semicolon

▶ Tropical Storm Irene caused major flooding in the Northeast *;* hundreds of roads and bridges were damaged or destroyed.

Adding a transition after the semicolon such as *therefore* or *however,* followed by a comma, can help make explicit how the two clauses relate.

▶ Tropical Storm Irene caused major flooding in the Northeast *; as a result,* hundreds of roads and bridges were damaged or destroyed.

Revise One Clause as a Subordinate Clause

▶ *When* Tropical Storm Irene caused major flooding in the Northeast *,* hundreds of roads and bridges were damaged or destroyed.

MAKE THE CLAUSES INTO TWO SEPARATE SENTENCES

▶ The number of landline telephones is decreasing, *. More* ~~more~~ and more people have only a cell phone.

▶ Why build a new stadium, *? The* ~~the~~ existing stadium is just fine.

LINK CLAUSES WITH COMMA + *AND, BUT, OR, NOR, FOR, SO,* OR *YET*

▶ The 2011 Japanese tsunami produced five million tons of trash, *and* most of it stayed near the Japanese coastline.

▶ Some adoptees would like to find their birth parents *, but* they are often thwarted by laws protecting the privacy of the parents.

▶ Many jobs today are not tied to a particular physical location *, so* employees can work anywhere online.

LINK THE CLAUSES WITH A SEMICOLON

▶ Green tea has been gaining in popularity in recent years *;* it has less caffeine than black tea and is seen as a more healthful alternative.

▶ Global warming could have serious consequences, *; for example,* many countries and cities might be threatened by rising ocean levels.

REVISE ONE CLAUSE AS A SUBORDINATE CLAUSE

▶ Small Midwestern towns have been losing population, *because* young people go elsewhere to find jobs.

▶ *Although* *Moby-Dick* got terrible reviews when it was first published, many people now consider it the greatest American novel ever written.

PREPOSITIONS

ABOUT, AT, BY, FOR, FROM, IN, ON, TO—these are all prepositions, words that show relationships between other words. Imagine you've got a book *about* your mom, *by* your mom, *for* your mom, or *from* your mom; each means something different, and the difference is all in the prepositions. Not all languages use prepositions, and if English is not your primary language, they can be a challenge to learn. Following are some tips and examples that can help with three of the most widely used prepositions: *at, in,* and *on.* Remember, though, that are there are many exceptions; if in doubt, consult a dictionary.

Prepositions of Place

AT *a specific address:* the house *at* 54 Main Street

a general kind of place: at home, *at* work, *at* school

a general kind of event: at a concert, *at* a party

IN *an enclosed space: in* the closet, *in* my pocket, *in* a cup

a geographical area: in Brazil, *in* Chicago, *in* Africa

a printed work: an article *in* a journal, a chapter *in* a book

ON *a surface:* sitting *on* the bench, a fly *on* the wall, papers *on* a desk

a street: driving *on* Route 17, a restaurant *on* Maple Avenue

an electronic medium: on the web, *on* TV, *on* the radio

Prepositions of Time

AT *a specific point in time: at* 4:46 a.m., *at* noon, *at* sunrise

IN *a part of a day: in* the morning, *in* the evening (but *at* night)

a year, month, or season: in 2012, *in* January, *in* the spring

a period of time: graduated *in* three years, return *in* an hour

ON *a day of the week or month: on* Thursday, *on* March 13

a holiday: travel *on* Thanksgiving, a parade *on* Memorial Day

PREPOSITIONS OF PLACE

▶ Dylan Thomas once lived *in* New York, *at* the Chelsea Hotel *on* Twenty-third Street.

▶ People *in* the neighborhood often rent rooms *in* their homes to students.

▶ Dogs are not allowed *in* most grocery stores *in* the United States.

▶ The story *on* the radio was about the growth of Pentecostal religion *in* South America.

▶ The money *in* the tip jar was divided among the employees.

▶ An accident *on* Interstate 81 injured three people.

▶ Put your papers *in* the envelope *on* my office door.

PREPOSITIONS OF TIME

▶ The Beatles first came to the United States *in* 1964.

▶ Betsye takes classes *in* the evening.

▶ Jamaica Kincaid was the Grinnell College commencement speaker *on* May 21, 2012.

▶ The performance will be *on* July 25 *at* noon.

▶ The Occupy Wall Street movement began *in* 2011.

▶ Juliet Rose was born *on* April 15, 2012.

▶ The Kenyon Gospel Choir will perform *on* Martin Luther King Jr.'s birthday.

IF YOU'VE EVER BEEN READING SOMETHING and stumbled over a word like *he* or *which* because you couldn't tell what it referred to, you've discovered a problem with pronoun reference. Pronouns need to have a clear antecedent, a specific word that they refer to—and to agree with that antecedent in gender and number, as the following example demonstrates:

▶ *Coffee shops* are good places to work because *they* offer quiet spaces and comforting beverages.

Clear Pronoun Reference

A pronoun should refer clearly to one and only one antecedent.

AMBIGUOUS Although Lady Gaga and Madonna are often compared, she is more accomplished as a musician.

Who's more accomplished, Lady Gaga or Madonna? To eliminate the ambiguity, revise the sentence to use pronouns that refer clearly to one woman or the other or to eliminate the need for a pronoun.

EDITED Although she is often compared to Madonna, Lady Gaga is more accomplished as a musician.

EDITED Although often compared to Madonna, Lady Gaga is more accomplished as a musician.

This, That, Which

Be sure the pronouns *this*, *that*, and *which* refer to a specific antecedent rather than to an idea or a sentence. Because the context often makes the meaning obvious, this kind of vague reference is common in conversation, but in writing you should eliminate the pronoun or provide a clear antecedent.

▶ Cable television has consistently challenged the domination of the major
        a trend that
networks, ~~which~~ has benefited viewers.
        ^

▶ Cable provides many more programming options than the networks can,
           variety
and viewers appreciate this.
           ^

CLEAR PRONOUN REFERENCE

▶ In the climax of the play, the central character tells his brother
the brother
that ~~he~~ will never measure up to their father.
   ^

▶ The management representatives reached a tentative agreement on a new
management's
contract with the unions, but ~~their~~ tough negotiating stance on the details
   ^

made a final settlement difficult.

▶ The management representatives reached a tentative agreement on a new
the unions'
contract with the unions, but ~~their~~ tough negotiating stance on the details
   ^

made a final settlement difficult.

THIS, THAT, WHICH

▶ Most scientists believe that global warming is occurring at least partly
idea
because of human activity, but most conservatives reject that.
   ^

drop in price
▶ Solar energy is becoming cheaper, and this will eventually make it
   ^
competitive with fossil fuels.

and therefore are
▶ Most Americans have to drive to work~~, which makes them~~ extremely
   ^
sensitive to gasoline prices.

a fact that
▶ Most Americans have to drive to work, ~~which~~ makes them extremely
   ^
sensitive to gasoline prices.

They, It, You

In informal contexts, we often use *they, it,* or *you* without any antecedent. In academic writing, however, *they* and *it* should always have a specific antecedent, and *you* should be used only to refer specifically to the reader.

▶ At some airports, ~~they~~ do not ask passengers to remove belts to go

    TSA agents

    through the security check.

▶ ~~On the~~ website,~~it~~ identifies the author as a former speechwriter for

    The

    Stephen Colbert.

▶ ~~In many states, you must~~ go through a law enforcement background

    Many states require people to

    check before ~~you~~ can work with children.

    they

    This use of you *could be appropriate in some rhetorical situations—in a manual for day-care workers, for instance—but is inappropriate in most academic writing.*

Implied antecedents

In informal contexts, we often use pronouns that refer to words clearly implied but not directly stated in a sentence. In academic writing, however, do not use such implied antecedents.

▶ I had planned to bike to class yesterday, but it had a flat tire.

    ride my

    Although the pronoun it *implies that* bike *is a noun, it was used as a verb. The revision makes it into a noun.*

▶ In ~~Edward Ball's~~ *Slaves in the Family,* he writes about finding and interviewing

    Edward Ball

    the African American descendants of his white slave-owning ancestors.

THEY, IT, YOU

► At some airports, ~~they do not ask~~ *are not asked* passengers to remove belts

to go through the security check.

► ~~On the website, it~~ *The "Contributors" link* identifies the author as a former speechwriter for

Stephen Colbert.

► In many states, ~~you~~ *job applicants* must go through a law enforcement background check

before ~~you~~ *they* can work with children.

► ~~On the~~ *The* voter registration form ~~they ask you for your~~ *asks for the voter's* home address

and phone number.

► ~~In the~~ *The* advertisement, ~~it~~ claims that the company will pay the shipping

charges for returning items for any reason.

IMPLIED ANTECEDENTS

► The children spent the afternoon sledding until a runner broke off of ~~it~~ *the sled*.

► The contractor repaired several holes in the wall and did not charge for

~~them~~ *that part of the work*.

► The inscription on Thomas Jefferson's tombstone does not mention that ~~he~~ *Jefferson*

was president of the United States.

Pronoun-Antecedent Agreement

A pronoun has to agree with its antecedent in gender and number.

GENDER   As Speaker of the House of Representatives, *John Boehner* was known for *his* candor and for letting *his* emotions show, sometimes choking up during debates about issues that mattered a lot to *him*.

NUMBER   *Speakers* must often exert *themselves* to persuade *their* party's representatives to side with *them*.

Compound antecedents

Compound antecedents joined with *and* take a plural pronoun unless they are preceded by *each* or *every*.

▶ Because of security concerns, when *the president and vice president* travel to the same event, *they* rarely travel together.

▶ *Every* U.S. *president and vice president* has needed to decide how to define *his* political role.

When a compound antecedent is joined with *or* or *nor*, the pronoun should agree with the nearest antecedent. If the antecedents are different genders or numbers, you might want to edit the sentence to keep it from being awkward.

AWKWARD   Neither Serena Williams nor Roger Federer was at his best.

EDITED   Serena Williams wasn't at her best, and Roger Federer wasn't either.

AWKWARD   Either the teachers or the principal needs to use his authority.

EDITED   Either the principal or the teachers need to use their authority.

Collective nouns as antecedents

collective nouns such as *team* or *audience* or the others listed on the facing page take a singular pronoun when the pronoun refers to the unit as a whole but a plural pronoun when the pronoun refers to multiple parts of the unit.

SINGULAR   The *band* changed *its* name to try to attract a different fan base.

PLURAL   The band left *their* instruments in the music room.

PRONOUN-ANTECEDENT AGREEMENT

Compound antecedents

▶ *Every fruit and vegetable* labeled "organic" has to be certified by ~~their~~ *its* grower.

▶ *Each manager and salesperson* is required to set ~~their~~ *his or her* personal goals each year.

▶ Neither Angela Merkel nor François Hollande felt politically secure enough to risk offending *domestic* public opinion ~~in his own country~~ during the EU crisis.

▶ Under the Articles of Confederation, either the ~~states~~ *national government* or the ~~national government~~ *states* could issue ~~its~~ *their* own currency.

Collective nouns as antecedents

COMMON COLLECTIVE NOUNS

audience	herd	faculty	chorus
crowd	family	congregation	jury
team	couple	choir	panel

▶ The *committee* took *their* seats, and the meeting began.

▶ The judge told the *jury* to consider only the facts of the case in reaching *its* verdict.

Indefinite pronouns as antecedents

Most indefinite pronouns such as *anybody, everyone, nobody,* or *someone* take a singular pronoun.

▶ *Everyone* involved in the negotiations had *his or her* own agenda.

If you find *his or her* awkward, revise the sentence to make both pronouns plural or to eliminate the indefinite pronouns.

▶ *All* of those involved in the negotiations had *their* own agendas.

▶ The *individuals* involved in the negotiations all had *their* own agendas.

In informal conversation, words like *everybody, someone,* and *nobody* are often used with plural pronouns: *Somebody left their coat on the chair.* In academic writing, however, stick to the singular for such references.

Noun antecedents that could be either male or female

If an antecedent could be either male or female, do not use masculine pronouns such as *he* or *him* to refer to it. Use *he or she, her or his,* and so on, or edit the sentence to make the antecedent and pronoun both plural or to eliminate the pronoun.

▶ A *Speaker of the House* has to be good at enforcing party discipline; it is an important part of *his or her* job.

▶ *Speakers of the House* have to be good at enforcing party discipline; it is an important part of *their* job.

▶ A *Speaker of the House* has to be good at enforcing party discipline; it is an important part of *the* job.

Indefinite pronouns as antecedents

SINGULAR INDEFINITE PRONOUNS

another	each	much	one
any	either	neither	other
anybody	everybody	nobody	somebody
anyone	everyone	no one	someone
anything	everything	nothing	something

► ~~Anyone who uses~~ Facebook ~~has~~ to remember to set up their primary

settings carefully.

(Users of) *(have)*

► Everybody on the girls' volleyball team *was* expected to buy ~~their~~ own
uniform.

(her)

► *Someone* who has served in the military should not have to worry about
losing *his or her* health insurance.

► *People* in my generation once thought that going to college would guarantee
their financial security.

Noun antecedents that could be either male or female

(or her)

► A college student often chooses his major on the basis of its expected
financial rewards.

(a)

► A college student often chooses ~~his~~ major on the basis of its expected
financial rewards.

(College students often choose their)

► ~~A college student often chooses his~~ major on the basis of its expected

financial rewards.

A SENTENCE FRAGMENT OCCURS when something less than a sentence is capitalized and punctuated as if it were a complete sentence. Fragments are common in advertising, where they serve to grab the attention of readers and sometimes to create memorable slogans. For example:

▶ A unique mix of clothing and accessories you don't even know you want yet!
—Lizard Lounge ad, *Willamette Week*

As common as they are in many informal contexts, fragments are frowned upon in academic writing. In these contexts, they are considered errors because readers see them as violating the basic rules of sentence structure—and as evidence that the author doesn't know what those rules are.

A sentence fragment occurs when some essential element is missing, usually a subject or a verb—or when it begins with a subordinating word like *which* or *because* and is merely a subordinate clause. To be a sentence, there must be at least one main clause.

NO SUBJECT	Many people could not resist buying homes at very low interest rates. As a result, took on too much debt.
NO VERB	Bank loans available with little or no down payment.
SUBORDINATE CLAUSE	In Ireland, many new homes remain empty. Because the real estate bubble burst.

To edit most fragments, you need to do one of two things: (1) make the fragment into a complete sentence, or (2) attach it to a nearby sentence.

Make the Fragment into a Complete Sentence

ADD A SUBJECT	*they* As a result, took on too much debt.
ADD A VERB	*became* Bank loans available with little or no down payment.
DELETE THE SUBORDINATING WORD	*because* In Ireland, many new homes remain empty. ~~Because~~ the real estate bubble burst.

MAKE THE FRAGMENT INTO A COMPLETE SENTENCE

▶ *I had*
  ~~Had~~ an accident in my truck and had to spend a lot of money on repairs.
  ^

▶ U.S. companies have come under increasing pressure to cut costs. *Many of them have* ~~Have~~

  outsourced jobs to China, India, and other Asian countries.

▶ The U.S. housing market still *is* extremely depressed. *The president and Congress need* ~~Need~~ to figure out a
  ^   ^

  way to help millions of homeowners who cannot pay their mortgages.

▶ The program showed glaciers melting as a result of global warming. Many *are*
  ^

  disappearing faster than predicted a few years ago.

▶ My sister's room *was* always a mess, crammed with posters, athletic
  ^

  equipment, and clothes thrown on the floor.

▶ *It was*
  ~~Was~~ really exciting and stimulating to live in Tokyo.
  ^

▶ The Semester at Sea students and their instructors sailed around the world
  They visited
  on the *MV Explorer.* ~~Visiting~~ twelve countries in 106 days.
  ^

▶ *The Best Exotic Marigold Hotel* *starred* ~~starring~~ Judi Dench, Maggie Smith, Bill
  ^

  Nighy, and Tom Wilkinson in an extravagant Indian adventure.

▶ Dad explained how to write checks and balance my checkbook. *He also taught me* ~~Also~~ how
  ^
  to scramble eggs.

▶ Nick worked as an intern at a consulting firm for six months after graduating.
  He did so to
  ~~To~~ get experience and perhaps to get a permanent position there.
  ^

▶ He eventually decided to move to New York. *He thought he'd* ~~Because he~~ find more job
  ^
  opportunities there.

Attach the Fragment to a Nearby Sentence

▶ A growing number of "medical tourists" travel abroad to have cosmetic

               or

surgery. ~~Or~~ other medical procedures that are much cheaper outside the

United States.

▶ Michael Moore's movie *Sicko* made the American health-care system a topic

                           , although

of national conversation. ~~Although~~ even many who share his politics

criticized him for playing fast and loose with the facts.

                                     nomination,

▶ In 1968, George Romney tried for the Republican presidential ~~nomination.~~

   which

~~Which~~ his son Mitt won forty-four years later.

                           television, we decided

▶ Tired of the same old reality shows and reruns on ~~television. Decided~~

to go to an a cappella concert on campus.

ATTACH THE FRAGMENT TO A NEARBY SENTENCE

▶ Older Americans are often nostalgic for the 1950s. ~~When~~ *, when* families and

jobs seemed more stable.

▶ The average family size has dropped sharply. ~~Because~~ *because* people are

marrying at later ages and having fewer children than in the baby boom era.

▶ In the 1970s, the United States began losing manufacturing jobs to overseas

competitors. ~~Has~~ *, a trend that has* only recently been reversed.

▶ In recent years, India has begun to develop its own high-tech ~~economy.~~ *economy,*

~~Which~~ *which* is centered in the city of Bangalore.

▶ ABC is broadcasting the 2012 NBA finals. ~~With,~~ *with* a panel of experts

breaking down the games afterward.

▶ The farmers market opens every Sunday morning at 9:00. ~~And~~ *and* closes at

1:00.

▶ Much of the country is suffering from a heat wave. ~~Which~~ *, which* makes many

of us especially irritable.

YOU'LL OFTEN HAVE REASON to shift gears when you write, as when you shift from one verb tense to another.

▶ The National Weather Service issued a freeze warning, saying that temperatures will dip into the 20s tomorrow.

This sentence refers to actions occurring at different times, so they require different tenses. But unnecessary shifts in tense—or point of view—can confuse readers.

Shifts in Tense

It's sometimes necessary to shift verb tenses to refer to actions that take place at different times.

▶ The play that *opened* yesterday *will be reviewed* in newspapers tomorrow.

Readers may be confused, however, if you shift from one tense to another in referring to things that happen in the same time frame.

SHIFT   The editorial *noted* the increases in college tuition this year and also *discusses* the causes of skyrocketing tuition costs over the last few decades.

This sentence starts out using the past tense (*noted*) and then switches to the present tense (*discusses*). To eliminate the shift, make both verbs either past tense or present:

▶ The editorial *noted* the increases in college tuition this year and also *discussed* the causes of skyrocketing tuition costs over the last few decades.

▶ The editorial *notes* the increases in college tuition this year and also *discusses* the causes of skyrocketing tuition costs over the last few decades.

Be careful to use the present tense when you're writing about a literary work—and not to accidentally shift to the past tense.

▶ Fitzgerald portrays Gatsby as a boy from a poor family who eventually becomes rich enough to buy a mansion, where he ~~threw~~ *throws* huge extravagant parties in the hope of impressing Daisy.

SHIFTS IN TENSE

▶ After Pearl Harbor, U.S. authorities wrongly suspected that Japanese
  Americans living near the Pacific coast ~~are~~ *were* a security risk.

▶ According to several studies, women are more likely than men to develop
  the disease, but their symptoms ~~tended~~ *tend* to be less severe.

▶ In many cities, the Occupy protesters came into conflict with police and
  in some cases ~~are~~ *were* injured by pepper spray and other crowd-control tactics.

▶ In *Moneyball,* Brad Pitt plays Billy Beane, general manager of the Oakland A's,
  and ~~showed~~ *shows* how he uses statistics to find undervalued ball players.

▶ Only a few countries are major contributors to global warming, but this
  phenomenon ~~affected~~ *affects* everyone in the world.

▶ Miguel was paddling swiftly to the pier deep in the Amazon rainforest; he
  ~~misses~~ *missed* a stroke and almost ~~falls~~ *fell* overboard.

▶ Chen competed successfully for the women's Olympics semifinal in aerial
  acrobatics, but then she ~~fails~~ *failed* to attain the title in the end.

Shifts in Point of View

Sometimes you may have good reason to shift between first person (*I, we*), second person (*you*), or third person (*he, she, they*).

▶ *You* may think that you clearly remember the details of an event, but *scientists* who have studied eyewitness testimony in court cases have found that witnesses' memories are often extremely faulty.

In this sentence, the writer is contrasting readers' beliefs about something with research findings about the same topic, so a shift from second person (*you*) to third (*scientists*) is appropriate. Shifting from one point of view to another when referring to the same subjects, however, would be inconsistent—and could confuse your audience.

SHIFT   *Employees* were stunned by the huge increases in health-insurance premiums. *You* had no choice, though, but to pay or to lose coverage.

Here the point of view shifts from *employees* to *you*, even though both sentences refer to the same group of people. To eliminate the inconsistency, revise one of the sentences to use the same point of view as the other.

▶ *Employees* were stunned by the huge increases in health-insurance premiums. *They* had no choice, though, but to pay or to lose coverage.

Some shifts in number are actually problems in agreement between a pronoun and its antecedent. Such a shift is often the result of an effort to avoid using *he* to refer to both men and women—or to avoid the awkward *he or she* construction. Here's an example from this book, shown as it was in the first draft, then as it was edited to eliminate the confusing shift.

SHIFT   Today, *anyone* with access to a computer can publish what *they* write.

EDITED   Today, if you have access to a computer, you can publish what you write.

SHIFTS IN POINT OF VIEW

▶ *If you decide*   *, you have*
  ~~A person who decides~~ to become a vegetarian ~~has~~ to pay careful attention
  to your diet to make sure you are getting essential nutrients.

▶ Many Americans want the government to provide services that benefit
  they
  them, but ~~we~~ do not want to pay for these services through taxes.

▶ The library is so quiet during exams week that one can hear a sheet of paper
  one's
  fall on the floor or ~~your~~ fingers tapping on a laptop.

▶ When you get to college, you have to grow up and do laundry, balance a
  you're on
  checkbook, and keep track of all your courses, so for the first time, ~~I'm on~~
  your
  ~~my~~ own.

▶ Students working on service-learning projects in Ghana or Kenya or South
  they have
  Africa are making a difference, even though ~~a student has~~ little power to
  change the world.

  economists
▶ Even though ~~an economist~~ may understand what's wrong with the economy,
  they don't necessarily know how to fix it.

▶ Teachers who speak more than one language are in great demand, and
  teachers who speak   *have*
  ~~a teacher who speaks~~ Spanish in particular probably ~~has~~ many job
  opportunities.

▶ Our relay team practiced passing the baton over and over and over again
  Runners need
  before the Penn Relays. ~~A runner needs~~ to hand the baton off very carefully
  so that no one drops it.

VERBS NEED TO AGREE (that is, match up) with their subjects in number (singular or plural) and person (first, second, or third): *I smile, you smile, he or she smiles, we smile, they smile.* Sometimes getting subjects and verbs to agree can be tricky, however, especially when other words come between them: *The best paintings in the show were watercolors.* Following are guidelines to help you check for subject-verb agreement in your writing.

When Other Words Come between Subject and Verb

Sometimes the subject is separated from the verb by other words. Be careful that the verb agrees with the subject, not with a word that falls in between.

> ▶ The *contents* of the old family photo album ~~has~~ *have* provided many clues in our genealogical research.

> ▶ The *mayor* as well as the taxpayers ~~support~~ *supports* the stadium proposal.

Compound Subjects

If two or more subjects are joined by *and*, they generally take a plural verb.

> ▶ My math textbook and workbook ~~costs~~ *cost* more than all my other books combined.

However, if two words joined by *and* are considered a single unit, like *fish and chips*, they take a singular verb.

> ▶ Fish and chips ~~are~~ *is* a dish found on menus everywhere in England.

If two or more subjects are joined by *or* or *nor*, the verb should agree with the closest subject.

> ▶ Neither the legislators nor the governor ~~were~~ *was* willing to take a stand.

A sentence like this, where the subject includes both singular and plural parts, may read more smoothly if you revise to put the plural part closest to the verb: *Neither the governor nor the legislators were willing to take a stand.*

WHEN OTHER WORDS COME BETWEEN SUBJECT AND VERB

▶ *Institutions* of higher education *continue* to think of creative ways to increase income.

▶ The *laughter* of the children watching the clowns *was* soothing.

▶ *Produce* grown using organic methods *is* more expensive.

▶ A bowl of ripe yellow pears, which created a delicious smell in the kitchen, ~~were~~ *was* part of the strategy to make the house more inviting to potential buyers.

COMPOUND SUBJECTS

▶ *Peanut butter and pizza are* my favorite foods.

▶ *Peanut butter and jelly,* however, *is* my favorite sandwich.

▶ I love Justin Bieber, but *neither "All around the World" nor "Boyfriend" lives* up to all the hype about his new album.

▶ *The president or the chancellor or the trustees have* the power to overturn decisions of the faculty senate.

▶ *A blanket and a pillow* ~~was~~ *were distributed* to each camper.

▶ Either the workers on the renovation project *or their supervisor* ~~are~~ *is* responsible for the damage.

▶ Neither she nor I know~~s~~ the answer to your question.

Subjects That Follow Verbs

Although verbs usually follow their subjects in English sentences, sometimes this order is reversed. In a sentence that begins with *there is* or *there are*, the subject always follows the verb. In the following example, the subject is *problems*.

▶ There ~~is~~ ^{are} undoubtedly many unresolved problems with the current proposal.

Sentences that begin with a prepositional phrase followed by a verb may also cause problems. In the following sentence, the subject is *rights*, not *importance*.

▶ Of greatest importance ~~is~~ ^{are} the rights to the performers' videos.

Collective Nouns Such as *Audience* or *Team*

In American English, collective nouns like *audience, team,* and *crowd* are usually treated as singular. Sometimes, however, when they refer to individuals in a group rather than to the group as a unit, they take a plural verb.

SINGULAR The *team wins* convincingly each week.

PLURAL   The *committee disagree* about the report's suggestions.

The members of the committee disagree with each other. If a sentence like this sounds awkward, you can revise to make it clear that you are referring to individuals, not the unit: *The committee members disagree about the report's suggestions.*

COMMON COLLECTIVE NOUNS

audience	herd	faculty	chorus
crowd	family	congregation	jury
team	couple	choir	panel
committee	board (of directors, of trustees, etc.)		

SUBJECTS THAT FOLLOW VERBS

▶ There *are a desk and a computer* for each of the temporary employees.

▶ Here *~~is~~* *the plan* for the renovation *and a list* of items to buy.
     are

▶ Behind the stage *~~was~~* *a dressing room and storage space* for costumes.
     were

COLLECTIVE NOUNS SUCH AS *AUDIENCE* OR *TEAM*

▶ In criminal cases, a *jury needs* to reach a unanimous verdict to convict or acquit; otherwise, a mistrial is declared.

▶ In criminal cases, the *members* of a jury *need* to reach a unanimous verdict to convict or acquit; otherwise, a mistrial is declared.

▶ The *audience were chatting* with one another as they waited for the performance to begin.

▶ The *cast* for the San Francisco production of *The Book of Mormon was* different from the one in New York.

▶ For the last few performances, the audience *~~were~~* made up almost entirely
     was

of people who had gotten deeply discounted or even free tickets.

▶ The cast of a Broadway show sometimes agrees to reduce their salaries to try to keep the show running longer.

Indefinite Pronouns Such as *Everyone* or *Nobody*

Most indefinite pronouns—words like *anyone, anything, each, everyone, nobody, no one,* and *something*—take a singular verb, even those that seem to have plural meanings (and are often treated as plural in casual conversation).

▶ *Everyone* at the Academy Awards *likes* to make a fashion statement.

▶ *Each* of the nominees *prepares* an acceptance speech and *hopes* to use it.

A few indefinite pronouns, including *both, few, many, others,* and *several,* are plural and take plural verbs.

▶ *Many* of the athletes in the Ironman Triathlon *have trained* for years.

Some indefinite pronouns, including *all, any, none, some, more, most,* and *enough,* take a singular verb when they refer to a singular noun or a plural verb when they refer to a plural noun.

SINGULAR *None* of the information given on the site *identifies* the sponsor.

PLURAL   *None* of the Greeks interviewed for the article *expect* the country's economic problems to improve in the next few years.

Words Such as *News* That Look Plural But Are Usually Singular

Words such as *news* and *athletics* look plural because they end in *–s,* but they are generally treated as singular. Some such words, notably *physics, mathematics, statistics, politics,* and *economics,* can be singular or plural, depending on the context.

SINGULAR Statistics *is* a required course for political science majors.

PLURAL   Statistics *show* that texting while driving is extremely dangerous.

INDEFINITE PRONOUNS SUCH AS *EVERYONE* OR *NOBODY*

▶ *Everyone,* it seems, *wants* to be on a reality show.

▶ *All of the candidates were* nervous about having to take a position on the immigration reform issue.

▶ *All of the media attention was focused* on the female candidates' appearance and the male candidates' sex life.

▶ *Some of the service members* discharged under the "don't ask, don't tell" policy *have reapplied* to the military.

▶ *Some of the debate* over the issues involved *was* similar to the debate over racial integration of the military in the 1940s.

▶ Each of the traditional neighborhoods in Chicago contributes distinctive qualities to the city.

WORDS SUCH AS *NEWS* THAT LOOK PLURAL
BUT ARE USUALLY SINGULAR

▶ *News travels* across the globe in a matter of seconds over the internet.

▶ German *measles* ~~are~~ is especially dangerous to pregnant women.

▶ *Economics* ~~have~~ has become one of the most popular majors at many colleges.

▶ The *economics* of higher education in the United States *puts* great financial pressure on families with average incomes.

Who, That, Which

The relative pronouns *who, that,* and *which* take singular verbs when they refer to a singular noun and plural verbs when they refer to a plural noun.

SINGULAR   Solar energy *technology* that *is* cheap and easy to install is growing in popularity.

PLURAL   *Cows,* which *produce* methane gas, play a surprisingly important part in global warming.

Problems sometimes occur with the expressions *one of the* and *the only one of the.* Phrases beginning with *the only one of the* always take a singular verb. Those beginning with *one of the* usually take a plural verb.

▶   *The only one of the* candidates who *was* appealing to younger voters was Ron Paul.

▶   A lack of safe drinking water is *one of the* main factors that *reduce* life expectancy in some developing countries.

Subjects That Are Titles

Subjects that are titles of books, movies, and so on use a singular verb even if the title is plural in form.

▶   *The Chronicles of Narnia* ~~have~~ has been cited as an influence by J. K. Rowling, author of the Harry Potter series.

WHO, THAT, WHICH

▶ Walter Isaacson has written *biographies* of Albert Einstein, Henry Kissinger, Benjamin Franklin, and Steve Jobs that *have* brought him much acclaim.

▶ Makers of flooring are increasingly turning to *bamboo*, which *is* easy to grow and harvest and is environmentally sustainable.

▶ PETA is one of the organizations that oppose*s* using animals in scientific experiments.

▶ Johnson is the only one of the presidential candidates who support*s* legalizing marijuana.

SUBJECTS THAT ARE TITLES

▶ *Friday Night Lights captures* perfectly the atmosphere of a small Texas town and its high school football team.

▶ Released in 1963, Alfred Hitchcock's thriller *The Birds is* still giving moviegoers nightmares half a century later.

▶ *Angry Birds* ~~have~~ *has* become tremendously popular through what Wikipedia calls "its successful combination of addictive gameplay, comical style, and low price."

WHAT'S THE DIFFERENCE between *lie* and *lay?* When would you re-membered *to study*, and when would you say you remembered *studying?* Why would you say you'd do something *if you had time* when you know you won't have time? These are all questions about verbs, the subject of this section.

Verb Forms

Every English verb has four forms: base, past tense, past participle, and pres-ent participle. For regular verbs, the past tense and past participle are both formed by adding -*ed* or -*d* to the base (and sometimes dropping a silent *e* or doubling a final consonant): *worked, danced, chatted.* For all verbs, the pres-ent participle is formed by adding –*ing* to the base form (again, sometimes dropping an *e* or doubling a consonant): *working, dancing, chatting.*

The problems that some writers have with verb forms are mostly with the past tense and past participle of irregular verbs, which do not follow the -*ed* or -*d* pattern and thus have to be memorized. A list of the forms of some common irregular verbs appears on the facing page.

Be careful not to confuse the past tense with the past participle. The past tense is used alone, whereas the past participle must be used together with one or more helping verbs such as *have* or *be.*

▶ When the maple tree *fell* in the storm, it *broke* the kitchen window.

▶ If other trees *had fallen*, more damage *would have been done.*

Forms of be. The verb *be* is especially irregular, with eight forms that simply must be learned.

BASE FORM	be
PRESENT TENSE	am, is, are
PAST TENSE	was, were
PRESENT PARTICIPLE	being
PAST PARTICIPLE	been

Some Common Irregular Verbs

BASE FORM	PAST TENSE	PAST PARTICIPLE	PRESENT PARTICIPLE
begin	began	begun	beginning
broadcast	broadcast	broadcast	broadcasting
choose	chose	chosen	choosing
do	did	done	doing
eat	ate	eaten	eating
find	found	found	finding
fly	flew	flown	flying
give	gave	given	giving
go	went	gone	going
grow	grew	grown	growing
have	had	had	having
know	knew	known	knowing
lay	laid	laid	laying
lie (recline)	lay	lain	lying
make	made	made	making
prove	proved	proved, proven	proving
read	read	read	reading
rise	rose	risen	rising
set	set	set	setting
sit	sat	sat	sitting
show	showed	showed, shown	showing
think	thought	thought	thinking
win	won	won	winning
take	took	taken	taking
write	wrote	written	writing

Verb Tenses

English verbs have three tenses to indicate time: present, past, and future.

PRESENT	PAST	FUTURE
I smile	I smiled	I will smile
I speak	I spoke	I will speak

Each tense has progressive forms, which indicate continuing actions.

PRESENT PROGRESSIVE   I *am smiling* in my class photo.

PAST PROGRESSIVE   I *was smiling* when it was taken.

FUTURE PROGRESSIVE   We *will* still *be working* on this book next week.

In addition, each tense has perfect forms. The *present perfect* indicates actions that happened at an indefinite time in the past or that began in the past and continue in the present. The *past perfect* indicates actions that took place before another past action. The *future perfect* indicates actions that will occur in the future before some other action.

PRESENT PERFECT   We *have spoken* about this situation repeatedly.

PAST PERFECT   She *had finished* before I arrived.

FUTURE PERFECT   By this time next year, we *will have been* to Paris.

Verbs can also be both perfect and progressive: I *have been working* late for many months now. This section focuses on several issues with verbs that often cause confusion in academic writing.

Verb Tenses

PRESENT	We *work* hard and *play* hard.
PAST	He *worked* at Northern Trust many years ago.
FUTURE	I *will* never again *work* this hard!
PRESENT PROGRESSIVE	It's midnight, and we *are* just *eating!*
PAST PROGRESSIVE	When I saw her, she *was making* cupcakes.
FUTURE PROGRESSIVE	Our take-out food *will be arriving* soon.
PRESENT PERFECT	That building *has been* empty for many months.
PAST PERFECT	This house *had been* empty for months when we rented it.
FUTURE PERFECT	Tomorrow we *will have been married* a year.
PRESENT PERFECT PROGRESSIVE	She *has been talking* since age two.
PAST PERFECT PROGRESSIVE	I *had been hoping* to see you.
FUTURE PERFECT PROGRESSIVE	We *will be seeing* you soon.

Use the present tense for scientific or general facts, even if the main clause of the sentence is in the past tense.

▶ Magellan's voyage proved conclusively that the world *is* round.

Use the present perfect tense to indicate a past action that continues in the present or to specify an action that took place in an indefinite time in the past.

▶ According to the 2010 census, the United States *has become* a predominantly urban nation.

Use the past tense to indicate a specific time in the past.

▶ Once the children moved out, we *decided* to move back to the city.

If you're writing about literature, use the present tense to discuss a text and the past tense to discuss its historical context.

▶ In *Pride and Prejudice and Zombies,* Elizabeth Bennet and Mr. Darcy *defeat* a field of zombies and then *settle* down to live happily ever after.

▶ According to author Seth Grahame-Smith, *Pride and Prejudice was* "just ripe for gore and senseless violence" ("Zombies Literature").

If you're following MLA, use the present tense in signal phrases introducing sources. But if you mention the date of the source, use the past tense.

▶ In his book *Spaghetti Westerns,* Christopher Frayling *observes* that "*Once Upon a Time* is concerned with the 'language' and 'syntax' of the Western" (213).

▶ As Pauline Kael *wrote* in her 1965 book *Kiss Kiss Bang Bang,* "*Stagecoach* had a mixture of reverie and reverence about the American past that made the picture seem almost folk art; we wanted to believe in it even if we didn't" (52).

If you're following APA, use the past tense or the present perfect tense in identifying a source:

▶ Zikmund-Fisher, Smith, Ubel, and Fagerlin (2007) *suggested* that numerical aptitude leads to better risk comprehension.

▶ Research *has proven* that higher mathematical aptitude leads to higher achievement on risk comprehension tasks (Zikmund-Fisher et al., 2007).

Use the present tense for scientific or general facts

▶ Galileo demonstrated that the earth *revolves* around the sun.

Use the present perfect to indicate a past action that continues in the present

▶ Since she finished school, Carolina *has had* three different jobs.

▶ She *has received* a big promotion since we last saw her.

▶ Since we arrived in Hong Kong, rents *have* almost *doubled*.

If you're writing about literature

▶ In *Native Son,* Chang-rae Lee *tells* the story of Henry Park, a man of two worlds who fears he belongs to neither one.

▶ Published to great acclaim in 1995, it *was* Lee's first novel.

If you're citing sources MLA style

▶ In his book *Crowded Prairie: American National Identity in the Hollywood Western,* Michael Coyne *explains* the significance of *Stagecoach* to the Western genre and its influence in solidifying the genre's archetypes.

▶ In her 1993 essay on landscape photography, Deborah Bright *argued* that landscape photography has reinforced certain formulaic myths about landscape.

If you're citing sources APA style

▶ Bonari et al. (2005) *found* that pregnant women are more likely to discontinue using antidepressants during pregnancy if their risk assessments are too high.

Gerunds and Infinitives

A gerund is the *-ing* form of a verb that functions as a noun: *walking, thinking*. An infinitive is *to* + the base form of a verb that's also used as a noun: *to walk, to think*. Deciding when to use a gerund or an infinitive can be a challenge, but in general, use gerunds to state facts and use infinitives to state intentions, desires, or expectations.

Use gerunds after verbs that express facts

admit	enjoy	practice	suggest
consider	finish	recall	tolerate
discuss	imagine	resist	understand

▶ Susanna had always *enjoyed making* things, so none of us were at all surprised that she majored in art.

Use infinitives after verbs that express intentions, desires, or expectations

ask	decide	intend	plan
agree	expect	manage	promise
claim	hope	offer	want

▶ She *decided to major* in art.

A few verbs can be followed by either a gerund or an infinitive: *begin, continue, hate, like, love, prefer,* and *start*. In some cases—*forget, remember, stop, try*—the choice of a gerund or infinitive affects the meaning.

▶ He remembered *to call* his mom on her birthday.

He intended to call, and he did.

▶ He remembered *calling* his mother for her birthday.

He remembered that he had made the call.

Always use a gerund, not an infinitive, after a preposition

▶ She got college credit *for passing* the Advanced Placement calculus exam.

INFINITIVES

▶ Television *started to get* big in the US in 1948 with the incredible success of Milton Berle's show, which was so popular that the reservoir levels in Detroit dropped every Tuesday night at 9 p.m. because everyone *waited* until the show was over *to go* to the toilet. —FRANK ROSE, *The Art of Immersion*

▶ The foods *I like to eat* the best, like pizza and hamburgers and ice cream, are not always things that I should eat.

▶ Most students at Grinnell *plan to study* abroad during their junior year. Some students *hope to learn* a new language, while others simply *want to travel*.

▶ Those with double majors usually can't *manage to take* a semester abroad.

▶ We *decided to get* Dad a shredder for Father's Day when we realized he was burning return-address labels in the barbecue.

▶ Environmentalists *hoped to convince* people that long-life fluorescent bulbs were a good investment.

GERUNDS

▶ Whatever a man's age may be, he can reduce it several years *by putting* a bright-colored flower in his button-hole. —MARK TWAIN

▶ Roger Clemens never *admitted using* steroids, and the jury believed him.

▶ In her most stressful moments, she *imagined being* in Paris.

▶ Who doesn't *enjoy taking* time off every now and then to relax?

▶ *By comparing* the food served in Chinese restaurants in five different countries, Yunshu made progress *in answering* her question about why Chinese food is so universally popular.

▶ In high school, I *avoided taking* courses that *required* a lot of *writing*.

▶ Switzerland has many famous resorts *for skiing*.

Mood

English has three moods: indicative, imperative, and subjunctive. Use the indicative to state facts, opinions, or questions. Use the imperative to give commands. Use the subjunctive to express wishes, requests, and conditions that are hypothetical, unlikely, or contrary to fact. Use modal helping verbs such as *may, might,* or *would* to indicate likelihood or probability.

INDICATIVE	Megastores *have spread* across the country.
IMPERATIVE	*Shop* at Walmart to save money.
SUBJUNCTIVE	I would shop at Target if there *were* one in my hometown.

Writers are sometimes confused by conditional sentences, especially ones with a clause starting with *if.* Use the indicative if the condition in the *if* clause is possible; use the subjunctive if it's unlikely.

When the if clause expresses a condition that is possible, use the present tense in the *if* clause and a modal such as *may, might,* or *will* plus the base form of a verb in the other clause.

▶ If our school *wins* the conference championship, applications *will go* up.

When the if clause expresses a condition that is unlikely, hypothetical, or contrary to fact, use the past tense in the *if* clause and *would* or another modal such as *might* plus the base form of a verb in the other clause. Use *were* rather than *was* in the *if* clause.

UNLIKELY	If I *won* the lottery, I *would buy* a house.
CONTRARY TO FACT	If I *were* you, I *would* not *shop* at Target.

In clauses expressing a wish, use the past tense of the verb—use *were* for *be.*

▶ I *wish* I *were* three inches taller and twenty pounds lighter.

MOOD

Conditions that are possible

▶ If temperatures next winter *are* warmer than usual, we *will save* on heating bills.

▶ If I *have* time, I *will be* happy to help.

▶ According to the directions on the box, your teeth *will become* white if you *apply* the whitening strips for a half hour a day.

▶ If the company ~~will match~~ ^matches^ my other offer, I will stay.

Conditions that are unlikely or hypothetical

▶ If Costco *opened* a store here, my family's store *might not survive*.

▶ If our college *had* a larger endowment, it *could reduce* class sizes.

▶ I *wouldn't do* that if I *were* you!

▶ If it ~~wasn't~~ ^weren't^ against the law, we would visit Cuba.

Wishful thinking

▶ I *wish* that I *were* able to attend college full-time.

▶ My mother *wishes* my sisters and I *lived* closer to home.

▶ We *wish* that it *didn't cost* so much to live in Rio.

▶ "If wishes *were* horses, beggars *would ride*" is a nursery rhyme often used to suggest that it is better to act than to wish.

SIXTEEN

Assembling a Portfolio

FOR HIS FIRST-YEAR WRITING CLASS, Julio Martinez was required to build a portfolio of his work to demonstrate how his writing had improved during the term. He included the drafts and final revision of a rhetorical analysis, along with two peer reviews he received from fellow students; an annotated bibliography; and the drafts and final revision of a research report. Finally, he wrote a cover letter to his instructor in which he described, evaluated, and reflected on his writing—and set out several goals to work on after the term was over. He submitted his portfolio in print.

Not so Susanna Moller, an art major, who created a website to host the portfolio of her artwork. She included only finished works, organized by subject and style. When she had her first solo show, she posted the review from the college newspaper. As graduation approached, she put her résumé on the site—and added the URL to résumés she sent to potential employers so they could see her work.

Deborah Burke began her portfolio with a first-year essay she was very proud of. The next year, she wrote a radio essay on the same topic, which became the second item in her portfolio. Continuing her research, she wrote a play and added the script to her portfolio, along with a video of herself performing a scene from the play. Finally, she added her résumé and a statement reflecting on her work in college. This portfolio helped her to get an internship—and later a job.

You may be required to keep a portfolio of your work for a writing course as a way of thinking about what you've learned, demonstrating to your instructor what you've done, and assessing your strengths and weaknesses as a writer. Even if you're not required to do so, keeping a portfolio is one of the best ways of demonstrating what you've learned and showcasing your best work. Portfolios can make powerful statements to prospective employers about your abilities and accomplishments, and they can be an important part of how your work is assessed. Whatever your purpose, assembling a portfolio offers an excellent opportunity to reflect on your writing and to chart future goals for yourself as a writer. This chapter provides guidelines to help you compile a portfolio for a writing class.

What to Include in a Writing Portfolio

Your portfolio should represent your best work and demonstrate your growth as a writer, so you'll probably include some of the following materials:

- A number of your best papers
- Writing in several genres and media
- Freewriting and other notes
- Various drafts, from first to final
- Response from readers
- A statement reflecting on your work

Your instructor may specify what you need to include, but often you'll get to choose. In that case, what you include will depend on what you're trying to show. If you're trying to show your best work, you might include three pieces that you like best; if, on the other hand, you're trying to show a range of what you've written, you would probably choose writing in various genres and media. If you're trying to show how you've improved, you'll want to include papers in several drafts. Just remember that your portfolio is an opportunity for *you* to evaluate and present your own writing: Choose work that demonstrates what you want to show.

Collecting Your Work

Start working on your portfolio early in the term. Organization is critical, so create a specific computer folder for the portfolio and save it with a file name (like "My Portfolio") where you can easily find it; inside the folder, create sub-folders, one for each piece of writing you include. Identify all drafts with a title and date, as shown in the following example.

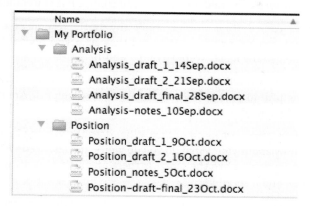

If you're required to include a statement reflecting on your writing, take notes on your process and your work *throughout the term*. If you receive any peer response, keep copies in your file.

Reflecting on Your Writing

An essential component is a statement that introduces and reflects on the work that's included in the portfolio. Such a statement should describe your writing process, explain what's included and why you included the pieces you did, and reflect on your development as a writer.

Writing such a statement gives you the opportunity to take a good look at your writing and to evaluate it on your own terms. Maybe the essay on which you received your lowest grade was one where you experienced a breakthrough in your writing process—even if the grade it earned doesn't reflect that. You may well want to discuss this breakthrough in your statement. Did you discover that freewriting worked better than outlining as a way to generate ideas? These are the kinds of insights you can weave into your statement, demonstrating to your instructor that you have thought carefully about both your writing and your writing process. Following are some prompts to help you think about your writing with a critical eye:

- *Review each piece of writing in your portfolio.* What are the strengths and the weaknesses? Which is your best piece? Explain why it is the best and what it demonstrates about what you've learned. Which would you say is the weakest—and how would you change it if you could?

- *Analyze your writing process.* Study any drafts, responses, and other materials you're including. How did they help you revise? Which of them helped the most? Were any not helpful?

- *Describe the strategies and techniques you use.* Which ones have proved most helpful to you, and which have been less helpful? Are there any you really enjoy?

- *Reflect on your work as an author.* What does the writing in your portfolio show about you? What do you do well—and less well? What kinds of writing do you like the most? Is there any kind of writing that you dislike—and if so, why?

- *Define goals.* What has assembling and reflecting on your portfolio helped you better understand about yourself as a writer? What strengths or weaknesses do you see that you didn't see before? Based on this analysis, what do you now want to work on?

Budget plenty of time for writing and revising your statement, and try to get feedback from classmates or a tutor at the writing center. Ask them to read with an eye for what the statement says about you as a writer. Remember that the statement itself demonstrates your writing ability: Write it thoughtfully and carefully.

This statement is usually written either as a letter or an essay. Whatever form it takes, it should describe your work, reflect on your development as a writer, assess what you have learned, and perhaps establish goals for yourself. You may or may not have an explicit thesis, but it needs to be clear what your portfolio demonstrates about you as a writer.

December 7, 2011

Dear Reader,

Writing used to be one of those things I never gave much time to. I'd get it done but without thinking much about how to do it better. It wasn't until coming to Ball State and taking a class with Professor Clark-Upchurch that writing started to be more than just a nuisance. For the first time, I was forced to look at the inner workings of formal writing, picking it apart and examining each part, learning what each part is supposed to contribute and why it's important. Slowly over the course of this semester, I have moved beyond the simple five-paragraph style of writing I learned in high school. All in all, I have become a stronger writer.

Writing the first paper, the literacy narrative, came easily to me . . . or so I thought. When my paper came back to me with Professor Clark-Upchurch's questions about my thesis and organization, some irrelevant incidents I included, a lack of illustrations to support my points, and comments about my "repetitive and simplistic sentence structures," I knew I needed to work harder. On the second paper, an analysis of a magazine ad, my thesis was clear and my paragraphs "flowed, one into the next" with good examples from the ad as support, but I still needed to work on using a variety of sentences to "make the reader want to read on."

It was on my last paper, the research-based essay, that I finally pulled everything together: an engaging introduction, a clear thesis, logical organization, solid development with lots of supporting examples, and (finally!) varied sentences.

Although my writing style has improved and my understanding of all that goes into a paper is at an all-time high, I still struggle with writing a proposal. I'm not sure why, but for some reason writing an essay about writing a future essay leaves me confused. I'd rather just write the essay in the first place than waste time and effort proposing what I'm going to write about. As a result,

I never really made a decent effort at the third writing project—
the proposal for the research paper. Thus I have decided to
exclude that paper from my portfolio as I am sure it is my
weakest.

In addition to these three papers, I include drafts with peer
responses and Professor Clark-Upchurch's suggestions in order
to provide a clear picture of how much I learned this term. One
of the most helpful parts of the class was the peer responding
sessions, when we analyzed each other's essays. Doing this
allowed me to see that writing in college is for more than just
pleasing the teacher and getting a grade.

The essays you are about to read are just a stepping-stone,
a sturdy base for me to continue developing my writing into
something more. But now the seed has been planted, whether
willingly or unwillingly. Now whenever I need to write a formal
paper, I have some tools I have learned and can use instead of
simply scraping by on whatever I can muster.

Sincerely,
Kameron Wiles

Organizing a Portfolio

The way you organize and present your portfolio is important, part of how you present yourself as a writer. There's no one way to organize a portfolio, but it needs to be carefully organized so that it's easy to read. Be sure you know if your instructor expects a certain format or system.

Print portfolios can go in a folder (for a small portfolio) or a binder (for a longer one). Begin with a title page that includes your name, the course title and number, the instructor's name, the date, and the portfolio's title. Follow the title page with a table of contents. Next comes your statement and then the writing. Organize the portfolio by assignments, putting all the materials from each assignment together, with the final draft on top. Label everything. If you're using a binder, add tabbed dividers, one for each assignment. Number the pages consecutively, and be sure each item is labeled.

E-portfolios can be as basic as uploading *Word* documents to *Blackboard* or some other online course management system. Or you might post texts to an e-portfolio platform such as *Digication*.

There are many other platforms where you can create an e-portfolio, from *Google Docs* or *Google Sites* to blogging sites like *WordPress, Scribd,* and *Tumblr.* Here are a few things to keep in mind when working on a portfolio that will be submitted online:

- Figure out exactly what you're going to put in your portfolio before uploading anything.

- Be sure you know what system your instructor expects you to use, and contact your school's IT help desk in case you need assistance.

- If you need to upload files, know what type of file you should use, *Word* documents or PDFs.

- Double-check that the version you are uploading is the final version.

- If you are working on an e-portfolio website, set up a homepage with your basic information and include links to your statement and to each piece of writing, each on its own page.

- To be sure all of the links work and everything looks the way you expect, check your site in different browsers and on different computers (laptops and desktops); you don't want to find out after you've submitted it that links don't work or some parts aren't visible.

- If you'd like to preserve your e-portfolio or continue to add to it, ask your instructor or IT help desk if it will remain online after the term ends. If you find it will be deleted, you will need to move it to a more permanent platform.

Portfolios are becoming increasingly necessary, both in school and on the job. Your portfolio is more than an archive of your writing—it's a way of looking systematically at your work. Keeping a portfolio of your work enables you to reflect on your development as a writer and to build connections between that self and your professional self after graduation. Working portfolios establish connections—between what you've learned and what you need to work on, and between your work as a student and your future as a professional.

Readings

Readings

University Undergraduate Learning Outcomes
UNLV

THE FIVE UNIVERSITY UNDERGRADUATE LEARNING OUTCOMES (UULOs) define what all UNLV students should know and be able to do when they graduate. Because students engage with the UULOs in both their general education and academic majors, the UULOs help make the undergraduate experience intentional and coherent.

The UULOs create a purposeful sequence of learning from the first year, to the middle years, to the senior year. Student learning develops through both curricular and co-curricular experiences which expose students to the UULOs in diverse contexts.

UNLV defines specific student outcomes for each UULO. Jump to each UULO's section to read its description and specific outcomes.

Intellectual Breadth and Lifelong Learning

Graduates are able to understand and integrate basic principles of the natural sciences, social sciences, humanities, fine arts, and health sciences, and develop skills and a desire for lifelong learning. Specific outcomes for all students include:

1. Demonstrate in-depth knowledge and skills in at least one major area.
2. Identify the fundamental principles of the natural and health sciences, social sciences, humanities and fine arts.
3. Apply the research methods and theoretical models of the natural and health sciences, social sciences, humanities and fine arts to define, solve, and evaluate problems.
4. Transfer knowledge and skills gained from general and specialized studies to new settings and complex problems.
5. Demonstrate life-long learning skills, including the ability to place problems in personally meaningful contexts, reflect on one's own understanding, demonstrate awareness of what needs to be learned, articulate a learning plan, and act independently on the plan using appropriate resources.
6. Achieve success in one's chosen field or discipline, including applying persistence, motivation, interpersonal communications, leadership, goal setting, and career skills.

Inquiry and Critical Thinking

Graduates are able to identify problems, articulate questions, and use various forms of research and reasoning to guide the collection, analysis, and use of information related to those problems. Specific outcomes for all students include:

1. Identify problems, articulate questions or hypotheses, and determine the need for information.
2. Access and collect the needed information from appropriate primary and secondary sources.
3. Use quantitative and qualitative methods, including the ability to recognize assumptions, draw inferences, make deductions, and interpret information to analyze problems in context and draw conclusions.
4. Recognize complexity of problems and identify different perspectives from which problems and questions can be viewed.
5. Evaluate and report on conclusions, including discussing the basis for and strength of findings, and identify areas where further inquiry is needed.
6. Identify, analyze, and evaluate reasoning and construct and defend reasonable arguments and explanations.

Communication

Graduates are able to write and speak effectively to both general and specialized audiences, create effective visuals that support written or spoken communication, and use electronic media common to one's field or profession. Specific outcomes for all students include:

1. Demonstrate general academic literacy, including how to respond to needs of audiences and to different kinds of rhetorical situations, analyze and evaluate reasons and evidence, and construct research-based arguments using Standard Written English.
2. Effectively use the common genres and conventions for writing within a particular discipline or profession.
3. Prepare and deliver effective oral presentations.
4. Collaborate effectively with others to share information, solve problems, or complete tasks.
5. Produce effective visuals using different media.
6. Apply the up-to-date technologies commonly used to research and communicate within one's field.

Global/Multicultural Knowledge and Awareness

Graduates will have developed knowledge of global and multicultural societies and an awareness of their place in and effect on them. Specific outcomes for all students include:

1. Demonstrate knowledge of the history, philosophy, arts and geography of world cultures.
2. Respond to diverse perspectives linked to identity, including age, ability, religion, politics, race, gender, ethnicity, and sexuality, both in American and international context.
3. Apply the concept of social justice.
4. Demonstrate familiarity with a non-native language or experience living in a different culture.
5. Function effectively in diverse groups.
6. Demonstrate awareness of one's own place in and effect on the world.

Citizenship and Ethics

Graduates are able to participate knowledgeably and actively in the public life of our communities and make informed, responsible, and ethical decisions in their personal and professional lives. Specific outcomes for all students include:

1. Acquire knowledge of political, economic, and social institutions.
2. Identify the various rights and obligations that citizens have in their communities.
3. Apply various forms of citizenship skills such as media analysis, letter writing, community service and lobbying.
4. Explain the concept of sustainability as it impacts economic, environmental, and social concerns.
5. Examine various concepts and theories of ethics and how to deliberate and assess claims about ethical issues.
6. Apply ethical concepts and theories to specific ethical dilemmas students will experience in their personal and professional lives.

Can You Be Educated from a Distance?

JAMES BARSZCZ

BY ALMOST ANY MEASURE, there is a boom in Internet-based instruction. In just a few years, 34 percent of American colleges and universities have begun offering some form of what's called "distance learning" (DL), and among the larger schools, it's closer to 90 percent. If you doubt the popularity of the trend, you probably haven't heard of the University of Phoenix. It grants degrees entirely on the basis of online instruction. It enrolls 90,000 students, a statistic used to support its claim to be the largest private university in the country.

While the kinds of instruction offered in these programs will differ, DL usually signifies a course in which the instructors post syllabi, reading assignments, and schedules on Web sites, and students send in their written assignments by e-mail. Other forms of communication often come into play, such as threaded messaging, which allows for posting questions and comments that are publicly viewable, as a bulletin board would, as well as chat rooms for real-time interchanges. Generally speaking, face-to-face communication with an instructor is minimized or eliminated altogether.

The attraction for students might at first seem obvious. Primarily,

JAMES BARSZCZ (b. 1955) has worked in the Internet industry since 1995. After earning both his BA and his PhD in English literature from Rutgers University and his MA from Indiana University, he taught a variety of courses in literature and composition at Rutgers. Barszcz has since moved on to the telecommunications field, but he continues to publish essays on literary topics and is the founding editor of the *College Hill Review*, an online quarterly magazine.

Barszcz's essay "Can You Be Educated from a Distance?" was first printed in 2003, as online courses began to establish themselves in higher education. Barszcz considers some common arguments for "distance learning" and offers his own argument in favor of on-site education. While online classes can indeed provide a student with information, he says, a "true education" is about much more than simply acquiring information. As you read, ask yourself what you consider to be the most important features of your education and what your education really *educes*, or "draws out," from you.

there's the convenience promised by courses on the Net: you can do the work, as they say, in your pajamas. But figures indicate that the reduced effort results in a reduced commitment to the course. While attrition rates for all freshmen at American universities are around 20 percent, the rate for online students is 35 percent. Students themselves seem to understand the weaknesses inherent in the setup. In a survey conducted for eCornell, the DL division of Cornell University, less than a third of the respondents expected the quality of the online course to be as good as the classroom course.

Clearly, from the schools' perspective, there's a lot of money to be saved. Although some of the more ambitious programs require new investments in servers and networks to support collaborative software, most DL courses can run on existing or minimally upgraded systems. The more students who enroll in a course but don't come to campus, the more the school saves on keeping the lights on in the classrooms, paying custodians, and maintaining parking lots. And, while there's evidence that instructors must work harder to run a DL course for a variety of reasons, they won't be paid any more, and might well be paid less.

But as a rule, those who champion distance learning don't base their arguments on convenience or cost savings. More often, they claim DL signals an advance in the effectiveness of education. Consider the vigorous case made by Fairleigh Dickinson University (FDU), in Madison, New Jersey, where students—regardless of their expectations or desires—are now required to take one DL course per year. By setting this requirement, they say, FDU recognizes the Internet as "a premier learning tool" of the current technological age. Skill in using online resources "prepares our students, more than others, for life-long learning—for their jobs, their careers, and their personal growth." Moreover, Internet-based courses will connect FDU students to a "global virtual faculty," a group of "world-class scholars, experts, artists, politicians, and business leaders around the world."

Sounds pretty good. But do the claims make much sense? First, it should be noted that students today and in the future might well use the Internet with at least as much facility as the faculty. It's not at all clear that they need to be taught such skills. More to the point, how much time and effort do you suppose "world-class scholars" (much less politicians and business leaders) will expend for the benefit of students they never meet or even see? Probably a lot less than they're devoting to the books, journal articles, and position papers that are already available to anyone with access to a library.

Another justification comes from those who see distance learning as the next step in society's progress toward meritocracy. A recent article in *Forbes* magazine cites Professor Roger Schank of Northwestern University, who predicts that soon "students will be able to shop around, taking a course from any institution that offers a good one. . . . Quality education will be available to all. Students will learn what they want to learn rather than what some faculty committee decided was the best practical compromise." In sum, says Professor Schank, who is also chairman of a distance-learning enterprise called CognitiveArts, "Education will be measured by what you know rather than by whose name appears on your diploma."

Statements like these assume education consists in acquiring information ("what you know"). Accept that and it's hard to disagree with the conclusions. After all, what does it matter how, or through what medium, you get the information? But few truly educated people hold such a mechanistic view. Indeed, traditionally, education was aimed at cultivating intellectual and moral values, and the "information" you picked up was decidedly secondary. It was commonplace for those giving commencement speeches to note that, based on etymology, education is a drawing out, not a putting in. That is, a true education *educes,* or draws out, from within a person qualities of intellect and character that would otherwise have remained hidden or dormant.

Exactly how this kind of educing happens is hard to pin down. Only in part does it come from watching professors in the classroom present material and respond to student questions, the elements of education that can be translated to the Net with reasonable fidelity. Other educational experiences include things like watching how professors joke with each other (or not!) in the hallways, seeing what kinds of pictures are framed in a professor's office, or going out for coffee after class with people in your dorm. Such experiences, and countless others, are sometimes labeled (and dismissed) as "social life on campus." But they also contribute invaluably to education. Through them, you learn a style, in the noblest sense of that term, a way of regarding the information you acquire and the society you find yourself in. This is what the philosopher Alfred North Whitehead meant when he called style the ultimate acquisition of a cultivated mind. And it's the mysterious ways of cultivating that style that the poet Robert Frost meant when he said that all that a college education requires is that you "hang around until you catch on." Hanging around, that is, on campus, not lurking on the Net.

Study Questions

1. What unusual requirement must students at Fairleigh Dickinson University fulfill?

2. How does Barszcz define a "true education"? Why is this definition important to his argument?

3. What arguments does Barszcz cite for distance learning? How does he refute these arguments? What is the main reason he is against distance learning?

4. *For Writing.* Consider how and where you learn as you receive your education. Drawing on your own experience, write an argument in which you take a position on distance learning. You may argue for it, against it, or for some combination of the two (you might be for certain aspects of it but against others, for instance).

Preparing for a Career

DEREK BOK

VOCATIONAL COURSES have long been a burr under the saddle of those who teach the liberal arts. According to one survey, 60 percent of Arts and Sciences professors do not even think that preparing for a good job is a particularly important goal for undergraduates. In sharp contrast, almost three-fourths of entering freshmen regard it as the *most* important reason for going to college. One can easily understand why students feel this way. Most of them will spend more time making a living over the next several decades than they will doing anything else. The careers they choose and the success they achieve at work will have a great deal to do with defining who they are, how satisfied they feel about their lives, and how comfortably they will live. No wonder they take their careers so seriously. The puzzle is that so few liberal arts teachers seem to agree.

Why are these professors so cool to the vocational needs of their students? How can they educate young people in so many ways and for so many purposes yet refuse to help prepare them for the work that will shape their future lives so profoundly?

DEREK BOK (b. 1930) earned his BA at Stanford University in 1951, his law degree at Harvard Law School in 1954, and his MA at George Washington University in 1958. After teaching law at Harvard, he served as the dean of the law school from 1968 until 1971, when he became the university's president, a position he held for twenty years. His books on education include *Beyond the Ivory Tower* (1984), *Universities and the Future of America* (1990), and *Universities in the Marketplace* (2003).

In "Preparing for a Career," Bok challenges what he considers to be the elitist notion that vocational training has no place in a liberal arts curriculum. In fact, he argues, the vocational and the liberal arts could merge, producing a student who is better prepared for the world of work. As you read, consider Bok's ethos as the president of one of the most elite liberal arts colleges in the United States. How persuasive is his argument? Should the vocational and the liberal arts be integrated?

Part of the explanation, surely, is the tendency of much vocational education to offer training without intellectual depth.[1] However worthy their place in the economic order, hotel management, mortuary science, and public relations do not engage the frontiers of thought in the same way as mathematics, physics, or philosophy. Much of what students need to prepare for these callings takes the form of practical skills rather than the kinds of knowledge that are the intellectual's stock in trade. To many liberal arts professors, such competencies should be either learned on the job or taught in some kind of trade school, but surely not studied in a university under the tutelage of scholars.

Another contributing cause is the fear that students will be so concerned about their careers that, once vocational education gains a foothold in the college, it will spread like crabgrass and eventually take over the entire curriculum. Money and commercialization already exert undue influence over university behavior. Making room for vocational training will arguably exacerbate these worrisome trends. Undergraduates are deeply preoccupied with succeeding in their careers, especially in a world they perceive as increasingly competitive and in constant flux. Given the opportunity, they may well neglect other purposes of undergraduate education in their eagerness to take any course that promises to give them a competitive edge in the struggle for success and financial security.

At the same time, the threat posed by vocational courses cannot be 5 removed by simply ignoring their existence. Denying vocational concerns any place in the curriculum will diminish the chance to help undergraduates think about their careers in terms broader than simply making money. Moreover, such opposition is impractical in any event. Since students can choose which college to attend, market pressures force institutions to give them the practical training they desire. University officials who worry about filling the seats in the college cannot afford the fantasy that finding a job is a matter of little consequence. They understand full well the depth of student desire to prepare for a career. As a result, apart from a few score institutions that remain wholly dedicated to the liberal arts, virtually all

---

1. It should be noted that evidence is mixed on whether the vocational emphasis of a college either helps or hinders the development of cognitive ability (including critical thinking skills); Ernest T. Pascarella and Patrick T. Terenzini, *How College Affects Students*, Vol. 2, pp. 172–73. [Author's note.]

colleges have established vocational majors, often separated from Arts and Sciences in schools of their own.

The question, then, is not whether to banish all vocational courses but whether to join in giving students a larger view of the professions that goes beyond mere skills training. Unfortunately, in universities with both liberal arts and vocational faculties, cooperation has been conspicuous by its absence. According to one report, "In many colleges and universities, a lamentable chasm separates the liberal arts college and professional departments. Competition for resources is keen, autonomy is jealously guarded, and cross-disciplinary discourse is fraught with difficulty."

Liberal arts faculties have paid a heavy price for their ostrich-like response to the demand for practical courses. Given a choice, students have deserted the traditional disciplines in droves. Today 60 percent of all college seniors are majoring in a vocational program. Whereas substantial majorities once chose a liberal arts concentration, only about one-third do so now. The rest must often make their way through programs that receive little help from Arts and Sciences faculties to ensure that the courses students take outside their vocational majors afford them the full benefit of a first-rate liberal education.

These disadvantages have finally begun to persuade some Arts and Sciences faculties to reexamine their connections with vocational education and think about responding to students' employment concerns in new and creative ways. The challenge is critical, and not just for practical reasons. Successfully met, it could invigorate both the liberal arts and vocational programs while accomplishing much to serve the needs of undergraduates.

* * *

Vocational Majors

Most college seniors do not move directly to an advanced degree program after they graduate; they look for work. Since the average length of time people stay in their first job has shrunk dramatically, more and more employers want their employees to "hit the ground running" without having to receive costly training from the company. As a result, undergraduates today are more likely than ever to feel that they must not only choose a career but also prepare themselves for a job while still in college. Spurred by competition for students, university officials have responded by mounting a wide array of vocational majors ranging from traditional staples, such as business and engineering, to such exotic entries as prison administration, sports management, and even video game design.

There has long been disagreement over whether vocational majors are actually better preparation for a career than a liberal arts degree. In most cases, the answer depends on the line of work a student wishes to pursue. Undergraduates who plan to move directly into a highly specialized or technical career had best enroll in vocational programs. No employer looking for an engineer or a hospital technician will be eager to hire someone with a major in English literature. On the other hand, students who expect to take a professional degree in law or medicine will be well advised to follow a liberal arts program in college and leave their vocational training for later. The choice is not so clear, however, for undergraduates who want to find some sort of managerial or supervisory job in business without acquiring an M.B.A. Should such students select a business major or take a traditional liberal arts degree? Since many thousands of undergraduates face this choice every year, the question has considerable practical importance.

A number of researchers have tried to supply an answer. Their work seems to show that vocational majors have an easier time than liberal arts graduates in finding an initial job in business and tend to advance faster and earn more money during their first 10 years of work. After 10 years, the picture becomes more complicated. As time goes on, the technical and practical skills that vocational majors learn in college become less important to continued success. Such abilities as communication skills, human relations, creativity, and "big-picture thinking" matter more. Since liberal arts faculties appear to do a better job than their vocational colleagues in fostering these qualities, graduates with traditional Arts and Sciences majors begin to gain ground. Within the ranks of top management, neither liberal arts nor vocational majors have an advantage.

Studies also show that the nature of one's education has a bearing on *what kind* of position one will occupy in business. Management and engineering majors tend to gravitate toward careers in accounting, production, and finance. Their comparative advantage seems to lie in manufacturing companies. Liberal arts majors are more likely to specialize in marketing, human resources, or public affairs and to move into companies in the service sector.

Future trends are harder to predict. Corporations are becoming more technical and science based, trends that favor business and engineering majors. On the other hand, companies also seem destined to witness faster change, more frequent career shifts, increasingly diverse workforces, and expanding global operations, all of which favor a broad liberal arts education.

In light of these findings, what can one say about the choice between liberal arts and vocational degrees? All in all, though many undergraduates may be excessively concerned with getting a job and earning money, it is hard to fault them for choosing vocational programs. The degrees they earn are essential for many technical jobs and offer advantages in business for at least a decade following graduation. Even in the longer run, there is little indication that students with business degrees will suffer a disadvantage. The practical question, then, is not whether many students are unwisely choosing vocational majors but whether *both* liberal arts *and* vocational programs could do a better job of reconciling the career needs of students with the other goals of a rounded undergraduate education.

How should vocational majors be constructed to respect the other important aims of college? In principle, the guidelines seem fairly clear. Like all majors, vocational programs should not take up so much space in the curriculum that other important educational goals must be sacrificed. Professors should not spend valuable time teaching skills better learned at work, nor ought they to be excessively preoccupied with teaching competencies that may be relevant to a first job but will soon become obsolete. Since critical thinking is as important to almost every occupation as it is to the liberal arts, instructors should try to use active methods of teaching with appropriate feedback. Moreover, because there is more to a calling than making money, vocational concentrations should offer breadth and perspective by including material on the history of the profession, its current role in society, and the recurring moral dilemmas that practitioners face in carrying out their work. Finally, like all majors, vocational programs should include some sort of culminating project that gives students an opportunity to increase their powers of reasoning and analysis by exploring a challenging problem in depth.

How successful are the more prominent occupational majors in meeting these specifications?[2]

Liberal Arts Majors

Many undergraduates who plan to move directly to a job and know what sort of job they want still seek a liberal arts degree. What, if anything, should colleges do to prepare these students for their careers? This issue rarely arises in debates about liberal education. While participants often question whether vocational programs are consistent with a suitably rounded education, they seldom inquire whether liberal arts programs are sufficiently respectful of undergraduates' desire for a successful, satisfying career. More's the pity. A well-crafted college curriculum, even if it offers no vocational majors, can do much to help students find jobs and fare well in their chosen careers.

The most important step that Arts and Sciences faculties can take is simply to do a better job of achieving the traditional goals of liberal education. As previously noted, when business leaders describe what they most need from the young managers and engineers they employ, they regularly stress not only strong communications skills and an ability to think critically and solve problems, but also a capacity to collaborate with others and work with diverse populations, a sensitivity to ethical problems, a strong self-discipline, and—for increasing numbers of companies—an appreciation of global issues and an ability to understand foreign cultures. These are all important aims of a liberal education and are accepted by almost every col-

2. In a section omitted here because of space concerns, Bok details the requirements of the three most prominent occupational majors. Of these, engineering is considered the most academically rigorous because of the many required math, science, and technical courses. However, engineering programs are often criticized for doing little to help their students develop communication skills, cultural sensitivity, ethical guidelines, or the ability to collaborate—all important components of a well-rounded education. Education programs, on the other hand, while meeting many of the requirements of a well-rounded education because of their recommended course work in the liberal arts, are criticized for not being rigorous enough. Courses in education history, pedagogy, and curriculum planning are perceived as poorly conceived and shallow. Finally, business schools offer the most popular occupational degree, but here too there is concern over curricular breadth and depth. While business colleges do require students to take a number of liberal arts courses, employers have found that business graduates have poor writing and speaking skills, poor critical thinking skills, and poor leadership skills, and lack "ethical sensitivity."

lege faculty. As previous chapters have pointed out, however, many students graduate having made only modest progress in acquiring these capabilities. That is why employers who complain about the college graduates they hire grumble not only about the lack of sufficient technical and vocational skills but also about deficiencies in speaking, writing, and other competencies long associated with a traditional college education.

A very different complaint from employers is that many of the young B.A. recipients they hire are lacking in self-discipline. According to their superiors, they often have difficulty being on time, working hard enough to do each job well, or listening carefully and following instructions. In view of these concerns, it is worth asking whether faculties themselves are not partially to blame by permitting a certain laxity to become entrenched on many campuses. Colleges have allowed widespread grade inflation and shown increased tolerance of late or incomplete work. As George Kuh points out after surveying hundreds of colleges, "There seems to be a breakdown of shared responsibility for learning—on the part of faculty members who allow students to get by with far less than maximal effort, and on the part of students who are not taking full advantage of the resources institutions provide." If undergraduates can receive high marks for sloppy work, routinely get extensions for assignments not completed on time, and escape being penalized for various forms of minor misconduct, it is hardly a surprise that employers find them lacking in self-discipline. Doing something to remedy this problem is not a crass concession to commercial interests but a useful reform that serves the interests of faculties and students as well as employers.

A much more controversial step would be to allow undergraduates to 20 take a small number of elective courses in practical vocational subjects, such as accounting, marketing, or finance. Arguably even two or three courses of this kind would help undergraduates decide what kind of business career to pursue and improve their prospects for employment. Recognizing these advantages, a number of colleges have already begun to provide this opportunity, but some liberal arts faculties still resist, fearing that any vocational courses they provide will become a beachhead for undermining the entire liberal arts curriculum and subverting the larger purposes it serves.

Barring all vocational courses makes little difference in colleges where almost all seniors go on to graduate or professional school. The consequences are more serious, however, for the majority of colleges in which most liberal arts students go directly into the workforce. Some companies have begun paying business schools to give a summer "crash course" in the basics of management for the new liberal arts graduates they have hired. While this step may solve the problem for some undergraduates, it does nothing for seniors seeking employment in companies that cannot or will not sponsor a program of this kind. Without any exposure to the skills and knowledge of the business world, such students could easily find themselves at a disadvantage in competing for jobs when they graduate.

At present, most business majors take at least half their courses in the liberal arts. In contrast, liberal arts majors have traditionally taken an average of less than 2 percent of their total courses in business. In effect, therefore, many undergraduates are choosing between a curriculum entirely devoted to the liberal arts and a vocational program that reserves half the curriculum for the liberal arts and half for courses specifically related to a career. It is not at all clear that such a choice is helpful for students or even in the best interest of Arts and Sciences faculties. A mere two or three elective courses in business or some other practical pursuit could help many undergraduates prepare for work without interfering significantly with the broader values of a liberal education. By encouraging such courses, faculties might even attract some undergraduates who would prefer a liberal arts curriculum but fear the consequences when they have to look for a job.

The Critical Challenge

Efforts to prepare students for a career are pulled in different directions by the two most powerful forces shaping American undergraduate education: the views of the faculty, on the one hand, and, on the other, the market pressures that students exert through their power to choose which institutions to attend. A few colleges have enough prestige that their faculties are not much bound by student opinion, leaving them reasonably free to build their educational programs according to their own ideas of what is appropriate. At most colleges, however, faculties must pay close heed to what prospective students want in order to attract enough applicants to fill their classrooms with undergraduates of adequate ability and promise.

Unfortunately neither faculty nor students can be counted upon to make fully appropriate choices about the role of vocation in a rounded undergraduate education. Arts and Sciences professors tend to attach too little importance to student career needs. Undergraduates, and the vocational faculties that prepare them for work, often neglect educational goals that serve the larger community, such as moral sensitivity and civic responsibility, and take too narrow a view of the competencies needed to succeed in a career. Achieving an ideal balance, then, requires a collaborative effort on the part of everyone involved.

Most universities have not yet managed to reconcile these two conflicting tendencies. Liberal arts programs seldom take adequate account of the crucial importance of students' careers—careers that will inevitably affect what kind of persons they become, how well they balance the claims of work and family, and what opportunities they have to serve others besides themselves. Vocational faculties, either by choice or because they have been rebuffed by their liberal arts colleagues, do not collaborate enough with Arts and Sciences faculties to prepare their students well for purposes other than performing the tasks demanded by their jobs.

The pressure to respond appropriately to vocational needs will not diminish in the foreseeable future. Liberal arts professors are unlikely to find their students becoming less preoccupied with their careers. The growing numbers of older and part-time students and the continuing high priority freshmen place on making money promise to keep vocational concerns at the forefront of their minds. At the same time, vocational faculties do not merely encounter pressure to pay more attention to specific practical skills; instead they are being urged to do a better job of developing precisely the competencies and qualities of mind traditionally associated with a liberal education.

The evolving priorities of employers make it easier for vocational programs and Arts and Sciences departments to collaborate, since the needs they serve increasingly overlap. Both faculties have good reason to cooperate. Without the help of liberal arts colleagues, vocational programs are likely to fall far short both in meeting the needs of employers and in preparing students for a rich, fulfilling life outside of work. Without paying greater attention to the career needs of their students, Arts and Sciences faculties seem destined to go on serving a minority of undergraduates while leaving the rest to vocational programs that deny them the full benefits of a rounded college education. Only if both faculties recognize the cost of going their separate ways will they achieve the full potential of both the liberal arts and vocational education in serving all the needs of their students.

Study Questions

1. Why, according to Bok, has vocational training been dismissed by instructors at liberal arts colleges? What role does Bok think that it *should* play in higher education?

2. Identify Bok's thesis. Is it stated directly or implied?

3. How does Bok attempt to persuade his readers that vocational training can and should be integrated into the liberal arts curriculum? Are his arguments convincing? Why or why not?

4. What rhetorical strategies does Bok use to lay out his argument? What purpose do the subheadings in the essay serve?

5. *For Writing.* Write an essay in which you argue for or against—or both— Bok's thesis, drawing on personal experience and using concrete examples to support your ideas.

Hal and Me

NICHOLAS CARR

"**D**AVE, STOP. Stop, will you? Stop, Dave. Will you stop?" So the supercomputer HAL pleads with the implacable astronaut Dave Bowman in a famous and weirdly poignant scene toward the end of Stanley Kubrick's *2001: A Space Odyssey*. Bowman, having nearly been sent to a deep-space death by the malfunctioning machine, is calmly, coldly disconnecting the memory circuits that control its artificial brain. "Dave, my mind is going," HAL says, forlornly. "I can feel it. I can feel it."

I can feel it too. Over the last few years I've had an uncomfortable sense that someone, or something, has been tinkering with my brain, remapping the neural circuitry, reprogramming the memory. My mind isn't going—so far as I can tell—but it's changing. I'm not thinking the way I used to think. I feel it most strongly when I'm reading. I used to find it easy to immerse myself in a book or a lengthy article. My mind would get caught up in the twists of the narrative or the turns of the argument, and I'd spend hours stroll-

---

NICHOLAS CARR (b. 1959) is an American journalist and author who specializes in writing about the connection between technology, economics, and culture. He earned a BA from Dartmouth College and an MA in English and American literature and language from Harvard University. His work has appeared in a number of newspapers and magazines, including the *Guardian*, the *Times* of London, the *New York Times*, the *Wall Street Journal*, and *Wired*. In addition, he is the author of four books on information technology, including *The Big Switch: Rewiring the World, from Edison to Google* (2008) and *The Shallows: What the Internet Is Doing to Our Brains* (2011), which was a finalist for the Pulitzer Prize.

"Hal and Me," taken from *The Shallows*, describes Carr's thoughts on how the Internet alters its users' minds in ways that are both subtle and profound. Among other things, he argues that using the Internet changes the ways in which we read and absorb information—on the one hand, we read more quickly and more widely, but on the other hand, we rarely explore topics as deeply as we do when reading and researching with print sources. As you read, take note of how Carr compares his experiences using the Internet with other people's stories and the research that he has done on the topic.

ing through long stretches of prose. That's rarely the case anymore. Now my concentration starts to drift after a page or two. I get fidgety, lose the thread, begin looking for something else to do. I feel like I'm always dragging my wayward brain back to the text. The deep reading that used to come naturally has become a struggle.

I think I know what's going on. For well over a decade now, I've been spending a lot of time online, searching and surfing and sometimes adding to the great databases of the Internet. The Web's been a godsend to me as a writer. Research that once required days in the stacks or periodical rooms of libraries can now be done in minutes. A few Google searches, some quick clicks on hyperlinks, and I've got the telltale fact or the pithy quote I was after. I couldn't begin to tally the hours or the gallons of gasoline the Net has saved me. I do most of my banking and a lot of my shopping online. I use my browser to pay my bills, schedule my appointments, book flights and hotel rooms, renew my driver's license, send invitations and greeting cards. Even when I'm not working, I'm as likely as not to be foraging in the Web's data thickets—reading and writing e-mails, scanning headlines and blog posts, following Facebook updates, watching video streams, downloading music, or just tripping lightly from link to link to link.

The Net has become my all-purpose medium, the conduit for most of the information that flows through my eyes and ears and into my mind. The advantages of having immediate access to such an incredibly rich and easily searched store of data are many, and they've been widely described and duly applauded. "Google," says Heather Pringle, a writer with *Archaeology* magazine, "is an astonishing boon to humanity, gathering up and concentrating information and ideas that were once scattered so broadly around the world that hardly anyone could profit from them."[1] Observes *Wired's* Clive Thompson, "The perfect recall of silicon memory can be an enormous boon to thinking."[2]

The boons are real. But they come at a price. As McLuhan[3] suggested, 5 media aren't just channels of information. They supply the stuff of thought, but they also shape the process of thought. And what the Net seems to be

1. Heather Pringle, "Is Google Making Archaeologists Smarter?" *Beyond Stone & Bone* blog (Archaeological Institute of America), February 27, 2009, archaeology.org/blog/?p=322. [All notes are the author's unless otherwise indicated.]
2. Clive Thompson, "Your Outboard Brain Knows All," *Wired*, October 2007.
3. Herbert Marshall McLuhan (1911–1980), Canadian philosopher and media theorist known for his view that "the medium is the message." [Editor's note.]

doing is chipping away my capacity for concentration and contemplation. Whether I'm online or not, my mind now expects to take in information the way the Net distributes it: in a swiftly moving stream of particles. Once I was a scuba diver in the sea of words. Now I zip along the surface like a guy on a Jet Ski.

Maybe I'm an aberration, an outlier. But it doesn't seem that way. When I mention my troubles with reading to friends, many say they're suffering from similar afflictions. The more they use the Web, the more they have to fight to stay focused on long pieces of writing. Some worry they're becoming chronic scatterbrains. Several of the bloggers I follow have also mentioned the phenomenon. Scott Karp, who used to work for a magazine and now writes a blog about online media, confesses that he has stopped reading books altogether. "I was a lit major in college, and used to be [a] voracious book reader," he writes. "What happened?" He speculates on the answer: "What if I do all my reading on the Web not so much because the way I read has changed, i.e. I'm just seeking convenience, but because the way I THINK has changed?"[4]

Bruce Friedman, who blogs about the use of computers in medicine, has also described how the Internet is altering his mental habits. "I now have almost totally lost the ability to read and absorb a longish article on the Web or in print," he says.[5] A pathologist on the faculty of the University of Michigan Medical School, Friedman elaborated on his comment in a telephone conversation with me. His thinking, he said, has taken on a "staccato" quality, reflecting the way he quickly scans short passages of text from many sources online. "I can't read *War and Peace* anymore," he admitted. "I've lost the ability to do that. Even a blog post of more than three or four paragraphs is too much to absorb. I skim it."

Philip Davis, a doctoral student in communication at Cornell who contributes to the Society for Scholarly Publishing's blog, recalls a time back in the 1990s when he showed a friend how to use a Web browser. He says he was "astonished" and "even irritated" when the woman paused to read the text on the sites she stumbled upon. "You're not supposed to read Web pages,

4. Scott Karp, "The Evolution from Linear Thought to Networked Thought," *Publishing 2.0* blog, February 9, 2008, publishing2.com/2008/02/09/the-evolution-from-linear-thought-to-networked-thought.
5. Bruce Friedman, "How Google Is Changing Our Information-Seeking Behavior," *Lab Soft News* blog, February 6, 2008, labsoftnews.typepad.com/lab_soft_news/2008/02/how-google-is-c.html.

just click on the hypertexted words!" he scolded her. Now, Davis writes, "I read a lot—or at least I should be reading a lot—only I don't. I skim. I scroll. I have very little patience for long, drawn-out, nuanced arguments, even though I accuse others of painting the world too simply."[6]

Karp, Friedman, and Davis—all well-educated men with a keenness for writing—seem fairly sanguine about the decay of their faculties for reading and concentrating. All things considered, they say, the benefits they get from using the Net—quick access to loads of information, potent searching and filtering tools, an easy way to share their opinions with a small but interested audience—make up for the loss of their ability to sit still and turn the pages of a book or a magazine. Friedman told me, in an e-mail, that he's "never been more creative" than he has been recently, and he attributes that "to my blog and the ability to review/scan 'tons' of information on the Web." Karp has come to believe that reading lots of short, linked snippets online is a more efficient way to expand his mind than reading "250-page books," though, he says, "we can't yet recognize the superiority of this networked thinking process because we're measuring it against our old linear thought process."[7] Muses Davis, "The Internet may have made me a less patient reader, but I think that in many ways, it has made me smarter. More connections to documents, artifacts, and people means more external influences on my thinking and thus on my writing."[8] All three know they've sacrificed something important, but they wouldn't go back to the way things used to be.

For some people, the very idea of reading a book has come to seem old- 10 fashioned, maybe even a little silly—like sewing your own shirts or butchering your own meat. "I don't read books," says Joe O'Shea, a former president of the student body at Florida State University and a 2008 recipient of a Rhodes Scholarship. "I go to Google, and I can absorb relevant information quickly." O'Shea, a philosophy major, doesn't see any reason to plow through chapters of text when it takes but a minute or two to cherry-pick the pertinent passages using Google Book Search. "Sitting down and going through a book from cover to cover doesn't make sense," he says. "It's not a good use of my time, as I can get all the information I need faster through

6. Philip Davis, "Is Google Making Us Stupid? Nope!" *The Scholarly Kitchen* blog, June 16, 2008, scholarlykitchen.sspnet.org/2008/06/16/is-google-making-us-stupid-nope.

7. Scott Karp, "Connecting the Dots of the Web Revolution," *Publishing 2.0* blog, June 17, 2008, publishing2.com/2008/06/17/connecting-the-dots-of-the-web-revolution.

8. Davis, "Is Google Making Us Stupid? Nope!"

the Web." As soon as you learn to be "a skilled hunter" online, he argues, books become superfluous.[9]

O'Shea seems more the rule than the exception. In 2008, a research and consulting outfit called nGenera released a study of the effects of Internet use on the young. The company interviewed some six thousand members of what it calls "Generation Net"—kids who have grown up using the Web. "Digital immersion," wrote the lead researcher, "has even affected the way they absorb information. They don't necessarily read a page from left to right and from top to bottom. They might instead skip around, scanning for pertinent information of interest."[10] In a talk at a recent Phi Beta Kappa meeting, Duke University professor Katherine Hayles confessed, "I can't get my students to read whole books anymore."[11] Hayles teaches English; the students she's talking about are students of literature.

People use the Internet in all sorts of ways. Some are eager, even compulsive adopters of the latest technologies. They keep accounts with a dozen or more online services and subscribe to scores of information feeds. They blog and they tag, they text and they twitter. Others don't much care about being on the cutting edge but nevertheless find themselves online most of the time, tapping away at their desktop, their laptop, or their mobile phone. The Net has become essential to their work, school, or social lives, and often to all three. Still others log on only a few times a day—to check their e-mail, follow a story in the news, research a topic of interest, or do some shopping. And there are, of course, many people who don't use the Internet at all, either because they can't afford to or because they don't want to. What's clear, though, is that for society as a whole the Net has become, in just the twenty years since the software programmer Tim Berners-Lee wrote the code for the World Wide Web, the communication and information medium of choice. The scope of its use is unprecedented, even by the standards of the mass media of the twentieth century. The scope of its influence is equally broad. By choice or necessity, we've embraced the Net's uniquely rapid-fire mode of collecting and dispensing information.

9. Don Tapscott, "How Digital Technology Has Changed the Brain," *Business Week Online*, November 10, 2008, www.businessweek.com/technology/content/nov2008/tc2008117_0345 17.htm.
10. Don Tapscott, "How to Teach and Manage 'Generation Net,'" *BusinessWeek Online*, November 30, 2008, www.businessweek.com/technology/content/nov2008/tc20081130_713563.htm.
11. Quoted in Naomi S. Baron, *Always On: Language in an Online and Mobile World* (Oxford: Oxford University Press, 2008), 204.

We seem to have arrived, as McLuhan said we would, at an important juncture in our intellectual and cultural history, a moment of transition between two very different modes of thinking. What we're trading away in return for the riches of the Net—and only a curmudgeon would refuse to see the riches—is what Karp calls "our old linear thought process." Calm, focused, undistracted, the linear mind is being pushed aside by a new kind of mind that wants and needs to take in and dole out information in short, disjointed, often overlapping bursts—the faster, the better. John Battelle, a onetime magazine editor and journalism professor who now runs an online advertising syndicate, has described the intellectual frisson he experiences when skittering across Web pages: "When I am performing bricolage in real time over the course of hours, I am 'feeling' my brain light up, I [am] 'feeling' like I'm getting smarter."[12] Most of us have experienced similar sensations while online. The feelings are intoxicating—so much so that they can distract us from the Net's deeper cognitive consequences.

For the last five centuries, ever since Gutenberg's[13] printing press made book reading a popular pursuit, the linear, literary mind has been at the center of art, science, and society. As supple as it is subtle, it's been the imaginative mind of the Renaissance, the rational mind of the Enlightenment, the inventive mind of the Industrial Revolution, even the subversive mind of Modernism. It may soon be yesterday's mind.

·   ·   ·

The HAL 9000 computer was born, or "made operational," as HAL himself humbly put it, on January 12, 1992, in a mythical computer plant in Urbana, Illinois. I was born almost exactly thirty-three years earlier, in January of 1959, in another midwestern city, Cincinnati, Ohio. My life, like the lives of most Baby Boomers and Generation Xers, has unfolded like a two-act play. It opened with Analogue Youth and then, after a quick but thorough shuffling of the props, it entered Digital Adulthood.

When I summon up images from my early years, they seem at once comforting and alien, like stills from a G-rated David Lynch film. There's the bulky mustard-yellow telephone affixed to the wall of our kitchen, with its

12. John Battelle, "Google: Making Nick Carr Stupid, but It's Made This Guy Smarter," *John Battelle's Searchblog*, June 10, 2008, battellemedia.com/archives/004494.php.
13. Johannes Gutenberg (c. 1398–1468), German developer of the first movable-type printing press, which revolutionized publishing by making mass-produced books possible. [Editor's Note.]

rotary dial and long, coiled cord. There's my dad fiddling with the rabbit ears on top of the TV, vainly trying to get rid of the snow obscuring the Reds game. There's the rolled-up, dew-dampened morning newspaper lying in our gravel driveway. There's the hi-fi console in the living room, a few record jackets and dust sleeves (some from my older siblings' Beatles albums) scattered on the carpet around it. And downstairs, in the musty basement family room, there are the books on the bookshelves—lots of books—with their many-colored spines, each bearing a title and the name of a writer.

In 1977, the year *Star Wars* came out and the Apple Computer company was incorporated, I headed to New Hampshire to attend Dartmouth College. I didn't know it when I applied, but Dartmouth had long been a leader in academic computing, playing a pivotal role in making the power of data-processing machines easily available to students and teachers. The college's president, John Kemeny, was a respected computer scientist who in 1972 had written an influential book called *Man and the Computer*. He had also, a decade before that, been one of the inventors of BASIC, the first programming language to use common words and everyday syntax. Near the center of the school's grounds, just behind the neo-Georgian Baker Library with its soaring bell tower, squatted the single-story Kiewit Computation Center, a drab, vaguely futuristic concrete building that housed the school's pair of General Electric GE-635 mainframe computers. The mainframes ran the groundbreaking Dartmouth Time-Sharing System, an early type of network that allowed dozens of people to use the computers simultaneously. Time-sharing was the first manifestation of what we today call personal computing. It made possible, as Kemeny wrote in his book, "a true symbiotic relationship between man and computer."[14]

I was an English major and went to great lengths to avoid math and science classes, but Kiewit occupied a strategic location on campus, midway between my dorm and Fraternity Row, and on weekend evenings I'd often spend an hour or two at a terminal in the public teletype room while waiting for the keg parties to get rolling. Usually, I'd fritter away the time playing one of the goofily primitive multiplayer games that the undergraduate programmers—"sysprogs," they called themselves—had hacked together. But I did manage to teach myself how to use the system's cumbersome word-processing program and even learned a few BASIC commands.

That was just a digital dalliance. For every hour I passed in Kiewit, I

---

14. John G. Kemeny, *Man and the Computer* (New York: Scribner, 1972), 21.

must have spent two dozen next door in Baker. I crammed for exams in the library's cavernous reading room, looked up facts in the weighty volumes on the reference shelves, and worked part-time checking books in and out at the circulation desk. Most of my library time, though, went to wandering the long, narrow corridors of the stacks. Despite being surrounded by tens of thousands of books, I don't remember feeling the anxiety that's symptomatic of what we today call "information overload." There was something calming in the reticence of all those books, their willingness to wait years, decades even, for the right reader to come along and pull them from their appointed slots. *Take your time*, the books whispered to me in their dusty voices. *We're not going anywhere.*

It was in 1986, five years after I left Dartmouth, that computers entered   20
my life in earnest. To my wife's dismay, I spent nearly our entire savings, some $2,000, on one of Apple's earliest Macintoshes—a Mac Plus decked out with a single megabyte of RAM, a 20-megabyte hard drive, and a tiny black-and-white screen. I still recall the excitement I felt as I unpacked the little beige machine. I set it on my desk, plugged in the keyboard and mouse, and flipped the power switch. It lit up, sounded a welcoming chime, and smiled at me as it went through the mysterious routines that brought it to life. I was smitten.

The Plus did double duty as both a home and a business computer. Every day, I lugged it into the offices of the management consulting firm where I worked as an editor. I used Microsoft Word to revise proposals, reports, and presentations, and sometimes I'd launch Excel to key in revisions to a consultant's spreadsheet. Every evening, I carted it back home, where I used it to keep track of the family finances, write letters, play games (still goofy, but less primitive), and—most diverting of all—cobble together simple databases using the ingenious HyperCard application that back then came with every Mac. Created by Bill Atkinson, one of Apple's most inventive programmers, HyperCard incorporated a hypertext system that anticipated the look and feel of the World Wide Web. Where on the Web you click links on pages, on HyperCard you clicked buttons on cards—but the idea, and its seductiveness, was the same.

The computer, I began to sense, was more than just a simple tool that did what you told it to do. It was a machine that, in subtle but unmistakable ways, exerted an influence over you. The more I used it, the more it altered the way I worked. At first I had found it impossible to edit anything on-screen. I'd print out a document, mark it up with a pencil, and type the revisions back into the digital version. Then I'd print it out again and take another pass with the pencil. Sometimes I'd go through the cycle a dozen times a day. But at some point—and abruptly—my editing routine changed. I found I could no longer write or revise anything on paper. I felt lost without the Delete key, the scrollbar, the cut and paste functions, the Undo command. I *had* to do all my editing on-screen. In using the word processor, I had become something of a word processor myself.

Bigger changes came after I bought a modem, sometime around 1990. Up to then, the Plus had been a self-contained machine, its functions limited to whatever software I installed on its hard drive. When hooked up to other computers through the modem, it took on a new identity and a new role. It was no longer just a high-tech Swiss Army knife. It was a communications medium, a device for finding, organizing, and sharing information. I tried all the online services—CompuServe, Prodigy, even Apple's short-lived eWorld—but the one I stuck with was America Online. My original AOL subscription limited me to five hours online a week, and I would painstakingly parcel out the precious minutes to exchange e-mails with a small group of friends who also had AOL accounts, to follow the conversations on a few bulletin boards, and to read articles reprinted from newspapers and magazines. I actually grew fond of the sound of my modem connecting through the phone lines to the AOL servers. Listening to the bleeps and clangs was like overhearing a friendly argument between a couple of robots.

By the mid-nineties, I had become trapped, not unhappily, in the "upgrade cycle." I retired the aging Plus in 1994, replacing it with a Macintosh Performa 550 with a color screen, a CD-ROM drive, a 500-megabyte hard drive, and what seemed at the time a miraculously fast 33-megahertz processor. The new computer required updated versions of most of the programs I used, and it let me run all sorts of new applications with the latest multimedia features. By the time I had installed all the new software, my hard drive was full. I had to go out and buy an external drive as a supplement. I added a Zip drive too—and then a CD burner. Within a couple of years, I'd bought another new desktop, with a much larger monitor and a much faster chip, as well as a portable model that I could use while traveling. My employer had, in the meantime, banished Macs in favor of Windows PCs, so I was using two different systems, one at work and one at home.

It was around this same time that I started hearing talk of something 25 called the Internet, a mysterious "network of networks" that promised, according to people in the know, to "change everything." A 1994 article in

Wired declared my beloved AOL "suddenly obsolete." A new invention, the "graphical browser," promised a far more exciting digital experience: "By following the links—click, and the linked document appears—you can travel through the online world along paths of whim and intuition."[15] I was intrigued, and then I was hooked. By the end of 1995 I had installed the new Netscape browser on my work computer and was using it to explore the seemingly infinite pages of the World Wide Web. Soon I had an ISP account at home as well—and a much faster modem to go with it. I canceled my AOL service.

You know the rest of the story because it's probably your story too. Ever-faster chips. Ever-quicker modems. DVDs and DVD burners. Gigabyte-sized hard drives. Yahoo and Amazon and eBay. MP3s. Streaming video. Broadband. Napster and Google. BlackBerrys and iPods. Wi-Fi networks. YouTube and Wikipedia. Blogging and micro-blogging. Smartphones, thumb drives, netbooks. Who could resist? Certainly not I.

When the Web went 2.0 around 2005, I went 2.0 with it. I became a social networker and a content generator. I registered a domain, roughtype .com, and launched a blog. It was exhilarating, at least for the first couple of years. I had been working as a freelance writer since the start of the decade, writing mainly about technology, and I knew that publishing an article or a book was a slow, involved, and often frustrating business. You slaved over a manuscript, sent it off to a publisher, and assuming it wasn't sent back with a rejection slip, went through rounds of editing, fact checking, and proofreading. The finished product wouldn't appear until weeks or months later. If it was a book, you might have to wait more than a year to see it in print. Blogging junked the traditional publishing apparatus. You'd type something up, code a few links, hit the Publish button, and your work would be out there, immediately, for all the world to see. You'd also get something you rarely got with more formal writing: direct responses from readers, in the form of comments or, if the readers had their own blogs, links. It felt new and liberating.

Reading online felt new and liberating too. Hyperlinks and search engines delivered an endless supply of words to my screen, alongside pictures, sounds, and videos. As publishers tore down their pay-walls, the flood of free content turned into a tidal wave. Headlines streamed around the clock through my Yahoo home page and my RSS feed reader. One click on a link

15. Gary Wolfe, "The (Second Phase of the) Revolution Has Begun," *Wired*, October 1994.

led to a dozen or a hundred more. New e-mails popped into my in-box every minute or two. I registered for accounts with MySpace and Facebook, Digg and Twitter. I started letting my newspaper and magazine subscriptions lapse. Who needed them? By the time the print editions arrived, dew-dampened or otherwise, I felt like I'd already seen all the stories.

Sometime in 2007, a serpent of doubt slithered into my info-paradise. I began to notice that the Net was exerting a much stronger and broader influence over me than my old stand-alone PC ever had. It wasn't just that I was spending so much time staring into a computer screen. It wasn't just that so many of my habits and routines were changing as I became more accustomed to and dependent on the sites and services of the Net. The very way my brain worked seemed to be changing. It was then that I began worrying about my inability to pay attention to one thing for more than a couple of minutes. At first I'd figured that the problem was a symptom of middle-age mind rot. But my brain, I realized, wasn't just drifting. It was hungry. It was demanding to be fed the way the Net fed it—and the more it was fed, the hungrier it became. Even when I was away from my computer, I yearned to check e-mail, click links, do some Googling. I wanted to be *connected*. Just as Microsoft Word had turned me into a flesh-and-blood word processor, the Internet, I sensed, was turning me into something like a high-speed data-processing machine, a human HAL.

I missed my old brain.   30

Study Questions

1. Describe how Carr traces his own history of Internet use.

2. Consider Carr's use of multiple forms of evidence—he utilizes his own story, other people's experiences, and statistical data. How does this combination of sources affect the rhetorical impact of the essay?

3. How would you describe the overall tone of the piece? As you read the essay, what sense did you get about Carr's feelings about the Internet and his use of it? What are some specific examples from the essay that demonstrate how he establishes that tone?

4. *For Writing.* In a short essay, describe how *you* use the Internet, and how your Internet use has affected your life and school work.

The Obligation to Endure

RACHEL CARSON

THE HISTORY OF LIFE ON EARTH has been a history of interaction between living things and their surroundings. To a large extent, the physical form and the habits of the earth's vegetation and its animal life have been molded by the environment. Considering the whole span of earthly time, the opposite effect, in which life actually modifies its surroundings, has been relatively slight. Only within the moment of time represented by the present century has one species—man—acquired significant power to alter the nature of his world.

During the past quarter century this power has not only increased to one of disturbing magnitude but it has changed in character. The most alarming of all man's assaults upon the environment is the contamination of air, earth, rivers, and sea with dangerous and even lethal materials. This pollution is for the most part irrecoverable; the chain of evil it initiates not only in the world that must support life but in living tissues is for the most part irreversible. In this now universal contamination of the environment, chemicals are the sinister and little-recognized partners of radiation in changing the very nature of the world—the very nature of its life. Strontium

---

RACHEL CARSON (1907–1964) was born in Springdale, Pennsylvania, graduated from Pennsylvania College for Women in 1929, and received her MA in zoology from Johns Hopkins University in 1932. After writing three books on oceanic topics, she refocused her attention to the effects of pesticides on humans and the environment. In 1962 she published *Silent Spring*, a work that explained the way chemicals affect the ecosystem and helped launch the modern environmentalism movement. Before her death from breast cancer she testified in congressional hearings and called for new policies to regulate chemicals in the environment and to protect human health.

In this chapter from *Silent Spring*, Carson translates her research into accessible prose. She begins by presenting information, but she gradually produces so much evidence to support her claims that her expository writing subtly takes on a persuasive tone, revealing the dangers that humanity both creates and experiences when using chemicals to control the environment.

90, released through nuclear explosions into the air, comes to earth in rain or drifts down as fallout, lodges in soil, enters into the grass or corn or wheat grown there, and in time takes up its abode in the bones of a human being, there to remain until his death. Similarly, chemicals sprayed on croplands or forests or gardens lie long in soil, entering into living organisms, passing from one to another in a chain of poisoning and death. Or they pass mysteriously by underground streams until they emerge and, through the alchemy of air and sunlight, combine into new forms that kill vegetation, sicken cattle, and work unknown harm on those who drink from once-pure wells. As Albert Schweitzer[1] has said, "Man can hardly even recognize the devils of his own creation."

It took hundreds of millions of years to produce the life that now inhabits the earth—eons of time in which that developing and evolving and diversifying life reached a state of adjustment and balance with its surroundings. The environment, rigorously shaping and directing the life it supported, contained elements that were hostile as well as supporting. Certain rocks gave out dangerous radiation; even within the light of the sun, from which all life draws its energy, there were short-wave radiations with power to injure. Given time—time not in years but in millennia—life adjusts, and a balance has been reached. For time is the essential ingredient; but in the modern world there is no time.

The rapidity of change and the speed with which new situations are created follow the impetuous and the heedless pace of man rather than the deliberate pace of nature. Radiation is no longer merely the background radiation of rocks, the bombardment of cosmic rays, the ultraviolet of the sun that have existed before there was any life on earth; radiation is now the unnatural creation of man's tampering with the atom. The chemicals to which life is asked to make its adjustment are no longer merely the calcium and silica and copper and all the rest of the minerals washed out of the rocks and carried in rivers to the sea; they are the synthetic creations of man's inventive mind, brewed in his laboratories, and having no counterparts in nature.

To adjust to these chemicals would require time on the scale that is nature's; it would require not merely the years of a man's life but the life of generations. And even this, were it by some miracle possible, would be futile, for the new chemicals come from our laboratories in an endless stream; almost

1. French-German doctor (1875–1965) and philosopher.

500 annually find their way into actual use in the United States alone. The figure is staggering and its implications are not easily grasped—500 new chemicals to which the bodies of men and animals are required somehow to adapt each year, chemicals totally outside the limits of biologic experience.

Among them are many that are used in man's war against nature. Since the mid-1940's over 200 basic chemicals have been created for use in killing insects, weeds, rodents, and other organisms described in the modern vernacular as "pests"; and they are sold under several thousand different brand names.

These sprays, dusts, and aerosols are now applied almost universally to farms, gardens, forests, and homes—nonselective chemicals that have the power to kill every insect, the "good" and the "bad," to still the song of birds and the leaping of fish in the streams, to coat the leaves with a deadly film, and to linger on in soil—all this though the intended target may be only a few weeds or insects. Can anyone believe it is possible to lay down such a barrage of poisons on the surface of the earth without making it unfit for all life? They should not be called "insecticides," but "biocides."

The whole process of spraying seems caught up in an endless spiral. Since DDT[2] was released for civilian use, a process of escalation has been going on in which ever more toxic materials must be found. This has happened because insects, in a triumphant vindication of Darwin's principle of the survival of the fittest, have evolved super races immune to the particular insecticide used, hence a deadlier one has always to be developed—and then a deadlier one than that. It has happened also because, for reasons to be described later, destructive insects often undergo a "flareback," or resurgence, after spraying, in numbers greater than before. Thus the chemical war is never won, and all life is caught in its violent crossfire.

Along with the possibility of the extinction of mankind by nuclear war, the central problem of our age has therefore become the contamination of man's total environment with such substances of incredible potential for harm—substances that accumulate in the tissues of plants and animals and even penetrate the germ cells to shatter or alter the very material of heredity upon which the shape of the future depends.

Some would-be architects of our future look toward a time when it will 10
be possible to alter the human germ plasm by design. But we may easily be

2. Dichloro-Diphenyl-Trichloroethane, a synthetic pesticide banned in the United States in 1972.

doing so now by inadvertence, for many chemicals, like radiation, bring about gene mutations. It is ironic to think that man might determine his own future by something so seemingly trivial as the choice of an insect spray.

All this has been risked—for what? Future historians may well be amazed by our distorted sense of proportion. How could intelligent beings seek to control a few unwanted species by a method that contaminated the entire environment and brought the threat of disease and death even to their own kind? Yet this is precisely what we have done. We have done it, moreover, for reasons that collapse the moment we examine them. We are told that the enormous and expanding use of pesticides is necessary to maintain farm production. Yet is our real problem not one of *overproduction?* Our farms, despite measures to remove acreages from production and to pay farmers *not* to produce, have yielded such a staggering excess of crops that the American taxpayer in 1962 is paying out more than one billion dollars a year as the total carrying cost of the surplus-food storage program. And is the situation helped when one branch of the Agriculture Department tries to reduce production while another states, as it did in 1958, "It is believed generally that reduction of crop acreages under provisions of the Soil Bank will stimulate interest in use of chemicals to obtain maximum production on the land retained in crops"?

All this is not to say there is no insect problem and no need of control. I am saying, rather, that control must be geared to realities, not to mythical situations, and that the methods employed must be such that they do not destroy us along with the insects.

The problem whose attempted solution has brought such a train of disaster in its wake is an accompaniment of our modern way of life. Long before the age of man, insects inhabited the earth—a group of extraordinarily varied and adaptable beings. Over the course of time since man's advent, a small percentage of the more than half a million species of insects have come into conflict with human welfare in two principal ways: as competitors for the food supply and as carriers of human disease.

Disease-carrying insects become important where human beings are crowded together, especially under conditions where sanitation is poor, as in time of natural disaster or war or in situations of extreme poverty and deprivation. Then control of some sort becomes necessary. It is a sobering fact, however, as we shall presently see, that the method of massive chemical control has had only limited success, and also threatens to worsen the very conditions it is intended to curb.

Under primitive agricultural conditions the farmer had few insect problems. These arose with the intensification of agriculture—the devotion of immense acreages to a single crop. Such a system set the stage for explosive increases in specific insect populations. Single-crop farming does not take advantage of the principles by which nature works; it is agriculture as an engineer might conceive it to be. Nature has introduced great variety into the landscape, but man has displayed a passion for simplifying it. Thus he undoes the built-in checks and balances by which nature holds the species within bounds. One important natural check is a limit on the amount of suitable habitat for each species. Obviously then, an insect that lives on wheat can build up its population to much higher levels on a farm devoted to wheat than on one in which wheat is intermingled with other crops to which the insect is not adapted.

The same thing happens in other situations. A generation or more ago, the towns of large areas of the United States lined their streets with the noble elm tree. Now the beauty they hopefully created is threatened with complete destruction as disease sweeps through the elms, carried by a beetle that would have only limited chance to build up large populations and to spread from tree to tree if the elms were only occasional trees in a richly diversified planting.

Another factor in the modern insect problem is one that must be viewed against a background of geologic and human history: the spreading of thousands of different kinds of organisms from their native homes to invade new territories. This worldwide migration has been studied and graphically described by the British ecologist Charles Elton in his recent book *The Ecology of Invasions.* During the Cretaceous Period, some hundred million years ago, flooding seas cut many land bridges between continents and living things found themselves confined in what Elton calls "colossal separate nature reserves." There, isolated from others of their kind, they developed many new species. When some of the land masses were joined again, about 16 million years ago, these species began to move out into new territories—a movement that is not only still in progress but is now receiving considerable assistance from man.

The importation of plants is the primary agent in the modern spread of species, for animals have almost invariably gone along with the plants, quarantine being a comparatively recent and not completely effective innovation. The United States Office of Plant Introduction alone has introduced almost 200,000 species and varieties of plants from all over the world. Nearly half of the 180 or so major insect enemies of plants in the United States are accidental imports from abroad, and most of them have come as hitchhikers on plants. In new territory, out of reach of the restraining hand of the natural enemies that kept down its numbers in its native land, an invading plant or animal is able to become enormously abundant. Thus it is no accident that our most troublesome insects are introduced species.

These invasions, both the naturally occurring and those dependent on human assistance, are likely to continue indefinitely. Quarantine and massive chemical campaigns are only extremely expensive ways of buying time. We are faced, according to Dr. Elton, "with a life-and-death need not just to find new technological means of suppressing this plant or that animal"; instead we need the basic knowledge of animal populations and their relations to their surroundings that will "promote an even balance and damp down the explosive power of outbreaks and new invasions." Much of the necessary knowledge is now available but we do not use it. We train ecologists in our universities and even employ them in our governmental agencies but we seldom take their advice. We allow the chemical death rain to fall as though there were no alternative, whereas in fact there are many, and our ingenuity could soon discover many more if given opportunity.

Have we fallen into a mesmerized state that makes us accept as inevi- 20 table that which is inferior or detrimental, as though having lost the will or the vision to demand that which is good? Such thinking, in the words of the ecologist Paul Shepard, "idealizes life with only its head out of water, inches above the limits of toleration of the corruption of its own environment. . . . Why should we tolerate a diet of weak poisons, a home in insipid surroundings, a circle of acquaintances who are not quite our enemies, the noise of motors with just enough relief to prevent insanity? Who would want to live in a world which is just not quite fatal?"

Yet such a world is pressed upon us. The crusade to create a chemically sterile, insect-free world seems to have engendered a fanatic zeal on the part of many specialists and most of the so-called control agencies. On every hand there is evidence that those engaged in spraying operations exercise a ruthless power. "The regulatory entomologists . . . function as prosecutor, judge and jury, tax assessor and collector and sheriff to enforce their own orders," said Connecticut entomologist Neely Turner. The most flagrant abuses go unchecked in both state and federal agencies.

It is not my contention that chemical insecticides must never be used. I do contend that we have put poisonous and biologically potent chemicals indiscriminately into the hands of persons largely or wholly ignorant of their potentials for harm. We have subjected enormous numbers of people to contact with these poisons, without their consent and often without their knowledge. If the Bill of Rights contains no guarantee that a citizen shall be secure against lethal poisons distributed either by private individuals or by public officials, it is surely only because our forefathers, despite their considerable wisdom and foresight, could conceive of no such problem.

I contend, furthermore, that we have allowed these chemicals to be used with little or no advance investigation of their effect on soil, water, wildlife, and man himself. Future generations are unlikely to condone our lack of prudent concern for the integrity of the natural world that supports all life.

There is still very limited awareness of the nature of the threat. This is an era of specialists, each of whom sees his own problem and is unaware of or intolerant of the larger frame into which it fits. It is also an era dominated by industry, in which the right to make a dollar at whatever cost is seldom challenged. When the public protests, confronted with some obvious evidence of damaging results of pesticide applications, it is fed little tranquilizing pills of half-truth. We urgently need an end to these false assurances, to the sugar coating of unpalatable facts. It is the public that is being asked to assume the risks that the insect controllers calculate. The public must decide whether it wishes to continue on the present road, and it can do so only when in full possession of the facts. In the words of Jean Rostand,[3] "The obligation to endure gives us the right to know."

3. French biologist and philosopher (1894–1977).

Study Questions

1. According to Carson, "the history of life on earth has been a history of interaction between living things and their surroundings." However, humanity's presence has changed this interaction in fundamental ways. Explain what she means. How have human beings affected life on earth?

2. Characterize Carson's tone. Is her language overtly persuasive or more expository? How would you use language to make claims similar to those Carson makes? Choose one section of the essay in which she writes about dangers to life, and rewrite it to reflect your own writing style.

3. Reread paragraph 2. Carson uses some strong language to convince the reader about humanity's part in harming the environment. Identify the key sentence that presents her thesis, and show how she supports her claim in that paragraph and in the following paragraphs. Has she convinced you? Explain.

4. *For Writing.* Visit your local grocery store, hardware store, drugstore, or other store that sells items that contain chemicals, such as hair spray, hair dyes, insecticides, fertilizers, and paint removers. Choose a category of items—e.g., cosmetics or pesticides—to examine thoroughly. Read not only the ingredients but also any warnings that are on the labels. Research the ingredients of the products you have chosen. Write an expository or a persuasive essay about the dangers found in everyday products that Carson did not mention in her chapter.

Only Daughter

SANDRA CISNEROS

O NCE, **SEVERAL YEARS AGO,** when I was just starting out my writing career, I was asked to write my own contributor's note for an anthology I was part of. I wrote: "I am the only daughter in a family of six sons. That explains everything."

Well, I've thought about that ever since, and yes, it explains a lot to me, but for the reader's sake I should have written: "I am the only daughter in a Mexican family of six sons." Or even: "I am the only daughter of a Mexican father and a Mexican-American mother." Or: "I am the only daughter of a working-class family of nine." All of these had everything to do with who I am today.

I was/am the only daughter and *only* a daughter. Being an only daughter in a family of six sons forced me by circumstance to spend a lot of time by myself because my brothers felt it beneath them to play with a *girl* in public.

SANDRA CISNEROS (b. 1954) is a writer, teacher, and community activist. She was raised in both Chicago, the city in which she was born, and Mexico City. After earning her undergraduate degree in English at Loyola University in Chicago, Cisneros obtained an MFA in creative writing at the University of Iowa. A writer of poetry, fiction, and essays, Cisneros won the American Book Award in 1985 for her first novel, *The House on Mango Street* (1983). She has also published two volumes of poetry, a collection of short stories, a children's book, and a second novel, *Caramelo* (2002). During her career, Cisneros has taught writing at every level above first grade and has been a visiting writer at many universities. In 2000 she established the Alfredo Cisneros Del Moral Foundation to honor the memory of her father; each year, the foundation awards grants to writers born in Texas, writing about Texas, or living in Texas.

In the following essay, first published in *Glamour* magazine in 1990, Cisneros explores the play on words of its title: she describes her life as an only daughter in a large Mexican American family and as, from her father's perspective, "only a daughter." As you read, consider the contrasts Cisneros notes—in language, in meaning, and in expectations—and how these disparities contribute to the development of the essay.

But that aloneness, that loneliness, was good for a would-be writer—it allowed me time to think and think, to imagine, to read and prepare myself.

Being only a daughter for my father meant my destiny would lead me to become someone's wife. That's what he believed. But when I was in the fifth grade and shared my plans for college with him. I was sure he understood. I remember my father saying, "*Que bueno, mi'ja*, that's good." That meant a lot to me, especially since my brothers thought the idea hilarious. What I didn't realize was that my father thought college was good for girls—good for finding a husband. After four years in college and two more in graduate school, and still no husband, my father shakes his head even now and says I wasted all that education.

In retrospect, I'm lucky my father believed daughters were meant for 5 husbands. It meant it didn't matter if I majored in something silly like English. After all, I'd find a nice professional eventually, right? This allowed me the liberty to putter about embroidering my little poems and stories without my father interrupting with so much as a "What's that you're writing?"

But the truth is, I wanted him to interrupt. I wanted my father to understand what it was I was scribbling, to introduce me as "My only daughter, the writer." Not as "This is only my daughter. She teaches." *Es maestra*—teacher. Not even *profesora.*

In a sense, everything I have ever written has been for him, to win his approval even though I know my father can't read English words, even though my father's only reading includes the brown-ink *Esto* sports magazines from Mexico City and the bloody *¡Alarma!* magazines that feature yet another sighting of *La Virgen de Guadalupe* on a tortilla[1] or a wife's revenge on her philandering husband by bashing his skull in with a *molcajete* (a kitchen mortar made of volcanic rock). Or the *fotonovelas*, the little picture paperbacks with tragedy and trauma erupting from the characters' mouths in bubbles.

My father represents, then, the public majority. A public who is disinterested in reading, and yet one whom I am writing about and for, and privately trying to woo.

When we were growing up in Chicago, we moved a lot because of my father. He suffered bouts of nostalgia. Then we'd have to let go our flat, store

---

1. That is, the legendary appearance of an image of the Virgin of Guadalupe (Mary, mother of Jesus) in the texture of a toasted tortilla.

the furniture with mother's relatives, load the station wagon with baggage and bologna sandwiches and head south. To Mexico City.

We came back, of course. To yet another Chicago flat, another Chicago 10 neighborhood, another Catholic school. Each time, my father would seek out the parish priest in order to get a tuition break, and complain or boast: "I have seven sons."

He meant *siete hijos,* seven children, but he translated it as "sons." "I have seven sons." To anyone who would listen. The Sears Roebuck employee who sold us the washing machine. The short-order cook where my father ate his ham-and-eggs breakfasts. "I have seven sons." As if he deserved a medal from the state.

My papa. He didn't mean anything by that mistranslation, I'm sure. But somehow I could feel myself being erased. I'd tug my father's sleeve and whisper: "Not seven sons. Six! and *one daughter.*"

When my oldest brother graduated from medical school, he fulfilled my father's dream that we study hard and use this—our heads, instead of this— our hands. Even now my father's hands are thick and yellow, stubbed by a history of hammer and nails and twine and coils and springs. "Use this," my father said, tapping his head, "and not this," showing us those hands. He always looked tired when he said it.

Wasn't college an investment? And hadn't I spent all those years in college? And if I didn't marry, what was it all for? Why would anyone go to college and then choose to be poor? Especially someone who had always been poor.

Last year, after ten years of writing professionally, the financial re- 15 wards started to trickle in. My second National Endowment for the Arts Fellowship. A guest professorship at the University of California, Berkeley. My book, which sold to a major New York publishing house.

At Christmas, I flew home to Chicago. The house was throbbing, same as always: hot *tamales* and sweet *tamales* hissing in my mother's pressure cooker, and everybody—my mother, six brothers, wives, babies, aunts, cousins—talking too loud and at the same time, like in a Fellini film, because that's just how we are.

I went upstairs to my father's room. One of my stories had just been translated into Spanish and published in an anthology of Chicano writing, and I wanted to show it to him. Ever since he recovered from a stroke two years ago, my father likes to spend his leisure hours horizontally. And that's how I found him, watching a Pedro Infante[2] movie on Galavision and eating rice pudding.

There was a glass filmed with milk on the bedside table. There were several vials of pills and balled Kleenex. And on the floor, one black sock and a plastic urinal that I didn't want to look at but looked at anyway. Pedro Infante was about to burst into song, and my father was laughing.

I'm not sure if it was because my story was translated into Spanish, or because it was published in Mexico, or perhaps because the story dealt with Tepeyac, the *colonia* my father was raised in and the house he grew up in, but at any rate, my father punched the mute button on his remote control and read my story.

I sat on the bed next to my father and waited. He read it very slowly. As if he were reading each line over and over. He laughed at all the right places and read lines he liked out loud. He pointed and asked questions: "Is this So-and-so?" "Yes," I said. He kept reading.

When he was finally finished, after what seemed like hours, my father looked up and asked: "Where can we get more copies of this for the relatives?"

Of all the wonderful things that happened to me last year, that was the most wonderful.

2. José Pedro Infante Cruz (1917–57), Mexican actor and singer. *Galavision:* Spanish-language cable channel.

Study Questions

1. Why does Cisneros's father believe college can be worthwhile for her? How does he view her actual college experience?

2. In paragraph 8, Cisneros writes that her father represents "the public majority," which she envisions as the audience for her writing. Based on what she says about her father, how would you characterize that audience? How can you tell Cisneros is writing for them? What clues do you find in the way she addresses the reader and in her tone and diction?

3. Cisneros vividly describes her father's hands. Why? What significance do his hands have for her story?

4. *For Writing.* Have you ever been frustrated trying to gain someone's approval for an activity that is very important to you? Have you ever had a difficult time understanding someone else's devotion to an activity that means a lot to him or her—but not, personally, to you? Write a narrative in which you select one of these experiences and relate the main events associated with it, using vivid descriptions to make your characters real to your readers.

Framework for Success in Postsecondary Writing

CWPA, NCTE, AND NWP

Executive Summary

The concept of "college readiness" is increasingly important in discussions about students' preparation for postsecondary education.

This Framework describes the rhetorical and twenty-first-century skills as well as habits of mind and experiences that are critical for college success. Based in current research in writing and writing pedagogy, the Framework was written and reviewed by two- and four-year college and high school writing faculty nationwide and is endorsed by the Council of Writing Pro-

---

"Framework for Success in Postsecondary Writing" is a joint publication of three professional organizations: the Council of Writing Program Administrators (CWPA), the National Council of Teachers of English (NCTE), and the National Writing Project (NWP). The three groups were founded to meet specific needs of English teachers and their students. The oldest of the three, NCTE, was established in 1911 with the goal of giving high school and college English teachers a greater voice in what students are taught. NWP was founded in 1974 to foster collaboration between colleges and teachers of grades K-12, in order to improve writing education across all grade levels. CWPA was formed in 1977 to help directors of writing programs at the university level work together to establish common goals for writing classes at different colleges and universities.

In the following passage from the Framework, the authors lay out their definition of the goals for a college education as it relates to writing. Rather than defining successful writing as simply a matter of grammatical correctness or fulfilling the requirements of individual assignments, the authors assert that successful student writers must master a set of mental processes that can be applied in a variety of academic settings. As you read, think about how the authors' "habits of mind" match up with your own experiences with writing and with your education up to this point. How has developing these habits—or not developing them—affected the progress of your own academic career? Do these lists help you to clarify your academic goals?

gram Administrators, the National Council of Teachers of English, and the National Writing Project.

Habits of mind refers to ways of approaching learning that are both intellectual and practical and that will support students' success in a variety of fields and disciplines. The Framework identifies eight habits of mind essential for success in college writing:

- Curiosity—the desire to know more about the world.
- Openness—the willingness to consider new ways of being and thinking in the world.
- Engagement—a sense of investment and involvement in learning.
- Creativity—the ability to use novel approaches for generating, investigating, and representing ideas.
- Persistence—the ability to sustain interest in and attention to short- and long-term projects.
- Responsibility—the ability to take ownership of one's actions and understand the consequences of those actions for oneself and others.
- Flexibility—the ability to adapt to situations, expectations, or demands.
- Metacognition—the ability to reflect on one's own thinking as well as on the individual and cultural processes used to structure knowledge.

The Framework then explains how teachers can foster these habits of mind through **writing, reading, and critical analysis** experiences. These experiences aim to develop students'

- Rhetorical knowledge—the ability to analyze and act on understandings of audiences, purposes, and contexts in creating and comprehending texts;
- Critical thinking—the ability to analyze a situation or text and make thoughtful decisions based on that analysis, through writing, reading, and research;
- Writing processes—multiple strategies to approach and undertake writing and research;
- Knowledge of conventions—the formal and informal guidelines that

define what is considered to be correct and appropriate, or incorrect and inappropriate, in a piece of writing; and

- Ability to compose in multiple environments—from traditional pen and paper to electronic technologies.

Study Questions

1. According to the summary of the Framework, what is "college readiness" and how does it relate to composition (writing) classes?

2. What criteria do the authors present for evaluating students' development as writers?

3. How do the authors establish their ethos in the document—that is, how do they show that their recommendations can be trusted?

4. *For Writing.* Think about your own writing. In a brief essay, explain which of the Framework's "habits of mind" you consider to be your strongest abilities, and which ones you think you most need to work on developing.

The Bayou and the Ship Channel: Finding Place and Building Community in Houston, Texas

TERRELL F. DIXON AND LISA SLAPPEY

MOST AMERICANS VIEW OUR CITIES as having a sort of built-in place-lessness. Cities are mainly freeways, and malls, and chain restaurants. The real Places, the ones that matter, are the Grand Canyon, and Old Faithful, and Rocky Mountain National Park. Once we allow for differences in weather, one American city is pretty much like another.

Our students share this general sense that place is somewhere outside the city. To counteract this viewpoint, to get the students thinking about cities in a different way, we each have chosen to focus our "Literature and the Environment" classes on the city where we teach: Houston. At first, it sounds like an overwhelming challenge: how can we make the epitome of the placeless city a place that lives for them? The solution is simple: get them out in it.

TERRELL F. DIXON (b. 1940) and Lisa Slappey (b. 1969) are both university professors dedicated to making environmental awareness part of the English curriculum. Dixon received his BA at the University of Oklahoma and his PhD at Indiana University. He has taught at Indiana University, Southern Methodist University, and the University of Houston, where he currently teaches undergraduate and graduate courses in environmental literature. Dixon's books include *Being in the World: An Environmental Reader for Writers* (1993, co-edited with Scott H. Slovic), *John Graves: Writer* (2007, co-edited with Mark Busby), and *City Wilds: Essays and Stories about Urban Nature* (2002). Slappey received her BA from Florida State University and her MA and PhD from Rice University. Now a professor at Rice, she focuses mainly on environmental literature and Native American literature.

In "The Bayou and the Ship Channel," Dixon and Slappey take readers through the experiences their students had as they got out of the classroom and visited Houston's Ship Channel and Buffalo Bayou, sharing their reactions and responses to various sights and, notably, smells they encountered in the course of their fieldwork. Through a close examination of Houston from the perspective of college teachers and students, Dixon and Slappey explore the idea of place and how we shape and interact with our environment.

What follows is a distillation of our experiences in teaching urban nature in Houston. Lisa works with undergraduate students, mostly non-English majors, at Rice University; Terrell works with graduate students in creative writing and literature at the University of Houston. We share the desire to help our students discover the nature of place in the city. Taking Rice students to the Ship Channel and University of Houston students to Buffalo Bayou makes Houston both our subject and our classroom.

The Ship Channel

When I ask students where they imagine living after college, few say Houston. As a small private university within Houston's metropolis, Rice University can often seem dissociated, both physically and culturally, from the surrounding city. Rice boasts a strong residential-college system, and even commuting students need not stray far from campus. Students rarely see this city as a desirable living place, nor do they realize how many Rice graduates either stay in or return to Houston to work in our medical center, our petrochemical industry, or our shiny downtown buildings. Many will make their fortunes and raise their families right here. To begin to instill in them an awareness of Houston as a wonderfully complex place, we go outside for a look at the city they will call home for at least four years.

What they see is not always pretty. A trip to the Ship Channel may pro- 5
vide the most revealing, if the least aesthetically pleasing, vision of Houston. Though we may also visit Buffalo Bayou, Brazos Bend State Park, or the Galleria, the Ship Channel takes us to the source of so much of the filthy lucre available here. Many of the social, economic, and environmental challenges facing Houston are evident in this segment of the waterway that connects Buffalo Bayou to the Gulf of Mexico. The place itself is a history lesson. In 1836, Sam Houston's forces defeated Santa Anna's[1] Mexican Army at the Battle of San Jacinto, opening the way for an influx of American settlers into the new Republic of Texas. Most of those early arrivals to the city founded by the Allen brothers[2] and bearing Houston's name came by this water route. The

1. Antonio López de Santa Anna (1794–1876), Mexican revolutionary leader, army general, and seven-time president. Sam Houston: American politician and soldier (1793–1863), governor of Tennessee, two-time president of the Republic of Texas, and governor of the state of Texas.
2. Augustus Chapman Allen (1806–64) and John Kirby Allen (1810–38), land speculators.

outcome of that 1836 contest of international wills set the stage for Houston's emergence as not merely a Southern cotton exchange or oil-refining boomtown but as a global-commerce headquarters as well.

Houston houses the nation's second-busiest port and the world's second-largest petrochemical complex. Proud of those designations, the city offers a free public relations boat tour of the Houston Ship Channel. Taking my students on the ninety-minute tour aboard the MV[3] *Sam Houston* to meet our petrochemical neighbors requires that we make reservations, bring identification, and clear Homeland Security. Bureaucracy aside, everyone associated with the Ship Channel has always welcomed us, though I warn the class not to expect the "unforgettably spectacular waterborne adventure" promised on the Port of Houston's official Web site. We journey from our little urban oasis across the 610 Ship Channel Bridge and onto Clinton Drive, passing parking lots full of shiny imported cars on one side and ramshackle housing on the other. Ship Channel neighborhoods lack the Rice area's affluence. Those who can afford to live elsewhere do. Environmental justice begins to take human form.

Students ask why Houston would market this view of itself to tourists, and yet the ship's register is full of visitors. This area interests our guests more than it interests the locals. Over the years, only two of my local students had taken the boat tour before our field trips. Virtually all admit to a basic lack of awareness of the Ship Channel's functions. Some are surprised to learn that we are a port city; certainly they are oblivious to the port's past and present connections to Rice University. Marie Phelps McAshan describes in romantic terms the 1874 port "dream" of Houston as a cotton exporter. This economic and engineering feat required "the narrow tortuous channel choked with logs, infested with alligators, and full of all kinds of debris" (100–101) to be dredged to a depth of twenty-five feet; it succeeded because "these men of great vision and indomitable energy persevered" (101). The project was completed in 1914. The leaders in the later stages included Baldwin Rice, Houston mayor and nephew of Rice University's founder, and Jesse H. Jones, namesake of Rice's Graduate School of Management.

Overwhelmed by the Ship Channel, the noxious smells, noise, smoke, the huge refineries, the filth in the water and along the banks, my students begin to understand Houston's prominence in the global petrochemical economy. Oil and gas politics underpin many national strategies, and the

3. Merchant Vessel

Port of Houston, at once dangerous, powerful, and vulnerable, becomes a significant place. Recognizing the port as neighbor makes us notice when, for example, refineries explode, as they do, faithfully and conveniently, at least once a semester.

For those who live and die by the petrochemical industry, there is nothing convenient about the constant threats and occasional eruptions serving as student lessons. Once students understand that we all face environmental perils daily, they ask how individuals can initiate change when corporations seem so powerful. Sandra Steingraber reminds us in *Living Downstream* that "with the right to know comes the duty to inquire" (xxii) and, ultimately, "the obligation to act" (117). This is not easy, since closing ranks is industry's typical response to disaster.

On February 6, 2006, explosions at Akzo Nobel Chemicals in Deer Park 10 sent one employee to the burn unit. Officials shut down nearby roads while attempting to determine the danger level; instead of calling the city's firefighters, the plant's in-house fire crew handled the situation. When one student investigated this incident for her midterm project, neither Akzo Nobel nor OSHA provided any information relating to the fire, so she exercised her right to know and fulfilled her duty to inquire by filing for disclosure under the Freedom of Information Act.

On the boat, we wonder that the industries lining the shore do not have more frequent mishaps than those making the evening news. Perhaps nothing less than spectacular tragedy will force our attention, however briefly, to what occurs along the Ship Channel. How many of us know or care about the chemical processes and political maneuvers that keep the Ship Channel—and therefore much of Houston—generating growth and income? Who pays attention to the daily Air Quality Index, monitors particulate matter, or worries about toxins in the water? Should a hurricane wind its way up the Ship Channel, what sort of unnatural disaster might ensue? In November 2004, *Texas Monthly* magazine's executive editor S.C. Gwynne described the Ship Channel as a "prime terrorist target" because "it is both ground zero for the nation's petrochemical industry and home to unfathomably large quantities of the deadliest, most combustible, disease-causing, lung-exploding, chromosome-annihilating, and metal-dissolving substances known to man," yet until the Bush administration planned in 2006 to award management of several U.S. ports (Houston was not among them) to Dubai Ports World, how many citizens recognized the port systems' vulnerability to any form of terrorism?

Despite its activity level, there is a depressing, even desolate quality to the Ship Channel. Advocates of retrofitting industrial plants could build their cases here: much of the equipment seems old, rusted, and run-down; some structures, such as the Houston Lighting and Power building, are simply abandoned and falling apart. Add a few dark clouds, and the view becomes downright ominous with silhouetted spires belching toxicity into the air. Here, where the hot, hard, dirty work takes place, the effect of heavy industry cannot be disguised. Unless we are doing that work, unless we live in the communities where such work takes place, it is easy enough to disregard it. On the boat's return trip, we see Houston's glassy, expensive downtown rising in the background.

The Ship Channel provides olfactory as well as visual stimuli. One class suggests renaming the boat trip "The Tour of Smells." Author Bill Minutaglio recounts a "joke" popular in Texas City in the 1940s: *"What brought you here?" "Shit, that's an easy answer. It's the stink. The stink of money"* (7). The Port Authority takes pride in "generating more than $10 billion in business each year and supporting nearly 300,000 jobs." In 2005, Exxon Mobil alone, whose Baytown, Texas, plant is the largest refinery in the United States, posted a staggering $36.13 billion profit ("Exxon Mobil . . .").

Although it is easy to revile petrochemical giants for their avarice, they are not the port's only financial beneficiaries. According to *The Port of Houston Magazine*, each year more than 6,000 vessels carrying 15 million tons of containers loaded with consumer products pass through the facility. They are destined not only or even primarily for metropolitan Houston, but for all of the pretty places in our nation's interior. The port's motto, "The Port Delivers the Goods," could not be more appropriate. Many of us sell these goods; all of us use them. The boat tour reminds us that everyone is implicated in the activities of the Port of Houston and the Houston Ship Channel. The stench, which is often what students recall long after the tour, clings to all of us, no matter how far we distance ourselves from the Ship Channel.

Environmental lawyer Jim Blackburn lectures in the Department of Civil and Environmental Engineering at Rice University and opposes the massive new Bayport Container Facility. In his beautiful text, *The Book of Texas Bays*, he urges us to consider the personal implications at the intersection of ecology and economy: 15

We Texans are on a path whereby the full costs of our projects—our water supply, our shipping channels, our water pollutants—are not

being paid today. . . . Our most pressing need is to find a different
way of thinking about economics and ecology, one that is serious
about protecting life on our living planet, one that provides for an
accounting of the full cost of our current activities. (56–57)

Blackburn's work, including a federal lawsuit to stop the Bayport project,
reveals the highly politicized issues surrounding the Houston Ship Channel. Although the suit was rejected, at least the Port Authority's Web site
now includes a nod toward environmental consciousness. At forty-five feet
deep and 530 feet wide and crowded with hundreds of industrial facilities,
today's Ship Channel bears little resemblance to that wildly lush, narrow
channel through which early settlers journeyed up Buffalo Bayou to Houston. It is a fine place to account for the costs not just of our projects but of our
way of life.

Buffalo Bayou

As Houston has grown, its bayous have suffered. Some very early city plans
followed the flow of the bayous, but after that our bayous have more often
than not been degraded and ignored. Some remarkably sinuous streams that
once threaded the landscape of the coastal plain have been "channelized"
(that is, in a process as ugly as the word itself, reshaped into a straight line
and then cemented). Others have been made unappealing ditches, dumping
grounds for trash, homes to nests of plastic bags, shopping carts, abandoned
cars, and the occasional murder victim. Though we citizens usually choose
not to really see our bayous, we were sometimes inadvertently implicated
in a drive-by bayou sighting. We glimpse part of a bayou, usually from the
corner of our eye, from a car speeding down a crowded freeway. Such hap-
penings have inspired us, not to stop, look, and walk but to keep on going.
In a revealing synecdoche that signifies how we Houstonians have treated
our home landscape, the nickname Space City has mostly supplanted the
original, place-based Bayou City. We have chosen to look away.

The problem has been, I think, that the bayous were not part of the aesthetic vocabulary of most Americans. Without peaks and rushing streams,
it took us some time to learn how to read their beauty.

Houstonians were prodded into this recognition process by two disparate things. One was popular culture on the national level; the other was

the work of Richard Florida, a Carnegie Mellon professor who is a special-
ist on urban economies. The popular culture provocation was the late-night
television world of Jay Leno and David Letterman. Houston has always been
an exceedingly image-conscious city, mindful of its status relative to other
cities and determined to advance its place in the great, fluid hierarchy of city
reputations.

Thus what transpired during the presidential election of 2000 had a
huge impact: Leno and Letterman made fun of Houston! The jokes began
with a George W. Bush campaign promise that he "would do for the country
what he did for Texas." The talk show hosts tied that phrase to then current
news stories about Houston's number one ranking in air pollution, Houston's traffic gridlock, etc. For Houston power brokers, the ridicule translated into a loss of face and, even worse, a potential loss of business. At last,
change had to be considered.

My seminar students at the University of Houston come from all parts   20
of the country, and they begin the seminar with the Jay Leno humorous
view of Houston. No need to teach it. They have already discovered poor
public transportation, high heat and humidity. It is a big, hot city, and they
mostly try not to get out in it, except in an air-conditioned automobile.

The change in the city's attitude toward bayous also stems from the
theories of Richard Florida. Sometimes we read his work; most often I summarize it. Florida has developed—with appropriate data, charts, etc.—a pro-
file of what he designates the "creative class."[4] This class of young people,
he says, now drives the economic engines of the cities where they *choose* to
live. "Choose" is the key word here; Florida believes that those who make up
the creative class seek more than a well-paying job. They take the ability to
earn a good income as a given. What they look for, instead, is something that
Florida describes as "quality of place." Quality of place for these young people
has many different components, but foremost among them are such "ameni-
ties" as diversity. To them, diversity means everything from an ethnically
mixed population, to varied kinds of restaurants, to active gay and lesbian
communities, to an atmosphere where current artistic creation flourishes
(not the big museums that emphasize the work from other times and places).

4. Richard Florida's thesis is developed in *The Rise of the Creative Class* (New York: Basic Books,
2002). The Houston Quality of Life Coalition Web page presents (under the heading "Additional
Resources") a fifty-page essay that includes many but not all of his ideas: "Competing in the
Age of Talent: Quality of Place and the New Economy." [Author's note.]

It also encompasses opportunities for outdoor activity, and natural places conducive to outdoor recreation are a high priority in this group's evaluation.

Clearly, high air pollution and traffic gridlock will not attract this group. And, just as clearly, the landscape feature in Houston that has the most potential is the bayou system. It seemed no accident that Richard Florida's work began to appear on the Web site for a relatively new organization, one whose membership overlapped greatly with that of the Greater Houston Partnership (formerly called the Houston Chamber of Commerce). This organization calls itself the Quality of Life Coalition, and, since a fifty-page essay written by Florida is part of the Web site, the echo of his phrase seems deliberate. The negative push of Leno and Letterman and the positive pull of Florida's argument combined to have a powerful impact. At last, a substantial change in Houston's long-term complacency about ongoing landscape degradation seems to be happening.

My graduate students' notion of what a city can and should be also changes as they learn Florida's views. Their sense of Houston, however, changes most with the group field-study segment of the seminar. This usually involves two visits, the first to a cement-bottomed bayou not far from campus, complete with high-wire lines and rusted pipes over the bayou. This serves as my example of a "bad," that is, "unrestored" Houston bayou. During one recent early-spring visit, however, there were great blue herons in the water, and a sharp-eyed student spotted huckleberries growing along the bank, enough for two very tasty pies—reminders that it is hard to completely eradicate nature. We may have to work to see it, but it is there, even in the heavily industrialized city.

This changing sense of what was best for Houston crystallized in "Buffalo Bayou and Beyond: Visions, Strategies, and Actions for the Twenty-first Century." A long title for a huge plan. The project is, both in scope and in finances, typical of Houston at its most ambitious: the redevelopment of some ten miles of downtown bayou, to be completed over a twenty-year period, at a projected expense of $800 million.

The plan also was a stunningly attractive departure from business as usual in Houston—a needed fulcrum for how the city treats nature. It is by no means the first plan to beautify this bayou; there were at least twenty such proposals, of varying scopes, during the twentieth century. None of those earlier plans had either the range or the backing of this one, and most of them got nowhere. This was good news. It also has made it more uplifting to use the city as environmental text.

With the new plan, it suddenly seemed as if Houston was ready to move into a new growth stage, a maturity that honored, rather than degraded, the natural world. I went to the announcement, noted that several people talked with pride about "greening Houston," and left with only one nagging question. Some dignitary mentioned an aquarium, but I couldn't find it on my expensive, detailed take-home rendition of the plan. I wondered: do we need an aquarium there, right on the banks of the bayou? Even if the aquarium is presumed to have educational value, doesn't that make either one or the other of the two bodies of water—either the real bayou or the man-made aquarium—redundant?

I soon found out. On October 20, 2002, less than a month after the big introduction of "Buffalo Bayou and Beyond," the *Houston Chronicle* featured a front-page story praising a new draw for tourism and a boost for the economy: the Downtown Aquarium. The news that morning seemed so far from the elaborate press conference presentations that I had to read it several times. That was because the Downtown Aquarium is a mammoth business venture—a $38 million aquatic-themed entertainment center spread over six acres, featuring the following: a huge seafood restaurant, a 200,000-gallon shark tank with a mini-train running through it, the capacity to hold three thousand people at a time, and a merry-go-round with sea life rider seats near a ninety-foot Ferris wheel. At night, the Ferris wheel glows bright blue neon. This place is, beneath the self-serving designation of itself as an aquarium, a very large and Disney-fied Landry's seafood restaurant, one with a permanent carnival attached and several large fish tanks squeezed into a small space below the restaurant and gift shop. It was the first bayou project after the September "Buffalo Bayou and Beyond" announcement, *and* it was to be on six acres of public land. The land deal was so blatant that the Houston papers—even the alternative one—dodged the underlying issue.

The argument, widely circulated by word of mouth, was that the Ferris wheel and the carnival were needed to draw "more people" downtown. "To thereby build community as we build downtown." A key point was that "not everyone would go to the Wortham Center Opera House across the street."

Students study this decision, the company involved in it and its political connections, and what was written about it. We talk about the culture's need, first, to do away with nature and then to build commercial, profit-generating simulations of it, about what happens when city governments try to outsource the responsibility to provide parks for its citizens. The rationale for the city's aquarium decision, as I suggest to students before we walk this section of the bayou, underestimates both the power of nature and the priorities of the majority of those Houstonians who are working class or middle class. A real park could build a more inclusive community; the city's decision assumed, and thereby strengthened, a socioeconomic- (and often color-) based separation. People from all walks of life desire and deserve parks, both to enjoy the natural world and to enjoy sharing space with someone who is not just exactly like them.

Since the 2002 announcement, Buffalo Bayou has prospered. Two stages   30 of a beautiful and environmentally helpful redevelopment are done (and the two stages do include some areas with diverse residential demographics). Though I still contend that the permanent "seafood" carnival detracts from downtown and trashes the bayou, the overall Buffalo Bayou redevelopment progress has been good. Houston, downtown, on Buffalo Bayou, is making progress. It is green and spacious, with a good view of a mostly beautiful sky- line (marred only by the bright neon Ferris wheel) in the distance, good trails, a great dog park, and the chance to see large turtles sunning themselves on bayou logs and many migrating birds in the spring and fall. I urge my stu- dents to walk there at least several times during the semester.

There is a certain pleasure and heuristic value, however, in the field study trip when the seminar goes downtown to walk the bayou. The dis- cussions and readings work well, but the main field study segment of the class helps multiply the impact of the students' library and classroom work. However contradictory the term "urban nature walk" may sound, it works. It remains the best teaching tool that I have.

We start at Sabine Street and stroll down toward the aquarium. This juxtaposition of Buffalo Bayou and the aquarium entertainment complex built on its banks does have one redeeming virtue. It creates a serendipi- tous site for students to observe and learn about contemporary American culture and urban nature's contested place in it. On our way, we see turtles and birds—herons as well as egrets. Often, we see alligators. Students have already read a funny short story by Donald Barthelme, a legendary teacher in our graduate program. Barthelme's "Return" creates a contemporary ur- ban everyman who returns to Houston and tries to connect with the city through nature, but who finally settles for a simulation of Southern nature, a nine-hundred-foot steel azalea.

When we get to the "aquarium," we note the exhibition room that dis- plays stuffed or glassed-in versions of the local wildlife that we have just seen. The name over that door says "Louisiana Swamp." We pass it, and then head back up Buffalo Bayou. Students sometimes ask, "Where do they keep the steel azalea?"

Most of these seminar students will leave Houston. Only one or two from a class of fifteen will teach and write here. But whether they settle in small college towns or teach in urban universities across the country, they do leave with a sense of one city's efforts to re-green itself, and of its missteps and its successes. The degree of commitment will vary, but they are all to some degree part of a larger community that has started to recognize the importance of urban nature. They can take with them the knowledge that more than 80 percent of their students will live in cities, that city wilds and walks within these wilds are crucial if we are to expand America's environmental consciousness.

Conclusion

The Ship Channel and the bayou embody the two central attitudes that 35 the city of Houston has had toward the natural world—the Ship Channel expresses Houston's past build-and-develop-the-hell-out-of-this-place-and-damn-the-consequences attitudes. It may someday get cleaned up a bit.

Upstream and uptown, there is Buffalo Bayou, increasingly seen as an "amenity," a way to attract the labor force, those imaginative city builders of the future—beautiful in itself and becoming developed, mostly, in ways that will enhance that beauty and the city's enjoyment of it. Houston's future, we hope, will include the beautification of other bayous. But certainly this is progress. Houston is not now and never will be Portland, or Boulder, or San Francisco. It is, however, now a city where community has begun to coalesce and grow around the idea of finding the place—the bayous, the trees, the neighborhoods—once hidden beneath our decades of determined growth into placelessness.

Cities, wild places before they became urban centers, can be made green again, and our students at the University of Houston and at Rice can someday support such a process wherever they live. They learn that they want a city with jobs and homes, *and* places that can embody what Terry Tempest Williams calls "the open space of democracy." They seek places where citizens of all kinds can go to renew their human connections and discover a larger sense of community, their ties to the green world that undergirds and supports the life of the city.

Works Cited

Barthelme, Donald. "Return." *The Teachings of Don B.* New York: Turtle Bay Books, 1992. Print.

Blackburn, Jim. *The Book of Texas Bays.* College Station: Texas A&M University Press, 2004. Print.

"Exxon Mobil Posts Largest Annual Profit for U.S. Company." *New York Times* 31 Jan. 2006. Web. 2 Sept. 2006.

Florida, Richard. *The Rise of the Creative Class.* New York: Basic Books, 2002. Print.

Gwynne, S. C. "Attack Here." *Texas Monthly* Nov. 2004. Posted on the Houston Architecture Info Forum, 1 Nov. 2004. Web. 4 Sept. 2006.

McAshan, Marie Phelps. *A Houston Legacy: On the Corner of Main and Texas.* Houston: Hutchins House, 1985. Print.

Minutaglio, Bill. *City on Fire: The Explosion That Devastated a Texas Town and Ignited a Historic Legal Battle.* New York: Perennial, 2004. Print.

The Port of Houston Magazine Jan./Feb. 2006. Print.

Sam Houston Boat Tour. The Port of Houston Authority, 2009. Web. 3 Sept. 2006.

Steingraber, Sandra. *Living Downstream.* New York: Vintage Books, 1997. Print.

Turner, Allan. "CEO Casts His Net for Downtown." *Houston Chronicle* 20 October 2002: A1. Web.

Williams, Terry Tempest. *The Open Space of Democracy.* Barrington, MA: Orion Society, 2004. Print.

Study Questions

1. Identify the authors of each section and explain where each took their classes. How do you think they each feel about Houston? Support your response with passages from the essay.

2. When some authors write in collaboration with others, the work takes on one voice and does not distinguish who writes what part. In this essay, however, readers can clearly tell that Slappey wrote one section and Dixon wrote the other. Evaluate their method of collaboration and determine if two voices detract from or add to the unity of the essay. Would you prefer reading an essay written in this way or one that has one voice? How would you prefer to write a collaborative essay?

3. What is the authors' thesis? Where is it stated most directly? How do they support that thesis?

4. Description appears throughout the essay, with lots of concrete, specific details painting a picture of various places in Houston. What dominant impression of Houston do the authors create? What details contribute to this impression?

5. *For Writing.* Select a place that you feel is representative of the town you live in now or of your hometown—for instance, a local landmark, a natural feature like a beach or a mountain, or a well-known building. Write an essay in which you describe this place, creating an overall impression of it, and explain how it is representative of the town.

Sex, Drugs, Disasters, and the Extinction of Dinosaurs
STEPHEN JAY GOULD

S CIENCE, IN ITS MOST FUNDAMENTAL DEFINITION, is a fruitful mode of inquiry, not a list of enticing conclusions. The conclusions are the consequence, not the essence. My greatest unhappiness with most popular presentations of science concerns their failure to separate fascinating claims from the methods that scientists use to establish the facts of nature. Journalists, and the public, thrive on controversial and stunning statements. But science is, basically, a way of knowing—in P. B. Medawar's apt words, "the art of the soluble." If the growing corps of popular science writers would focus on how scientists develop and defend those fascinating claims, they would make their greatest possible contribution to public understanding.

Consider three ideas, proposed in perfect seriousness to account for that greatest of all titillating puzzles—the extinction of dinosaurs. These three notions invoke the primarily fascinating themes of our culture—sex,

---

STEPHEN JAY GOULD (1941–2002) was born in New York City; he earned his undergraduate degree at Antioch College in Ohio and his PhD at Columbia University. For thirty-five years Gould was a professor at Harvard University. However, he is best known for his ability to explain complex scientific topics in ways that make them accessible to a general audience, often by writing articles in popular magazines and by advising (and often appearing in) television programs like PBS's *NOVA*. He collected his columns from the magazine *Natural History* into several book-length collections, including *Hen's Teeth and Horse's Toes* (1983), *The Flamingo's Smile* (1985), and *Bully for Brontosaurus* (1991). The recipient of dozens of honorary degrees, Gould was a finalist for the Pulitzer Prize for his book *Wonderful Life: The Burgess Shale and the Nature of History* (1989).

The following essay, originally published in *Discover Magazine* in 1984, presents three potential hypotheses for the extinction of the dinosaurs and analyzes each for its scientific value. As you read, think about how the essay is organized and how Gould incorporates humor into a serious discussion. How might these qualities contribute to Gould's reputation as a writer who excels at presenting scientific topics to a general audience?

drugs, and violence—and I want to show why two of them rank as silly speculation, and why the other represents science at its grandest and most useful.

Science works with testable hypotheses. If, after much compilation and scrutiny of data, new information continues to affirm a hypothesis, we may accept it provisionally and gain confidence as further evidence mounts. We can never be completely sure that a hypothesis is right, though we may be able to show with confidence that it is wrong. The best scientific hypotheses are also generous and expansive: they suggest extensions and implications that enlighten related, and even far distant, subjects. Simply consider how the idea of evolution has influenced virtually every intellectual field.

Useless speculation, on the other hand, is restrictive. It generates no testable hypothesis, proposes no way to obtain potentially refuting evidence. Please note that I am not speaking of truth or falsity. The speculation may well be true; still, if it provides, in principle, no material for affirmation or rejection, we can make nothing of it. It must simply stand forever as an intriguing idea. Useless speculation turns in on itself and leads nowhere; good science reaches out. But, enough preaching. Let's move on to dinosaurs, and the three proposed causes of their extinction.

1. Sex: Testes function only in a narrow range of temperature (those of   5 mammals hang externally in a scrotal sac because they need to be cooler than the body). A worldwide rise in temperature at the close of the Cretaceous period caused the testes of dinosaurs to stop functioning and led to their extinction by sterilization of males.

2. Drugs: Angiosperms (flowering plants) first evolved toward the end of the dinosaurs' reign. Many of these plants contain psychoactive agents, avoided by mammals today because of their bitter taste. Dinosaurs had neither means to taste the bitterness, nor livers effective enough to detoxify the substances. They died of massive overdoses.

3. Disasters: A huge asteroid struck the earth some 65 million years ago, lofting a cloud of dust into the sky and blocking sunlight, thereby suppressing photosynthesis and so drastically lowering world temperatures that dinosaurs and hosts of other creatures became extinct.

Before analyzing these three tantalizing statements, we must establish a basic ground rule often violated in proposals for the dinosaurs' demise. *There is no separate problem of the extinction of dinosaurs.* Too often we divorce specific events from their wider contexts and systems of cause and effect. The fundamental fact of dinosaur extinction is that it coincided with

the demise of many other groups across a wide range of habitats, from terrestrial to marine.

The history of life has been punctuated by brief episodes of mass extinction. A recent analysis by University of Chicago paleontologists Jack Sep-
koski and Dave Raup, based on the best and most exhaustive tabulation of
data ever assembled, shows clearly that five episodes of mass dying stand
well above the "background" extinctions of normal times. The Cretaceous
debacle, occurring 65 million years ago and separating the Mesozoic and
Cenozoic eras of our geological time scale, ranks prominently among the
five. Nearly all the marine plankton (single-celled floating creatures) died
suddenly, at least in geological terms; among marine invertebrates, close to
15 percent of all families perished, including many previously dominant
groups, especially the ammonites (relatives of squids in coiled shells). On
land, the dinosaurs disappeared after more than 100 million years of un-
challenged domination.

In this context, speculations limited to dinosaurs alone ignore the ₁₀
larger phenomenon. We need a coordinated explanation for a system of
events that includes the extinction of dinosaurs as one component. Thus
it makes little sense, though it may fuel our desire to view mammals as inevitable inheritors of the earth, to guess that dinosaurs died because small
mammals ate their eggs (a perennial untestable speculation). It seems
most unlikely that some disaster peculiar to dinosaurs befell these massive
beasts—and that the debacle happened to strike just when one of history's
five great dyings had enveloped the earth for completely different reasons.

The testicular theory, an old favorite from the 1940s, had its root in
an interesting and thoroughly respectable study of temperature tolerances
in the American alligator, published in the staid *Bulletin of the American
Museum of Natural History* in 1946 by three experts on living and fossil
reptiles—E. H. Colbert, my own first teacher in paleontology, R. B. Cowles,
and C. M. Bogert.

The first sentence of their summary reveals a purpose beyond alligators: "This report describes an attempt to infer the reactions of extinct reptiles, especially the dinosaurs, to high temperatures as based upon reactions
observed in the modern alligator." They studied, by rectal thermometry, the
body temperatures of alligators under changing conditions of heating and
cooling. (Well, let's face it, you wouldn't want to try sticking a thermometer
under a 'gator's tongue.) The predictions under test go way back to an old
theory first stated by Galileo in the 1630s—the unequal scaling of surfaces

and volumes. As an animal, or any object, grows (provided its shape doesn't change), surface areas must increase more slowly than volumes—since surfaces get larger as length squared, volumes much more rapidly, as length cubed. Therefore, small animals have high ratios of surface to volume, while large animals cover themselves with relatively little surface.

Among cold-blooded animals lacking any physiological mechanism for keeping their temperatures constant, small creatures have a hell of a time keeping warm—because they lose so much heat through their relatively large surfaces. On the other hand, large animals, with their relatively small surfaces, may lose heat so slowly that, once warm, they may maintain effectively constant temperatures against ordinary fluctuations of climate. (In fact, the resolution of the "hot-blooded dinosaur" controversy of a few years back may simply be that, while large dinosaurs possessed no physiological mechanism for constant temperature, and so were not warm-blooded in the technical sense, their size and relatively small surface area kept them warm.)

Colbert, Cowles, and Bogert compared the warming rates of small and large alligators. As predicted, the small fellows heated up (and cooled down) more quickly. When exposed to a warm sun, a tiny 50-gram (1.76-ounce) alligator heated up one degree Celsius every minute and a half, while a large alligator, 260 times bigger at 13,000 grams (28.7 pounds), took seven and a half minutes to gain a degree. Extrapolating up to an adult ten-ton dinosaur, they concluded that a one-degree rise in body temperature would take 86 hours. If large animals absorb heat so slowly (through their relatively small surfaces), they will also be unable to shed any excess heat gained when temperatures rise above a favorable level.

The authors then guessed that large dinosaurs lived at or near their op- 15 timum temperatures; Cowles suggested that a rise in global temperatures just before the Cretaceous extinction caused the dinosaurs to heat up beyond their optimal tolerance—and, being so large, they couldn't shed the unwanted heat. (In a most unusual statement for a scientific paper, Colbert and Bogert explicitly disavowed this speculative extension of their empirical work on alligators.) Cowles conceded that this excess heat probably wasn't enough to kill or even to enervate the great beasts, but since testes often function only within a narrow range of temperature, he proposed that this global rise might have sterilized all the males, causing extinction by natural contraception.

The overdose theory has recently been supported by UCLA psychiatrist

Ronald K. Siegel. Siegel has observed, he claims, more than 2,000 animals that can give themselves various drugs—from a swig of alcohol to massive doses of the big H.[1] Elephants will swill the equivalent of twenty beers at a time, but do not like alcohol in concentrations greater than 7 per cent. In a silly bit of anthropocentric speculation, Siegel states that "elephants drink, perhaps, to forget . . . the anxiety produced by shrinking rangeland and the competition for food."

Since fertile imaginations can apply almost any hot idea to the extinction of dinosaurs, Siegel found a way. Flowering plants did not evolve until late in the dinosaurs' reign. These plants also produced an array of aromatic, amino-acid-based alkaloids—the major group of psychoactive agents. Most mammals are "smart" enough to avoid these potential poisons. The alkaloids simply don't taste good (they are bitter), and in any case we mammals have livers happily supplied with the capacity to detoxify them. But, Siegel speculates, perhaps dinosaurs could neither taste the bitterness nor detoxify the substances once ingested. Speaking of their extinction, he recently told members of the American Psychological Association: "I'm not suggesting that all dinosaurs OD'd on plant drugs, but it certainly was a factor." He also argued that death by overdose may help explain why so many dinosaur fossils are found in contorted positions. (Do not go gentle into that good night.)[2]

Extraterrestrial catastrophes have long pedigrees in the popular literature of extinction, but the subject exploded again after a long lull three years ago when the father-son, physicist-geologist team of Luis and Walter Alvarez proposed that an asteroid, about six miles in diameter, struck the earth 65 million years ago. Most asteroids circle the sun in an orbit between Mars and Jupiter but some, the so-called Apollo objects, take a more eccentric route, actually crossing the earth's orbit in their path around the sun. The chance of a collision at any crossing is minuscule, but the number of Apollo objects and the immensity of geological time virtually guarantee that impacts will occur once in a great while.

The force of such a collision would be immense, greater by far than the megatonnage of all the world's nuclear weapons. In trying to reconstruct a scenario that would explain the simultaneous dying of dinosaurs on land and so many creatures in the sea, the Alvarezes proposed that a gigantic dust cloud, generated by particles blown aloft in the impact, would so

1. Slang term for heroin.
2. Repeated line (and title) of a poem by Welsh poet Dylan Thomas (1914–53).

darken the earth that photosynthesis would cease and temperatures drop precipitously. (Rage, rage against the dying of the light.)[3] The single-celled photosynthetic oceanic plankton, with life cycles measured in weeks, would perish outright, but land plants might survive through the dormancy of their seeds (land plants were not much affected by the Cretaceous extinction, and any adequate theory must account for the curious pattern of differential survival). Dinosaurs would die by starvation and freezing; small, warm-blooded mammals, with more modest requirements for food and better regulation of body temperature, would squeak through.

All three theories, testicular malfunction, psychoactive overdosing, and asteroidal zapping, grab our attention mightily. As pure statements, they rank about equally high on any hit parade of primal fascination. Yet one represents expansive science, the others restrictive and untestable speculation.

How could we possibly decide whether the hypothesis of testicular frying is right or wrong? We would have to know things that the fossil record cannot provide. What temperatures were optimal for dinosaurs? Could the beasts avoid the absorption of excess heat by staying in the shade, or in caves? At what temperatures did their testicles cease to function? Were late Cretaceous climates ever warm enough to drive the internal temperatures of dinosaurs close to this ceiling? Testicles simply don't fossilize, and how could we infer their temperature tolerances even if they did? In short, Cowles's hypothesis is simply an intriguing speculation leading nowhere. The most damning statement against it appeared right in the conclusion of Colbert, Cowles, and Bogert's paper, when they admitted: "It is difficult to advance any definite arguments against this hypothesis." My statement may seem paradoxical—isn't a hypothesis really good if you can't devise any arguments against it? Quite the contrary. It is simply untestable and unusable.

Siegel's overdosing has even less going for it. At least Cowles extrapolated his conclusion from some good data on alligators. And he didn't completely violate the primary guideline of explaining dinosaur extinction in the context of a general mass dying—for rise in temperature could be the root cause of a general catastrophe, zapping dinosaurs by testicular malfunction and different groups for other reasons. But Siegel's speculation cannot touch the extinction of ammonites or oceanic plankton (diatoms make their own food with good sweet sunlight; they don't OD on the chemicals of

3. Another repeating line in Thomas's poem.

terrestrial plants). It is simply a gratuitous, attention-grabbing guess. It cannot be tested, for how can we know what dinosaurs tasted and what their livers could do?

The hypothesis doesn't even make any sense in its own context. Angiosperms were in full flower tens of millions of years before dinosaurs went the way of all flesh. Why did it take so long? As for the pains of a chemical death recorded in contortions of fossils, I regret to say (or rather I'm pleased to note for the dinosaurs' sake) that Siegel's knowledge of geology must be a bit deficient: muscles contract after death and geological strata rise and fall with motions of the earth's crust after burial—more than enough reason to distort a fossil's pristine appearance.

The asteroid story, on the other hand, has a basis in evidence. It can be tested, extended, refined and, if wrong, disproved. The Alvarezes did not just construct an arresting guess for public consumption. They proposed their hypothesis after laborious geochemical studies with Frank Asaro and Helen Michel had revealed a massive increase of iridium in rocks deposited right at the time of extinction. Iridium, a rare metal of the platinum group, is virtually absent from indigenous rocks of the earth's crust; most of our iridium comes from extraterrestrial objects that hit the earth.

The Alvarez hypothesis bore immediate fruit. Based originally on evidence found in rocks at two sites in Europe, it led geochemists throughout the world to examine other sediments of the same age. They found abnormally high amounts of iridium everywhere—from continental rocks of the western United States to deep sea cores from the South Atlantic. 25

Cowles proposed his testicular hypothesis in the mid-1940s. Where has it gone since then? Absolutely nowhere, because scientists can do nothing with it. It merely stands as a curious appendage to a solid study of alligators. Siegel's overdose scenario will also win a few press notices and fade into oblivion. The Alvarezes' asteroid falls into a different category altogether, and much of the popular commentary has missed this essential distinction by focusing on the impact and its attendant results, and forgetting what is really important to a scientist—the iridium. If you talk just about asteroids, dust, and darkness, you simply tell stories better and no more entertaining than fried testicles or terminal trips. It is the iridium—the source of testable evidence—that counts and forges the crucial distinction between speculation and science.

The proof, to twist a phrase, lies in the doing. In thirty-five years, Cowles's hypothesis led to no further advances toward our understanding of dinosaurian extinction. In three years, the Alvarez hypothesis has spawned hundreds of studies, a major conference, and attendant publications. Geologists are fired up. They are looking for iridium at all other extinction boundaries and, by the way, have not (with one exception) found any marked increases—thus proving that a good hypothesis also shows its worth by failing to work in other situations. Every week exposes a new wrinkle in the scientific press. In November a group of Yale scientists supported the hypothesis by finding a "cosmic signature" for isotopes of osmium in Cretaceous boundary rocks (a ratio of isotopes found in extraterrestrial material but not in crustal rocks produced on earth). Then, in December, chemists from the University of Maryland cast some doubt by reporting that volcanic eruptions of Kilauea on Hawaii had belched forth unexpectedly high levels of iridium; perhaps an extraterrestrial source need not be sought.

My point is simply this: whatever the eventual outcome (I suspect it will be positive), the Alvarez hypothesis is exciting, fruitful science because it generates tests, provides us with things to do, and expands outward. We are having fun, battling back and forth, moving toward a resolution, and extending the hypothesis beyond its original scope.

As just one example of the unexpected, distant cross-fertilization that good science engenders, the Alvarez hypothesis made a major contribution to a theme that has riveted public attention in the past few months—so-called nuclear winter. In a speech delivered in April 1982, Luis Alvarez calculated the energy that a six-mile asteroid would release on impact. He compared such an explosion with a full nuclear exchange and implied that all-out atomic war might unleash similar consequences.

This theme of impact leading to massive dust clouds and falling temperatures was an important factor in the decision of Carl Sagan and a group of colleagues to model the climatic consequences of nuclear holocaust. We have, of course, long known that a full nuclear exchange could kill half of humanity outright and cannot be deemed acceptable on any grounds. But some of us still had lurking in our minds the hope that, if we hunkered down in our shelters and lived far from military sites or cities, at least we could survive after the initial fallout dropped.

Apparently, it is not necessarily so. Full nuclear exchange would probably generate the same kind of dust cloud and darkening that may have wiped out the dinosaurs. Temperatures would drop precipitously and agriculture might become impossible. Avoidance of nuclear war is fundamentally an ethical and political problem, but we must know the factual consequences to make firm judgments. Is this not a heartening thought: a recognition of the very phenomenon that made our evolution possible by exterminating the previously dominant dinosaurs and clearing a way for the evolution of large mammals, including us, might actually help to save us from joining those magnificent beasts in contorted poses among the strata of the earth.

Study Questions

1. Gould explores three possible explanations for the extinction of the dinosaurs. Which one of these does he think is best, and why?

2. What criteria does Gould use to evaluate each of the three hypotheses? What other criteria might he have used? How would changing the criteria change the outcome of his evaluation? What makes for "good science," according to Gould?

3. Gould's writing is often praised as "accessible"—that is, he presents scientific information in a way that makes it understandable for nonscientists. The organization of this essay and its use of humor are two elements that help make it accessible; how is each suited for a general audience? How would the essay have been different if it were written for an audience of scientists?

4. *For Writing.* Select a topic for which there are multiple causes or explanations and do research to uncover common arguments for each explanation. In an essay, address a few of those causes or explanations and argue for the superiority of one of them. Be sure to document your sources using the citation style assigned.

Hidden Intellectualism

GERALD GRAFF

EVERYONE KNOWS SOME YOUNG PERSON who is impressively "street smart" but does poorly in school. What a waste, we think, that one who is so intelligent about so many things in life seems unable to apply that intelligence to academic work. What doesn't occur to us, though, is that schools and colleges might be at fault for missing the opportunity to tap into such street smarts and channel them into good academic work.

Nor do we consider one of the major reasons why schools and colleges overlook the intellectual potential of street smarts: the fact that we associate those street smarts with anti-intellectual concerns. We associate the educated life, the life of the mind, too narrowly and exclusively with subjects and texts that we consider inherently weighty and academic. We assume that it's possible to wax intellectual about Plato, Shakespeare, the French Revolution, and nuclear fission, but not about cars, dating, fashion, sports, TV, or video games.

The trouble with this assumption is that no necessary connection has ever been established between any text or subject and the educational depth and weight of the discussion it can generate. Real intellectuals turn any subject, however lightweight it may seem, into grist for their mill through the thoughtful questions they bring to it, whereas a dullard will find a way to drain the interest out of the richest subject. That's why a George Orwell writing on the cultural meanings of penny postcards is infinitely more substantial than the cogitations of many professors on Shakespeare or globalization.

Students do need to read models of intellectually challenging writing—and Orwell is a great one—if they are to become intellectuals themselves. But they would be more prone to take on intellectual identities if we encouraged

GERALD GRAFF, a professor of English and education at the University of Illinois at Chicago, is best known for his books *Professing Literature: An Institutional History*, *Beyond the Culture Wars: How Teaching the Conflicts Can Revitalize American Education*, *Clueless in Academe: How Schooling Obscures the Life of the Mind*, and (with Cathy Birkenstein) *"They Say / I Say": The Moves That Matter in Academic Writing*. This essay was written for *Clueless* in 2003.

them to do so at first on subjects that interest them rather than ones that interest us.

I offer my own adolescent experience as a case in point. Until I entered 5 college, I hated books and cared only for sports. The only reading I cared to do or could do was sports magazines, on which I became hooked, becoming a regular reader of *Sport* magazine in the late forties, *Sports Illustrated* when it began publishing in 1954, and the annual magazine guides to professional baseball, football, and basketball. I also loved the sports novels for boys of John R. Tunis and Clair Bee and autobiographies of sports stars like Joe DiMaggio's *Lucky to Be a Yankee* and Bob Feller's *Strikeout Story*. In short, I was your typical teenage anti-intellectual—or so I believed for a long time. I have recently come to think, however, that my preference for sports over schoolwork was not anti-intellectualism so much as intellectualism by other means.

In the Chicago neighborhood I grew up in, which had become a melting pot after World War II, our block was solidly middle class, but just a block away—doubtless concentrated there by the real estate companies—were African Americans, Native Americans, and "hillbilly" whites who had recently fled postwar joblessness in the South and Appalachia. Negotiating this class boundary was a tricky matter. On the one hand, it was necessary to maintain the boundary between "clean-cut" boys like me and working-class "hoods," as we called them, which meant that it was good to be openly smart in a bookish sort of way. On the other hand, I was desperate for the approval of the hoods, whom I encountered daily on the playing field and in the neighborhood, and for this purpose it was not at all good to be book-smart. The hoods would turn on you if they sensed you were putting on airs over them: "Who you lookin' at, smart ass?" as a leather-jacketed youth once said to me as he relieved me of my pocket change along with my self-respect.

I grew up torn, then, between the need to prove I was smart and the fear of a beating if I proved it too well; between the need not to jeopardize my respectable future and the need to impress the hoods. As I lived it, the conflict came down to a choice between being physically tough and being verbal. For a boy in my neighborhood and elementary school, only being "tough" earned you complete legitimacy. I still recall endless, complicated debates in this period with my closest pals over who was "the toughest guy in the school." If you were less than negligible as a fighter, as I was, you settled for the next best thing, which was to be inarticulate, carefully hiding telltale marks of literacy like correct grammar and pronunciation.

In one way, then, it would be hard to imagine an adolescence more thoroughly anti-intellectual than mine. Yet in retrospect, I see that it's more complicated, that I and the 1950s themselves were not simply hostile toward intellectualism, but divided and ambivalent. When Marilyn Monroe married the playwright Arthur Miller in 1956 after divorcing the retired baseball star Joe DiMaggio, the symbolic triumph of geek over jock suggested the way the wind was blowing. Even Elvis, according to his biographer Peter Guralnick, turns out to have supported Adlai over Ike in the presidential election of 1956. "I don't dig the intellectual bit," he told reporters. "But I'm telling you, man, he knows the most."

Though I too thought I did not "dig the intellectual bit," I see now that I was unwittingly in training for it. The germs had actually been planted in the seemingly philistine debates about which boys were the toughest. I see now that in the interminable analysis of sports teams, movies, and toughness that my friends and I engaged in—a type of analysis, needless to say, that the real toughs would never have stooped to—I was already betraying an allegiance to the egghead world. I was practicing being an intellectual before I knew that was what I wanted to be.

It was in these discussions with friends about toughness and sports, I think, and in my reading of sports books and magazines, that I began to learn the rudiments of the intellectual life: how to make an argument, weigh different kinds of evidence, move between particulars and generalizations, summarize the views of others, and enter a conversation about ideas. It was in reading and arguing about sports and toughness that I experienced what it felt like to propose a generalization, restate and respond to a counter-argument, and perform other intellectualizing operations, including composing the kind of sentences I am writing now.

Only much later did it dawn on me that the sports world was more compelling than school because it was *more intellectual than school*, not less. Sports after all was full of challenging arguments, debates, problems for analysis, and intricate statistics that you could care about, as school conspicuously was not. I believe that street smarts beat out book smarts in our culture not because street smarts are nonintellectual, as we generally suppose, but because they satisfy an intellectual thirst more thoroughly than school culture, which seems pale and unreal.

They also satisfy the thirst for community. When you entered sports debates, you became part of a community that was not limited to your family and friends, but was national and public. Whereas schoolwork isolated you from others, the pennant race or Ted Williams's .400 batting average was something you could talk about with people you had never met. Sports introduced you not only to a culture steeped in argument, but to a public argument culture that transcended the personal. I can't blame my schools for failing to make intellectual culture resemble the Super Bowl, but I do fault them for failing to learn anything from the sports and entertainment worlds about how to organize and represent intellectual culture, how to exploit its gamelike element and turn it into arresting public spectacle that might have competed more successfully for my youthful attention.

For here is another thing that never dawned on me and is still kept hidden from students, with tragic results: that the real intellectual world, the one that existed in the big world beyond school, is organized very much like the world of team sports, with rival texts, rival interpretations and evaluations of texts, rival theories of why they should be read and taught, and elaborate team competitions in which "fans" of writers, intellectual systems, methodologies, and -isms contend against each other.

To be sure, school contained plenty of competition, which became more invidious as one moved up the ladder (and has become even more so today with the advent of high-stakes testing). In this competition, points were scored not by making arguments, but by a show of information or vast reading, by grade-grubbing, or other forms of oneupmanship. School competition, in short, reproduced the less attractive features of sports culture without those that create close bonds and community.

And in distancing themselves from anything as enjoyable and absorb- 15 ing as sports, my schools missed the opportunity to capitalize on an element of drama and conflict that the intellectual world shares with sports. Consequently, I failed to see the parallels between the sports and academic worlds that could have helped me cross more readily from one argument culture to the other.

Sports is only one of the domains whose potential for literacy training (and not only for males) is seriously underestimated by educators, who see sports as competing with academic development rather than a route to it. But if this argument suggests why it is a good idea to assign readings and topics that are close to students' existing interests, it also suggests the limits of this tactic. For students who get excited about the chance to write about their passion for cars will often write as poorly and unreflectively on that topic as on Shakespeare or Plato. Here is the flip side of what I pointed out before: that there's no necessary relation between the degree of interest a student shows in a text or subject and the quality of thought or expression such a student manifests in writing or talking about it. The challenge, as college professor Ned Laff has put it, "is not simply to exploit students' nonacademic interests, but to get them to see those interests through academic eyes."

To say that students need to see their interests "through academic eyes" is to say that street smarts are not enough. Making students' nonacademic interests an object of academic study is useful, then, for getting students' attention and overcoming their boredom and alienation, but this tactic won't in itself necessarily move them closer to an academically rigorous treatment of those interests. On the other hand, inviting students to write about cars, sports, or clothing fashions does not have to be a pedagogical cop-out as long as students are required to see these interests "through academic eyes," that is, to think and write about cars, sports, and fashions in a reflective, analytical way, one that sees them as microcosms of what is going on in the wider culture.

If I am right, then schools and colleges are missing an opportunity when they do not encourage students to take their nonacademic interests as objects of academic study. It is self-defeating to decline to introduce any text or subject that figures to engage students who will otherwise tune out academic work entirely. If a student cannot get interested in Mill's *On Liberty* but will read *Sports Illustrated* or *Vogue* or the hip-hop magazine *Source* with absorption, this is a strong argument for assigning the magazines over the classic. It's a good bet that if students get hooked on reading and writing by doing term papers on *Source*, they will eventually get to *On Liberty*. But even if they don't, the magazine reading will make them more literate and reflective than they would be otherwise. So it makes pedagogical sense to develop classroom units on sports, cars, fashions, rap music, and other such topics. Give me the student anytime who writes a sharply argued, sociologically acute analysis of an issue of *Source* over the student who writes a lifeless explication of *Hamlet* or Socrates' *Apology*.

Study Questions

1. Gerald Graff's principal evidence in this essay is his own personal experience. How and how well does he present other supporting evidence? How and how well does he present the views that he is arguing against?

2. Graff notes that Laff suggests that students be encouraged to view what interests them "through academic eyes" (16). What do you and your friends discuss

frequently? Sports stats? Relative merits of various cosmetics brands or video games? Who is the best dancer? rapper? Have you ever thought and written about those interests "in a reflective, analytical way" (16)? Is doing so an appealing possibility? What tools or assistance might you need in order to be able to do so effectively?

3. In introducing his argument, Graff makes frequent use of the first-person plural—"we think," "we associate," and so on (1, 2). Who is this "we"—whom does he see as his audience: professors? parents? absolutely everybody? Explain the reasoning behind your answer, and provide evidence from the text. Why might Graff have chosen to use "we" this way? How does it affect your response to his argument? How do you think it would affect the response of his audience in general?

4. Graff argues that a student who learns to take an academic approach to *Sports Illustrated*, *Vogue*, *Source*, or other popular periodicals will eventually be likely to want to read traditionally academic material. Do you agree with that argument?

5. Graff recollects growing up "torn . . . between the need to prove I was smart and the fear of a beating if I proved it too well" (7). Did you have any similar experiences growing up, possibly involving fear of social rather than physical harm? Write an essay in which you describe the prevailing (and perhaps conflicting) attitudes toward academic success among your friends, family members, and neighbors. Once you establish the context, write about your strategies and experiences in navigating the attitudes of those around you.

My Mind Is a Web Browser:
How People with Autism Think
TEMPLE GRANDIN

SINCE WRITING *THINKING IN PICTURES*, which described my visual way of thinking, I have gained further insights into how my thought processes are different when compared to those of people who think in language. At autism meetings, I am often asked, "How can you be effective at public speaking when you think in pictures that are like video tapes in your imagination?" It is almost as though I have two levels of consciousness that operate separately. Only by interviewing people did I learn that many of them think primarily in words, and that their thoughts are linked to emotion. In my brain, words act as a narrator for the visual images in my imagination. I can see the pictures in my memory files.

To use a computer analogy: The language part of my brain is the computer operator, and the rest of my brain is the computer. In most people, the brain's computer operator and the computer are merged into one seamless consciousness; but in me they are separate. I hypothesize that the frontal cortex of my brain is the operator and the rest of my brain is the computer.

TEMPLE GRANDIN (b. 1947) was born in Boston, Massachusetts, and was diagnosed with autism when she was three years old. She did not begin to speak until she was four, but later attended a boarding school for gifted children in New Hampshire, graduating in 1966. She earned a BS in psychology from Franklin Pierce College in 1970, an MS in animal science from Arizona State University in 1975, and a PhD in animal science from the University of Illinois at Urbana-Champaign in 1989. A professor at Colorado State University, Grandin designs livestock-handling facilities and is an advocate for animal welfare. She also advocates for autism rights and has been outspoken about this issue in the media. HBO made a dramatic film about her life, released in 2010, starring Claire Danes, which won five Emmys.

"My Mind Is a Web Browser: How People with Autism Think" analyzes Grandin's thought process: she thinks in images, not words; indeed, she has said that words are her second language. As you read, consider your own thought process. How do you think in words, images, or both?

When I lecture, the language itself is mostly "downloaded" out of memory from files that are like tape recordings. I use slides or notes to trigger opening the different files. When I am talking about something for the first time, I look at the visual images on the "computer monitor" in my imagination, then the language part of me describes those images. After I have given the lecture several times, the new material in language is switched over into "audio tape-recording files." When I was in high school, other kids called me "tape recorder."

Non-autistic people seem to have a whole upper layer of verbal thinking that is merged with their emotions. By contrast, unless I panic, I use logic to make all decisions; my thinking can be done independently of emotion. In fact, I seem to lack a higher consciousness composed of abstract verbal thoughts that are merged with emotion. Researchers have learned that people with autism have a decreased metabolism in the area in the frontal cortex that connects the brain's emotional centers with higher thinking (the anterior cingulate).[1] The frontal cortex is the brain's senior executive, like the CEO of a corporation. Brain scans indicate that people with autism use problem-solving circuits in social situations. Unlike non-autistic people, the emotion center in their amygdala is not activated, for example, when they judge expressions in another person's eyes.[2]

My Mind Is a Web Browser

Now let me explain how the language part of my brain and the "thinking 5 in pictures" part of my brain seem to interact. My mind works just like an Internet Web browser. A Web browser finds specific words; by analogy, my mind looks for picture memories that are associated with a word. It can also go off on a tangent in the same way as a Web browser, because visual thinking is non-linear, associative thinking.

To demonstrate how my mind works, at an autism meeting I asked a member of the audience to name a thing for me to invent. I wanted to show

1. Haznedar MM, Buchsbaum MS, Metzer M, et al. Anterior cingulate gyrus volume and glucose metabolism in autistic disorder. *American Journal of Psychiatry.* 1997: 154:1047–1050.
2. Baron-Cohen S, Ring HA, Wheelwright S. Social intelligence in the normal and autistic brain: an FMRI study. *European Journal of Neuroscience.* 1999: 11:1891–1898.

how the visual part of my brain and the language part worked separately. Somebody said, "invent a better paper clip." The language part of my brain said, "I can do that," and pictures immediately started flashing into my imagination of all kinds of paper clips I have seen. My "Web browser" searched the picture memory files; many paper clip pictures flashed through my imagination like slides. I could stop on any one picture and study it. I saw an odd, plastic paper clip that was on a scientific paper from Europe. At this point, I got off the subject and saw pictures of the first scientific meeting I had attended in Spain. The language voice inside me said: "Get back on the subject of paper clips." The language part of me is a manager who uses simple nondescriptive language to tell the rest of my brain what to do.

Often, the best ideas for inventing things come just as I am drifting off to sleep. The pictures are clearer then. It is as though I can access the most concrete, vivid memory files with the most detailed images. The language part of my brain is completely shut off at night.

To get ideas for new paper clip designs, I can pull up pictures of clothes pins and other clip-like things, such as mouse traps and C clamps used in woodworking. I start thinking that inventing a better clip for holding a thick pile of papers together might be more marketable than a new paper clip design. Existing spring binder clips tend to rip envelopes when papers are mailed, because the clips have protruding edges. When I think about this, I see ripped envelopes. The language part of my mind says, "Design a flat binder clip for thick documents." When I say this, I see a mailed document in an undamaged envelope. My visual imagination then sees a large plastic clip that I saw in Japan. Japanese apartment dwellers who do not have clothes driers use large, plastic clips to hold blankets and other laundry on balcony railings. A small version of the Japanese balcony clip may make a better paper clip for holding many pages.

When I was responding to the paper clip inquiry, I knew that I could visually associate all day about paper clips. The language part of my mind then said, "That is enough," and I resumed my lecture. But as I corrected the first draft of this article, I saw a one-piece molded plastic binder clip that would lay flat on a thick bunch of papers.

I do have the ability to control the rate at which pictures come onto the 10 "computer screen" in my imagination. Some people with autism are not able to do this. One person with autism told me that images explode into a web of a pictures that are interrelated. The decision-making process can become "locked up" and overloaded with pictures coming in all at once.

Unmasking Talent

I have been fascinated with research indicating that the detailed, realistic pictures that autistic savants—autistic individuals with extraordinary talent in a specific area—make may be created by directly accessing primary memory areas deep in the brain. Researchers in Australia hypothesize that autistic savants may have privileged access to lower levels of information.[3] A study with a non-autistic "human calculator," who could solve multiplication problems twice as quickly as a normal person, indicated that his brain had enhanced low-level processing.[4] EEG recordings of his brain waves showed that brain activity was greatest, as compared with a normal person, when the multiplication problem was first flashed on the screen.

I hypothesize that I am able to access primary visual files in my brain. When designing livestock equipment in my business, I can do three-dimensional, full-motion videos of equipment and can test-run the equipment in my imagination. I can walk around it or fly over it. My ability to rotate the image is slow. I move my mind's eye around or over the image.

When I read an article in *Neurology* about frontal temporal lobe dementia, I became extremely excited. It provided a scientific foundation for the idea of hidden visual thinking under a layer of verbal thinking. Research on frontal temporal lobe dementia, an Alzheimer's-like condition that destroys language and social areas in the brain, demonstrated that, as the condition progressed, visual skills in art emerged in people who had no interest in art.[5] The increase in creativity was always visual, never verbal. Brain scans found the highest activity in the visual cortex. As the patient's cognitive abilities deteriorated, the art became more photo realistic. Artwork published with the journal article looks like the art of autistic savants.

3. Snyder AW, Mitchell JD. Is integer arithmetic fundamental to mental processing? The mind's secret arithmetic. *Proceedings of the Royal Society of London.* 1999:266: 587–592.
4. Birbaumer N. Rain Man's revelations. *Nature.* 1999:399:211–212.
5. Miller BL, Cummings J, Mishkin F. Emergence of artistic talent in froniotemporal dementia. *Neurology.* 1998:51:978–982.

I See the Decision Process

I see the decision-making process in my mind in a way most people do not. When I tried to explain this to a person who thinks in language, he just didn't get it. How my decision-making works is most clearly seen in an emergency.

On a bright, sunny day, I was driving to the airport when an elk ran into ₁₅ the highway just ahead of my car. I had only three or four seconds to react. During those few seconds, I saw images of my choices. The first image was of a car rear-ending me. This is what would have happened if I had made the instinctive panic response and slammed on the brakes. The second image was of an elk smashing through my windshield. This is what would have happened if I had swerved. The last image showed the elk passing by in front of my car. The last choice was the one I could make if I inhibited the panic response and braked just a little to slow the car. I mentally "clicked" on slowing down and avoided an accident. It was like clicking a computer mouse on the desired picture.

Animal Decision Making

I speculate that the decision-making process I used to avoid the accident may be similar to the process animals use. From my work with animals, I've come to believe that consciousness originally arose from the orienting response. When a deer sees a person, it will often freeze and look at him. This is the deer's orienting response. During this time, it decides either to run away or to keep grazing. It does not act as a programmed robot, governed by instinct or reflexes; it has the flexibility to make a decision. One of the things that has helped me to understand animals is that, more than most people, I think and feel like one. The more "animal" parts of the normal human brain may be covered by layers of language-based thinking.

Thinking in Audio Tapes

In connection with my lectures, I have talked with autistic people who are not visual thinkers. They seem to think in audio tape clips. Audio tape thinking does not have to involve language; instead of using visual images to form memories, these people store very specific audio clips. I suspect that, for them, hearing is easier than seeing. Dr. John Stein and his colleagues at Oxford University have discovered that some people have difficulty seeing rapidly changing visual scenes. They find reading is difficult because the print appears jumbled.[6] This results from defects in brain circuits that process motion.[7] The eye is fine; the circuits between brain and eyes malfunction.

One person I know who is expert at training animals told me that she hears the animal's behavior instead of seeing it. She has audio tapes in her memory with little sound details. For example, she knows that the animal is relaxed or agitated by listening to its breathing or footsteps. She reads audio signals instead of body posture.

Piecing the Details Together

People with autism, and animals as well, pay more attention to details. As I described in *Thinking in Pictures*, all my thinking goes from the specific to the general. I look at lots of little details and piece them together to make a concept. The first step in forming an idea is to make categories. For example, the most primary level is sorting objects by color or shape. The next step is sorting things by less obvious features, as when we categorize cats and dogs. When I was five years old, I figured out that a miniature dachshund was not a cat because it had a dog's nose; all dogs had certain features that were visually recognizable.

My mind seeks these categories amidst an array of little details. In problem solving, my thinking process is like that of an epidemiologist tracking down a disease. The epidemiologist collects lots of little pieces of information and finally figures out the common factor that caused certain people to fall ill. For example, they may all have eaten strawberries from a certain place.   20

Also, I understand concepts visually. For example, all objects classified as keys will open locks. I realize that the word "key" can also be used metaphorically, when we say, "the key to success is positive thinking." When I think about that phrase, I see Norman Vincent Peale's book, *The Power of Positive Thinking*, and I see myself back at my aunt's ranch reading it. I then see a stage where a person is getting an award and I see a large cardboard key.

6. Clayton J. Lost for Words. *New Scientist*. April 24, 1999. pp. 27–30.
7. Eden GF, Van Meter JW, Ramsey J, et al. Abnormal processing of artistic talent in dyslexia revealed by functional brain imaging. *Nature*. 1996:382:66–69.

Even in this situation, the key still unlocks the door to success. The ability to form categories is the beginning of the ability to form concepts. Keys in their physical form open physical locks but abstract keys can open many things, such as a scientific discovery or career success.

In teaching people to understand animal behavior, I have to help them to learn how to observe details that seem insignificant. Animals notice details in their environment that most people do not see, such as a branch that moves slightly or a shadow. In my work with livestock facilities, I try to get the language-based thinkers of the world to be more observant of little details that spook cattle. A cow may balk at entering a vaccinating chute because it sees a piece of jiggling chain that most people ignore, but which is significant in the cow's environment.

That little chain attracts the cow's attention because it moves quickly. Rapid movement activates the amygdala, the brain's emotion center.[8] In a prey species such as cattle, rapid movement elevates fear because, in the wild, things that move rapidly are often dangerous. Something moving quickly in the bushes may be a lion. On the other hand, a predatory animal, such as a dog, is attracted to rapid movement. This may explain why some dogs attack joggers. Rapid movement triggers chasing and attacking in a predatory animal, but it triggers flight in a prey species such as deer or cattle.

Objects that move rapidly also attract the attention of people with autism. When I was younger, I liked to play with automatic doors at supermarkets. I enjoyed watching the rapid opening movement. Elevator doors were not interesting; they did not move fast enough to be pleasurable to watch. Tests of my visual tracking indicate that I have a slight abnormality in my eye's ability to track a moving object. Children and adults with autism who never learn to speak have graver defects in their nervous system. The automatic doors that I liked to watch cause many nonverbal autistics to put their hands over their eyes. The rapid movement of the doors hurts their eyes. Possibly, a small defect in eye tracking makes rapidly moving things attractive to me, while a more serious neurological defect makes them unpleasant to other autistics. As a child, my favorite things all made rapid movements. I liked flapping flags, kites, and model airplanes that flew.

8. LeDoux J. *The Emotional Brain*. Simon and Schuster; 1996.

Disturbing Sounds

I have always felt that my senses were more like those of an animal. Does 25 my brain have deeper access to the ancient anti-predator circuits that humans share with animals? At night, I cannot get to sleep if I hear high-pitched, intermittent noise such as a backup alarm on a truck or children yelling in the next hotel room; they make my heart race. Thunder or airport noise does not bother me, but the little high-pitched noises cannot be shut out. Recent research with pigs has confirmed that intermittent sounds are more disturbing to them than steady sounds.[9]

Why are high-pitched sounds disturbing to animals (and to me), while airport noises and thunder are not? I speculate that in nature the rumble of thunder is not dangerous but a high-pitched noise would be an animal's distress call. Beeping backup alarms and car alarms are electronic distress calls, which activate my nervous system even though I know they are harmless. It is almost as though these animal circuits in my brain have been laid bare.

Proportional Thinking

A recent report in *Science* indicated that activities involving numbers are processed in at least two different parts of the brain.[10] Precise calculations are dependent on language and are processed in the frontal areas; proportional figuring is processed in visual areas. Proportional thinking is figuring out if one object is less or more than another. For example, three marbles are more than one marble. Animals can do proportional thinking. They can easily determine that 10 pieces of food are more than two. It is likely that proportional thinking is the kind of number processing that humans share with animals.

In school, math was a tough subject for me. Finding the precisely correct answer is difficult because I mix up numbers. On the other hand, I am very good at proportional thinking, coming up with an accurate approxi-

9. Talling JC, Waran NK, Wathes CM. Sound avoidance by domestic pigs depends on the characteristics of the signal. *Applied Animal Behavior Science*. 1998: 58: 255–266.
10. Dehaene S, Spelke E, Pinel P, Stanescu R, Tsivkin S. Sources of mathematical thinking: Behavioral and brain imaging evidence. *Science*. 1999: 284:970–973.

mate answer. In my scientific work, I often convert numerical differences between my control and experimental groups to percentage differences. Percentage differences can be visualized on a pie chart. When I present data, I like to use charts and graphs so I can see the proportional differences between different sets of data.

When I did cost estimating for cattle industry construction projects, I never tried to calculate projects to the penny. Instead, I estimated the cost of a new job by figuring out its proportional cost in relation to other finished projects. This was mainly a visual process. I would look at the drawing and build the entire project in my imagination. I then would put it up on the video screen in my imagination and compare it in size to other completed projects that had complete cost figures. In my mind, I could compare four or five completed projects with the drawing I was estimating. The project being estimated might be equal to two-thirds of a cattle-handling facility that I designed at Red River Feedlot and about 25 percent bigger than a corral I designed for Lone Mountain Ranch.

For money to have meaning to me, it must be related to something I can   30
buy with it, otherwise it is too abstract. For example, $3 is equal to lunch at McDonald's, $20 is a tank of gas, and $1000 can buy a computer. Big tables full of figures make little sense to me. Some more severely autistic people do not understand money at all. For me to understand a billion dollars, I have to have a picture in my mind of something that cost a billion dollars. One billion is one quarter of the cost of the new Denver Airport. When President Clinton announced part way through the war in Kosovo that it had cost $2 billion, I figured that half a Denver Airport worth of money had been spent. Different amounts of money have different visual values. It is interesting that proportional thinking for numbers is in the visual parts of the brain.

In proportional thinking, as in creating something new, making a decision, and forming concepts, my thinking relies on more direct access to the primary visual memory areas in my brain. There is a whole higher level of abstract thinking seamlessly linked to emotion that I do not have.

Study Questions

1. What is the difference between a verbal and a visual way of thinking? What role does emotion play in each? Why?

2. How effective is the metaphor of the web browser that Grandin uses for describing how her mind works?

3. What is the function of the subheadings in this essay? Are the subheadings effective? What other ways might Grandin have supplied transitions and other signposts to the reader?

4. How does Grandin think in pictures? Analyze the process of her "visual way of thinking."

5. *For Writing.* Consider your thought process by testing two of Grandin's examples. How would you go about designing a paper clip? How would you deal with an elk that suddenly entered your path? In an essay, explore the way that you would come to a solution. What does your process say about you?

What Is College For?

GARY GUTTING

MOST AMERICAN COLLEGE STUDENTS are wrapping up yet another semester this week. For many of them, and their families, the past months or years in school have likely involved considerable time, commitment, effort and expense. Was it worth it?

Some evidence suggests that it was. A Pew Research survey this year found that 74 percent of graduates from four-year colleges say that their education was "very useful in helping them grow intellectually." Sixty-nine percent said that "it was very useful in helping them grow and mature as a person" and 55 percent claimed that "it was very useful in helping prepare them for a job or career." Moreover, 86 percent of these graduates think "college has been a good investment for them personally."

Nonetheless, there is incessant talk about the "failure" of higher education. (Anthony Grafton at The New York Review of Books provides an ex-

---

GARY GUTTING is an American academic and writer. He serves as a professor and chairperson in the philosophy department at the University of Notre Dame, having received his doctorate in philosophy from Saint Louis University. Gutting's scholarship focuses on French philosophy and the connections among faith, science, and society. He is the author of a number of books, including *Religious Belief and Religious Skepticism* (1982), *What Philosophers Know: Case Studies in Recent Analytical Philosophy* (2009), and *Thinking the Impossible: French Philosophy Since 1960* (2011). In addition to his scholarly work, Gutting has written essays and editorials on matters of education, philosophy, politics, and religion for popular publications.

"What Is College For?" was published in the *New York Times* in 2011. In the essay, Gutting discusses the real importance of colleges and college education, as well as the argument that college serves little useful purpose for many students. While acknowledging that there are factors that can limit some students' intellectual development during their college years, Gutting argues that college can and should be a valuable experience for students, provided that both they and their teachers approach classes with the mindset that higher education is inherently "worth it," for students and for the society at large. As you read, note the factors that hold some students back, as well as those that can help students to thrive.

cellent survey of recent discussions.) Much of this has to do with access: it's too expensive, admissions policies are unfair, the drop-out rate is too high. There is also dismay at the exploitation of graduate students and part-time faculty members, the over-emphasis on frills such as semi-professional athletics or fancy dorms and student centers, and the proliferation of expensive and unneeded administrators. As important as they are, these criticisms don't contradict the Pew Survey's favorable picture of the fundamental value of students' core educational experience.

But, as Grafton's discussion also makes clear, there are serious concerns about the quality of this experience. In particular, the university curriculum leaves students disengaged from the material they are supposed to be learning. They see most of their courses as intrinsically "boring," of value only if they provide training relevant to future employment or if the teacher has a pleasing (amusing, exciting, "relevant") way of presenting the material. As a result, students spend only as much time as they need to get what they see as acceptable grades (on average, about 12 to 14 hour a week for all courses combined). Professors have ceased to expect genuine engagement from students and often give good grades (B or better) to work that is at best minimally adequate.

This lack of academic engagement is real, even among schools with the 5 best students and the best teachers, and it increases dramatically as the quality of the school decreases. But it results from a basic misunderstanding—by both students and teachers—of what colleges are for.

First of all, they are not simply for the education of students. This is an essential function, but the raison d'être of a college is to nourish a world of intellectual culture; that is, a world of ideas, dedicated to what we can know scientifically, understand humanistically, or express artistically. In our society, this world is mainly populated by members of college faculties: scientists, humanists, social scientists (who straddle the humanities and the sciences properly speaking), and those who study the fine arts. Law, medicine and engineering are included to the extent that they are still understood as "learned professions," deploying practical skills that are nonetheless deeply rooted in scientific knowledge or humanistic understanding. When, as is often the case in business education and teacher training, practical skills far outweigh theoretical understanding, we are moving beyond the intellectual culture that defines higher education.

Our support for higher education makes sense only if we regard this intellectual culture as essential to our society. Otherwise, we could provide job-training and basic social and moral formation for young adults far more efficiently and cheaply, through, say, a combination of professional and trade schools, and public service programs. There would be no need to support, at great expense, the highly specialized interests of, for example, physicists, philosophers, anthropologists and art historians. Colleges and universities have no point if we do not value the knowledge and understanding to which their faculties are dedicated.

This has important consequences for how we regard what goes on in college classrooms. Teachers need to see themselves as, first of all, intellectuals, dedicated to understanding poetry, history, human psychology, physics, biology—or whatever is the focus of their discipline. But they also need to realize that this dedication expresses not just their idiosyncratic interest in certain questions but a conviction that those questions have general human significance, even apart from immediately practical applications. This is why a discipline requires not just research but also teaching. Non-experts need access to what experts have learned, and experts need to make sure that their research remains in contact with general human concerns. The classroom is the primary locus of such contact.

Students, in turn, need to recognize that their college education is above all a matter of opening themselves up to new dimensions of knowledge and understanding. Teaching is not a matter of (as we too often say) "*making* a subject (poetry, physics, philosophy) interesting" to students but of students coming to see how such subjects are *intrinsically* interesting. It is more a matter of students moving beyond their interests than of teachers fitting their subjects to interests that students already have. Good teaching does not make a course's subject more interesting; it gives the students more interests—and so makes them more interesting.

Students readily accept the alleged wisdom that their most important 10 learning at college takes place outside the classroom. Many faculty members—thinking of their labs, libraries or studies—would agree. But the truth is that, for both students and faculty members, the classroom is precisely where the most important learning occurs.

Study Questions

1. According to Gutting's essay, what are some factors that may hamper the college experience for some students, and what are some factors that can foster student engagement with their education?

2. What evidence does Gutting provide for why he thinks college is important and "worth it"?

3. How does Gutting describe successful students and teachers? What are some of the qualities that members of the two groups possess?

4. *For Writing.* Gutting argues that for students to succeed they need to be engaged—and to engage themselves—with their subjects. Consider your own educational career to this point, and write a brief essay in which you examine your own level of engagement with your classes. In which classes do you find yourself most engaged, and how can you cultivate the same kind of enthusiasm for your work in other courses?

Keeping Close to Home: Class and Education

BELL HOOKS

W E ARE BOTH AWAKE in the almost dark of 5 a.m. Everyone else is sound asleep. Mama asks the usual questions. Telling me to look around, make sure I have everything, scolding me because I am uncertain about the actual time the bus arrives. By 5:30 we are waiting outside the closed station. Alone together, we have a chance to really talk. Mama begins. Angry with her children, especially the ones who whisper behind her back, she says bitterly, "Your childhood could not have been that bad. You were fed and clothed. You did not have to do without—that's more than a lot of folks have and I just can't stand the way y'all go on." The hurt in her voice saddens me. I have always wanted to protect mama from hurt, to ease her burdens. Now I am part of what troubles. Confronting me, she says accusingly, "It's not just the other children. You talk too much about the past. You don't just listen." And I do talk. Worse, I write about it.

Mama has always come to each of her children seeking different responses. With me she expresses the disappointment, hurt, and anger of betrayal: anger that her children are so critical, that we can't even have the

---

BELL HOOKS (b. 1952) is the pen name of Gloria Watkins; it is the combination of her mother's and grandmother's names and is uncapitalized in order to draw attention to her written work, rather than to herself as the author. hooks earned her BA at Stanford University, her MA at the University of Wisconsin, and her PhD at the University of Santa Cruz, where she wrote her dissertation on Toni Morrison. She is a prolific cultural critic who has published more than thirty books on subjects such as black masculinity, feminist analyses of visual culture, and her own life. hooks has taught at Yale University, Oberlin College, and the City College of New York. In 2004 she returned to Kentucky, where she was born, to become a professor at Berea College.

In the following selection from *Talking Back: Thinking Feminist, Thinking Black* (1989), hooks examines and challenges intertwined assumptions about race, class, and academia. As you read, consider the relationship between class and education: who has the opportunity to attend college? What assumptions do we make about fellow students? What does a college education "mean" in different communities?

sense to like the presents she sends. She says, "From now on there will be no presents. I'll just stick some money in a little envelope the way the rest of you do. Nobody wants criticism. Everybody can criticize me but I am supposed to say nothing." When I try to talk, my voice sounds like a twelve year old. When I try to talk, she speaks louder, interrupting me, even though she has said repeatedly, "Explain it to me, this talk about the past." I struggle to return to my thirty-five-year-old self so that she will know by the sound of my voice that we are two women talking together. It is only when I state firmly in my very adult voice, "Mama, you are not listening," that she becomes quiet. She waits. Now that I have her attention, I fear that my explanations will be lame, inadequate. "Mama," I begin, "people usually go to therapy because they feel hurt inside, because they have pain that will not stop, like a wound that continually breaks open, that does not heal. And often these hurts, that pain has to do with things that have happened in the past, sometimes in childhood, often in childhood, or things that we believe happened." She wants to know, "What hurts, what hurts are you talking about?" "Mom, I can't answer that. I can't speak for all of us, the hurts are different for everybody. But the point is you try to make the hurt better, to heal it, by understanding how it came to be. And I know you feel mad when we say something happened or hurt that you don't remember being that way, but the past isn't like that, we don't have the same memory of it. We remember things differently. You know that. And sometimes folk feel hurt about stuff and you just don't know or didn't realize it, and they need to talk about it. Surely you understand the need to talk about it."

Our conversation is interrupted by the sight of my uncle walking across the park toward us. We stop to watch him. He is on his way to work dressed in a familiar blue suit. They look alike, these two who rarely discuss the past. This interruption makes me think about life in a small town. You always see someone you know. Interruptions, intrusions are part of daily life. Privacy is difficult to maintain. We leave our private space in the car to greet him. After the hug and kiss he has given me every year since I was born, they talk about the day's funerals. In the distance the bus approaches. He walks away knowing that they will see each other later. Just before I board the bus I turn, staring into my mother's face. I am momentarily back in time, seeing myself eighteen years ago, at this same bus stop, staring into my mother's face, continually turning back, waving farewell as I returned to college—that experience which first took me away from our town, from family. Departing was as painful then as it is now. Each movement away makes return harder. Each separation intensifies distance, both physical and emotional.

To a southern black girl from a working-class background who had never been on a city bus, who had never stepped on an escalator, who had never travelled by plane, leaving the comfortable confines of a small town Kentucky life to attend Stanford University was not just frightening; it was utterly painful. My parents had not been delighted that I had been accepted and adamantly opposed my going so far from home. At the time, I did not see their opposition as an expression of their fear that they would lose me forever. Like many working-class folks, they feared what college education might do to their children's minds even as they unenthusiastically acknowledged its importance. They did not understand why I could not attend a college nearby, an all-black college. To them, any college would do. I would graduate, become a school teacher, make a decent living and a good marriage. And even though they reluctantly and skeptically supported my educational endeavors, they also subjected them to constant harsh and bitter critique. It is difficult for me to talk about my parents and their impact on me because they have always felt wary, ambivalent, mistrusting of my intellectual aspirations even as they have been caring and supportive. I want to speak about these contradictions because sorting through them, seeking resolution and reconciliation has been important to me both as it affects my development as a writer, my effort to be fully self-realized, and my longing to remain close to the family and community that provided the groundwork for much of my thinking, writing, and being.

Studying at Stanford, I began to think seriously about class differences. To be materially underprivileged at a university where most folks (with the exception of workers) are materially privileged provokes such thought. Class differences were boundaries no one wanted to face or talk about. It was easier to downplay them, to act as though we were all from privileged backgrounds, to work around them, to confront them privately in the solitude of one's room, or to pretend that just being chosen to study at such an institution meant that those of us who did not come from privilege were already in transition toward privilege. To not long for such transition marked one as rebellious, as unlikely to succeed. It was a kind of treason not to believe that it was better to be identified with the world of material privilege than with the world of the working class, the poor. No wonder our working-class parents from poor backgrounds feared our entry into such a world, intuiting perhaps that we might learn to be ashamed of where we had come from, that we might never return home, or come back only to lord it over them.

Though I hung with students who were supposedly radical and chic, we did not discuss class. I talked to no one about the sources of my shame, how it hurt me to witness the contempt shown the brown-skinned Filipina maids who cleaned our rooms, or later my concern about the $100 a month I paid for a room off-campus which was more than half of what my parents paid for rent. I talked to no one about my efforts to save money, to send a little something home. Yet these class realities separated me from fellow students. We were moving in different directions. I did not intend to forget my class background or alter my class allegiance. And even though I received an education designed to provide me with a bourgeois sensibility, passive acquiescence was not my only option. I knew that I could resist. I could rebel. I could shape the direction and focus of the various forms of knowledge available to me. Even though I sometimes envied and longed for greater material advantages (particularly at vacation times when I would be one of few if any students remaining in the dormitory because there was no money for travel), I did not share the sensibility and values of my peers. That was important—class was not just about money; it was about values which showed and determined behavior. While I often needed more money, I never needed a new set of beliefs and values. For example, I was profoundly shocked and disturbed when peers would talk about their parents without respect, or would even say that they hated their parents. This was especially troubling to me when it seemed that these parents were caring and concerned. It was often explained to me that such hatred was "healthy and normal." To my white, middle-class California roommate, I explained the way we were taught to value our parents and their care, to understand that they were not obligated to give us care. She would always shake her head, laughing all the while, and say, "Missy, you will learn that it's different here, that we think differently." She was right. Soon, I lived alone, like the one Mormon student who kept to himself as he made a concentrated effort to remain true to his religious beliefs and values. Later in graduate school I found that classmates believed "lower class" people had no beliefs and values. I was silent in such discussions, disgusted by their ignorance.

Carol Stack's anthropological study, *All Our Kin*, was one of the first books I read which confirmed my experiential understanding that within black culture (especially among the working class and poor, particularly in southern states), a value system emerged that was counter-hegemonic, that challenged notions of individualism and private property so important to the maintenance of white-supremacist, capitalist patriarchy. Black folk created in marginal spaces a world of community and collectivity where resources were shared. In the preface to *Feminist Theory: From Margin to Center*, I talked about how the point of difference, this marginality, can be the space for the formation of an oppositional world view. That world view must be articulated, named if it is to provide a sustained blueprint for change. Unfortunately, there has existed no consistent framework for such naming. Consequently both the experience of this difference and documentation of it (when it occurs) gradually lose presence and meaning.

Much of what Stack documented about the "culture of poverty," for example, would not describe interactions among most black poor today irrespective of geographical setting. Since the black people she described did not acknowledge (if they recognized it in theoretical terms) the oppositional value of their world view, apparently seeing it more as a survival strategy determined less by conscious efforts to oppose oppressive race and class biases than by circumstance, they did not attempt to establish a framework to transmit their beliefs and values from generation to generation. When circumstances changed, values altered. Efforts to assimilate the values and beliefs of privileged white people, presented through media like television, undermine and destroy potential structures of opposition.

Increasingly, young black people are encouraged by the dominant culture (and by those black people who internalize the values of this hegemony) to believe that assimilation is the only possible way to survive, to succeed. Without the framework of an organized civil rights or black resistance struggle, individual and collective efforts at black liberation that focus on the primacy of self-definition and self-determination often go unrecognized. It is crucial that those among us who resist and rebel, who survive and succeed, speak openly and honestly about our lives and the nature of our personal struggles, the means by which we resolve and reconcile contradictions. This is no easy task. Within the educational institutions where we learn to develop and strengthen our writing and analytical skills, we also learn to think, write, and talk in a manner that shifts attention away from personal experience. Yet if we are to reach our people and all people, if we are to remain connected (especially those of us whose familial backgrounds are poor and working-class), we must understand that the telling of one's personal story provides a meaningful example, a way for folks to identify and connect.

Combining personal with critical analysis and theoretical perspectives 10
can engage listeners who might otherwise feel estranged, alienated. To
speak simply with language that is accessible to as many folks as possible is
also important. Speaking about one's personal experience or speaking with
simple language is often considered by academics and/or intellectuals (irrespective of their political inclinations) to be a sign of intellectual weakness
or even anti-intellectualism. Lately, when I speak, I do not stand in place—
reading my paper, making little or no eye contact with audiences—but instead make eye contact, talk extemporaneously, digress, and address the
audience directly. I have been told that people assume I am not prepared,
that I am anti-intellectual, unprofessional (a concept that has everything to
do with class as it determines actions and behavior), or that I am reinforcing
the stereotype of black people as non-theoretical and gutsy.

Such criticism was raised recently by fellow feminist scholars after a
talk I gave at Northwestern University at a conference on "Gender, Culture,
Politics" to an audience that was mainly students and academics. I deliber-
ately chose to speak in a very basic way, thinking especially about the few
community folks who had come to hear me. Weeks later, Kum-Kum Sangari, a
fellow participant who shared with me what was said when I was no longer
present, and I engaged in quite rigorous critical dialogue about the way my
presentation had been perceived primarily by privileged white female academics. She was concerned that I not mask my knowledge of theory, that
I not appear anti-intellectual. Her critique compelled me to articulate concerns that I am often silent about with colleagues. I spoke about class allegiance and revolutionary commitments, explaining that it was disturbing
to me that intellectual radicals who speak about transforming society, ending the domination of race, sex, class, cannot break with behavior patterns
that reinforce and perpetuate domination, or continue to use as their sole
reference point how we might be or are perceived by those who dominate,
whether or not we gain their acceptance and approval.

This is a primary contradiction which raises the issue of whether or not
the academic setting is a place where one can be truly radical or subversive.
Concurrently, the use of a language and style of presentation that alienates
most folks who are not also academically trained reinforces the notion that
the academic world is separate from real life, that everyday world where
we constantly adjust our language and behavior to meet diverse needs.
The academic setting is separate only when we work to make it so. It is a
false dichotomy which suggests that academics and/or intellectuals can

only speak to one another, that we cannot hope to speak with the masses. What is true is that we make choices, that we choose our audiences, that we choose voices to hear and voices to silence. If I do not speak in a language that can be understood, then there is little chance for dialogue. This issue of language and behavior is a central contradiction all radical intellectuals, particularly those who are members of oppressed groups, must continually confront and work to resolve. One of the clear and present dangers that exists when we move outside our class of origin, our collective ethnic experience, and enter hierarchical institutions which daily reinforce domination by race, sex, and class, is that we gradually assume a mindset similar to those who dominate and oppress, that we lose critical consciousness because it is not reinforced or affirmed by the environment. We must be ever vigilant. It is important that we know who we are speaking to, who we most want to hear us, who we most long to move, motivate, and touch with our words.

When I first came to New Haven to teach at Yale, I was truly surprised by the marked class divisions between black folks—students and professors—who identify with Yale and those black folks who work at Yale or in surrounding communities. Style of dress and self-presentation are most often the central markers of one's position. I soon learned that the black folks who spoke on the street were likely to be part of the black community and those who carefully shifted their glance were likely to be associated with Yale. Walking with a black female colleague one day, I spoke to practically every black person in sight (a gesture which reflects my upbringing), an action which disturbed my companion. Since I addressed black folk who were clearly not associated with Yale, she wanted to know whether or not I knew them. That was funny to me. "Of course not," I answered. Yet when I thought about it seriously, I realized that in a deep way, I knew them for they, and not my companion or most of my colleagues at Yale, resemble my family. Later that year, in a black women's support group I started for undergraduates, students from poor backgrounds spoke about the shame they sometimes feel when faced with the reality of their connection to working-class and poor black people. One student confessed that her father is a street person, addicted to drugs, someone who begs from passersby. She, like other Yale students, turns away from street people often, sometimes showing anger or contempt; she hasn't wanted anyone to know that she was related to this kind of person. She struggles with this, wanting to find a way to acknowledge and affirm this reality, to claim this connection. The group asked me and one another what we do to remain connected, to honor the bonds we have with working-class and poor people even as our class experience alters.

Maintaining connections with family and community across class boundaries demands more than just summary recall of where one's roots are, where one comes from. It requires knowing, naming, and being ever-mindful of those aspects of one's past that have enabled and do enable one's self-development in the present, that sustain and support, that enrich. One must also honestly confront barriers that do exist, aspects of that past that do diminish. My parents' ambivalence about my love for reading led to intense conflict. They (especially my mother) would work to ensure that I had access to books, but would threaten to burn the books or throw them away if I did not conform to other expectations. Or they would insist that reading too much would drive me insane. Their ambivalence nurtured in me a like uncertainty about the value and significance of intellectual endeavor which took years for me to unlearn. While this aspect of our class reality was one that wounded and diminished, their vigilant insistence that being smart did not make me a "better" or "superior" person (which often got on my nerves because I think I wanted to have that sense that it did indeed set me apart, make me better) made a profound impression. From them I learned to value and respect various skills and talents folk might have, not just to value people who read books and talk about ideas. They and my grandparents might say about somebody, "Now he don't read nor write a lick, but he can tell a story," or as my grandmother would say, "call out the hell in words."

Empty romanticization of poor or working-class backgrounds under-   15
mines the possibility of true connection. Such connection is based on understanding difference in experience and perspective and working to mediate and negotiate these terrains. Language is a crucial issue for folk whose movement outside the boundaries of poor and working-class backgrounds changes the nature and direction of their speech. Coming to Stanford with my own version of a Kentucky accent, which I think of always as a strong sound quite different from Tennessee or Georgia speech, I learned to speak differently while maintaining the speech of my region, the sound of my family and community. This was of course much easier to keep up when I returned home to stay often. In recent years, I have endeavored to use various speaking styles in the classroom as a teacher and find it disconcerts those who feel that the use of a particular patois excludes them as listeners, even if there is translation into the usual, acceptable mode of speech. Learning

to listen to different voices, hearing different speech challenges the notion that we must all assimilate—share a single, similar talk—in educational institutions. Language reflects the culture from which we emerge. To deny ourselves daily use of speech patterns that are common and familiar, that embody the unique and distinctive aspect of our self is one of the ways we become estranged and alienated from our past. It is important for us to have as many languages on hand as we can know or learn. It is important for those of us who are black, who speak in particular patois as well as standard English to express ourselves in both ways.

Often I tell students from poor and working-class backgrounds that if you believe what you have learned and are learning in schools and universities separates you from your past, this is precisely what will happen. It is important to stand firm in the conviction that nothing can truly separate us from our pasts when we nurture and cherish that connection. An important strategy for maintaining contact is ongoing acknowledgement of the primacy of one's past, of one's background, affirming the reality that such bonds are not severed automatically solely because one enters a new environment or moves toward a different class experience.

Again, I do not wish to romanticize this effort, to dismiss the reality of conflict and contradiction. During my time at Stanford, I did go through a period of more than a year when I did not return home. That period was one where I felt that it was simply too difficult to mesh my profoundly disparate realities. Critical reflection about the choice I was making, particularly about why I felt a choice had to be made, pulled me through this difficult time. Luckily I recognized that the insistence on choosing between the world of family and community and the new world of privileged white people and privileged ways of knowing was imposed upon me by the outside. It is as though a mythical contract had been signed somewhere which demanded of us black folks that once we entered these spheres we would immediately give up all vestiges of our underprivileged past. It was my responsibility to formulate a way of being that would allow me to participate fully in my new environment while integrating and maintaining aspects of the old.

One of the most tragic manifestations of the pressure black people feel to assimilate is expressed in the internalization of racist perspectives. I was shocked and saddened when I first heard black professors at Stanford downgrade and express contempt for black students, expecting us to do poorly, refusing to establish nurturing bonds. At every university I have attended as a student or worked at as a teacher, I have heard similar attitudes expressed with little or no understanding of factors that might prevent brilliant black students from performing to their full capability. Within universities, there are few educational and social spaces where students who wish to affirm positive ties to ethnicity—to blackness, to working-class backgrounds—can receive affirmation and support. Ideologically, the message is clear—assimilation is the way to gain acceptance and approval from those in power.

Many white people enthusiastically supported Richard Rodriguez's[1] vehement contention in his autobiography, *Hunger of Memory,* that attempts to maintain ties with his Chicano background impeded his progress, that he had to sever ties with community and kin to succeed at Stanford and in the larger world, that family language, in his case Spanish, had to be made secondary or discarded. If the terms of success as defined by the standards of ruling groups within white-supremacist, capitalist patriarchy are the only standards that exist, then assimilation is indeed necessary. But they are not. Even in the face of powerful structures of domination, it remains possible for each of us, especially those of us who are members of oppressed and/or exploited groups as well as those radical visionaries who may have race, class, and sex privilege, to define and determine alternative standards, to decide on the nature and extent of compromise. Standards by which one's success is measured, whether student or professor, are quite different for those of us who wish to resist reinforcing the domination of race, sex, and class, who work to maintain and strengthen our ties with the oppressed, with those who lack material privilege, with our families who are poor and working-class.

When I wrote my first book, *Ain't I a Woman: Black Women and Feminism,* the issue of class and its relationship to who one's reading audience might be came up for me around my decision not to use footnotes, for which I have been sharply criticized. I told people that my concern was that footnotes set class boundaries for readers, determining who a book is for. I was shocked that many academic folks scoffed at this idea. I shared that I went into working-class black communities as well as talked with family and friends to survey whether or not they ever read books with footnotes and found that they did not. A few did not know what they were, but most folks saw them as indicating that a book was for college-educated people. These responses influenced my decision. When some of my more radical, college-educated friends freaked out about the absence of footnotes, I seriously questioned how we could ever imagine revolutionary transformation

20

---

1. American author and commentator (b. 1944).

of society if such a small shift in direction could be viewed as threatening. Of course, many folks warned that the absence of footnotes would make the work less credible in academic circles. This information also highlighted the way in which class informs our choices. Certainly I did feel that choosing to use simple language, absence of footnotes, etc. would mean I was jeopardizing the possibility of being taken seriously in academic circles but then this was a political matter and a political decision. It utterly delights me that this has proven not to be the case and that the book is read by many academics as well as by people who are not college-educated.

Always our first response when we are motivated to conform or compromise within structures that reinforce domination must be to engage in critical reflection. Only by challenging ourselves to push against oppressive boundaries do we make the radical alternative possible, expanding the realm and scope of critical inquiry. Unless we share radical strategies, ways of rethinking and revisioning with students, with kin and community, with a larger audience, we risk perpetuating the stereotype that we succeed because we are the exception, different from the rest of our people. Since I left home and entered college, I am often asked, usually by white people, if my sisters and brothers are also high achievers. At the root of this question is the longing for reinforcement of the belief in "the exception" which enables race, sex, and class biases to remain intact. I am careful to separate what it means to be exceptional from a notion of "the exception."

Frequently I hear smart black folks, from poor and working-class backgrounds, stressing their frustration that at times family and community do not recognize that they are exceptional. Absence of positive affirmation clearly diminishes the longing to excel in academic endeavors. Yet it is important to distinguish between the absence of basic positive affirmation and the longing for continued reinforcement that we are special. Usually liberal white folks will willingly offer continual reinforcement of us as exceptions— as special. This can be both patronizing and very seductive. Since we often work in situations where we are isolated from other black folks, we can easily begin to feel that encouragement from white people is the primary or only source of support and recognition. Given the internalization of racism, it is easy to view this support as more validating and legitimizing than similar support from black people. Still, nothing takes the place of being valued and appreciated by one's own, by one's family and community. We share a mutual and reciprocal responsibility for affirming one another's successes. Sometimes we have to talk to our folks about the fact that we need their ongoing support and affirmation, that it is unique and special to us. In some cases we may never receive desired recognition and acknowledgement of specific achievements from kin. Rather than seeing this as a basis for estrangement, for severing connection, it is useful to explore other sources of nourishment and support.

I do not know that my mother's mother ever acknowledged my college education except to ask me once, "How can you live so far away from your people?" Yet she gave me sources of affirmation and nourishment, sharing the legacy of her quilt-making, of family history, of her incredible way with words. Recently, when our father retired after more than thirty years of work as a janitor, I wanted to pay tribute to this experience, to identify links between his work and my own as writer and teacher. Reflecting on our family past, I recalled ways he had been an impressive example of diligence and hard work, approaching tasks with a seriousness of concentration I work to mirror and develop, with a discipline I struggle to maintain. Sharing these thoughts with him keeps us connected, nurtures our respect for each other, maintaining a space, however large or small, where we can talk.

Open, honest communication is the most important way we maintain relationships with kin and community as our class experience and backgrounds change. It is as vital as the sharing of resources. Often financial assistance is given in circumstances where there is no meaningful contact. However helpful, this can also be an expression of estrangement and alienation. Communication between black folks from various experiences of material privilege was much easier when we were all in segregated communities sharing common experiences in relation to social institutions. Without this grounding, we must work to maintain ties, connection. We must assume greater responsibility for making and maintaining contact, connections that can shape our intellectual visions and inform our radical commitments.

The most powerful resource any of us can have as we study and teach in university settings is full understanding and appreciation of the richness, beauty, and primacy of our familial and community backgrounds. Maintaining awareness of class differences, nurturing ties with the poor and working-class people who are our most intimate kin, our comrades in struggle, transforms and enriches our intellectual experience. Education as the practice of freedom becomes not a force which fragments or separates, but one that brings us closer, expanding our definitions of home and community.

Boston, 1989

Study Questions

1. How does hooks's mother feel when her daughter leaves for Stanford? How does hooks feel about her parents when she is away at college? Why does she claim that, at institutions such as Stanford, black people feel the need to assimilate? How does hooks differ from her classmates, and later, from her professional colleagues?

2. In this essay hooks challenges rigidly held notions of economic, social, and academic classification. How does she find herself being classified by her family, her classmates, her professional colleagues, and by academic readers of her books? How does she challenge these classifications?

3. *For Writing.* Consider the various ways in which you have been classified—perhaps by gender, race, ethnicity, region of origin, social class, or interests and activities. Choose one or two of these classifications and write an essay in which you analyze how and why you were classified. Your essay might be serious or humorous. What are the implications of being classified in such a manner?

The Gettysburg Address

ABRAHAM LINCOLN

FOUR SCORE AND SEVEN YEARS AGO our fathers brought forth on this continent, a new nation, conceived in Liberty, and dedicated to the proposition that all men are created equal.

Now we are engaged in a great civil war, testing whether that nation, or any nation so conceived and so dedicated, can long endure. We are met on a great battle-field of that war. We have come to dedicate a portion of that field, as a final resting place for those who here gave their lives that that nation might live. It is altogether fitting and proper that we should do this.

But, in a larger sense, we can not dedicate—we can not consecrate—we can not hallow—this ground. The brave men, living and dead, who struggled here, have consecrated it, far above our poor power to add or detract. The world will little note, nor long remember what we say here, but it can never forget what they did here. It is for us the living, rather, to be dedicated here to the unfinished work which they who fought here have thus far so nobly advanced. It is rather for us to be here dedicated to the great task remaining before us—that from these honored dead we take increased devotion to that cause for which they gave the last full measure of devotion—that we here highly resolve that these dead shall not have died in vain—that this nation,

---

ABRAHAM LINCOLN (1809–1865), before he was elected president in 1860, was a country lawyer and then a political leader in Illinois. As the sixteenth president of the United States, he worked to abolish slavery by issuing the Emancipation Proclamation and urging passage of the Thirteenth Amendment to the Constitution, abolishing slavery. He is remembered for his steady leadership during the Civil War as well as his simple eloquence.

The Gettysburg Address, delivered in 1863 at the dedication of a cemetery for soldiers killed at the Battle of Gettysburg, is one of the shortest speeches ever made by a president. But beyond officially dedicating the Gettysburg National Cemetery, Lincoln had another intention: to sound a rallying cry to all Americans to preserve the Union. Through the skillful use of pathos, he reminds his audience of those who died fighting for their country, and he calls upon all Americans to persevere in their noble struggle.

under God, shall have a new birth of freedom—and that government of the people, by the people, for the people, shall not perish from the earth.

Study Questions

1. Lincoln tells his audience that they "have come to dedicate a portion" of the battlefield as a cemetery. But who does he say has already consecrated the ground? How have they consecrated it? Why does Lincoln use the word *consecrated*, which is usually associated with holiness?

2. One of Lincoln's rhetorical strategies is the repetition of a parallel structure— repeating several words in similiarly constructed phrases. Identify the two examples of this parallel structure and explain their effect.

3. Lincoln also repeats the word "dedicate" six times in different forms. Find each use of the word and explain how its meaning differs in each context. What other words does he repeat? What effect does this technique have for listeners?

4. *For Writing.* Edward Everett, a senator during Lincoln's presidency, delivered his own speech immediately before Lincoln delivered the Gettysburg Address. Find a copy of Everett's speech and write a rhetorical analysis, comparing and contrasting the two speeches, arriving at a conclusion in your final paragraph.

Are Too Many People Going to College?

CHARLES MURRAY

To **ASK WHETHER** too many people are going to college requires us to think about the importance and nature of a liberal education. "Universities are not intended to teach the knowledge required to fit men for some special mode of gaining their livelihood," John Stuart Mill told students at the University of St. Andrews in 1867. "Their object is not to make skillful lawyers, or physicians, or engineers, but capable and cultivated human beings." If this is true (and I agree that it is), why say that too many people are going to college? Surely a mass democracy should encourage as many people as possible to become "capable and cultivated human beings" in Mill's sense. We should not restrict the availability of a liberal education to a rarefied intellectual elite. More people should be going to college, not fewer.

Yes and no. More people should be getting the basics of a liberal education. But for most students, the places to provide those basics are elementary and middle school. E. D. Hirsch Jr. is the indispensable thinker on this topic, beginning with his 1987 book *Cultural Literacy: What Every American Needs to Know*. Part of his argument involves the importance of a body of core knowledge in fostering reading speed and comprehension. With regard to a liberal education, Hirsch makes three points that are germane here:

Full participation in any culture requires familiarity with a body of core knowledge. To live in the United States and not recognize Teddy Roosevelt, Prohibition, the Minutemen, Wall Street, smoke-filled rooms, or Gettysburg is like trying to read without knowing some of the ten thousand most commonly used words in the language. It signifies a degree of cultural illitera-

---

CHARLES MURRAY is the W. H. Brady Scholar at the American Enterprise Institute, a conservative think tank in Washington, D.C., and describes himself as a libertarian. He is the coauthor, with Richard Herrnstein, of *The Bell Curve* (1994) and author, most recently, of *Coming Apart* (2012). This essay, adapted from his book, *Real Education: Four Simple Truths for Bringing America's Schools Back to Reality* (2008), first appeared on September 8, 2008, in *The American*, the journal of the American Enterprise Institute.

cy about America. But the core knowledge transcends one's own country. Not to recognize Falstaff, Apollo, the Sistine Chapel, the Inquisition, the twenty-third Psalm, or Mozart signifies cultural illiteracy about the West. Not to recognize the solar system, the Big Bang, natural selection, relativity, or the periodic table is to be scientifically illiterate. Not to recognize the Mediterranean, Vienna, the Yangtze River, Mount Everest, or Mecca is to be geographically illiterate.

This core knowledge is an important part of the glue that holds the culture together. All American children, of whatever ethnic heritage, and whether their families came here 300 years ago or three months ago, need to learn about the Pilgrims, Valley Forge, Duke Ellington, Apollo 11, Susan B. Anthony, George C. Marshall, and the Freedom Riders. All students need to learn the iconic stories. For a society of immigrants such as ours, the core knowledge is our shared identity that makes us Americans together rather than hyphenated Americans.

K–8 are the right years to teach the core knowledge, and the effort should 5 **get off to a running start in elementary school.** Starting early is partly a matter of necessity: There's a lot to learn, and it takes time. But another reason is that small children enjoy learning myths and fables, showing off names and dates they have memorized, and hearing about great historical figures and exciting deeds. The educational establishment sees this kind of curriculum as one that forces children to memorize boring facts. That conventional wisdom is wrong on every count. The facts can be fascinating (if taught right); a lot more than memorization is entailed; yet memorizing things is an indispensable part of education, too; and memorizing is something that children do much, much better than adults. The core knowledge is suited to ways that young children naturally learn and enjoy learning. Not all children will be able to do the reading with the same level of comprehension, but the fact-based nature of the core knowledge actually works to the benefit of low-ability students—remembering facts is much easier than making inferences and deductions. The core knowledge curriculum lends itself to adaptation for students across a wide range of academic ability.

In the 20 years since *Cultural Literacy* was published, Hirsch and his colleagues have developed and refined his original formulation into an inventory of more than 6,000 items that approximate the core knowledge broadly shared by literate Americans. Hirsch's Core Knowledge Foundation has also developed a detailed, grade-by-grade curriculum for K–8, complete with lists of books and other teaching materials.

The Core Knowledge approach need not stop with eighth grade. High school is a good place for survey courses in the humanities, social sciences, and sciences taught at a level below the demands of a college course and accessible to most students in the upper two-thirds of the distribution of academic ability. Some students will not want to take these courses, and it can be counterproductive to require them to do so, but high school can put considerable flesh on the liberal education skeleton for students who are still interested.

Liberal Education in College

Saying "too many people are going to college" is not the same as saying that the average student does not need to know about history, science, and great works of art, music, and literature. They do need to know—and to know more than they are currently learning. So let's teach it to them, but let's not wait for college to do it.

Liberal education in college means taking on the tough stuff. A high-school graduate who has acquired Hirsch's core knowledge will know, for example, that John Stuart Mill was an important 19th-century English philosopher who was associated with something called Utilitarianism and wrote a famous book called *On Liberty*. But learning philosophy in college, which is an essential component of a liberal education, means that the student has to be able to read and understand the actual text of *On Liberty*. That brings us to the limits set by the nature of college-level material. Here is the first sentence of *On Liberty*: "The subject of this essay is not the so-called liberty of the will, so unfortunately opposed to the misnamed doctrine of philosophical necessity; but civil, or social liberty: the nature and limits of the power which can be legitimately exercised by society over the individual." I will not burden you with *On Liberty*'s last sentence. It is 126 words long. And Mill is one of the more accessible philosophers, and *On Liberty* is one of Mill's more accessible works. It would be nice if everyone could acquire a fully formed liberal education, but they cannot.

Specifically: When College Board researchers defined "college readiness" as the SAT score that is associated with a 65 percent chance of getting 10 at least a 2.7 grade point average in college during the freshman year, and then applied those criteria (hardly demanding in an era of soft courses and grade inflation) to the freshmen in a sample of 41 major colleges and universities, the threshold "college readiness" score was found to be 1180 on the combined SAT math and verbal tests. It is a score that only about 10 percent of American 18-year-olds would achieve if they all took the SAT, in an age when more than 30 percent of 18-year-olds go to college.

Should all of those who do have the academic ability to absorb a college-level liberal education get one? It depends. Suppose we have before us a young woman who is in the 98th percentile of academic ability and wants to become a lawyer and eventually run for political office. To me, it seems essential that she spend her undergraduate years getting a rigorous liberal education. Apart from a liberal education's value to her, the nation will benefit. Everything she does as an attorney or as an elected official should be informed by the kind of wisdom that a rigorous liberal education can encourage. It is appropriate to push her into that kind of undergraduate program.

But the only reason we can get away with pushing her is that the odds are high that she will enjoy it. The odds are high because she is good at this sort of thing—it's no problem for her to read *On Liberty* or *Paradise Lost*. It's no problem for her to come up with an interesting perspective on what she's read and weave it into a term paper. And because she's good at it, she is also likely to enjoy it. It is one of Aristotle's central themes in his discussion of human happiness, a theme that John Rawls later distilled into what he called the Aristotelian Principle: "Other things equal, human beings enjoy the exercise of the irrealized capacities (their innate or trained abilities), and this enjoyment increases the more the capacity is realized, or the greater its complexity." And so it comes to pass that those who take the hardest majors and who enroll in courses that look most like an old fashioned liberal education are concentrated among the students in the top percentiles of academic ability. Getting a liberal education consists of dealing with complex intellectual material day after day, and dealing with complex intellectual material is what students in the top few percentiles are really good at, in the same way that other people are really good at cooking or making pottery. For these students, doing it well is fun.

Every percentile down the ability ladder—and this applies to all abilities, not just academic—the probability that a person will enjoy the hardest aspects of an activity goes down as well. Students at the 80th percentile of academic ability are still smart kids, but the odds that they will respond to a course that assigns Mill or Milton are considerably lower than the odds that a student in the top few percentiles will respond. Virtue has nothing to do with it. Maturity has nothing to do with it. Appreciation of the value of a liberal education has nothing to do with it. The probability that a student will enjoy *Paradise Lost* goes down as his linguistic ability goes down, but so does the probability that he works on double acrostic puzzles in his spare time or regularly plays online Scrabble, and for the identical reason. The lower down the linguistic ladder he is, the less fun such activities are.

And so we return to the question: Should all of those who have the academic ability to absorb a college-level liberal education get one? If our young woman is at the 80th percentile of linguistic ability, should she be pushed to do so? She has enough intellectual capacity, if she puts her mind to it and works exceptionally hard.

The answer is no. If she wants to, fine. But she probably won't, and there's no way to force her. Try to force her (for example, by setting up a demanding core curriculum), and she will transfer to another school, because she is in college for vocational training. She wants to write computer code. Start a business. Get a job in television. She uses college to take vocational courses that pertain to her career interests. A large proportion of people who are theoretically able to absorb a liberal education have no interest in doing so.

And reasonably so. Seen dispassionately, getting a traditional liberal education over four years is an odd way to enjoy spending one's time. Not many people enjoy reading for hour after hour, day after day, no matter what the material may be. To enjoy reading *On Liberty* and its ilk—and if you're going to absorb such material, you must in some sense enjoy the process—is downright peculiar. To be willing to spend many more hours writing papers and answers to exam questions about that material approaches masochism.

We should look at the kind of work that goes into acquiring a liberal education at the college level in the same way that we look at the grueling apprenticeship that goes into becoming a master chef: something that understandably attracts only a few people. Most students at today's colleges choose not to take the courses that go into a liberal education because the capabilities they want to develop lie elsewhere. These students are not lazy, any more than students who don't want to spend hours learning how to chop carrots into a perfect eighth-inch dice are lazy. A liberal education just doesn't make sense for them.

For Learning How to Make a Living, the Four-Year Brick-and-Mortar Residential College Is Increasingly Obsolete

We now go from one extreme to the other, from the ideal of liberal education to the utilitarian process of acquiring the knowledge that most students go to college to acquire—practical and vocational. The question here is not whether the traditional four-year residential college is fun or valuable as a place to grow up, but when it makes sense as a place to learn how to make a living. The answer is: in a sensible world, hardly ever.

Start with the time it takes—four years. Assuming a semester system with four courses per semester, four years of class work means 32 semester-long courses. The occupations for which "knowing enough" requires 32 courses are exceedingly rare. For some professions—medicine and law are the obvious examples—a rationale for four years of course work can be concocted (combining pre-med and pre-law undergraduate courses with three years of medical school and law school), but for every other occupation, the body of knowledge taught in classrooms can be learned more quickly. Even Ph.D.s don't require four years of course work. The Ph.D. is supposed to signify expertise, but that expertise comes from burrowing deep in to a specialty, not from dozens of courses.

Those are the jobs with the most stringent academic requirements. For the student who wants to become a good hotel manager, software designer, accountant, hospital administrator, farmer, high-school teacher, social worker, journalist, optometrist, interior designer, or football coach, four years of class work is ridiculous. Actually becoming good in those occupations will take longer than four years, but most of the competence is acquired on the job. The two-year community college and online courses offer more flexible options for tailoring course work to the real needs of the job.

A brick-and-mortar campus is increasingly obsolete. The physical infrastructure of the college used to make sense for three reasons. First, a good library was essential to higher learning, and only a college faculty and student body provided the economies of scale that made good libraries affordable. Second, scholarship flourishes through colleagueships, and the college campus made it possible to put scholars in physical proximity to each other. Third, the best teaching requires interaction between teachers and students, and physical proximity was the only way to get it. All three rationales for the brick-and-mortar campus are fading fast.

The rationale for a physical library is within a few years of extinction. Even now, the Internet provides access, for a price, to all the world's significant technical journals. The books are about to follow. Google is scanning the entire text of every book in the libraries of Harvard, Princeton, Stanford, Oxford, the New York Public Library, the Bavarian State Library, Ghent University Library, Keio Library (Tokyo), the National Library of Catalonia, University of Lausanne, and an expanding list of others. Collectively, this project will encompass close to the sum total of human knowledge. It will be completely searchable. Everything out of copyright will be free. Everything still under copyright will be accessible for a fee. Libraries will still be a selling point for colleges, but as a place for students to study in pleasant surroundings—an amenity in the same way that an attractive student union is an amenity. Colleges and universities will not need to exist because they provide libraries.

The rationale for colleges based on colleagueships has eroded. Until a few decades ago, physical proximity was important because correspondence and phone calls just weren't as good. As email began to spread during the 1980s, physical proximity became less important. As the capacity of the Internet expanded in the 1990s, other mechanisms made those interactions richer. Now, regular emails from professional groups inform scholars of the latest publications in their field of interest. Specialized chat groups enable scholars to bounce new ideas off other people working on the same problems. Drafts are exchanged effortlessly and comments attached electronically. Whether physical proximity still has any advantages depends mostly on the personality of the scholar. Some people like being around other people during the workday and prefer face-to-face conversations to emails. For those who don't, the value of being on a college campus instead of on a mountaintop in Montana is nil. Their electronic access to other scholars is incomparably greater than any scholar enjoyed even within the world's premier universities before the advent of the Internet. Like the library, face-to-face colleagueships will be an amenity that colleges continue to provide. But colleges and universities will not need to exist because they provide a community of scholars.

The third rationale for the brick-and-mortar college is that it brings teachers together with students. Working against that rationale is the explosion in the breadth and realism of what is known as distance learning. The idea of distance learning is surprisingly old—Isaac Pitman was teaching his shorthand system to British students through the postal service in the 1840s, and the University of London began offering degrees for correspondence students in 1858—but the technology of distance learning changed little for the next century. The advent of inexpensive videocassettes in the 1980s opened up a way for students to hear and see lectures without being in the classroom. By the early 1990s, it was possible to buy college-level courses on audio or videotape, taught by first-rate teaching professors, on a wide range of topics, for a few hundred dollars. But without easy interaction between teacher and student, distance learning remained a poor second-best to a good college seminar.

Once again, the Internet is revolutionizing everything. As personal 25 computers acquired the processing power to show high-definition video and the storage capacity to handle big video files, the possibilities for distance learning expanded by orders of magnitude. We are now watching the early expression of those possibilities: podcasts and streaming videos in real time of professors' lectures, online discussions among students scattered around the country, online interaction between students and professors, online exams, and tutorials augmented by computer-aided instruction software.

Even today, the quality of student-teacher interactions in a virtual classroom competes with the interactions in a brick-and-mortar classroom. But the technology is still in its early stages of development and the rate of improvement is breathtaking. Compare video games such as Myst and SimCity in the 1990s to their descendants today; the Walkman you used in the 1990s to the iPod you use today; the cell phone you used in the 1990s to the BlackBerry or iPhone you use today. Whatever technical limitations might lead you to say, "Yes, but it's still not the same as being there in the classroom," are probably within a few years of being outdated.

College Isn't All It's Cracked Up to Be

College looms so large in the thinking of both parents and students because it is seen as the open sesame to a good job. Reaping the economic payoff for college that shows up in econometric analyses is a long shot for large numbers of young people.

When high-school graduates think that obtaining a B.A. will help them get a higher-paying job, they are only narrowly correct. Economists have established beyond doubt that people with B.A.s earn more on average than people without them. But why does the B.A. produce that result? For whom does the B.A. produce that result? For some jobs, the economic premium for a degree is produced by the actual education that has gone into getting the degree. Lawyers, physicians, and engineers can earn their high incomes only by deploying knowledge and skills that take years to acquire, and degrees in law, medicine, and engineering still signify competence in those knowledges and skills. But for many other jobs, the economic premium for the B.A. is created by a brutal fact of life about the American job market: Employers do not even interview applicants who do not hold a B.A. Even more brutal, the advantage conferred by the B.A. often has nothing to do with the content of the education. Employers do not value what the student learned, just that the student has a degree.

Employers value the B.A. because it is a no-cost (for them) screening device for academic ability and perseverance. The more people who go to college, the more sense it makes for employers to require a B.A. When only a small percentage of people got college degrees, employers who required a B.A. would have been shutting themselves off from access to most of the talent. With more than a third of 23-year-olds now getting a B.A., many employers can reasonably limit their hiring pool to college graduates because bright and ambitious high-school graduates who can go to college usually do go to college. An employer can believe that exceptions exist but rationally choose not to expend time and money to identify them. Knowing this, large numbers of students are in college to buy their admission ticket—the B.A.

But while it is true that the average person with a B.A. makes more than 30 the average person without a B.A., getting a B.A. is still going to be the wrong economic decision for many high-school graduates. Wages within occupations form a distribution. Young people with okay-but-not-great academic ability who are thinking about whether to go after a B.A. need to consider the competition they will face after they graduate. Let me put these calculations in terms of a specific example, a young man who has just graduated from high school and is trying to decide whether to become an electrician or go to college and major in business, hoping to become a white-collar manager. He is at the 70th percentile in linguistic ability and logical mathematical ability—someone who shouldn't go to college by my standards, but who can, in today's world, easily find a college that will give him a degree. He is exactly average in interpersonal and intrapersonal ability. He is at the 95th percentile in the small-motor skills and spatial abilities that are helpful in being a good electrician.

He begins by looking up the average income of electricians and managers on the Bureau of Labor Statistics website, and finds that the mean annual income for electricians in 2005 was $45,630, only about half of the $88,450 mean for management occupations. It looks as if getting a B.A. will buy him a huge wage premium. Should he try to get the B.A. on economic grounds?

To make his decision correctly, our young man must start by throwing out the averages. He has the ability to become an excellent electrician and can reasonably expect to be near the top of the electricians' income distribution. He does not have it in him to be an excellent manager, because he is only average in interpersonal and intrapersonal ability and only modestly above average in academic ability, all of which are important for becoming a good manager, while his competitors for those slots will include many who are high in all of those abilities. Realistically, he should be looking at the incomes toward the bottom of the distribution of managers. With that in mind, he goes back to the Bureau of Labor Statistics website and discovers that an electrician at the 90th percentile of electricians' incomes made $70,480 in 2005, almost twice the income of a manager at the 10th percentile of managers' incomes ($37,800). Even if our young man successfully completes college and gets a B.A. (which is far from certain), he is likely to make less money than if he becomes an electrician.

Then there is job security to consider. A good way to make sure you always can find work is to be among the best at what you do. It also helps to have a job that does not require you to compete with people around the globe. When corporations downsize, they lay off mediocre managers before they lay off top electricians. When the economy gets soft, top electricians can find work when mediocre managers cannot. Low-level management jobs can often be outsourced to India, whereas electricians' jobs cannot.

What I have said of electricians is true throughout the American job market. The income for the top people in a wide variety of occupations that do not require a college degree is higher than the average income for many occupations that require a B.A. Furthermore, the range and number of such jobs are expanding rapidly. The need for assembly-line workers in factories (one of the most boring jobs ever invented) is falling, but the demand for skilled technicians of every kind—in healthcare, information technology, transportation networks, and every other industry that relies on high-tech equipment—is expanding. The service sector includes many low-skill, low-paying jobs, but it also includes growing numbers of specialized jobs that pay well (for example, in healthcare and the entertainment and leisure industries). Construction offers an array of high-paying jobs for people who are good at what they do. It's not just skilled labor in the standard construction trades that is in high demand. The increase in wealth in American society has increased the demand for all sorts of craftsmanship. Today's high-end homes and office buildings may entail the work of specialized skills in stonework, masonry, glazing, painting, cabinetmaking, machining, landscaping, and a dozen other crafts. The increase in wealth is also driving an increased demand for the custom-made and the exquisitely wrought, meaning demand for artisans in everything from pottery to jewelry to metalworking. There has never been a time in history when people with skills not taught in college have been in so much demand at such high pay as today, nor a time when the range of such jobs has been so wide. In today's America, finding a first-rate lawyer or physician is easy. Finding first-rate skilled labor is hard.

Intrinsic Rewards

The topic is no longer money but job satisfaction—intrinsic rewards. We re- 35
turn to our high-school graduate trying to decide between going to college and becoming an electrician. He knows that he enjoys working with his hands and likes the idea of not being stuck in the same place all day, but he also likes the idea of being a manager sitting behind a desk in a big office, telling people what to do and getting the status that goes with it.

However, he should face facts that he is unlikely to know on his own, but that a guidance counselor could help him face. His chances of getting the big office and the status are slim. He is more likely to remain in a cubicle, under the thumb of the boss in the big office. He is unlikely to have a job in which he produces something tangible during the course of the day.

If he becomes a top electrician instead, he will have an expertise that he exercises at a high level. At the end of a workday, he will often be able to see that his work made a difference in the lives of people whose problems he has solved. He will not be confined to a cubicle and, after his apprenticeship, will be his own supervisor in the field. Top electricians often become independent contractors who have no boss at all.

The intrinsic rewards of being a top manager can be just as great as those of a top electrician (though I would not claim they are greater), but the intrinsic rewards of being a mediocre manager are not. Even as people in white-collar jobs lament the soullessness of their work, the intrinsic rewards of exercising technical skills remain undiminished.

Finally, there is an overarching consideration so important it is hard to express adequately: the satisfaction of being good at what one does for a living (and knowing it), compared to the melancholy of being mediocre at what one does for a living (and knowing it). This is another truth about living a human life that a 17-year-old might not yet understand on his own, but that a guidance counselor can bring to his attention. Guidance counselors and parents who automatically encourage young people to go to college straight out of high school regardless of their skills and interests are being thoughtless about the best interests of young people in their charge.

The Dark Side of the B.A. as Norm

It is possible to accept all that I have presented as fact and still disagree with 40 the proposition that too many people are going to college. The argument goes something like this:

The meaning of a college education has evolved since the 19th century. The traditional liberal education is still available for students who want it, but the curriculum is appropriately broader now, and includes many courses for vocational preparation that today's students want. Furthermore, intellectual requirements vary across majors. It may be true that few students can complete a major in economics or biology, but larger proportions can handle the easier majors. A narrow focus on curriculum also misses the important nonacademic functions of college. The lifestyle on today's campuses may leave something to be desired, but four years of college still give youngsters in late adolescence a chance to encounter different kinds of people, to discover new interests, and to decide what they want to make of their lives. And if it is true that some students spend too much of their college years partying, that was also true of many Oxford students in the 18th century. Lighten up.

If the only people we had to worry about were those who are on college campuses and doing reasonably well, this position would have something to be said for it. It does not address the issues of whether four years makes sense or whether a residential facility makes sense; nevertheless, college as it exists is not an intrinsically evil place for the students who are there and are coping academically. But there is the broader American society to worry about as well. However unintentionally, we have made something that is still inaccessible to a majority of the population—the B.A.—into a symbol of first-class citizenship. We have done so at the same time that other class divisions are becoming more powerful. Today's college system is implicated in the emergence of class-riven America.

The problem begins with the message sent to young people that they should aspire to college no matter what. Some politicians are among the most visible offenders, treating every failure to go to college as an injustice that can be remedied by increasing government help. American educational administrators reinforce the message by instructing guidance counselors to steer as many students as possible toward a college-prep track (more than 90 percent of high-school students report that their guidance counselors encouraged them to go to college). But politicians and educators are only following the lead of the larger culture. As long as it remains taboo to acknowledge that college is intellectually too demanding for most young people, we will continue to create crazily unrealistic expectations among the next generation. If "crazily unrealistic" sounds too strong, consider that more than 90 percent of high school seniors expect to go to college, and more than 70 percent of them expect to work in professional jobs.

One aspect of this phenomenon has been labeled misaligned ambitions, meaning that adolescents have career ambitions that are inconsistent with their educational plans. Data from the Sloan Study of Youth and Social Development conducted during the 1990s indicate that misaligned ambitions characterized more than half of all adolescents. Almost always, the misalignment is in the optimistic direction, as adolescents aspire to be attorneys or physicians without understanding the educational hurdles they must surmount to achieve their goals. They end up at a four-year institution not because that is where they can take the courses they need to meet their career goals, but because college is the place where B.A.s are handed out, and everyone knows that these days you've got to have a B.A. Many of them drop out. Of those who entered a four-year college in 1995, only 58 percent had gotten their B.A. five academic years later. Another 14 percent were still enrolled. If we assume that half of that 14 percent eventually get their B.A.s, about a third of all those who entered college hoping for a B.A. leave without one.

If these numbers had been produced in a culture where the B.A. was a 45 nice thing to have but not a big deal, they could be interpreted as the result of young adults deciding that they didn't really want a B.A. after all. Instead, these numbers were produced by a system in which having a B.A. is a very big deal indeed, and that brings us to the increasingly worrisome role of the B.A. as a source of class division. The United States has always had symbols of class, and the college degree has always been one of them. But through the first half of the 20th century, there were all sorts of respectable reasons a person might not go to college—not enough money to pay for college; needing to work right out of high school to support a wife, parents, or younger siblings; or the commonly held belief that going straight to work was better preparation for a business career than going to college. As long as the percentage of college graduates remained small, it also remained true, and everybody knew it, that the majority of America's intellectually most able people did not have B.A.s.

Over the course of the 20th century, three trends gathered strength. The first was the increasing proportion of jobs screened for high academic ability due to the advanced level of education they require—engineers, physicians, attorneys, college teachers, scientists, and the like. The second was the increasing market value of those jobs. The third was the opening up of college to more of those who had the academic ability to go to college, partly because the increase in American wealth meant that more parents could afford college for their children, and partly because the proliferation of scholarships and loans made it possible for most students with enough academic ability to go.

The combined effect of these trends has been to overturn the state of affairs that prevailed through World War II. Now the great majority of America's intellectually most able people do have a B.A. Along with that transformation has come a downside that few anticipated. The acceptable excuses for not going to college have dried up. The more people who go to college, the more stigmatizing the failure to complete college becomes. Today, if you do not get a B.A., many people assume it is because you are too dumb or too lazy. And all this because of a degree that seldom has an interpretable substantive meaning.

Let's approach the situation from a different angle. Imagine that America had no system of postsecondary education and you were made a member of a task force assigned to create one from scratch. Ask yourself what you would think if one of your colleagues submitted this proposal:

First, we will set up a common goal for every young person that represents educational success. We will call it a B.A. We will then make it difficult or impossible for most people to achieve this goal. For those who can, achieving the goal will take four years no matter what is being taught. We will attach an economic reward for reaching the goal that often has little to do with the content of what has been learned. We will lure large numbers of people who do not possess adequate ability or motivation to try to achieve the goal and then fail. We will then stigmatize everyone who fails to achieve it.

What I have just described is the system that we have in place. There must be a better way. 50

Study Questions

1. The "I say" here is explicit: "too many people are going to college." We know what Charles Murray thinks. But why does he think this? In the rest of his essay, he tells us why. Summarize his argument, noting all the reasons and evidence he gives to support his claim.

2. Is Murray right—are too many people going to college? If you disagree, why? Whether or not you agree with him, do you find his argument persuasive?

3. In the middle of the essay is a lengthy narrative about someone who is trying to decide what to be when he grows up, an electrician or a manager. What does this narrative contribute to Murray's argument? Where would the argument be without the narrative?

4. In one or two paragraphs, reflect on why you chose your current school. Did you consider, first and foremost, how your college would help you "learn how to make a living," as Murray would recommend? Did you consider other potential benefits of your college education? If you could have a well-paying job without a college education, would you go to college anyway?

How I Came to Love the Veil

YVONNE RIDLEY

I **USED TO LOOK AT VEILED WOMEN** as quiet, oppressed creatures—until I was captured by the Taliban.

In September 2001, just fifteen days after the terrorist attacks on the United States, I snuck into Afghanistan, clad in a head-to-toe blue *burqa*, intending to write a newspaper account of life under the repressive regime. Instead, I was discovered, arrested, and detained for ten days. I spat and swore at my captors; they called me a "bad" woman but let me go after I promised to read the Koran and study Islam. (Frankly, I'm not sure who was happier when I was freed—they or I.)

Back home in London, I kept my word about studying Islam—and was amazed by what I discovered. I'd been expecting Koran chapters on how to beat your wife and oppress your daughters; instead, I found passages promoting the liberation of women. Two-and-a-half years after my capture, I converted to Islam, provoking a mixture of astonishment, disappointment, and encouragement among friends and relatives.

Now, it is with disgust and dismay that I watch here in Britain as former foreign secretary Jack Straw describes the Muslim *nikab*—a face veil that reveals only the eyes—as an unwelcome barrier to integration, with Prime Minister Tony Blair, writer Salman Rushdie, and even Italian Prime Minister Romano Prodi leaping to his defense.

YVONNE RIDLEY (b. 1964) is a British journalist who was taken captive by the Taliban, an Islamist militia that ruled Afghanistan from 1996 until their ouster by U. S. military forces in 2001. Ridley is the political editor of the Islam Channel TV in London and author of *In the Hands of the Taliban: Her Extraordinary Story* (2001).

In this article published as "A Conversion Unveiled" in the *Houston Chronicle* (October 29, 2005) and later in *The Washington Post* (October 22, 2006), Ridley reflects on the wearing of Muslim veils and the place of women in Islam. She describes the treatment of women in the Muslim world as well as the reaction she sparked in Great Britain when she began wearing the veil. As you read, keep track of the evidence Ridley provides to support her claim that Islam does not oppress women.

Having been on both sides of the veil, I can tell you that most Western ₅ male politicians and journalists who lament the oppression of women in the Islamic world have no idea what they are talking about. They go on about veils, child brides, female circumcision, honor killings, and forced marriages, and they wrongly blame Islam for all this—their arrogance surpassed only by their ignorance.

These cultural issues and customs have nothing to do with Islam. A careful reading of the Koran shows that just about everything that Western feminists fought for in the 1970s was available to Muslim women 1,400 years ago. Women in Islam are considered equal to men in spirituality, education, and worth, and a woman's gift for childbirth and child-rearing is regarded as a positive attribute.

When Islam offers women so much, why are Western men so obsessed with Muslim women's attire? Even British government ministers Gordon Brown and John Reid have made disparaging remarks about the *nikab*—and they hail from across the Scottish border, where men wear skirts.

When I converted to Islam and began wearing a headscarf, the repercussions were enormous. All I did was cover my head and hair—but I instantly became a second-class citizen. I knew I'd hear from the odd Islamophobe, but I didn't expect so much open hostility from strangers. Cabs passed me by at night, their "for hire" lights glowing. One cabbie, after dropping off a white passenger right in front of me, glared at me when I rapped on his window, then drove off. Another said, "Don't leave a bomb in the back seat" and asked, "Where's bin Laden[1] hiding?"

Yes, it is a religious obligation for Muslim women to dress modestly, but the majority of Muslim women I know like wearing the *hijab*, which leaves the face uncovered, though a few prefer the nikab. It is a personal statement: My dress tells you that I am a Muslim and that I expect to be treated respectfully, much as a Wall Street banker would say that a business suit defines him as an executive to be taken seriously. And, especially among converts to the faith like me, the attention of men who confront women with inappropriate, leering behavior is not tolerable.

I was a Western feminist for many years, but I've discovered that Mus- ₁₀ lim feminists are more radical than their secular counterparts. We hate those ghastly beauty pageants, and tried to stop laughing in 2003 when

---

1. Saudi Arabian leader of the Islamic militia group *al Qaeda,* in hiding after the American invasion of Afghanistan in 2001.

judges of the Miss Earth competition hailed the emergence of a bikini-clad Miss Afghanistan, Vida Samadzai, as a giant leap for women's liberation. They even gave Samadzai a special award for "representing the victory of women's rights."

Some young Muslim feminists consider the *hijab* and the *nikab* political symbols, too, a way of rejecting Western excesses such as binge drinking, casual sex, and drug use. What is more liberating: being judged on the length of your skirt and the size of your surgically enhanced breasts, or being judged on your character and intelligence? In Islam, superiority is achieved through piety—not beauty, wealth, power, position, or sex.

I didn't know whether to scream or laugh when Italy's Prodi joined the debate last week by declaring that it is "common sense" not to wear the *nikab* because it makes social relations "more difficult." Nonsense. If this is the case, then why are cellphones, landlines, e-mail, text messaging, and fax machines in daily use? And no one switches off the radio because they can't see the presenter's face.

Under Islam, I am respected. It tells me that I have a right to an education and that it is my duty to seek out knowledge, regardless of whether I am single or married. Nowhere in the framework of Islam are we told that women must wash, clean, or cook for men. As for how Muslim men are allowed to beat their wives—it's simply not true. Critics of Islam will quote random Koranic verses or *hadith*, but usually out of context. If a man does raise a finger against his wife, he is not allowed to leave a mark on her body, which is the Koran's way of saying, "Don't beat your wife, stupid."

It is not just Muslim men who must reevaluate the place and treatment of women. According to a recent National Domestic Violence Hotline survey, four million American women experience a serious assault by a partner during an average twelve-month period. More than three women are killed by their husbands and boyfriends every day—that is nearly 5,500 since 9/11.

Violent men don't come from any particular religious or cultural category; one in three women around the world has been beaten, coerced into sex, or otherwise abused in her lifetime, according to the hotline survey. This is a global problem that transcends religion, wealth, class, race, and culture.

But it is also true that in the West, men still believe that they are superior to women, despite protests to the contrary. They still receive better pay for equal work—whether in the mailroom or the boardroom—and women are still treated as sexualized commodities whose power and influence flow directly from their appearance.

And for those who are still trying to claim that Islam oppresses women, recall this 1992 statement from the Rev. Pat Robertson, offering his views on empowered women: Feminism is a "socialist, anti-family political movement that encourages women to leave their husbands, kill their children, practice witchcraft, destroy capitalism, and become lesbians."

Now you tell me who is civilized and who is not.

Study Questions

1. What did Ridley say was the reaction of others who saw her wearing a head scarf? What is the difference between a *hijab* and a *nikab*? How can they be interpreted as "political symbols"?

2. Reread Ridley's article and determine what her thesis is. Is it stated or implied? Working backward from the thesis, create a reverse cluster—one that is extracted from something that is already written. Does this help you understand the different points of her article? Explain.

3. *For Writing.* Ridley touches upon a number of controversial topics—multiculturalism, feminism, fundamentalism, religious conversion, and more. Choose one, discuss Ridley's position, and respond to it, either agreeing or disagreeing, using well-reasoned arguments supported with adequate evidence.

A Spirit Reborn

WILLIAM SAFIRE

ABRAHAM LINCOLN'S WORDS at the dedication of the Gettysburg cemetery will be the speech repeated at the commemoration of September 11 by the governor of New York and by countless other speakers across the nation.

The lips of many listeners will silently form many of the famous phrases. "Four score and seven years ago"—a sonorous way of recalling the founding of the nation eighty-seven years before he spoke—is a phrase many now recite by rote, as is "the last full measure of devotion."

But the selection of this poetic political sermon as the oratorical centerpiece of our observance need not be only an exercise in historical evocation, nonpolitical correctness, and patriotic solemnity. What makes this particular speech so relevant for repetition on this first anniversary of the worst bloodbath on our territory since Antietam Creek's waters ran red is this: now, as then, a national spirit rose from the ashes of destruction.

Here is how to listen to Lincoln's all-too-familiar speech with new ears.

In those 236 words, you will hear the word *dedicate* five times. The first s two times refer to the nation's dedication to two ideals mentioned in the Declaration of Independence, the original ideal of "liberty" and the ideal that became central to the Civil War: "that all men are created equal."

The third, or middle, *dedication* is directed to the specific consecration of the site of the battle of Gettysburg: "to dedicate a portion of that field as a final resting place." The fourth and fifth times Lincoln repeated *dedicate* reaffirmed those dual ideals for which the dead being honored fought: "to the unfinished work" and then "to the great task remaining before us" of securing freedom and equality.

Those five pillars of dedication rested on a fundament of religious metaphor. From a president not known for his piety—indeed, often criticized for

Just before the first anniversary of September 11, 2001, *New York Times* columnist WILLIAM SAFIRE analyzed the Gettysburg Address for what it meant to Americans after 9/11.

his supposed lack of faith—came a speech rooted in the theme of national resurrection. The speech is grounded in conception, birth, death, and rebirth.

Consider the barrage of images of birth in the opening sentence. The nation was "conceived in liberty" and "brought forth"—that is, delivered into life—by "our fathers" with all "created" equal. (In the nineteenth century, both "men" and "fathers" were taken to embrace women and mothers.) The nation was born.

Then, in the middle dedication, to those who sacrificed themselves, come images of death: "final resting place" and "brave men, living and dead."

Finally, the nation's spirit rises from this scene of death: "that this nation, under God, shall have a new birth of freedom." Conception, birth, death, rebirth. The nation, purified in this fiery trial of war, is resurrected. Through the sacrifice of its sons, the sundered nation would be reborn as one.

An irreverent aside: All speechwriters stand on the shoulders of orators past. Lincoln's memorable conclusion was taken from a fine oration by the Reverend Theodore Parker at an 1850 Boston antislavery convention. That social reformer defined the transcendental "idea of freedom" to be "a government of all the people, by all the people, for all the people."

Lincoln, thirteen years later, dropped the "alls" and made the phrase his own. (A little judicious borrowing by presidents from previous orators shall not perish from the earth.) In delivering that final note, the Union's defender is said to have thrice stressed the noun "people" rather than the prepositions "of," "by," and "for." What is to be emphasized is not rhetorical rhythm but the reminder that our government's legitimacy springs from America's citizens; the people, not the rulers, are sovereign. Not all nations have yet grasped that.

Do not listen on September 11 only to Lincoln's famous words and comforting cadences. Think about how Lincoln's message encompasses but goes beyond paying "fitting and proper" respect to the dead and the bereaved. His sermon at Gettysburg reminds "us the living" of our "unfinished work" and "the great task remaining before us"—to resolve that this generation's response to the deaths of thousands of our people leads to "a new birth of freedom."

Look at Your Fish: In the Laboratory with Agassiz

SAMUEL SCUDDER

IT WAS MORE THAN FIFTEEN YEARS AGO that I entered the laboratory of Professor Agassiz, and told him I had enrolled my name in the scientific school as a student of natural history. He asked me a few questions about my object in coming, my antecedents generally, the mode in which I afterwards proposed to use the knowledge I might acquire, and finally, whether I wished to study any special branch. To the latter I replied that while I wished to be well grounded in all departments of zoology, I purposed to devote myself specially to insects.

"When do you wish to begin?" he asked.

"Now," I replied.

This seemed to please him, and with an energetic "Very well," he reached from a shelf a huge jar of specimens in yellow alcohol.

"Take this *fish*," said he, "and look at it; we call it a Hæmulon; by and by ⁵ I will ask what you have seen."

SAMUEL SCUDDER (1837–1911) the first North American insect paleontologist, was born in Boston, Massachusetts, and educated at both Williams College, graduating in 1857, and Harvard University, graduating in 1862. Well known for advocating firsthand observation as an indispensable part of the scientific process, Scudder published extensively—more than seven hundred articles during the course of his career. He was twice president of the Boston Society of Natural History, cofounder of the Cambridge Entomological Club's journal *Psyche*, and the first editor of the journal *Science*.

In the following selection, Scudder recounts the story of his first encounter with the famed paleontologist Louis Agassiz at Harvard University. It tells of an impatient young biology student, bored after ten minutes of looking at a dead fish, who discovers that he cannot really begin to engage in science at all until he immerses himself in the process of observation, which can take days, even months, in order to understand something. Consider how well you think you know the physical structure or the behavior of a family member, a pet, or even yourself. Do you think you might learn something new with closer, longer observations?

With that he left me, but in a moment returned with explicit instructions as to the care of the object entrusted to me.

"No man is fit to be a naturalist," said he, "who does not know how to take care of specimens."

I was to keep the fish before me in a tin tray, and occasionally moisten the surface with alcohol from the jar, always taking care to replace the stopper tightly. Those were not the days of ground glass stoppers, and elegantly shaped exhibition jars; all the old students will recall the huge, neckless glass bottles with their leaky, wax-besmeared corks, half eaten by insects and begrimed with cellar dust. Entomology was a cleaner science than ichthyology, but the example of the professor, who had unhesitatingly plunged to the bottom of the jar to produce the fish, was infectious; and though this alcohol had "a very ancient and fish-like smell," I really dared not show any aversion within these sacred precincts, and treated the alcohol as though it were pure water. Still I was conscious of a passing feeling of disappointment, for gazing at a fish did not commend itself to an ardent entomologist. My friends at home, too, were annoyed, when they discovered that no amount of eau de cologne would drown the perfume which haunted me like a shadow.

In ten minutes I had seen all that could be seen in that fish, and started in search of the professor, who had however left the museum; and when I returned, after lingering over some of the odd animals stored in the upper apartment, my specimen was dry all over. I dashed the fluid over the fish as if to resuscitate the beast from a fainting-fit, and looked with anxiety for a return of the normal, sloppy appearance. This little excitement over, nothing was to be done but return to a steadfast gaze at my mute companion. Half an hour passed,—an hour,—another hour; the fish began to look loathsome. I turned it over and around; looked it in the face,—ghastly; from behind, beneath, above, sideways, at a three quarters' view,—just as ghastly. I was in despair; at an early hour I concluded that lunch was necessary; so, with infinite relief, the fish was carefully replaced in the jar, and for an hour I was free.

On my return, I learned that Professor Agassiz had been at the museum, ₁₀ but had gone and would not return for several hours. My fellow-students were too busy to be disturbed by continued conversation. Slowly I drew forth that hideous fish, and with a feeling of desperation again looked at it. I might not use a magnifying glass; instruments of all kinds were interdicted. My two hands, my two eyes, and the fish; it seemed a most limited field. I pushed my finger down its throat to feel how sharp the teeth were. I began to count the scales in the different rows until I was convinced that that was nonsense. At last a happy thought struck me—I would draw the fish; and now with surprise I began to discover new features in the creature. Just then the professor returned.

"That is right," said he; "a pencil is one of the best of eyes. I am glad to notice, too, that you keep your specimen wet and your bottle corked."

With these encouraging words, he added,—

"Well, what is it like?"

He listened attentively to my brief rehearsal of the structure of parts whose names were still unknown to me: the fringed gill-arches and movable operculum; the pores of the head, fleshy lips, and lidless eyes; the lateral line, the spinous fins, and forked tail; the compressed and arched body. When I had finished, he waited as if expecting more, and then, with an air of disappointment,—

"You have not looked very carefully; why," he continued, more ear- 15 nestly, "you haven't even seen one of the most conspicuous features of the animal, which is as plainly before your eyes as the fish itself; look again, look again!" and he left me to my misery.

I was piqued; I was mortified. Still more of that wretched fish! But now I set myself to my task with a will, and discovered one new thing after another, until I saw how just the professor's criticism had been. The afternoon passed quickly, and when, toward its close, the professor inquired,—

"Do you see it yet?"

"No," I replied, "I am certain I do not, but I see how little I saw before."

"That is next best," said he, earnestly, "but I won't hear you now; put away your fish and go home; perhaps you will be ready with a better answer in the morning. I will examine you before you look at the fish."

This was disconcerting; not only must I think of my fish all night, study- 20 ing, without the object before me, what this unknown but most visible feature might be; but also, without reviewing my new discoveries, I must give an exact account of them the next day. I had a bad memory; so I walked home by Charles River[1] in a distracted state, with my two perplexities.

The cordial greeting from the professor the next morning was reassuring; here was a man who seemed to be quite as anxious as I, that I should see for myself what he saw.

1. Massachusetts river between Boston and Cambridge.

"Do you perhaps mean," I asked, "that the fish has symmetrical sides with paired organs?"

His thoroughly pleased, "Of course, of course!" repaid the wakeful hours of the previous night. After he had discoursed most happily and enthusiastically—as he always did—upon the importance of this point, I ventured to ask what I should do next.

"Oh, look at your fish!" he said, and left me again to my own devices. In a little more than an hour he returned and heard my new catalogue.

"That is good, that is good!" he repeated; "but that is not all; go on;" and so for three long days he placed that fish before my eyes, forbidding me to look at anything else, or to use any artificial aid. "Look, look, look," was his repeated injunction.

This was the best entomological lesson I ever had,—a lesson, whose influence has extended to the details of every subsequent study; a legacy the professor has left to me, as he has left it to many others, of inestimable value, which we could not buy, with which we cannot part.

A year afterward, some of us were amusing ourselves with chalking outlandish beasts upon the museum blackboard. We drew prancing star-fishes; frogs in mortal combat; hydra-headed worms; stately crawfishes, standing on their tails, bearing aloft umbrellas; and grotesque fishes with gaping mouths and staring eyes. The professor came in shortly after, and was as amused as any, at our experiments. He looked at the fishes.

"Hæmulons, every one of them," he said; "Mr. —— [2] drew them."

True; and to this day, if I attempt a fish, I can draw nothing but Hæmulons.

The fourth day, a second fish of the same group was placed beside the first, and I was bidden to point out the resemblances and differences between the two; another and another followed, until the entire family lay before me, and a whole legion of jars covered the table and surrounding shelves; the odor had become a pleasant perfume; and even now, the sight of an old, six-inch, worm-eaten cork brings fragrant memories!

The whole group of Hæmulons was thus brought in review; and, whether engaged upon the dissection of the internal organs, the preparation and examination of the bony frame-work, or the description of the various parts, Agassiz' training in the method of observing facts and their

2. The article originally appeared anonymously—"BY A FORMER PUPIL."

orderly arrangement was ever accompanied by the urgent exhortation not to be content with them.

"Facts are stupid things," he would say, "until brought into connection with some general law."

At the end of eight months, it was almost with reluctance that I left these friends and turned to insects; but what I had gained by this outside experience has been of greater value than years of later investigation in my favorite groups

Study Questions

1. What is the student's initial mindset regarding lab work? How does it change? What sensory details enliven Scudder's description of his first days in the laboratory?

2. What kind of process does Professor Agassiz encourage? How is this process both challenging and helpful to the student?

3. What kind of organization does Scudder use to present the process of learning to observe? What other organization might he have used?

4. *For Writing.* Choose something to observe—perhaps an animal, a plant, or even yourself—and spend several days looking at it carefully. Then in an essay analyze your process of observation and what it yielded. What did you learn and how did you learn it?

How to Write (the Perfect) Email
DAVID SHIPLEY AND WILL SCHWALBE

THE FACT THAT EMAIL is a searchable, storable medium means that you have to compose your message with special care. And the fact that you are writing—constructing sentences, choosing words, making grammatical decisions, adding punctuation—with previously unimaginable swiftness makes the situation all the more vexed, as does the delusion that email, because it's electronic, is somehow more ephemeral than, say, a letter.

Also, because it's *often* acceptable to be lax about the rules of grammar on email, there's the misconception that it's *always* acceptable to be lax about them. That's not the case. We aren't going to offer a guide to style and usage here—lots of books have done that already and done it well. What we are going to do, though, is outline the implications of taking risks with your English in emails and review the stylistic traps that are peculiar to the medium.

DAVID SHIPLEY (b. 1963) is the Op-Ed editor of the *New York Times*. From 1995 to 1997 he served the Clinton administration as a special assistant to the president and speechwriter. Prior to his White House experience, he was the executive editor of the *New Republic*.

WILL SCHWALBE (b. 1962) works in the field of new media and served as senior vice president and editor-in-chief of both Hyperion Books and William Morrow. He is on the board of governors of Yale University Press. Schwalbe has a background in journalism and has written for such publications as the *New York Times*, *Ms.* magazine, and the *South China Morning Post*.

Shipley and Schwalbe collaborated on *Send: Why People Email So Badly and How to Do It Better* (2007). In the following selection from that book, the authors instruct readers on how to write the "perfect" e-mail, taking into account such elements as word choice, spelling, grammar, and emoticons. The key, they say, is to consider carefully your relationship to the person who will receive your message. As you read these instructions, think about the kind of e-mails that you send and receive on a daily basis. Do they follow Shipley and Schwalbe's guidelines? If not, why not?

Choosing the Right Words

In Japanese, the status of the person you are addressing governs the words you use. A sentence directed toward a peer, for instance, requires different word forms from one directed to someone higher or lower than you on the social ladder. (You use one word form when speaking to your boss, another to a colleague, yet another to a child.) Learning Japanese, then, requires learning multiple ways of saying the same thing. The need to remember which kind of word form to use is one of the elements that makes it hard for native English speakers to master Japanese.

What many people don't consider, however, is that in this respect English is arguably more complicated than Japanese—precisely because English doesn't offer the convenience of different words to signal that you know the nature of your social relationship to the person with whom you are speaking. In lieu of specific words to show deference—or familiarity—English relies heavily on the delicate manipulation of tone.

More than anything else, vocabulary conveys tone and reveals you as 5 boss or subordinate, buyer or seller, seeker or sage. The words you choose can be formal, casual, or somewhere in between; they can be literal or figurative; they can be precise or vague; understated, correct, or exaggerated; simple or complex; common or rare; prosaic or poetic; contracted or not.

Certainly, some words are inherently safer than others, but if you never venture beyond them you become yet another unmemorable correspondent, ceding the chance to make an impression in your email. Think of your own inbox. When wading through an ocean of emails, don't you yearn for one to jump out? After a hundred people email you that they "look forward to meeting you" so that they can share their "qualifications" or "describe the benefits of their product" or present you with a "business opportunity," you crave something by someone who took the time to choose words with personality, rather than simply cribbing phrases from the modern business lexicon. The trick is to be vivid and specific—even, perhaps, revealing—without forgetting your original relationship with the person to whom you're writing.

On the most elemental level, the deal is this. Before you set finger to keyboard, ask yourself one question (and don't write until you get the answer): *What is my relationship to the person I'm writing?* Then, make sure your word choice is appropriate.

. . .

Misspellings

If careful word choice is the ultimate goal, then accidental word choice is the ultimate pitfall. There is a big difference between poor spelling that reads as sloppiness and poor spelling that results in an entirely different word appearing from the one intended. As people have increasingly come to rely on computer spell-check programs, they've also become increasingly susceptible to creating documents where an entirely wrong, albeit correctly spelled, word has found its way into the text. When the word is obviously wrong ("sned," not "send"), then the recipient will probably guess correctly that you simply failed to proof the document. But when a word is more subtly wrong, then at best she may think you didn't know the meaning of the word you used; at worst she will assume the wrong word was the chosen one, and judge you accordingly.

A computer won't flag "affect" when you meant "effect." If you want your battery changed because it can no longer safely hold a charge, the ramifications if you accidentally ask for it to be charged instead of changed could be disastrous. Will once received an unintentionally humorous note about a film called *The Dangerous Lives of Alter Boys*, except that "Alter" was supposed to be "Altar." The sender intended the Subject line to refer to helpful Catholic children and not castrati.

A friend once received an email that said: 10

> am in Pqris trying to flog q book or 3—bugger French keyboqrds and
> forgive the ,istqkes: Will e,qil you over the weekend: Clips qrrived
> todqy qnd very many thqnks.

This is actually a charming example of what would otherwise be a disastrous piece of correspondence. It's saved because its meaning is still clear, it was among pals, and the misspellings are both ubiquitous and cheerfully acknowledged. The point is not that you should never misspell a word, but that you should be aware of how it will be received when you do.

Grammar

Grammar is as important in determining tone as word choice is. The very same words, in different combinations, may or may not mean the same thing. But even if they mean the same thing, they may or may not convey the same tone. The examples used here aren't confined to email because good writing is good writing, no matter the medium.

Bad grammar isn't always wrong. "It ain't over till it's over" isn't right, but it's both memorable and effective. But even good grammar has its pitfalls. A simple sentence can be direct and unvarnished and perfectly appropriate. Or it can come across as childish or dictatorial. A complex sentence can sound conversational or elegant; it can also seem blathering or pompous.

Here's how simple grammar can be used to great effect.

On February 15, 1963, President John F. Kennedy wrote the following memo to Robert McNamara, his secretary of defense, after he had learned that the new military attaché to Laos, a former French colony, had only limited knowledge of French. The memo draws its power from a series of spare sentences, one after another, most sharing the same grammatical pattern, all but the last starting with a first-person pronoun.

> I do not see how he can be effective in Laos without knowledge of the language. I would think that the Army must have many officers who have language facility. I would like to receive a report on whether attachés are expected to have a language facility in French or Spanish before they are sent to countries where these languages are spoken. I do not think we should expect an attaché to pick up the language upon his arrival there. Would you let me have your thoughts on this.

The president doesn't say he's annoyed, miffed, perplexed, or that he 15 never wants this to happen again. He doesn't need to, because his disapproval is conveyed by the grammar. The structure is austere; the language is plain; the message is clear. The last sentence, "Would you let me have your thoughts on this," translates to "Please make sure this never happens again."

Obviously, this tone is appropriate for a subordinate and not a peer. But even presidents have peers. When Kennedy wrote to Soviet premier Nikita Khrushchev on the subject of space travel, his grammar turned expansive, complex, almost lyrical.

Beyond these specific projects we are prepared now to discuss broader cooperation in the still more challenging projects which must be undertaken in the exploration of outer space. The tasks are so challenging, the costs so great, and the risks to the brave men who engage in space exploration so grave, that we must in all good conscience try every possibility of sharing these tasks and costs and of minimizing the risks.

In both cases, Kennedy knew who he wanted to be in relation to the person to whom he was writing—peeved boss to McNamara, visionary partner to fellow world leader Khrushchev.

But what if one of your peers gets out of line? Look at this letter from Kennedy to Khrushchev during the Cuban missile crisis, which echoes the note to McNamara in both structure and tone.

I have taken careful note of your statement that the events in Cuba might affect peace in all parts of the world. I trust that this does not mean that the Soviet government, using the situation in Cuba as a pretext, is planning to inflame other areas of the world. I would like to think that your government has too great a sense of responsibility to embark upon any enterprise so dangerous to general peace. . . . I believe, Mr. Chairman, that you should recognize that free peoples in all parts of the world do not accept the claim of historical inevitability for Communist revolution.

The Kennedy letters illustrate two surefire grammar guidelines, ones we'd all do well to keep in mind every time we dash off an email that's more than a sentence long:

1. Simple, short, repetitive grammar intensifies.
2. Complex, clause-filled, rhythmically varied sentences generally soften the message.

Punctuation

It's OK to be lax so long as you're on email and on familiar terms with the   20
person to whom you're writing. With handhelds and IMing, the rules are
even looser.

It's useful to remind ourselves that punctuation originated as a reading tool. It was developed at a time when anyone who could write wrote
by hand. Punctuation was a lifeline in a sea of poor handwriting and ink
blotches. But email is completely legible. Generally, you can understand
what someone is trying to tell you—even if periods and commas are dropped
and paragraphs are littered with dashes.

Still, relaxed punctuation can do damage in a way that heedless upper-
casing and lowercasing cannot. Punctuation is in some measure governed
by your relationship to the person you're writing. If it's someone senior to
you, punctuate correctly. If the email you received was properly punctuated, your correspondent deserves the same. This is something that's easy
to forget. The speed, fluidity, and back-and-forth of email make it easier for
all sorts of punctuation tics to creep into our writing. Witness, for example,
the (confounding) growth in the use of trailing punctuation. "See you next
summer . . ." or "We can just discuss this in the meeting . . ." or "I lost my balloon . . ." We realize that email is often an ongoing conversation, but what's
so bad about a period?

And note: any kind of relaxed punctuation is not appropriate in letters
or memos. Also, keep in mind that even in email, if you drop, for example, an
important comma, you can change the meaning of a sentence 180 degrees.

THE DANGERS OF MISSING PUNCTUATION

A friend of ours worked in an office where an email flame war
erupted over a missing period. The email in question read:

No thanks to you.

It was supposed to say:

No. Thanks to you.

Paragraphs

Keep them short.

Otherwise, people won't be able to read your emails easily on a com- 25 puter screen.

Make sure you break a paragraph when you shift topics.

The key point or instruction should never be buried in a long paragraph.

Don't fear white space.

Contractions

Our language comes with an option for paring the fat out of a sentence: contractions. But many people who constantly use contractions in speech will avoid them in writing. The colleague who says, "I don't know whether to get a cappuccino or a latte today," will minutes later write an email stating, "I do not know whether we should send the shipment today or tomorrow." The tone of the latter is more formal and can strike the ear as awkward or fussy; in addition, because it places more emphasis on the "not," it sounds more severe. Email—flat, informal, democratic email—should encourage us to use contractions in a way we'd never use them in formal letters.

In email, *not* contracting comes with a risk. As with so much else, it all 30 goes back to childhood. Parents tend to avoid contractions when teaching small children a lesson. "Do NOT put your fingers in the soup bowl, Elliott (or Ben or Natalie or Sophie); I am telling you that for the last time and I am NOT going to tell you again." The word "don't" is a warning; the phrase "do not" is both a warning and a reprimand. The uncontracted form puts the reader in young Elliott's place, and makes him feel as if he's being lectured by an authority figure. This can be useful when the warning you are giving is dire: the directive "Do not let the nuclear reactor overheat" is strengthened by the use of the freestanding "not." But "Do not make extra copies of the report" would probably be better served by a "don't," unless you mean to suggest that there will be dire consequences for doing so.

And this point isn't confined to contractions of the word "not." Many noncontractions manage to make the recipient feel scolded. The person who says, "I am upset," is probably more upset than the one who says, "I'm upset." In most general email correspondence, the contraction should be the default, the uncontracted form used for special emphasis.

Capitals

When words are written in CAPITAL LETTERS, it means that THE WRITER IS SHOUTING AT YOU. Since no one likes to be yelled at, and people generally shout when they feel that they can win only by intimidation and not by reason, it's a good rule never to compose entire emails in capitals, even cheery ones. For one thing, they're just that much harder to read because we aren't used to reading large blocks of capitalized text. And rarely is it a good idea to capitalize pejorative words—IDIOT, for example. These words are that much harsher when capitalized.

(You can, however, shout a word or two in joy or celebration. HOORAY is a word that is appropriately capitalized. It's a loud word that no one minds hearing louder. Ditto for CONGRATULATIONS and BON APPETIT.)

If you really want to aggravate someone, using all caps is an effective way to do it. A study of email users in the United States and Britain found that overuse of capitals was the thing that most irritated email recipients. (Emails that conveyed an overly friendly tone also made the most-annoying list, but only in the United Kingdom.)

Oddly, writing only in lowercase doesn't indicate the opposite of shouting—no one thinks you are whispering when you abstain from using capital letters. They just think you are too lazy to hit the Shift key from time to time. As with typos and abbreviations, people are more forgiving of this when they know you are sending them a message from a mobile device than when you are clearly at a desktop. There is, however, an implied casualness to all-lowercase communication. Generally, it's acceptable from an employer to an employee but not the other way around, among friends or colleagues, and especially in very short replies. But it's industry-specific—at many companies it's more the rule than the exception. When in doubt, though, capitalize normally, especially if someone wrote to you that way.

Emoticons

Even though we're well out of junior high, we like emoticons and think there are good uses for them. Pictographic smiling faces and those created out of punctuation marks—☺ and :)—bug many people but they make us smile. (So, of course, does sunshine on our shoulders.) Emoticons are an at-tempt to put a human face on faceless, quick communication. We also love the whole emoticon family, though we must admit that some of the more baroque manifestations can leave us perplexed—by what they are supposed to be and by when we'd use them. For example, =) :–)= is Abraham Lincoln and :OI is mouth full.

Emoticons are handy for the following:

1. They're great for text and instant messages and rapid-fire emails be-cause they're really just a kind of shorthand.
2. They're helpful if you want to be cute, ironic, or tongue-in-cheek when writing those with whom you've already established a comfortable electronic correspondence. Certainly, you can use them with others who have used them with you.

However, emoticons should never be deployed when:

1. You're writing any kind of formal email or electronic message.
2. You're trying to compensate for a barb, a risky joke, or a sarcastic com-ment; the addition of an emoticon doesn't guarantee that there won't be hurt feelings.

.　.　.

Abbreviations

Abbreviations are like emoticons. They have an important function. FWIW (for what it's worth), PCM (please call me), W8 (wait)—all these facilitate communication, and in some cases they either help to bond people together in a shared language or are simply taken for granted. Whether an abbre-viation seems silly or outlandish depends on where you sit. After all, is LOL, which some people sneer at, really inherently more opaque than FYI?

Of course, when the conversation is formal or you're not sure the other 40 person knows the code, spell words out.

.　.　.

Study Questions

1. The authors list a number of elements that comprise a "perfect" e-mail. Which do you think are the most important? The least important? Why? They also list a number of e-mail hazards. Which are the worst? Why?

2. Consider this selection as a piece of advice. Evaluate its tone, as well as the quality and quantity of examples provided. Are they effective? Are you likely to follow these authors' advice? Why or why not?

3. *For Writing.* Review a week's worth of e-mails that you have sent to your friends, instructors, and family. In an essay, analyze your writing style in each kind of e-mail. Do you see any kinds of patterns? How do you write differently for your different audiences? Does this analysis make you reconsider the way you write e-mail?

Language and Literature
from a Pueblo Indian Perspective
LESLIE MARMON SILKO

WHERE I COME FROM, the words most highly valued are those spoken from the heart, unpremeditated and unrehearsed. Among the Pueblo people, a written speech or statement is highly suspect because the true feelings of the speaker remain hidden as she reads words that are detached from the occasion and the audience. I have intentionally not written a formal paper because I want you to hear and to experience English in a structure that follows patterns from the oral tradition. For those of you accustomed to being taken from point A to point B to point C, this presentation may be somewhat difficult to follow. Pueblo expression resembles something like a spider's web—with many little threads radiating from the center, crisscrossing each other. As with the web, the structure emerges as it

LESLIE MARMON SILKO (b. 1948), novelist, poet, and essayist, was born in Albuquerque, New Mexico, and grew up as part of the Laguna Pueblo tribe. She received her BA from the University of New Mexico in 1969 and then attended law school before leaving to become a writer. Silko has commented on how her mixed-race ancestry—Native American, European, and Mexican—led her to live on the edge of Laguna Pueblo culture, but she notes that the traditional stories told to her by her grandmother and aunts helped her to embrace her Native American heritage. A recipient of a MacArthur "Genius" Grant in 1981, Silko often tells stories about storytelling, as in her debut novel *Ceremony* (1977). Her other novels include *Almanac of the Dead* (1991) and *Gardens of the Dunes* (1999). She has also published poetry and story collections, including *Laguna Women: Poems* (1974) and *Sacred Water: Narratives and Pictures* (1993).

In "Language and Literature from a Pueblo Indian Perspective," which originated as a speech, Silko recounts traditional Pueblo stories in order to demonstrate the significance of storytelling in the Pueblo community. Notice how Silko organizes her narratives in order to develop her point. After you read this essay, consider the stories that are important in your own family tradition. What meanings do they hold?

is made and you must simply listen and trust, as the Pueblo people do, that meaning will be made.

My task is a formidable one: I ask you to set aside a number of basic approaches that you have been using, and probably will continue to use, and instead, to approach language from the Pueblo perspective, one that embraces the whole of creation and the whole of history and time.

What changes would Pueblo writers make to English as a language for literature? I have some examples of stories in English that I will use to address this question. At the same time, I would like to explain the importance of storytelling and how it relates to a Pueblo theory of language.

So I will begin, appropriately enough, with the Pueblo Creation story, an all-inclusive story of how life began. In this story, Tséitsínako, Thought Woman, by thinking of her sisters, and together with her sisters, thought of everything that is. In this way, the world was created. Everything in this world was a part of the original creation; the people at home understood that far away there were other human beings, also a part of this world. The Creation story even includes a prophecy, which describes the origin of European and African peoples and also refers to Asians.

This story, I think, suggests something about why the Pueblo people are more concerned with story and communication and less concerned with a particular language. There are at least six, possibly seven, distinct languages among the twenty pueblos of the southwestern United States, for example, Zuñi and Hopi. And from mesa to mesa there are subtle differences in language. But the particular language spoken isn't as important as what a speaker is trying to say, and this emphasis on the story itself stems, I believe, from a view of narrative particular to the Pueblo and other Native American peoples—that is, that language *is* story.

I will try to clarify this statement. At Laguna Pueblo, for example, many individual words have their own stories. So when one is telling a story, and one is using words to tell the story, each word that one is speaking has a story of its own, too. Often the speakers or tellers will go into these word-stories, creating an elaborate structure of stories-within-stories. This structure, which becomes very apparent in the actual telling of a story, informs contemporary Pueblo writing and storytelling as well as the traditional narratives. This perspective on narrative—of story within story, the idea that one story is only the beginning of many stories, and the sense that stories never truly end—represents an important contribution of Native American cultures to the English language.

Many people think of storytelling as something that is done at bedtime, that it is something done for small children. But when I use the term *storytelling*, I'm talking about something much bigger than that. I'm talking about something that comes out of an experience and an understanding of that original view of creation—that we are all part of a whole; we do not differentiate or fragment stories and experiences. In the beginning, Tséitsínako, Thought Woman, thought of all things, and all of these things are held together as one holds many things together in a single thought.

So in the telling (and you will hear a few of the dimensions of this telling) first of all, as mentioned earlier, the storytelling always includes the audience, the listeners. In fact, a great deal of the story is believed to be inside the listener; the storyteller's role is to draw the story out of the listeners. The storytelling continues from generation to generation.

Basically, the origin story constructs our identity—within this story, we know who we are. We are the Lagunas. This is where we come from. We came this way. We came by this place. And so from the time we are very young, we hear these stories, so that when we go out into the world, when one asks who we are, or where we are from, we immediately know: we are the people who came from the north. We are the people of these stories.

In the Creation story, Antelope says that he will help knock a hole in the   10
earth so that the people can come up, out into the next world. Antelope tries and tries; he uses his hooves, but is unable to break through. It is then that Badger says, "Let me help you." And Badger very patiently uses his claws and digs a way through, bringing the people into the world. When the Badger clan people think of themselves, or when the Antelope people think of themselves, it is as people who are of *this* story, and this is *our* place, and we fit into the very beginning when the people first came, before we began our journey south.

Within the clans there are stories that identify the clan. One moves, then, from the idea of one's identity as a tribal person into clan identity, then to one's identity as a member of an extended family. And it is the notion of "extended family" that has produced a kind of story that some distinguish from other Pueblo stories, though Pueblo people do not. Anthropologists and ethnologists have, for a long time, differentiated the types of stories the Pueblos tell. They tended to elevate the old, sacred, and traditional stories and to brush aside family stories, the family's account of itself. But in Pueblo culture, these family stories are given equal recognition. There is no definite, present pattern for the way one will hear the stories of one's own family, but it is a very critical part of one's childhood, and the storytelling continues throughout one's life. One will hear stories of importance to the family—sometimes wonderful stories—stories about the time a maternal uncle got the biggest deer that was ever seen and brought it back from the mountains. And so an individual's identity will extend from the identity constructed around the family—"I am from the family of my uncle who brought in this wonderful deer and it was a wonderful hunt."

Family accounts include negative stories, too; perhaps an uncle did something unacceptable. It is very important that one keep track of all these stories—both positive and not so positive—about one's own family and other families. Because even when there is no way around it—old Uncle Pete *did* do a terrible thing—by knowing the stories that originate in other families, one is able to deal with terrible sorts of things that might happen within one's own family. If a member of the family does something that cannot be excused, one always knows stories about similar inexcusable things done by a member of another family. But this knowledge is not communicated for malicious reasons. It is very important to understand this. Keeping track of all the stories within the community gives us all a certain distance, a useful perspective, that brings incidents down to a level we can deal with. If others have done it before, it cannot be so terrible. If others have endured, so can we.

The stories are always bringing us together, keeping this whole together, keeping this family together, keeping this clan together. "Don't go away, don't isolate yourself, but come here, because we have all had these kinds of experiences." And so there is this constant pulling together to resist the tendency to run or hide or separate oneself during a traumatic emotional experience. This separation not only endangers the group but the individual as well—one does not recover by oneself.

Because storytelling lies at the heart of Pueblo culture, it is absurd to attempt to fix the stories in time. "When did they tell the stories?" or "What time of day does the storytelling take place?"—these questions are nonsensical from a Pueblo perspective, because our storytelling goes on constantly: as some old grandmother puts on the shoes of a child and tells her the story of a little girl who didn't wear her shoes, for instance, or someone comes into the house for coffee to talk with a teenage boy who has just been in a lot of trouble, to reassure him that someone else's son has been in that kind of trouble, too. Storytelling is an ongoing process, working on many different levels.

Here's one story that is often told at a time of individual crisis (and I   15 want to remind you that we make no distinctions between types of story—historical, sacred, plain gossip—because these distinctions are not useful when discussing the Pueblo *experience* of language). There was a young man who, when he came back from the war in Vietnam, had saved up his army pay and bought a beautiful red Volkswagen. He was very proud of it. One night he drove up to a place called the King's Bar right across the reservation line. The bar is notorious for many reasons, particularly for the deep *arroyo*[1] located behind it. The young man ran in to pick up a cold six-pack, but he forgot to put on his emergency brake. And his little red Volkswagen rolled back into the *arroyo* and was all smashed up. He felt very bad about it, but within a few days everybody had come to him with stories about other people who had lost cars and family members to that *arroyo*, for instance, George Day's station wagon, with his mother-in-law and kids inside. So everybody was saying, "Well, at least your mother-in-law and kids weren't in the car when it rolled in," and one can't argue with that kind of story. The story of the young man and his smashed-up Volkswagen was now joined with all the other stories of cars that fell into that *arroyo*.

Now I want to tell you a very beautiful little story. It is a very old story that is sometimes told to people who suffer great family or personal loss. This story was told by my Aunt Susie. She is one of the first generation of people at Laguna who began experimenting with English—who began working to make English speak for us—that is, to speak from the heart. (I come from a family intent on getting the stories told.) As you read the story, I think you will hear that. And here and there, I think, you will also hear the influence of the Indian school[2] at Carlisle, Pennsylvania, where my Aunt Susie was sent (like being sent to prison) for six years.

This scene is set partly in Acoma, partly in Laguna. Waithea was a little girl living in Acoma and one day she said, "Mother, I would like to have some *yashtoah* to eat." *Yashtoah* is the hardened crust of corn mush that curls up. *Yashtoah* literally means "curled up." She said, "I would like to have some *yashtoah*," and her mother said, "My dear little girl, I can't make you any *yashtoah* because we haven't any wood, but if you will go down off the mesa, down below, and pick up some pieces of wood and bring them home, I will make you some *yashtoah*." So Waithea was glad and ran down the precipi-

---

1. Ravine (Spanish).
2. The Carlisle Indian Industrial School, federally supported boarding school attended by more than 15,000 Native American children from 1879 to 1918.

tous cliff of Acoma mesa. Down below, just as her mother had told her, there were pieces of wood, some curled, some crooked in shape, that she was to pick up and take home. She found just such wood as these.

She brought them home in a little wicker basket. First she called to her mother as she got home, "*Nayah, deeni!* Mother, upstairs!" The Pueblo people always called "upstairs" because long ago their homes were two, three stories, and they entered from the top. She said, "*Deeni! UPSTAIRS!*" and her mother came. The little girl said, "I have brought the wood you wanted me to bring." And she opened her little wicker basket to lay out the pieces of wood but here they were snakes. They were snakes instead of crooked sticks of wood. And her mother said, "Oh my dear child, you have brought snakes instead!" She said, "Go take them back and put them back just where you got them." And the little girl ran down the mesa again, down below to the flats. And she put those snakes back just where she got them. They were snakes instead and she was very hurt about this and so she said, "I'm not going home. I'm going to *Kawaik*, the beautiful lake place, *Kawaik*, and drown myself in the lake, *byn'yah'nah* [the 'west lake']. I will go there and drown myself."

So she started off, and as she passed the Enchanted Mesa near Acoma she met an old man, very aged, and he saw her running, and he said, "My dear child, where are you going?" "I'm going to *Kawaik* and jump into the lake there." "Why?" "Well, because," she said, "my mother didn't want to make any *yashtoah* for me." The old man said, "Oh, no! You must not go, my child. Come with me and I will take you home." He tried to catch her, but she was very light and skipped along. And every time he would try to grab her she would skip faster away from him.

The old man was coming home with some wood strapped to his back 20 and tied with yucca. He just let the strap go and let the wood drop. He went as fast as he could up the cliff to the little girl's home. When he got to the place where she lived, he called to her mother. "*Deeni!*" "Come on up!" And he said, "I can't. I just came to bring you a message. Your little daughter is running away. She is going to *Kawaik* to drown herself in the lake there." "Oh my dear little girl!" the mother said. So she busied herself with making the *yashtoah* her little girl liked so much. Corn mush curled at the top. (She must have found enough wood to boil the corn meal and make the *yashtoah*.)

While the mush was cooking off, she got the little girl's clothing, her *manta* dress[3] and buckskin moccasins and all her other garments, and put them in a bundle—probably a yucca bag. And she started down as fast as she could on the east side of Acoma. (There used to be a trail there, you know. It's gone now, but it was accessible in those days.) She saw her daughter way at a distance and she kept calling: "Stsamaku! My daughter! Come back! I've got your *yashtoah* for you." But the little girl would not turn. She kept on ahead and she cried: "My mother, my mother, she didn't want me to have any *yashtoah*. So now I'm going to *Kawaik* and drown myself." Her mother heard her cry and said, "My little daughter, come back here!" "No," and she kept a distance away from her. And they came nearer and nearer to the lake. And she could see her daughter now, very plain. "Come back, my daughter! I have your *yashtoah*." But no, she kept on, and finally she reached the lake and she stood on the edge.

She had tied a little feather in her hair, which is traditional (in death they tie this feather on the head). She carried a feather, the little girl did, and she tied it in her hair with a piece of string, right on top of her head she put the feather. Just as her mother was about to reach her, she jumped into the lake. The little feather was whirling around and around in the depths below. Of course the mother was very sad. She went, grieved, back to Acoma and climbed her mesa home. She stood on the edge of the mesa and scattered her daughter's clothing, the little moccasins, the *yashtoah*. She scattered them to the east, to the west, to the north, to the south. And the pieces of clothing and the moccasions and *yashtoah*, all turned into butterflies. And today they say that Acoma has more beautiful butterflies: red ones, white ones, blue ones, yellow ones. They came from this little girl's clothing.

Now this is a story anthropologists would consider very old. The version I have given you is just as Aunt Susie tells it. You can occasionally hear some English she picked up at Carlisle—words like "precipitous." You will also notice that there is a great deal of repetition, and a little reminder about *yashtoah*, and how it is made. There is a remark about the cliff trail at Acoma—that it was once there, but is there no longer. This story may be told at a time of sadness or loss, but within this story many other elements are brought together. Things are not separated out and categorized; all things are brought together. So that the reminder about the *yashtoah* is valuable information that is repeated—a recipe, if you will. The information about

---

3. Square, blanketlike cloth used as a cloak.

the old trail at Acoma reveals that stories are, in a sense, maps, since even to this day there is little information or material about trails that is passed around with writing. In the structure of this story the repetitions are, of course, designed to help you remember. It is repeated again and again, and then it moves on.

The next story I would like to tell is by Simon Ortiz, from Acoma Pueblo. He is a wonderful poet who also works in narrative. One of the things I find very interesting in this short story is that if you listen very closely, you begin to hear what I was talking about in terms of a story never beginning at the beginning, and certainly never ending. As the Hopis sometimes say, "Well, it has gone this far for a while." There is always that implication of a continuing. The other thing I want you to listen for is the many stories within one story. Listen to the kinds of stories contained within the main story—stories that give one a family identity and an individual identity, for example. This story is called "Home Country":

> "Well, it's been a while. I think in 1947 was when I left. My husband had been killed in Okinawa[4] some years before. And so I had no more husband. And I had to make a living. O I guess I could have looked for another man but I didn't want to. It looked like the war had made some of them into a bad way anyway. I saw some of them come home like that. They either got drunk or just stayed around a while or couldn't seem to be satisfied anymore with what was there. I guess now that I think about it, that happened to me although I wasn't in the war not in the Army or even much off the reservation just that several years at the Indian School. Well there was that feeling things were changing not only the men the boys, but things were changing.
>
> "One day the home nurse the nurse that came from the Indian health service was at my mother's home my mother was getting near the end real sick and she said that she had been meaning to ask me a question. I said what is the question. And the home nurse said well your mother is getting real sick and after she is no longer around for you to take care of, what will you be doing you and her are the only ones here. And I said I don't know. But I was thinking

---

4. Southernmost Japanese island, site of fierce fighting between Japanese and American forces in World War II. .

about it what she said made me think about it. And then the next time she came she said to me Eloise the government is hiring Indians now in the Indian schools to take care of the boys and girls I heard one of the supervisors saying that Indians are hard workers but you have to supervise them a lot and I thought of you well because you've been taking care of your mother real good and you follow all my instructions. She said I thought of you because you're a good Indian girl and you would be the kind of person for that job. I didn't say anything I had not ever really thought about a job but I kept thinking about it.

"Well my mother she died and we buried her up at the old place the cemetery there it's real nice on the east side of the hill where the sun shines warm and the wind doesn't blow too much sand around right there. Well I was sad we were all sad for a while but you know how things are. One of my aunties came over and she advised me and warned me about being too sorry about it and all that she wished me that I would not worry too much about it because old folks they go along pretty soon life is that way and then she said that maybe I ought to take in one of my aunties' kids or two because there was a lot of them kids and I was all by myself now. But I was so young and I thought that I might do that you know take care of someone but I had been thinking too of what the home nurse said to me about working. Hardly anybody at our home was working at something like that no woman anyway. And I would have to move away.

"Well I did just that. I remember that day very well. I told my aunties and they were all crying and we all went up to the old highway where the bus to town passes by every day. I was wearing an old kind of bluish sweater that was kind of big that one of my cousins who was older had got from a white person a tourist one summer in trade for something she had made a real pretty basket. She gave me that and I used to have a picture of me with it on it's kind of real ugly. Yeah that was the day I left wearing a baggy sweater and carrying a suitcase that someone gave me too I think or maybe it was the home nurse there wasn't much in it anyway either. I was scared and everybody seemed to be sad I was so young and skinny then. My aunties said one of them who was real fat you make sure you eat now make your own tortillas drink the milk

25

and stuff like candies is no good she learned that from the nurse. Make sure you got your letter my auntie said. I had it folded into my purse. Yes I have one too a brown one that my husband when he was still alive one time on furlough he brought it on my birthday it was a nice purse and still looked new because I never used it.

"The letter said that I had a job at Keams Canyon the boarding school there but I would have to go to the Agency first for some papers to be filled and that's where I was going first. The Agency. And then they would send me out to Keams Canyon. I didn't even know where it was except that someone of our relatives said that it was near Hopi. My uncles teased me about watching out for the Hopi men and boys don't let them get too close they said well you know how they are and they were pretty strict too about those things and then they were joking and then they were not too and so I said aw they won't get near to me I'm too ugly and I promised I would be careful anyway.

"So we all gathered for a while at my last auntie's house and then the old man my grandfather brought his wagon and horses to the door and we all got in and sat there for a while until my auntie told her father okay father let's go and shook his elbow because the poor old man was old by then and kind of going to sleep all the time you had to talk to him real loud. I had about ten dollars I think that was a lot of money more than it is now you know and when we got to the highway where the Indian road which is just a dirt road goes off the pave road my grandfather reached into his blue jeans and pulled out a silver dollar and put it into my hand. I was so shocked. We were all so shocked. We all looked around at each other we didn't know where the old man had gotten it because we were real poor two of my uncles had to borrow on their accounts at the trading store for the money I had in my purse but there it was a silver dollar so big and shining in my grandfather's hand and then in my hand.

"Well I was so shocked and everybody was so shocked that we all started crying right there at the junction of that Indian road and the pave highway I wanted to be a little girl again running after the old man when he hurried with his long legs to the cornfields or went for water down to the river. He was old then and his eye was turned gray and he didn't do much anymore except drive the

wagon and chop a little bit of wood but I just held him and I just
held him so tightly.

"Later on I don't know what happened to the silver dollar it had
a date of 1907 on it but I kept it for a long time because I guess I
wanted to have it to remember when I left my home country. What
I did in between then and now is another story but that's the time
I moved away,"

is what she said.[5]

There are a great many parallels between Pueblo experiences and those 30
of African and Caribbean peoples—one is that we have all had the con-
queror's language imposed on us. But our experience with English has been
somewhat different in that the Bureau of Indian Affairs schools were not interested in teaching us the canon of Western classics. For instance, we never
heard of Shakespeare. We were given Dick and Jane,[6] and I can remember
reading that the robins were heading south for the winter. It took me a long
time to figure out what was going on. I worried for quite a while about our
robins in Laguna because they didn't leave in the winter, until I finally realized that all the big textbook companies are up in Boston and *their* robins do
go south in the winter. But in a way, this dreadful formal education freed us
by encouraging us to maintain our narratives. Whatever literature we were
exposed to at school (which was damn little), at home the storytelling, the
special regard for telling and bringing together through the telling, was going on constantly.

And as the old people say, "If you can remember the stories, you will be
all right. Just remember the stories." When I returned to Laguna Pueblo after
attending college, I wondered how the storytelling was continuing (anthropologists say that Laguna Pueblo is one of the more acculturated pueblos), so
I visited an English class at Laguna Acoma High School. I knew the students
had cassette tape recorders in their lockers and stereos at home, and that
they listened to Kiss and Led Zeppelin and were all informed about popular culture in general. I had with me an anthology of short stories by Native American writers, *The Man to Send Rain Clouds*. One story in the book is
about the killing of a state policeman in New Mexico by three Acoma Pueblo

5. Simon J Ortiz, *Howabah Indians* (Tucson: Blue Moon Press, 1978).
6. Characters in an early-reading series common in American schools from the 1930s through
the 1960s.

men in the early 1950s.[7] I asked the students how many had heard this story and steeled myself for the possibility that the anthropologists were right, that the old traditions were indeed dying out and the students would be ignorant of the story. But instead, all but one or two raised their hands—they had heard the story, just as I had heard it when I was young, some in English, some in Laguna.

One of the other advantages that we Pueblos have enjoyed is that we have always been able to stay with the land. Our stories cannot be separated from their geographical locations, from actual physical places on the land. We were not relocated like so many Native American groups who were torn away from their ancestral land. And our stories are so much a part of these places that it is almost impossible for future generations to lose them—there is a story connected with every place, every object in the landscape.

Dennis Brutus has talked about the "yet unborn" as well as "those from the past," and how we are still *all* in *this* place, and language—the storytelling—is our way of passing through or being with them, or being together again. When Aunt Susie told her stories, she would tell a younger child to go open the door so that our esteemed predecessors might bring in their gifts to us. "They are out there," Aunt Susie would say. "Let them come in. They're here, they're here with us *within* the stories."

A few years ago, when Aunt Susie was 106, I paid her a visit, and while I was there she said, "Well, I'll be leaving here soon. I think I'll be leaving here next week, and I will be going over to the Cliff House." She said, "It's going to be real good to get back over there." I was listening, and I was thinking that she must be talking about our house at Paguate Village, just north of Laguna. And she went on, "Well, my mother's sister (and she gave her Indian name) will be there. She has been living there. She will be there and we will be over there, and I will get a chance to write down these stories I've been telling you." Now you must understand, of course, that Aunt Susie's mother's sister, a great storyteller herself, has long since passed over into the land of the dead. But then I realized, too, that Aunt Susie wasn't talking about death the way most of us do. She was talking about "going over" as a journey, a journey that perhaps we can only begin to understand through an appreciation for the boundless capacity of language that, through story-

7. See Simon J. Ortiz, "The Killing of a State Cop," in *The Man to Send Rain Clouds*, ed. Kenneth Rosen (New York: Viking Press, 1974), 101–108.

telling, brings us together, despite great distances between cultures, despite great distances in time.

Study Questions

1. Why does Silko *not* write a traditional, linear narrative? What is the significance of storytelling to Laguna Pueblo peoples? How does it connect with the land on which they live?

2. Explain how Silko organizes her essay—that is, her collection of stories—to demonstrate the "spider's web" that she mentions in the opening paragraph.

3. *For Writing.* Consider the place of storytelling in your own life. In an essay, retell some stories that are important to your family and reflect on their meaning. Who tells these stories? To whom? Why are they told?

My Year as a Freshman:
Connections to the Path Ahead
CATHY SMALL

SOMETIME AROUND MY FIFTEENTH YEAR of university teaching, I realized that I was beginning to lose it. My examples did not seem to hit home anymore, and I had lost patience with the rerun stories about why assignments were not in on time. Why didn't students do the reading I assigned? Why were class discussions like pulling teeth? What was up with these students who ate meals during my lectures or, worse, went to sleep?

These questions were ongoing topics of discussion with my colleagues. Finally I stopped to listen to myself, realizing that our "kids today" rhetoric sounded a lot like what was said about my own generation growing up. I wondered whether I was missing something. And if you are an anthropologist like I am, what do you do when you encounter another culture whom you do not understand? You go live with them, learn their language and customs, and try to walk a mile in their shoes—just as I did in my life's work in the Kingdom of Tonga in the South Pacific. I discovered long ago that people seem baffling and alien only if you have not seen the world from their perspective.

Community is not automatic in the U.S. university, and it is often elu-

CATHY SMALL (b. 1953) earned her PhD in cultural anthropology at Temple University. For some fifteen years her research focused on the Kingdom of Tonga in the South Pacific. But as Small became more and more concerned about the level of engagement in her undergraduate classroom at Northern Arizona University, she decided to embark on some very local field research to investigate student culture: Small applied to her university, was accepted, and spent a year undercover as a first-year student.

The article reprinted here is based on Small's book detailing her experiences, *My Freshman Year: What a Professor Learned by Becoming a Student* (2005), published under the pseudonym Rebekah Nathan. She attempts to research the cause-and-effect relationship between students' lack of engagement in the classroom and their outside social lives, using both her firsthand experience and close observation of her peers. As you read, notice how Small refers to herself throughout the essay and think about the ethos or the persona that she presents.

sive. Typically no time is built in for meals, office hours, or campus events. Instead, we have countless options that individualize our schedules and make connection an effort, but, ironically, we then invest whole segments of the university with the job of "creating community." What happens as a result is something that I saw countless times as a student. Huge effort would be put into designing community events—such as dorm "movie night" or a Super Bowl party—to which few students (or none) would come after the first semester. The sparse turnout spurred even more effort in student affairs to create new activities that were "better," resulting in an even greater proliferation of choices, more pulls on limited time, and further fragmentation.

The frenetic character of the modern university had a curious corollary because, to deal with its confusion and demands, many students quickly formed a small network of two to six friends with whom they spent most of their time. No longer flocking to big organized events or communal spaces, students formed small, close, often closed networks of friends who connected in real and in virtual space and time, through vehicles such as cell phones, instant-messaging, and MySpace or Facebook Web pages. In the end, the realities of how students formed community had little in common with institutional visions, activities, and policies.

Social Networks, Homogeneity, and Intellectual Life

Who are the two to six people who make up a typical student's network? 5 Through interviews with students, I learned that their primary networks were composed of students very much like themselves in age, ethnicity, class, and nationality. They tended to meet early in their freshman year (and sometimes even before), usually not in classes but during university "experiences," both structured and informal, that often drew on their common background—thereby consolidating similarities in their social networks.

I saw repercussions of this pattern in both social and intellectual life at the university. Despite strides in minority admissions and in curricular requirements for diversity courses, daily life interactions—such as who eats with whom—are largely homogenous, as more than fifteen hundred observations of student-dining partners confirmed in my own data. These patterns were much more pronounced among white students than students of color, who were much more likely to maintain ethnically "mixed" personal networks and eat at mixed tables of diners.

So in the spring of 2002, using my high school transcripts, I applied and was accepted to my own university as a freshman. I declared my major as undecided, signed up for a full of load of courses with professors whom I did not know, bought a student-meal plan, and moved out of my house and into the dorms. I also traded in my faculty ID, faculty parking pass, and even my circle of family and friends (whom I did not see for more than a semester) so that I could have a better sense of what students go through without their support networks. Although I went through our Institutional Review Board (IRB) process, this was always more of a personal quest to see the world from my students' vantage point and improve my teaching than it was a research project.

What I discovered profoundly changed me as a professor, but it also allowed me to see relationships and to connect dots that I never had recognized before, despite my long association with the university I call AnyU. I keep thinking about these sets of connections and their implications as I speak this year with students, faculty, student-affairs personnel, and administrators around the country. In this article, I will trace some of the relationships I noticed in my life and observations as a student and suggest briefly where I think they point for the direction of higher education today.

Community, Choice, and Fragmentation

I came to my freshman year expecting instant community, and I seemed to find it during my first week or two as a student at AnyU, attending our summer and pre-class freshman-orientation programs. Upperclassmen resident assistants (RAs) had been there for a week designing activities and putting up posters and welcome messages. There were ice cream socials, touch football on the quad, and special lectures, and our RAs invited us for meals, seminars, and games and movies. It was a social whirlwind; people were calling me, and inviting me, and slipping notes under my door. But then, as real student life kicked in, I found that "community" rarely looked like this again. Once classes started, everyone's very optional and private lives began.

Students today, according to Constance Staley (*Focus on College Success* 10 2008, Wadsworth) are over-optionalized. Of a thousand freshmen who may attend the same summer orientation, each chooses from the plethora of alternatives: the hundred different majors, whether or not to pledge a sorority or fraternity, or live on campus, or be in honors, or get the meal plan, or join the volleyball club. By the time you have chosen from among the options, your life and schedule have taken shape in a way that matches no other person's on campus.

There was a connection, in my mind, between this lack of "intimate diversity" and the quality of intellectual life. Two patterns come to mind. The first was the surprise of international students who were consistently asked questions such as "Where exactly is India?" Many reported a pattern of both ignorance and isolation at the U.S. university. The second is in the pattern of "nonengagement" that I noticed in the discussions in my classes. The most common classroom "debate" of social issues was not the uncivil exchange of words that university officials feared; it was a class where each student expressed his or her opinion individually and sequentially, without any comment on or relationship to anyone else.

The right to one's opinion clearly trumped the exchange of ideas because, in my view, the university, by confining its diversity efforts to the classroom, had failed to structure the experiences that lead to open and respectful interaction. In so doing, university life relinquishes the tremendous educational potential that comes from drawing on its diversity of people and opinions.

Stress, Democracy, Debt, Practicality, and Academics

The lore surrounding college life is still that of *Animal House*. Media images of college life purvey these same portraits of excess, freedom, and abandon, and students appropriate these images and symbols of themselves. Walking down a dorm corridor, you will see doors decorated with a narrow set of themes: images of alcohol, music groups, sports, and friends partying; words of irreverence, sexuality, freedom, humor, and fun.

It is not that partying does not exist, but the ubiquitous symbols of "fun" cover the other reality of college life: its stress. It did not take me long as a student to realize that student life is busy, stressful, and demanding.

Students at AnyU reflected national statistics which suggest that stu-　15 dents are studying less, but they are also socializing less because they are pressed by other demands. Understanding these pressures requires recognizing who our students are and seeing that many of the university's contemporary challenges come not from our failures but from our successes.

Critics who decry our lowered math and science scores, for instance, often forget that in the twentieth century, our country began with a higher education system that educated 2 percent of the population and ended with one that served 61 percent of our high school graduates. In 2007, we can expect two out of every three high school graduates—a much wider cross-section of U.S. society—to go on for higher education. As a consequence, our students are less affluent, more female, more minority, more first-generation college, and more international, which means that many more of our entering students are less prepared by parents and early schooling for college and less familiar with the "cultural rules" of academe (such as, what is plagiarism?). These shifts have occurred, ironically, at the same time as funding cuts so massive that public education really is not public any more, resulting in the reality that today's students are more in debt from their educational outlays than at any point in history.

The pressures can be crippling. Most students today work; many have families. Moreover, freshman orientation programs make it clear that, if good jobs and graduate school are on the horizon, students must do more than succeed in classes; they must volunteer, join professional organizations, and pursue interests beyond their classes.

The result of these multiple demands is that academics must be fit into a smaller and smaller portion of student life, a compression of intellectual life that affects students differently, but predictably. Some students drown, becoming "probation" or drop-out stats; many more others become skilled jugglers of college life, what George Kuh (Indiana University) has called "maze smart." I call what I witnessed "college management," a strategy of controlling the forces of college—classes included—on one's time and resources.

College managers taught me much as a student: how to balance my tough requirements with an "easy A" course; how to "block schedule" and carve out a free day or two for myself (meaning that the time of courses becomes more important than the subject). They counseled me as to what books I could avoid buying, what classes I could ditch, and what readings I could skim or skip rather than read.

Pressed as they are, students become enormously efficient, and student culture becomes eminently practical. I came to admire skilled college managers, but I could see too that many of our students were managing to jump through all of the academic hoops at the cost of a real education. And our university systems often supported them. 20

Classes, Social Life, and the Real World

It was hard to continue intellectual life out of the classroom. I describe an incident in my book, *My Freshman Year,* in which a class ended in the middle of a heated debate, spurred by the professor. I walked out of class with fellow students fully expecting to continue our argument, but the moment we crossed into the hallway, the conversation was dropped as if it were a hot potato.

I realized in time that this is how college life is. Students do not talk typically about academic issues outside of class and are even constrained sometimes *in* class. Even discussions of philosophical, political, and spiritual issues had little place in most circles. The pockets of students who do entertain such talk—majors in women's and ethnic studies, environmental studies, or evangelical Christians—often feel as if they are waging an uphill battle against the norm.

Does this mean that today's students do not value learning? Absolutely not. Almost 80 percent of students, in anonymous postings, said that they would not take a degree if you just gave it to them because they came to college to learn. But here is the rub: Most students report that the majority of what they learn is *outside* of the classroom and, further, that most of what one learns in class is forgotten by the next semester. Ask students what they mean by "outside," and they will tell you: the "real world" and the peer group. I found that the classes students valued and remembered most were the ones that most fully connected to these.

The Path Ahead: Connections for the Future

To my anthropologist's eye, university culture is a system of interconnected parts, itself embedded in a larger system of societal and historical relationships. To change anything, one must be aware of the ways in which these internal parts link, and that is why I have taken the time in this article to connect some dots. Just as one cannot really address problems of "diversity" at the university without involving issues of community and the social/academic divide, one must be mindful of the larger forces—such as public funding—that constrain how effective university-level policy really can be. Change in higher education must be understood as a reformulation of relationships, limited by larger forces. That said, here are three sets of relationships that have great potential for change and for the future of our universities: between teachers and students, between social and intellectual life, and between the academy and the real world.

First and foremost, teachers must connect to their increasingly diverse and practical students, and it will take nothing short of a revolution in pedagogy to accomplish this. That revolution is already in progress. The greatest contribution of American education to the world will be the example that we set in teaching the bulk of our population effectively and compassionately, adjusting our own instruction to the ways in which our students learn. Such change will mean a pedagogy that is more experiential and peer-centered, as Mark Taylor (www.taylorprograms.org) argues, and that builds to the theoretical from the concrete and practical, as Charles Schroeder suggests ("New Students—New Learning Styles." *Change,* v. 25 (5): 21–27).[1] It will mean much more support (or scaffolding) that makes clearer to less elite students how to get to desired outcomes, with more flexibility in how students acquire and demonstrate learning, attuned to the wider range of students we teach.

It is a revolution that will involve more than the professoriate. As teachers move from deliverers of information to designers of learning experiences, administrators must put in place the structures that will allow professors to experiment and collaborate. At the same time, those who support our technology and build our buildings will become part of the pedagogical team.

Second, we must do more to bridge the divide between social and intellectual life at the university. Universities must reclaim their ground as a place of lively debate, deep learning, and diversity, and to do so means forging new relationships between living and learning. So-called "living-learning communities" that bundle cohorts and courses are but a beginning to innovations that may entail new concepts of university time and credit. Many of the opportunities for truly deep learning will come from efforts to blur the line between classes and dorms, the social and the academic: language immersion programs, academic scheduling in the dorms, credit-bearing activities that combine academic reflection with university events, field-research opportunities, peer mentoring, and diversity programs that draw on both in- and out-of-class contexts.

1. Mark Taylor is a psychotherapist and consultant to institutions of higher learning; Charles Schroeder is an education theorist and Vice Chancellor for Student Affairs at the University of Missouri–Columbia.

Integrating academic and social life must be grounded in a more real-istic picture of how students form community, and it will mean substantial shifts, as Clara Lovett has called for, in the way student-affairs personnel allocate their own time and resources ("Alternatives to the Smorgasbord: Linking Student Affairs With Learning," *Chronicle of Higher Education*, March 17, 2006). Student-affairs professionals and faculty must become partners in accomplishing the academic mission, meaning changes in priorities for both.

Finally, we must rethink the academy's connection to the "real" practical world. As the student body of U.S. colleges and universities has come to represent a greater cross-section of our country, our students arrive with different preparation, obligations, and motivation from in the past. Not only does one see a more concrete and practical orientation toward learning, but also one sees a more compelling sense of the significance of the university's role in professional preparation. Indeed, as a professor at a nonelite public institution, I feel proud to have a role in improving the life chances and career options of my students.

But I do not know yet what making the academy/real world connection 30 fully entails. While I have personally made many changes in my own teaching to make my material more concrete and relevant and to bring my classes into the real world, it is clear that the university outreach must extend beyond teaching methods and content. The expansion of internship programs and service-learning projects are steps in the right direction, and perhaps, as Arthur Levine (Columbia University) has suggested, we should consider reversing the order of general education and major courses. By immersing our practical students in hands-on professional courses and experiences early, we may offer a more inviting entree to university life and success in school.

The university community must have these conversations, but to do so we must first end the false dichotomy between liberal studies and professional preparation and the tensions within the university that this can generate. Such a division is no longer useful in a world where most of our students depend on the university as a stepping stone to a middle-class life and where it is increasingly apparent that having a liberal education—including competencies in reading, writing, speaking, critical thinking, problem solving, ethics, cross-cultural communication, and compassion—must be the foundation of contemporary professional life.

The town-gown relationship will be important to the emergent directions of higher education in funding and curriculum, but the university must be vigilant in maintaining its unique character and independent function in society. As I wrote in *My Freshman Year,* "we would not want a university to become so immersed in the world that it can neither critique that world nor proffer an ideal vision of how else it might be." Higher education can neither be simply a training ground for the workforce nor an ivory tower, and faculty in particular must be critically involved in finding the right balance point in between.

Study Questions

1. Why did the author become a student? As a first-year student, how did she experience "community" on campus? What surprised her about contemporary student life?

2. According to Small, what are some causes of students' behavior in the classroom? What kinds of university programs would bring about more desirable effects? What kind of educational environment does Small think would be best in a typical public university? Does she give adequate examples of what does and doesn't work to improve learning? Explain.

3. Who is Small's audience? How do you know? How might her essay have been different if it were written for an audience of first-year students? Of the parents of first-year students?

4. *For Writing.* Do you recognize your own college or university in Small's essay? Write an essay in which you take a position on how well your own school builds community and fosters learning, and then offer a proposal for positive change. What particular challenges would have to be met?

Mother Tongue

AMY TAN

I **AM NOT A SCHOLAR** of English or literature. I cannot give you much more than personal opinions on the English language and its variations in this country or others.

I am a writer. And by that definition, I am someone who has always loved language. I am fascinated by language in daily life. I spend a great deal of my time thinking about the power of language—the way it can evoke an emotion, a visual image, a complex idea, or a simple truth. Language is the tool of my trade. And I use them all—all the Englishes I grew up with.

Recently, I was made keenly aware of the different Englishes I do use. I was giving a talk to a large group of people, the same talk I had already given to half a dozen other groups. The talk was about my writing, my life, and my book *The Joy Luck Club,* and it was going along well enough, until I remembered one major difference that made the whole talk sound wrong. My mother was in the room. And it was perhaps the first time she had heard me give a lengthy speech, using the kind of English I have never used with her. I was saying things like "the intersection of memory and imagination" and "There is an aspect of my fiction that relates to thus-and-thus"—a speech

AMY TAN (b.1952), the daughter of parents who emigrated from China, grew up in Oakland, California. In defiance of her mother's plan for her to pursue a career in medicine, Tan chose to study linguistics and pursue a career writing fiction. Tan's relationship with her mother figures prominently in her work, most notably in *The Joy Luck Club* (1989), her first and best-selling novel. The mother/daughter relationship is also central to "Mother Tongue," which first appeared in *Threepenny Review.* Tan's other works include *The Kitchen God's Wife* (1991), *The Bonesetter's Daughter* (2001), and *The Opposite of Fate* (2003).

In "Mother Tongue," Tan explores the different kinds of English she speaks and understands, taking into consideration her mother's English, the results of her own English achievement tests, and the reasons we don't see more Asian American writers. A remarkable ear for dialogue plays an important role in all of Tan's writing, and "Mother Tongue" is no exception. Notice how she weaves storytelling and dialogue, not only to inform and persuade, but also, through carefully crafted anecdotes, to help us understand her mother.

filled with carefully wrought grammatical phrases, burdened, it suddenly seemed to me, with nominalized forms, past perfect tenses, conditional phrases, forms of standard English that I had learned in school and through books, the forms of English I did not use at home with my mother.

Just last week, as I was walking down the street with her, I again found myself conscious of the English I was using, the English I do use with her. We were talking about the price of new and used furniture, and I heard myself saying this: "Not waste money that way." My husband was with us as well, and he didn't notice any switch in my English. And then I realized why. It's because over the twenty years we've been together I've often used the same kind of English with him, and sometimes he even uses it with me. It has become our language of intimacy, a different sort of English that relates to family talk, the language I grew up with.

So that you'll have some idea of what this family talk sounds like, I'll s quote what my mother said during a conversation that I videotaped and then transcribed. During this conversation, she was talking about a political gangster in Shanghai who had the same last name as her family's, Du, and how in his early years the gangster wanted to be adopted by her family, who were rich by comparison. Later, the gangster became more powerful, far richer than my mother's family, and he showed up at my mother's wedding to pay his respects. Here's what she said in part:

> "Du Yusong having business like fruit stand. Like off-the-street kind. He is Du like Du Zong—but not Tsung-ming Island people. The local people call *putong*. The river east side, he belong to that side local people. That man want to ask Du Zong father take him in like become own family. Du Zong father wasn't look down on him, but didn't take seriously, until that man big like become a mafia. Now important person, very hard to inviting him. Chinese way, came only to show respect, don't stay for dinner. Respect for making big celebration, he shows up. Mean gives lots of respect. Chinese custom. Chinese social life that way. If too important won't have to stay too long. He come to my wedding. I didn't see, I heard it. I gone to boy's side, they have YMCA dinner. Chinese age I was nineteen."

You should know that my mother's expressive command of English belies how much she actually understands. She reads the *Forbes* report, listens to *Wall Street Week*, converses daily with her stockbroker, reads Shirley

MacLaine's books with ease—all kinds of things I can't begin to understand. Yet some of my friends tell me they understand fifty percent of what my mother says. Some say they understand eighty to ninety percent. Some say they understand none of it, as if she were speaking pure Chinese. But to me, my mother's English is perfectly clear, perfectly natural. It's my mother tongue. Her language, as I hear it, is vivid, direct, full of observation and imagery. That was the language that helped shape the way I saw things, expressed things, made sense of the world.

Lately I've been giving more thought to the kind of English my mother speaks. Like others, I have described it to people as "broken" or "fractured" English. But I wince when I say that. It has always bothered me that I can think of no way to describe it other than "broken," as if it were damaged and needed to be fixed, as if it lacked a certain wholeness and soundness. I've heard other terms used, "limited English," for example. But they seem just as bad, as if everything is limited, including people's perceptions of the limited-English speaker.

I know this for a fact, because when I was growing up, my mother's "limited" English limited my perception of her. I was ashamed of her English. I believed that her English reflected the quality of what she had to say. That is, because she expressed them imperfectly, her thoughts were imperfect. And I had plenty of empirical evidence to support me: the fact that people in department stores, at banks, and in restaurants did not take her seriously, did not give her good service, pretended not to understand her, or even acted as if they did not hear her.

My mother has long realized the limitations of her English as well. When I was a teenager, she used to have me call people on the phone and pretend I was she. In this guise, I was forced to ask for information or even to complain and yell at people who had been rude to her. One time it was a call to her stockbroker in New York. She had cashed out her small portfolio, and it just so happened we were going to New York the next week, our first trip outside California. I had to get on the phone and say in an adolescent voice that was not very convincing, "This is Mrs. Tan." 10

My mother was standing in the back whispering loudly, "Why he don't send me check, already two weeks late. So mad he lie to me, losing me money."

And then I said in perfect English on the phone, "Yes, I'm getting rather concerned. You had agreed to send the check two weeks ago, but it hasn't arrived."

Then she began to talk more loudly. "What he want, I come to New York tell him front of his boss, you cheating me?" And I was trying to calm her down, make her be quiet, while telling the stockbroker, "I can't tolerate any more excuses. If I don't receive the check immediately, I am going to have to speak to your manager when I'm in New York next week." And sure enough, the following week, there we were in front of this astonished stockbroker, and I was sitting there red-faced and quiet, and my mother, the real Mrs. Tan, was shouting at his boss in her impeccable broken English.

We used a similar routine more recently, for a situation that was far less humorous. My mother had gone to the hospital for an appointment to find out about a CAT scan she had had a month earlier. She said she had spoken very good English, her best English, no mistakes. Still, she said, the hospital staff did not apologize when they informed her they had lost the CAT scan and she had come for nothing. She said they did not seem to have any sympathy when she told them she was anxious to know the exact diagnosis, since both her husband and her son had died of brain tumors. She said they would not give her any more information until the next time and she would have to make another appointment for that. So she said she would not leave until the doctor called her daughter. She wouldn't budge. And when the doctor finally called her daughter, me, who spoke in perfect English—lo and behold—we had assurances the CAT scan would be found, promises that a conference call on Monday would be held, and apologies for any suffering my mother had gone through for a most regrettable mistake.

I think my mother's English almost had an effect on limiting my possibilities in life as well. Sociologists and linguists probably will tell you that a person's developing language skills are more influenced by peers than by family. But I do think that the language spoken in the family, especially in immigrant families which are more insular, plays a large role in shaping the language of the child. And I believe that it affected my results on achievement tests, IQ tests, and the SAT. While my English skills were never judged poor, compared with math, English could not be considered my strong suit. In grade school I did moderately well, getting perhaps B's, sometimes B-pluses, in English and scoring perhaps in the sixtieth or seventieth percentile on achievement tests. But those scores were not good enough to override the opinion that my true abilities lay in math and science, because in those areas I achieved A's and scored in the ninetieth percentile or higher.

This was understandable. Math is precise; there is only one correct answer. Whereas, for me at least, the answers on English tests were always a judgment call, a matter of opinion and personal experience. Those tests were constructed around items like fill-in-the-blank sentence completion, such as "Even though Tom was _____ Mary thought he was _____." And the correct answer always seemed to be the most bland combinations, for example, "Even though Tom was shy, Mary thought he was charming," with the grammatical structure "even though" limiting the correct answer to some sort of semantic opposites, so you wouldn't get answers like "Even though Tom was foolish, Mary thought he was ridiculous." Well, according to my mother, there were very few limitations as to what Tom could have been and what Mary might have thought of him. So I never did well on tests like that.

The same was true with word analogies, pairs of words for which you were supposed to find some logical semantic relationship, for instance, "Sunset is to nightfall as _____ is to_____." And here you would be presented with a list of four possible pairs, one of which showed the same kind of relationship: *red* is to *stoplight, bus* is to *arrival, chills* is to *fever, yawn* is to *boring.* Well, I could never think that way. I knew what the tests were asking, but I could not block out of my mind the images already created by the first pair, *sunset* is to *nightfall*—and I would see a burst of colors against a darkening sky, the moon rising, the lowering of a curtain of stars. And all the other pairs of words—*red, bus, stoplight, boring*—just threw up a mass of confusing images, making it impossible for me to see that saying "A sunset precedes nightfall" was as logical as saying "A chill precedes a fever." The only way I would have gotten that answer right was to imagine an associative situation, such as my being disobedient and staying out past sunset, catching a chill at night, which turned into feverish pneumonia as punishment—which indeed did happen to me.

I have been thinking about all this lately, about my mother's English, about achievement tests. Because lately I've been asked, as a writer, why there are not more Asian-Americans represented in American literature. Why are there few Asian-Americans enrolled in creative writing programs? Why do so many Chinese students go into engineering? Well, these are broad sociological questions I can't begin to answer. But I have noticed in surveys—in fact, just last week—that Asian-American students, as a whole, do significantly better on math achievement tests than on English tests. And this makes me think that there are other Asian-American students whose English spoken in the home might also be described as "broken" or "limited." And perhaps they also have teachers who are steering them away from writing and into math and science, which is what happened to me.

Fortunately, I happen to be rebellious and enjoy the challenge of disproving assumptions made about me. I became an English major my first year in college, after being enrolled as pre-med. I started writing nonfiction as a freelancer the week after I was told by my boss at the time that writing was my worst skill and I should hone my talents toward account management.

But it wasn't until 1985 that I began to write fiction. At first I wrote what I thought to be wittily crafted sentences, sentences that would finally prove I had mastery over the English language. Here's an example from the first draft of a story that later made its way into *The Joy Luck Club,* but without this line: "That was my mental quandary in its nascent state." A terrible line, which I can barely pronounce.

Fortunately, for reasons I won't get into here, I later decided I should envision a reader for the stories I would write. And the reader I decided on was my mother, because these were stories about mothers. So with this reader in mind—and in fact she did read my early drafts—I began to write stories using all the Englishes I grew up with: the English I spoke to my mother, which for lack of a better term might be described as "simple"; the English she used with me, which for lack of a better term might be described as "broken"; my translation of her Chinese, which could certainly be described as "watered down"; and what I imagined to be her translation of her Chinese if she could speak in perfect English, her internal language, and for that I sought to preserve the essence, but neither an English nor a Chinese structure. I wanted to capture what language ability tests could never reveal: her intent, her passion, her imagery, the rhythms of her speech and the nature of her thoughts. [20]

Apart from what any critic had to say about my writing, I knew I had succeeded where it counted when my mother finished reading my book and gave me her verdict: "So easy to read."

Study Questions

1. Explain the pun in the title of Tan's essay.

2. Identify the different "Englishes" Tan discusses. What does she want her reader to understand about these different dialects?

3. Tan writes, "Fortunately, for reasons I won't get into here, I later decided I should envision a reader for the stories I would write. And the reader I decided on was my mother, because these were stories about mothers." How might the mental picture of her mother reading her stories have affected Tan's voice? When writing for college, whom do you most often envision as your reader? How does this affect the decisions you make in your writing?

4. **For Writing.** Write an essay describing your own "Englishes." Even if English is your only language, it's likely that you speak differently with different people—using with some, for instance, more formal language than with others. Think of how you talk with friends, parents, grandparents, children, siblings, and professors. How does your diction and syntax vary with different people? Do you have a special "English" for a particular medium, such as text-messaging or letter-writing? Describe at least three different ways you use language for different audiences and mediums and explain why you talk or write the way you do in each instance.

The Joy of Texting

LYNNE TRUSS

A s SOMEONE WHO SENDS TEXTS MESSAGES more or less non-stop, I
enjoy one particular aspect of texting more than anything else: that
it is possible to sit in a crowded railway carriage laboriously spelling out
quite long words in full, and using an enormous amount of punctuation,
without anyone being aware of how outrageously subversive I am being.
My texts are of epic length. "SMS 4" I am notified on-screen, but I merely
smile inwardly at this warning against extravagance, and see if I can finish
(for once) without getting to "SMS 5." No one around me can tell, as I thumb
the keys, that my secret delight is to shorten no words, use no smiley faces,
eschew predictive text, and employ no handy abbreviations except for
"LOL"—which I always use, wilfully incorrectly, to signify "lots of love."

We pedants are supposed to hate texting, but we don't. We are in love
with effective communication, and there's nothing more effective than
sending a message direct from your phone to someone else's, sometimes
from the hairdresser's (which I mention for a reason). "I CANT BELIEVE U
PUT APOSTROPHE IN HAIRDRESSERS," a friend texted me recently (he obviously had a bit of time on his hands, too). "Oh, I felt the apostrophe was
required," I texted back, happily—in both upper and lower case, with regular
spacing, and a comma after "Oh."

I am aware that I am breaking unwritten rules all the time with texting. The etiquette is a bit baffling, so I err on the side of overdoing it. For
example, I reply on immediate receipt of texts, and I suspect that such overt
eagerness is probably desperately uncool. I have one friend who is, I think,
trying to train me in the proper (cool) art of texting, which involves waiting
a day or two before dispatching a response. But even if I get a text at 1:30
in the morning, I still write back within two minutes, because I'm just too

LYNNE TRUSS, an English writer and journalist, may be best known for her 2004
book *Eats, Shoots and Leaves: The Zero Tolerance Approach to Punctuation*. She has
also written several novels and comic radio dramas and is a regular columnist and
radio commentator. This piece was originally published in 2008 in the British newspaper the *Guardian*.

excited not to (and anyway, I've woken up and put the light on). I also consci-
entiously supply answers to questions, which I find is not the norm, either.
As with email, the recipient of a texted question seems to have the option to
ignore it, while nevertheless saying hello, lovely day, and so on.

There are deeper etiquette issues, of course. A friend of mine once received a text with the news that another friend had committed suicide.
This is not the right sort of information to convey by text; just as it wouldn't
be the right sort of news to leave on an answering machine. Texting is a
supremely secretive medium of communication—it's like passing a note—
and this means we should be very careful what we use it for. I have been
thinking about the great plots in our literature that would be improved
(or destroyed) by the use of texting. The convenient plot device of the
wrong-letter-in-envelope in Ian McEwan's *Atonement,* for example, would
be far more plausible as a text sent in error (Robbie had meant to save it in
"Drafts"!). But Tess's confession about her baby would be much too big to put
in a text to Angel Clare in *Tess of the d'Urbervilles.* Even in a world of texting,
Tess still has to put that letter under that fateful door.

Whether one should read texts in company is the trickiest issue. In ₅
America, now, where nearly everyone seems to own a BlackBerry, there is
a new facial expression I have observed which involves a fixed smile and
panicky swivelled eyes, which means, "I am still listening to you, but I can
see I have a message, but I am honestly still listening to you, I will read the
message later, so tell me again, what did you say, I wish I could read my eff-
ing message." Asking permission from fellow diners to read messages seems
fairly acceptable ("Ooh, can I just see who this is from?"), but nodding and
sniggering at the content, without sharing it, is not. Composing a quick reply
while in company is likewise quite rude. I often excuse myself and then text
feverishly from the lavatories, which seems less socially offensive, even if
I'm gone for at least 20 minutes (what with all the spelling out of long words,
punctuating and so on).

Texting is a fundamentally sneaky form of communication, which we
should despise, but it is such a boon we don't care. We are all sneaks now. It's
as if we have an endless supply of telegram boys who, in a matter of seconds,
can not only locate anyone on the planet on our behalf, but also tap him on
the shoulder and hand over a sealed envelope marked "For Your Eyes Only."
My favourite text—which I lovingly preserve—was sent to me by a friend
in Greece, when I was staying the other side of the harbour from his house.
"AM WAVING" it said, and I looked across with my binoculars, and so he was.

The oldest form of communication was thus served by the latest. It seemed daft, but also right.

Study Questions

1. Lynne Truss takes an analytic look at her own habits and standards of texting, while acknowledging that they are different from those of most people that she knows. Although your texting practices may be very different from hers, do you agree that she has identified the etiquette dilemmas that the medium raises? Why or why not?

2. While acknowledging that the medium is more conducive to messages that are very short, Truss describes the great pleasure she gets from creating very long texts and relates an astonished response from one of her correspondents. Do you enjoy getting long texts? Why or why not?

3. Truss takes a flippant and casual tone with a relatively serious topic. Does her tone enhance her authority on this topic? undermine it? neither? How would you describe the ethos that Truss constructs for herself in this article?

4. In a very short essay, Truss manages to both criticize and applaud SMS messages and the social practices of sending and receiving them. Are her arguments consistent with one another? How would you summarize her main point?

5. How do you use texting in your life? What social activities and interactions does it facilitate? Are there any ways that it makes your life more complicated? Write an essay in which you analyze your own texting and describe both how it facilitates and complicates your life. (Before you write, it may be helpful to keep a log of all your texts for forty-eight hours—sent and received—so that you have evidence to draw from.)

I Won't Hire People Who Use Poor Grammar. Here's Why.

KYLE WIENS

IF YOU THINK AN APOSTROPHE was one of the 12 disciples of Jesus, you will never work for me. If you think a semicolon is a regular colon with an identity crisis, I will not hire you. If you scatter commas into a sentence with all the discrimination of a shotgun, you might make it to the foyer before we politely escort you from the building.

Some might call my approach to grammar extreme, but I prefer Lynne Truss's more cuddly phraseology: I am a grammar "stickler." And like Truss—author of *Eats, Shoots & Leaves*—I have a "zero tolerance approach" to grammar mistakes that make people look stupid.

Now, Truss and I disagree on what it means to have "zero tolerance." She thinks that people who mix up their itses "deserve to be struck by lightning, hacked up on the spot and buried in an unmarked grave," while I just think they deserve to be passed over for a job—even if they are otherwise qualified for the position.

KYLE WIENS is an American businessman and writer. He is the founder of iFixit, a company that allows users to find and share information about repairing household items, and Dozuki, which produces owner's manuals for companies. He also has a strong interest in matters of web technology, business, and the law. His work as a writer has appeared in a number of publications, including the The Wall Street Journal, Wired, and the Atlantic.

"I Won't Hire People Who Use Bad Grammar. Here's Why." was published in the *Harvard Business Review* in 2012. In the essay, Wiens argues that the ability to write well is a necessity for all potential employees of his businesses. He goes so far as to say that a lack of certain grammatical skills is enough for him to disqualify job candidates regardless of their other skills—even for positions that do not require much writing. Wiens recognizes that some people will disagree with his stance on the matter, yet he insists that strong writing skills are essential for employees to be successful. As you read, note the reasons Wiens gives for feeling so strongly about writing, and note why he believes that people's writing skills are indicative of other mental abilities.

Everyone who applies for a position at either of my companies, iFixit or Dozuki, takes a mandatory grammar test. Extenuating circumstances aside (dyslexia, English language learners, etc.), if job hopefuls can't distinguish between "to" and "too," their applications go into the bin.

Of course, we write for a living. iFixit.com is the world's largest on-line repair manual, and Dozuki helps companies write their own techni-cal documentation, like paperless work instructions and step-by-step user manuals. So, it makes sense that we've made a preemptive strike against groan-worthy grammar errors.

But grammar is relevant for all companies. Yes, language is constantly changing, but that doesn't make grammar unimportant. Good grammar is credibility, especially on the internet. In blog posts, on Facebook statuses, in e-mails, and on company websites, your words are all you have. They are a projection of you in your physical absence. And, for better or worse, people judge you if you can't tell the difference between their, there, and they're.

Good grammar makes good business sense—and not just when it comes to hiring writers. Writing isn't in the official job description of most people in our office. Still, we give our grammar test to everybody, including our salespeople, our operations staff, and our programmers.

On the face of it, my zero tolerance approach to grammar errors might seem a little unfair. After all, grammar has nothing to do with job perfor-mance, or creativity, or intelligence, right?

Wrong. If it takes someone more than 20 years to notice how to prop-erly use "it's," then that's not a learning curve I'm comfortable with. So, even in this hyper-competitive market, I will pass on a great programmer who cannot write.

Grammar signifies more than just a person's ability to remember high school English. I've found that people who make fewer mistakes on a gram-mar test also make fewer mistakes when they are doing something com-pletely unrelated to writing—like stocking shelves or labeling parts.

In the same vein, programmers who pay attention to how they con-struct written language also tend to pay a lot more attention to how they code. You see, at its core, code is prose. Great programmers are more than just code monkeys; according to Stanford programming legend Donald Knuth they are "essayists who work with traditional aesthetic and literary forms." The point: programming should be easily understood by real human be-ings—not just computers.

And just like good writing and good grammar, when it comes to programming, the devil's in the details. In fact, when it comes to my whole business, details are everything.

I hire people who care about those details. Applicants who don't think writing is important are likely to think lots of other (important) things also aren't important. And I guarantee that even if other companies aren't issuing grammar tests, they pay attention to sloppy mistakes on résumés. After all, sloppy is as sloppy does.

That's why I grammar test people who walk in the door looking for a job. Grammar is my litmus test. All applicants say they're detail-oriented; I just make my employees prove it.

Study Questions

1. According to Wiens, why is the ability to write clearly and correctly so important?

2. How does writing ability affect potential employees' ethos when they apply for a job?

3. What evidence does Wiens provide to support his argument that writing skills are essential, even for non-writing positions?

4. *For Writing.* Think of your own strengths as a writer, and imagine that you are applying for a position with one of Wiens's companies. In a short essay, explain which aspect of your writing would make you an appealing candidate. What do you do well as a writer, and why do you feel that it would help you stand out to employers? What does your writing ability indicate about your other abilities?

A Homemade Education

MALCOLM X

IT WAS BECAUSE OF MY LETTERS that I happened to stumble upon starting to acquire some kind of a homemade education. I became increasingly
frustrated at not being able to express what I wanted to convey in letters
that I wrote, especially those to Mr. Elijah Muhammad.[1]

In the street, I had been the most articulate hustler out there—I had
commanded attention when I said something. But now, trying to write

---

1. African American religious leader (1897–1975); head of the Nation of Islam from 1934 to
1975.

MALCOLM X (1925–1965) was one of the most prominent and controversial
civil rights activists of the 1960s. Born Malcolm Little in Omaha, Nebraska, he
excelled in school until his eighth-grade teacher discouraged him from pursuing a
law career, saying it was not a "realistic goal" for an African American. Years later,
while serving a prison sentence for larceny and breaking and entering, he began
educating himself. "Language became an obsession with me," he remembered. "I
began to realize the meaning and the power of words." He also converted to the
Lost-Found Nation of Islam (the so-called Black Muslims) and upon his release
from prison, became its national spokesperson. Both the Nation and Malcolm X
were known for their radical stance on race relations. Splitting with mainstream
civil rights activists like Martin Luther King Jr., they supported segregation instead
of integration and called for the founding of a black nation. In 1964, Malcolm X left
the Nation of Islam, converted to Sunni Islam, and adopted the name El-Hajj Malik
El Shabazz. He was assassinated by Nation followers in 1965.

The following selection comes from the chapter "Saved" in *The Autobiography
of Malcolm X*. Frustrated by his inability to communicate effectively in the letters
he writes, Malcolm embarks on his "homemade education" by increasing his vocabulary and reading widely. In the process, he learns not only about the history
of American racism toward African Americans, but also about the experiences
of non-Western peoples in their struggles against oppression. As you read, pay
close attention to the readings he lists and the examples he uses when discussing
world history; think about how they relate to the social and political upheaval of
the 1960s in America.

simple English, I not only wasn't articulate, I wasn't even functional. How would I sound writing in slang, the way I would *say* it, something such as "Look, daddy, let me pull your coat about a cat, Elijah Muhammad—"

Many who today hear me somewhere in person, or on television, or those who read something I've said, will think I went to school far beyond the eighth grade. This impression is due entirely to my prison studies.

It had really begun back in the Charlestown Prison, when Bimbi[2] first made me feel envy of his stock of knowledge. Bimbi had always taken charge of any conversation he was in, and I had tried to emulate him. But every book I picked up had few sentences which didn't contain anywhere from one to nearly all of the words that might as well have been in Chinese. When I just skipped those words, of course, I really ended up with little idea of what the book said. So I had come to the Norfolk Prison Colony still going through only book-reading motions. Pretty soon, I would have quit even these motions, unless I had received the motivation that I did.

I saw that the best thing I could do was get hold of a dictionary—to study, to learn some words. I was lucky enough to reason also that I should try to improve my penmanship. It was sad. I couldn't even write in a straight line. It was both ideas together that moved me to request a dictionary along with some tablets and pencils from the Norfolk Prison Colony school.

I spent two days just riffling uncertainly through the dictionary's pages. I'd never realized so many words existed! I didn't know *which* words I needed to learn. Finally, just to start some kind of action, I began copying.

In my slow, painstaking, ragged handwriting, I copied into my tablet everything printed on that first page, down to the punctuation marks.

I believe it took me a day. Then, aloud, I read back, to myself, everything I'd written on the tablet. Over and over, aloud, to myself, I read my own handwriting.

I woke up the next morning, thinking about those words—immensely proud to realize that not only had I written so much at one time, but I'd written words that I never knew were in the world. Moreover, with a little effort, I also could remember what many of these words meant. I reviewed the words whose meanings I didn't remember, Funny thing, from the dictionary first page right now, that "aardvark" springs to my mind. The dictionary had a picture of it, a long-tailed, long-eared, burrowing African

2. A fellow prison inmate at Charleston (Massachusetts) State Prison who motivated Malcolm X to educate himself.

mammal, which lives off termites caught by sticking out its tongue as an anteater does for ants.

I was so fascinated that I went on—I copied the dictionary's next page. ₁₀ And the same experience came when I studied that. With every succeeding page, I also learned of people and places and events from history. Actually the dictionary is like a miniature encyclopedia. Finally the dictionary's A section had filled a whole tablet—and I went on into the B's. That was the way I started copying what eventually became the entire dictionary. It went a lot faster after so much practice helped me to pick up handwriting speed. Between what I wrote in my tablet, and writing letters, during the rest of my time in prison I would guess I wrote a million words.

I suppose it was inevitable that as my word-base broadened, I could for the first time pick up a book and read and now begin to understand what the book was saying. Anyone who has read a great deal can imagine the new world that opened. Let me tell you something: from then until I left that prison, in every free moment I had, if I was not reading in the library, I was reading on my bunk. You couldn't have gotten me out of books with a wedge. Between Mr. Muhammad's teachings, my correspondence, my visitors—usually Ella and Reginald[3]—and my reading of books, months passed without my even thinking about being imprisoned. In fact, up to then, I never had been so truly free in my life.

The Norfolk Prison Colony's library was in the school building. A variety of classes was taught there by instructors who came from such places as Harvard and Boston universities. The weekly debates between inmate teams were also held in the school building. You would be astonished to know how worked up convict debaters and audiences would get over subjects like "Should Babies Be Fed Milk?"

Available on the prison library's shelves were books on just about every general subject. Much of the big private collection that Parkhurst[4] had willed to the prison was still in crates and boxes in the back of the library— thousands of old books. Some of them looked ancient: covers faded, old-time parchment-looking binding. Parkhurst, I've mentioned, seemed to have been principally interested in history and religion. He had the money and the special interest to have a lot of books that you wouldn't have in general circulation. Any college library would have been lucky to get that collection.

---

3. Ella Collins and Reginald Little, Malcolm X's sister and brother.
4. Charles Henry Parkhurst (1842–1933), American clergyman and social reformer.

As you can imagine, especially in a prison where there was heavy emphasis on rehabilitation, an inmate was smiled upon if he demonstrated an unusually intense interest in books. There was a sizable number of well-read inmates, especially the popular debaters. Some were said by many to be practically walking encyclopedias. They were almost celebrities. No university would ask any student to devour literature as I did when this new world opened to me, of being able to read and *understand*.

I read more in my room than in the library itself. An inmate who was known to read a lot could check out more than the permitted maximum number of books. I preferred reading in the total isolation of my own room.

When I had progressed to really serious reading, every night at about ten P.M. I would be outraged with the "lights out." It always seemed to catch me right in the middle of something engrossing.

Fortunately, right outside my door was a corridor light that cast a glow into my room. The glow was enough to read by, once my eyes adjusted to it. So when "lights out" came, I would sit on the floor where I could continue reading in that glow.

At one-hour intervals the night guards paced past every room. Each time I heard the approaching footsteps, I jumped into bed and feigned sleep. And as soon as the guard passed, I got back out of bed onto the floor area of that light-glow, where I would read for another fifty-eight minutes—until the guard approached again. That went on until three or four every morning. Three or four hours of sleep a night was enough for me. Often in the years in the streets I had slept less than that.

The teachings of Mr. Muhammad stressed how history had been "whitened"—when white men had written history books, the black man simply had been left out. Mr. Muhammad couldn't have said anything that would have struck me much harder. I had never forgotten how when my class, me and all of those whites, had studied seventh grade United States history back in Mason, the history of the Negro had been covered in one paragraph, and the teacher had gotten a big laugh with his joke, "Negroes' feet are so big that when they walk, they leave a hole in the ground."

This is one reason why Mr. Muhammad's teachings spread so swiftly *all* over the United States, among all Negroes, whether or not they became followers of Mr. Muhammad. The teachings ring true—to every Negro. You can hardly show me a black adult in America—or a white one, for that matter—who knows from the history books anything like the truth about the black man's role. In my own case, once I heard of the "glorious history of the black man," I took special pains to hunt in the library for books that would inform me on details about black history.

I can remember accurately the very first set of books that really impressed me. I have since bought that set of books and have it at home for my children to read as they grow up. It's called *Wonders of the World*. It's full of pictures of archeological finds, statues that depict, usually, non-European people.

I found books like Will Durant's *Story of Civilization*.[5] I read H. G. Wells' *Outline of History*.[6] *Souls Of Black Folk* by W. E. B. Du Bois[7] gave me a glimpse into the black people's history before they came to this country. Carter G. Woodson's[8] *Negro History* opened my eyes about black empires before the black slave was brought to the United States, and the early Negro struggles for freedom.

J. A. Rogers' three volumes of *Sex and Race*[9] told about race-mixing before Christ's time; about Aesop being a black man who told fables; about Egypt's Pharaohs; about the great Coptic Christian Empires [10] about Ethiopia, the earth's oldest continuous black civilization, as China is the oldest continuous civilization.

Mr. Muhammad's teaching about how the white man had been created led me to *Findings In Genetics* by Gregor Mendel.[11] (The dictionary's G section was where I had learned what "genetics" meant.) I really studied this book by the Austrian monk. Reading it over and over, especially certain sections, helped me to understand that if you started with a black man, a white man could be produced; but starting with a white man, you never could produce

---

5. American historian (1885–1981), who, with his wife Ariel Durant (1889–1981), wrote *The Story of Civilization*, an eleven-volume work (1935–75).
6. English novelist and historian (1866–1946); his *The Outline of History, Being a Plain History of Life and Mankind* was published in two volumes in 1920.
7. Civil rights activist (1868–1963), first director of the NAACP, and author of the groundbreaking work *The Souls of Black Folk* (1903), a study of African Americans in the post-Reconstruction South.
8. African American historian (1875–1950) and creator of Negro History Week (now Black History Month).
9. Comprehensive treatise (1941–42) on race mixing throughout history by Joel Augustus Rogers, journalist and historian (1880–1966)
10. The Coptic Orthodox Church of Alexandria, a form of Christianity developed in Egypt, is one of the earliest Christian denominations, said to have been founded by the apostle Mark in the middle of the first century c.e.
11. Austrian priest and scientist (1822–84) whose breeding experiments with pea plants led him to formulate the basic laws of heredity.

a black man—because the white gene is recessive. And since no one disputes that there was but one Original Man, the conclusion is clear.

During the last year or so, in the *New York Times,* Arnold Toynbee[12] used 25 the word "bleached" in describing the white man. (His words were: "White (i.e. bleached) human beings of North European origin. . . .") Toynbee also referred to the European geographic area as only a peninsula of Asia. He said there is no such thing as Europe. And if you look at the globe, you will see for yourself that America is only an extension of Asia. (But at the same time Toynbee is among those who have helped to bleach history. He has written that Africa was the only continent that produced no history. He won't write that again. Every day now, the truth is coming to light.)

I never will forget how shocked I was when I began reading about slavery's total horror. It made such an impact upon me that it later became one of my favorite subjects when I became a minister of Mr. Muhammad's. The world's most monstrous crime, the sin and the blood on the white man's hands, are almost impossible to believe. Books like the one by Frederick Olmstead[13] opened my eyes to the horrors suffered when the slave was landed in the United States. The European woman, Fannie Kimball,[14] who had married a Southern white slaveowner, described how human beings were degraded. Of course I read *Uncle Tom's Cabin.*[15]

In fact, I believe that's the only novel I have ever read since I started serious reading.

Parkhurst's collection also contained some bound pamphlets of the Abolitionist Anti-Slavery Society of New England. I read descriptions of atrocities, saw those illustrations of black slave women tied up and flogged with whips; of black mothers watching their babies being dragged off, never to be seen by their mothers again; of dogs after slaves, and of the fugitive slave catchers, evil white men with whips and clubs and chains and guns. I read

---

12. British historian (1889–1975) and author of the twelve-volume *A Study of History,* an examination of world history analyzing the rise and fall of civilizations.
13. Antislavery journalist (1822–1903) who was commissioned by the *New York Times* to research slavery in the South; now better remembered as one of the principal landscape designers of New York City's Central Park.
14. Frances Ann (Fanny) Kemble (1809–93), English actress who wrote *Journal of a Residence on a Georgia Plantation* (1863) to encourage support in Britain for the abolitionist movement.
15. Subtitled *Life Among the Lowly* (1852), an immensely popular and influential antislavery novel by American author Harriet Beecher Stowe (1811–96).

about the slave preacher Nat Turner,[16] who put the fear of God into the white slavemaster. Nat Turner wasn't going around preaching pie-in-the-sky and "non-violent" freedom for the black man. There in Virginia one night in 1831, Nat and seven other slaves started out at his master's home and through the night they went from one plantation "big house" to the next, killing, until by the next morning fifty-seven white people were dead and Nat had about seventy slaves following him. White people, terrified for their lives, fled from their homes, locked themselves up in public buildings, hid in the woods, and some even left the state. A small army of soldiers took two months to catch and hang Nat Turner. Somewhere I have read where Nat Turner's example is said to have inspired John Brown[17] to invade Virginia and attack Harper's Ferry nearly thirty years later, with thirteen white men and five Negroes.

I read Herodotus,[18] "the father of History," or, rather, I read about him. And I read the histories of various nations, which opened my eyes gradually, then wider and wider, to how the whole world's white men had indeed acted like devils, pillaging and raping and bleeding and draining the whole world's non-white people. I remember, for instance, books such as Will Durant's story of Oriental civilization, and Mahatma Gandhi's[19] accounts of the struggle to drive the British out of India.

Book after book showed me how the white man had brought upon the 30 world's black, brown, red, and yellow peoples every variety of the sufferings of exploitation. I saw how since the sixteenth century, the so-called "Christian trader" white man began to ply the seas in his lust for Asian and African empires, and plunder, and power. I read, I saw, how the white man never has gone among the non-white peoples bearing the Cross in the true manner and spirit of Christ's teachings—meek, humble, and Christ-like.

I perceived, as I read, how the collective white man had been actually nothing but a piratical opportunist who used Faustian machinations to make his own Christianity his initial wedge in criminal conquests. First,

16. American slave and mystic (1800–1831) who, in 1831, led the antebellum South's most significant slave rebellion in Virginia's Southampton County.
17. American abolitionist (1800–1859) who led a raid of the U.S. arsenal and armory in Harpers Ferry, Virginia, in an attempt to spark a slave revolt that would spread across the South; he was hanged on December 2, 1859.
18. Greek historian (c. 484–c. 425 B.C.E.), best known for his *Histories*, which deserve the rise of the Persian Empire and the causes of the Greco-Persian Wars.
19. Mohandas Karamchand Gandhi (1869–1948), political and spiritual leader of the Indian Independence Movement, which finally achieved its goal in 1947 when Britain formally ceded independence to India; he was assassinated in 1948.

always "religiously," he branded "heathen" and "pagan" labels upon ancient non-white cultures and civilizations. The stage thus set, he then turned upon his non-white victims his weapons of war.

I read how, entering India—half a *billion* deeply religious brown people—the British white man, by 1759, through promises, trickery and manipulations, controlled much of India through Great Britain's East India Company. The parasitical British administration kept tentacling out to half of the subcontinent. In 1857, some of the desperate people of India finally mutinied—and, excepting the African slave trade, nowhere has history recorded any more unnecessary bestial and ruthless human carnage than the British suppression of the non-white Indian people.

Over 115 million African blacks—close to the 1930's population of the United States—were murdered or enslaved during the slave trade. And I read how when the slave market was glutted, the cannibalistic white powers of Europe next carved up, as their colonies, the richest areas of the black continent.[20]

And Europe's chancelleries for the next century played a chess game of naked exploitation and power from Cape Horn to Cairo.

Ten guards and the warden couldn't have torn me out of those books. 35 Not even Elijah Muhammad could have been more eloquent than those books were in providing indisputable proof that the collective white man had acted like a devil in virtually every contact he had with the world's collective non-white man. I listen today to the radio, and watch television, and read the headlines about the collective white man's fear and tension concerning China. When the white man professes ignorance about why the Chinese hate him so, my mind can't help flashing back to what I read, there in prison, about how the blood forebears of this same white man raped China at a time when China was trusting and helpless. Those original white "Christian traders" sent into China millions of pounds of opium. By 1839, so many of the Chinese were addicts that China's desperate government destroyed twenty thousand chests of opium. The first Opium War[21] was promptly declared by the white man. Imagine! Declaring *war* upon someone who objects to being narcotized! The Chinese were severely beaten, with Chinese-invented gunpowder.

---

20. In what became known as "The Scramble for Africa," European countries competed to conquer African territory from the 1880s until the beginning of the First World War (1914–18).
21. The First Opium War (1839–42), fought between Britain and the Qing Dynasty in China, ended with China's cession of Hong Kong Island to Britain.

The Treaty of Nanking made China pay the British white man for the destroyed opium; forced open China's major ports to British trade; forced China to abandon Hong Kong; fixed China's import tariffs so low that cheap British articles soon flooded in, maiming China's industrial development.

After a second Opium War,[22] the Tientsin Treaties legalized the ravaging opium trade, legalized a British-French-American control of China's customs. China tried delaying that Treaty's ratification; Peking was looted and burned.

"Kill the foreign white devils!" was the 1901 Chinese war cry in the Boxer Rebellion.[23]

Losing again, this time the Chinese were driven from Peking's choicest areas. The vicious, arrogant white man put up the famous signs, "Chinese and dogs not allowed."

Red China[24] after World War II closed its doors to the Western white   40 world. Massive Chinese agricultural, scientific, and industrial efforts are described in a book that *Life* magazine recently published. Some observers inside Red China have reported that the world never has known such a hate-white campaign as is now going on in this non-white country where, present birth-rates continuing, in fifty more years Chinese will be half the earth's population. And it seems that some Chinese chickens will soon come home to roost, with China's recent successful nuclear tests.

Let us face reality. We can see in the United Nations a new world order being shaped, along color lines—an alliance among the non-white nations. America's U.N. Ambassador Adlai Stevenson[25] complained not long ago that in the United Nations "a skin game" was being played. He was right. He was facing reality. A "skin game" *is* being played. But Ambassador Stevenson sounded like Jesse James accusing the marshal of carrying a gun. Because who in the world's history ever has played a worse "skin game" than the white man?

Mr. Muhammad, to whom I was writing daily, had no idea of what a

22. Joint British and French military action against the Qing Dynasty of China (1856–60).
23. An uprising against imperialism in China that was finally quashed by the so-called Eight-Nation Alliance, which included Japan, Britain, and the United States (1899–1901).
24. That is, the People's Republic of China, founded in 1949 by the Communist Party of China after the Chinese Civil War.
25. American politician and statesman (1900–65); who ran as Democratic candidate for president in 1952 and 1956; he served as U.S. ambassador to the United Nations from 1961 until his death.

new world had opened up to me through my efforts to document his teachings in books.

When I discovered philosophy, I tried to touch all the landmarks of philosophical development. Gradually, I read most of the old philosophers, Occidental and Oriental. The Oriental philosophers were the ones I came to prefer; finally, my impression was that most Occidental philosophy had largely been borrowed from the Oriental thinkers. Socrates,[26] for instance, traveled in Egypt. Some sources even say that Socrates was initiated into some of the Egyptian mysteries. Obviously Socrates got some of his wisdom among the East's wise men.

I have often reflected upon the new vistas that reading opened to me. I knew right there in prison that reading had changed forever the course of my life. As I see it today, the ability to read awoke inside me some long dormant craving to be mentally alive. I certainly wasn't seeking any degree, the way a college confers a status symbol upon its students. My homemade education gave me, with every additional book that I read, a little bit more sensitivity to the deafness, dumbness, and blindness that was afflicting the black race in America. Not long ago, an English writer telephoned me from London, asking questions. One was, "What's your alma mater?" I told him, "Books." You will never catch me with a free fifteen minutes in which I'm not studying something I feel might be able to help the black man.

Yesterday I spoke in London, and both ways on the plane across the Atlantic I was studying a document about how the United Nations proposes to insure the human rights of the oppressed minorities of the world. The American black man is the world's most shameful case of minority oppression. What makes the black man think of himself as only an internal United States issue is just a catch-phrase, two words, "civil rights." How is the black man going to get "civil rights" before first he wins his *human* rights? If the American black man will start thinking about his *human* rights, and then start thinking of himself as part of one of the world's great peoples, he will see he has a case for the United Nations. 45

I can't think of a better case! Four hundred years of black blood and sweat invested here in America, and the white man still has the black man begging for what every immigrant fresh off the ship can take for granted the minute he walks down the gangplank.

---

26. Classical Greek philosopher (c. 469–399 B.C.E.), regarded as one of the founders of Western philosophy; known primarily through the writings of his student, Plato

But I'm digressing. I told the Englishman that my alma mater was books, a good library. Every time I catch a plane, I have with me a book that I want to read—and that's a lot of books these days. If I weren't out here every day battling the white man, I could spend the rest of my life reading, just satisfying my curiosity—because you can hardly mention anything I'm not curious about. I don't think anybody ever got more out of going to prison than I did. In fact, prison enabled me to study far more intensively than I would have if my life had gone differently and I had attended some college. I imagine that one of the biggest troubles with colleges is there are too many distractions, too much panty-raiding, fraternities, and boola-boola and all of that. Where else but in a prison could I have attacked my ignorance by being able to study intensely sometimes as much as fifteen hours a day?

Study Questions

1. Where is Malcolm X when he writes, "up to then, I never had been so truly free in my life"? What does he mean?

2. The author notes that he read only one novel—as opposed to many nonfiction works—after he started "serious reading": *Uncle Tom's Cabin*. What, then, do you think was his goal for reading? How do different genres meet different needs for a reader?

3. Malcolm X describes and analyzes the process by which he became educated. How does he convey the value of this education for his post-prison life? What argument is he making about something other than the value of education?

4. How does Malcolm X distinguish between *civil* rights and *human* rights? What evidence does he present that leads to this distinction?

5. *For Writing.* Malcolm X writes about how, in his seventh-grade history textbook, African American history was covered in one paragraph while the history of nonwhite cultures was omitted altogether. How does cultural context determine what is taught in school? Does education necessarily privilege certain groups at the expense of others? Should schools be required to teach diversity? Write an essay in which you examine the role education serves—or should serve—in a society.

The Act of Writing: One Man's Method

WILLIAM ZINSSER

W RITING IS A DEEPLY PERSONAL PROCESS, full of mystery and surprise. No two people go about it in exactly the same way. We all have little devices to get us started, or to keep us going, or to remind us of what we think we want to say, and what works for one person may not work for anyone else. The main thing is to get something written—to get the words out of our heads. There is no "right" method. Any method that will do the job is the right method for you.

It helps to remember that writing is hard. Most non-writers don't know this; they think that writing is a natural function, like breathing, that ought to come easy, and they're puzzled when it doesn't. If you find that writing is hard, it's because it *is* hard. It's one of the hardest things that people do. Among other reasons, it's hard because it requires thinking. You won't write clearly unless you keep forcing yourself to think clearly. There's no escaping the question that has to be constantly asked: What do I want to say next?

So painful is this task that writers go to remarkable lengths to postpone their daily labor. They sharpen their pencils and change their typewriter ribbon and go out to the store to buy more paper. Now these sacred rituals, as IBM would say, have been obsoleted.

When I began writing this book on my word processor I didn't have any idea what would happen. Would I be able to write anything at all? Would it be any good? I was bringing to the machine what I assumed were wholly different ways of thinking about writing. The units massed in front of me looked cold and sterile. Their steady hum reminded me that they were waiting. They seemed to be waiting for information, not for writing. Maybe what I wrote would also be cold and sterile.

I was particularly worried about the absence of paper. I knew that I 5 would only be able to see as many lines as the screen would hold—twenty lines. How could I review what I had already written? How could I get a sense of continuity and flow? With paper it was always possible to flick through the preceding pages to see where I was coming from—and where I ought to be going. Without paper I would have no such periodic fix. Would this be a major hardship?

The only way to find out was to find out. I took a last look at my unsharpened pencils and went to work.

My particular hang-up as a writer is that I have to get every paragraph as nearly right as possible before I go on to the next paragraph. I'm somewhat like a bricklayer: I build very slowly, not adding a new row until I feel that the foundation is solid enough to hold up the house. I'm the exact opposite of the writer who dashes off his entire first draft, not caring how sloppy it looks or how badly it's written. His only objective at this early stage is to let his creative motor run the full course at full speed; repairs can always be made later. I envy this writer and would like to have his metabolism. But I'm stuck with the one I've got.

I also care how my writing looks while I'm writing it. The visual arrangement is important to me: the shape of the words, of the sentences, of the paragraphs, of the page. I don't like sentences that are dense with long words, or paragraphs that never end. As I write I want to see the design that my piece will have when the reader sees it in type, and I want that design to have a rhythm and a pace that will invite the reader to keep reading. O.K., so I'm a nut. But I'm not alone; the visual component is important to a large number of people who write.

One hang-up we visual people share is that our copy must be neat. My lifelong writing method, for instance, has gone like this. I put a piece of paper in the typewriter and write the first paragraph. Then I take the paper out and edit what I've written. I mark it up horribly, crossing words out and scribbling new ones in the space between the lines. By this time the paragraph has lost its nature and shape for me as a piece of writing. It's a mishmash of typing and handwriting and arrows and balloons and other directional symbols. So I type a clean copy, incorporating the changes, and then I take that piece of paper out of the typewriter and edit it. It's better, but not much better. I go over it with my pencil again, making more changes, which again make it too messy for me to read critically, so I go back to the typewriter for round three. And round four. Not until I'm reasonably satisfied do I proceed to the next paragraph.

This can get pretty tedious, and I have often thought that there must 10 be a better way. Now there is. The word processor is God's gift, or at least science's gift, to the tinkerers and the refiners and the neatness freaks. For me it was obviously the perfect new toy. I began playing on page 1—editing, cutting and revising—and have been on a rewriting high ever since. The burden of the years has been lifted.

Mostly I've been cutting. I would guess that I've cut at least as many words out of this book as the number that remain. Probably half of those words were eliminated because I saw that they were unnecessary—the sentence worked fine without them. This is where the word processor can improve your writing to an extent that you will hardly believe. Learn to recognize what is clutter and to use the DELETE key to prune it out.

How will you know clutter when you see it? Here's a device I used when I was teaching writing at Yale that my students found helpful; it may be a help here. I would put brackets around every component in a student's paper that I didn't think was doing some kind of work. Often it was only one word—for example, the useless preposition that gets appended to so many verbs (order up, free up), or the adverb whose meaning is already in the verb (blare loudly, clench tightly), or the adjective that tells us what we already know (smooth marble, green grass). The brackets might surround the little qualifiers that dilute a writer's authority (a bit, sort of, in a sense), or the countless phrases in which the writer explains what he is about to explain (it might be pointed out, I'm tempted to say). Often my brackets would surround an entire sentence—the sentence that essentially repeats what the previous sentence has said, or tells the reader something that is implicit, or adds a detail that is irrelevant. Most people's writing is littered with phrases that do no new work whatever. Most first drafts, in fact, can be cut by fifty percent without losing anything organic. (Try it; it's a good exercise.)

By bracketing these extra words, instead of crossing them out, I was saying to the student: "I may be wrong, but I think this can go and the meaning of the sentence won't be affected in any way. But *you* decide: read the sentence without the bracketed material and see if it works." In the first half of the term, the students' papers were festooned with my brackets. Whole paragraphs got bracketed. But gradually the students learned to put mental brackets around their many different kinds of clutter, and by the end of the term I was returning papers to them that had hardly any brackets, or none. It was always a satisfying moment. Today many of those students are professional writers. "I still see your brackets," they tell me. "They're following me through life."

You can develop the same eye. Writing is clear and strong to the extent that it has no superfluous parts. (So is art and music and dance and typography and design.) You will really enjoy writing on a word processor when you see your sentences growing in strength, literally before your eyes, as you get rid of the fat. Be thankful for everything that you can throw away.

I was struck by how many phrases and sentences I wrote in this book 15
that I later found I didn't need. Many of them hammered home a point
that didn't need hammering because it had already been made. This kind
of overwriting happens in almost everybody's first draft, and it's perfectly
natural—the act of putting down our thoughts makes us garrulous. Luckily, the act of editing follows the act of writing, and this is where the word
processor will bail you out. It intercedes at the point where the game can be
won or lost. With its help I cut hundreds of unnecessary words and didn't
replace them.

Hundreds of others were discarded because I later thought of a better
word—one that caught more precisely or more vividly what I was trying to
express. Here, again, a word processor encourages you to play. The English
language is rich in words that convey an exact shade of meaning. Don't get
stuck with a word that's merely good if you can find one that takes the reader by surprise with its color or aptness or quirkiness. Root around in your
dictionary of synonyms and find words that are fresh. Throw them up on
the screen and see how they look.

Also learn to play with whole sentences. If a sentence strikes you as
awkward or ponderous, move your cursor to the space after the period and
write a new sentence that you think is better. Maybe you can make it shorter.
Or clearer. Maybe you can make it livelier by turning it into a question or
otherwise altering its rhythm. Change the passive verbs into active verbs.
(Passive verbs are the death of clarity and vigor.) Try writing two or three
new versions of the awkward sentence and then compare them, or write a
fourth version that combines the best elements of all three. Sentences come
in an infinite variety of shapes and sizes. Find one that pleases you. If it's
clear, and if it pleases you and expresses who you are, trust it to please other
people. Then delete all the versions that aren't as good. Your shiny new sentence will jump into position and the rest of the paragraph will rearrange
itself as quickly and neatly as if you had never pulled it apart.

Another goal that the word processor will help you to achieve is unity.
No matter how carefully you write each sentence as you assemble a piece
of writing, the final product is bound to have some ragged edges. Is the tone
consistent throughout? And the point of view? And the pronoun? And the
tense? How about the transitions? Do they pull the reader along, or is the
piece jerky and disjointed? A good piece of writing should be harmonious
from beginning to end in the voice of the writer and the flow if its logic. But
the harmony usually requires some last-minute patching.

I've been writing this book by the bricklayer method, slowly and carefully. That's all very well as far as it goes—at the end of every chapter the individual bricks may look fine. But what about the wall? The only way to check your piece for unity is to go over it one more time from start to finish, preferably reading it aloud. See if you have executed all the decisions that you made before you started writing.

One such decision is in the area of tone. I decided, for instance, that I [20] didn't want this book to be a technical manual. I'm not a technician; I'm a writer and an editor. The book wouldn't work if I expected the reader to identify with the process of mastering a new technology. He would have to identify with me. The book would be first of all a personal journey and only parenthetically a manual. I knew that this was a hybrid form and that its unities would never be wholly intact. Still, in going over each finished chapter I found places where the balance could be improved—where instructional detail smothered the writer and his narrative, or, conversely, where the writer intruded on the procedures he was trying to explain. With a word processor it was easy to make small repairs—perhaps just a change of pronoun and verb—that made the balance less uneven.

The instructional portions of the book posed a problem of their own—one that I had never faced before. My hope was to try to explain a technical process without the help of any diagrams or drawings. Would this be possible? It would be possible only if I kept remembering one fundamental fact: writing is linear and sequential. This may seem so obvious as to be insulting: everybody knows that writing is linear and sequential. Actually everybody doesn't know. Most people under thirty don't know. They have been reared since early childhood on television—a kaleidoscope of visual images flashed onto their brain—and it doesn't occur to them that sentence B must follow sentence A, and that sentence C must follow sentence B, or all the elegant sentences in the world won't add up to anything but confusion.

I mention this because word processors are going to be widely used by people who need to impart technical information: matters of operating procedure in business and banking, science and technology, medicine and health, education and government and dozens of other specialized fields. The information will only be helpful if readers can grasp it quickly and easily. If it's muddy they will get discouraged or angry, or both, and will stop reading.

You can avoid this dreaded fate for your message, whatever it is, by making sure that every sentence is a logical sequel to the one that preceded it. One way to approach this goal is to keep your sentences short. A major reason why technical prose becomes so tangled is that the writer tries to make one sentence do too many jobs. It's a natural hazard of the first draft. But the solution is simple: see that every sentence contains only one thought. The reader can accommodate only one idea at a time. Help him by giving him only one idea at a time. Let him understand A before you proceed to B.

In writing this book I was eager to explain the procedures that I had learned, and I would frequently lump several points together in one sentence. Later, editing what I had written, I asked myself if the procedure would be clear to someone who was puzzling through it for the first time—someone who hadn't struggled to figure the procedure out. Often I felt that it wouldn't be clear. I was giving the reader too much. He was being asked to picture himself taking various steps that were single and sequential, and that's how he deserved to get them.

I therefore divided all troublesome long sentences into two short sentences, or even three. It always gave me great pleasure. Not only is it the fastest way for a writer to get out of a quagmire that there seems to be no getting out of; I also like short sentences for their own sake. There's almost no more beautiful sight than a simple declarative sentence. This book is full of simple declarative sentences that have no punctuation and that carry one simple thought. Without a word processor, I wouldn't have chopped as many of them down to their proper size, or done it with so little effort. This is one of the main clarifying jobs that your machine can help you to perform, especially if your writing requires you to guide the reader into territory that is new and bewildering.

Not all my experiences, of course, were rosy. The machine had disadvantages as well as blessings. Often, for instance, I missed not being able to see more than twenty lines at a time—to review what I had written earlier. If I wanted to see more lines I had to "scroll" them back into view.

But even this wasn't as painful as I had thought it would be. I found that I could hold in my head the gist of what I had written and didn't need to keep looking at it. Was this need, in fact, still another writer's hang-up that I could shed? To some extent it was. I discovered, as I had at so many other points in this journey, that various crutches I had always assumed I needed were really not necessary. I made a decision to just throw them away and found that I could still function. The only real hardship occurred when a paragraph broke at the bottom of the screen. This meant that the first lines of the paragraph were on one page and the rest were on the next page, and I had to keep flicking the two pages back and forth to read what I was writing. But again, it wasn't fatal. I learned to live with it and soon took it for granted as an occupational hazard.

The story that I've told in this chapter is personal and idiosyncratic: how the word processor helped one writer to write one book. In many of its details it's everybody's story. But all writers have different methods and psychological needs. Yours may be unlike mine in many ways. In which case, you'll want to know: "What will the word processor do for *me*?"

ILLUSTRATION CREDITS